NAVIGATING LIFE AND WORK IN OLD REPUBLIC SÃO PAULO

Navigating Life and Work in Old Republic São Paulo

MOLLY C. BALL

University of Florida Press

Gainesville

25 24 23 22 21 20   6 5 4 3 2 1

ISBN 978-1-68340-166-7 (cloth)
ISBN 978-1-68340-171-1 (paper)

Library of Congress Cataloging-in-Publication Data
Names: Ball, Molly C., author.
Title: Navigating life and work in Old Republic São Paulo / Molly C. Ball.
Description: Gainesville : University of Florida Press, 2020. | Includes
    bibliographical references and index.
Identifiers: LCCN 2020022852 (print) | LCCN 2020022853 (ebook) | ISBN
    9781683401667 (hardback) | ISBN 9781683401933 (pdf)
Subjects: LCSH: Labor market—Brazil—History. | São Paulo
    (Brazil)—Social conditions. | São Paulo (Brazil)—Social life and
    customs—History. | São Paulo (Brazil)—Economic conditions. |
    Brazil—Politics and government—History.
Classification: LCC F2521 .B165 2020 (print) | LCC F2521 (ebook) | DDC
    981/.61—dc23
LC record available at https://lccn.loc.gov/2020022852
LC ebook record available at https://lccn.loc.gov/2020022853

UF PRESS

UNIVERSITY
OF FLORIDA

University of Florida Press
2046 NE Waldo Road
Suite 2100
Gainesville, FL 32609
http://upress.ufl.edu

Dedicated to all working mothers,
especially my own, Sarah Johnston Ball

Contents

Figures

Tables

Acknowledgments

Writing acknowledgments is a humbling exercise. There is simply no way to adequately express my gratitude to all the individuals who proved instrumental in bringing this book to life. What started as an idea on an initial archive exploration has developed and matured over the course of three continents, six different homes, and thirteen years. Within that span, I have embarked on new experiences, including saying goodbye to my father and starting my own family. I received critical financial, intellectual, and emotional support at every step of the journey. *Navigating Life and Work in Old Republic São Paulo* would not have been possible without this support.

Funding from the Fulbright-Hays and National Security Education Program made extended research trips possible in the early phase of the project, and a fellowship from the Doris Q. Quinn Foundation provided a year of writing support. The Economic History Association, the UCLA Center for Economic History, and the UCLA Department of History also provided travel and research support. In the final phases of the manuscript preparation, the Textbook and Academic Authors Association and the University of Rochester and its history department provided assistance to cover editorial costs.

In the early phases of this project I found a supportive intellectual environment and a family in UCLA's Bunche Hall in the history and economics departments. I am especially grateful to the UCLA economic history proseminars and the all-UC economic history workshops for providing valuable feedback and a space to develop my research. William Summerhill proved to be a motivating and understanding adviser and mentor, providing comments, steering me toward grant opportunities, and always encouraging me to "forge ahead." Just as importantly, however, he understood that life is not all about academia and respected and supported my personal choices. Naomi Lamoreaux and Leah Boustan also read early drafts closely, providing a good roadmap for revisions. Ned Alpers gave me the opportunity to work on my first publication, which opened the door to a wealth of immigration history that has made its way into my teaching and this book. Confronting exams, grant applications, research trips, and the cost of living on Los Angeles's west side would have been impossible without the support of my fellow graduate students and friends. In particular, I would like to thank Antonio, Crystal, Regan, James, Gissele, Alan, Eboni, Veronica, Zeb, Zevi, Ros, Dana, Lino, Miriam, and Xochitl for their friendship and helping to make LA on a budget fun.

Once I embarked on my research journey in Brazil, I found an equally welcoming research and intellectual community. Renato Colistete welcomed me into his economic history workshop in the Faculdade de Administração e Economia at the Universidade de São Paulo and has been steadily enthusiastic about my research. He introduced me to Thomas Kang, who became a friend and colleague. My thanks go to Thomas, Eduardo, Ricardo, Joço, Raquel, and Carla for exploring São Paulo with me. I thank Eduardo in particular for those early morning runs that got me through the research phase. Archivists throughout the city also provided amazing support as I requested documents and we traded *figurinhas*. I appreciate Isabel and the staff at the Fundação de Energia e Saneamento do Estado de São Paulo; Társio, Anna, and Maurício at the APESP; the ALESP staff; Sônia at the ABIT library. I also met Ian Read, Alicia Monroe, Uri Rosenheck, and James Woodard in São Paulo as they were conducting their own individual research; I am thankful that those friendships did not just stay in São Paulo, and I appreciate these friends' insights and collegiality.

The work continued to develop in western New York. I am especially grateful to Anne Macpherson for connecting me to the New York State Latin American History Workshop and to a cohort of Latin American historians in Rochester, Isabel Córdova, Aiala Levy, and Ryan Jones. Anne, Isabel, and Ryan, along with Ruben Flores and Pablo Sierra Silva, provided valuable feedback on the introduction to the book, and Pablo was always willing to read chapters and point out both inconsistencies and strengths. Colleagues and friends in the University of Rochester history department, the Humanities Center's Grupo Latin American working group, Blair Tinker in the Digital Scholarship Lab, and the Susan B. Anthony Institute (SBAI) provided intellectual companionship. Since 2013 the history department at Rochester has welcomed me and supported my trajectory, and I am particularly grateful to Matt Lenoe, Laura Smoller, and Stanley Engerman for their support. The SBAI writing retreats and writing group provided me with literal companionship as I chipped away at the manuscript and revisions one goal at time. I am particularly indebted to my friend and writing partner Kate Mariner for organizing many of these events and for our Monday morning writing miniretreats that continued virtually during the pandemic. Many of my colleagues have also become dear friends, and I thank Rena Searle, Kate Mariner, Aiala Levy, Brianna Theobald, Jennifer Kyker, Tom Fleischman, Tanya Bakhmetyeva, and Jean Pederson.

As I worked through chapters and revisions, mentors and support were never far away. Cristo Dantini at the General Motors Heritage Center played a key role in facilitating access to materials housed in Brazil. Ian Read generously provided feedback on manuscript materials. Joel Wolfe encouraged me to develop the manuscript. The insightful suggestions that he and Anne Hanley provided on the entire manuscript draft greatly improved the final product. Gregg Bocketti, Cassia Roth, and Rio Corley took valuable time to share publication expertise, and Jennifer Eaglin patiently explained the processes and limitations of ethanol production. Alex Borucki generously organized and hosted a workshop for Southern California Brazilianists. Lynn Carlson's expertise helped bring my vision into cartographic form and Alyssa Rodriguez assisted with indexing. It has been a pleasure working with Stephanye Hunter at the University of Florida Press as an editor. She has demystified the publication process and clarified even my smallest questions. I also thank the entire press for their support and flexibility during the COVID-19 pandemic.

My writing role in *Navigating Life and Work in Old Republic São Paulo* has come to a close, but I know I may never have even started on this journey had it not been for the support of some key individuals. Stephanie Spacciante took me on a study-abroad trip to Chile that changed my life forever. Faculty in the Clemson history department nurtured my love of learning and convinced me that graduate school was a viable opportunity. Steven Marks, in particular, has served as a valuable mentor at several critical junctures along the way. I am also truly indebted to Guita Debert for supporting my special student status at the Universidade de Campinas as I learned Portuguese after graduating from Clemson. Then, there is my own family.

Historians strive to maintain objectivity, but the truth is that it is impossible to do so. My own privilege of having had multiple supportive families throughout this process has influenced my understanding of family. The Fadiga family, Edson, Maria Eugênia, Carol, and Bela, welcomed me into their home as I learned Portuguese and Brazilian culture and history. They are my Brazilian family, and their constant love, support, and hospitality are beacons when I return to Brazil. Elizabeth Johnson, Reese Ewing, and their children, Julian and Annika, have generously welcomed me into their home on multiple occasions. Elizabeth has been a listening friend and has generously shared her own knowledge and connections. While I was living in Mexico, my *familia política* became a crucial support network, as did my compadres Fidel Pichel and Pamela Zamorra Cobos and my dear friend Isis Zempoalteca. Then there is my family, which has supported and encouraged my decisions and passions no matter how crazy they may seem. To my brother and sister, distance has made me treasure our friendship and the bond we share. I thank Edward for his statistical expertise and for being able to listen at the right moments. I thank Laura for Bananagrams and for being my constant cheerleader. For my late father, it has been in the most isolating moments that I listen to a message he once left me and know that he is with me. For my mother, as each day passes, I appreciate more her incredible ability to support, encourage, and believe in me. Her confidence never faltered even when mine did. I hope that I will be able to do the same for my own children.

Brennen Quetzal, Cuauhtemoc Elias, and Carolina Angeles have inspired and distracted me at just the right moments. Carolina has only seen the final phases of this journey, but I have come to count on the joy on her face when I come home, even if it's from the "uni chiquita." Cuauhtemoc's hugs, imagination, and genuine compliments make me smile even on the grayest of days. Brennen has been along for half of this journey, and her resilience, curiosity, and caring nature have made the trip infinitely more exciting. Pablo Miguel Sierra Silva, my best friend, colleague, and husband, has witnessed nearly every step of this journey. His support is unwavering, be it in parenting, in academia, or in life. He has made me a better scholar, but more importantly, a better person. I look forward to where the future takes us.

Note on Orthography, Names, and Currency

Changes in Brazilian Portuguese orthography and spelling and grammatical errors in immigrant letters lead to considerable spelling variation. In most instances I use the modern equivalent, such as Brás instead of Braz. Notable exceptions include bibliographic entries and the Fiação, Tecelagem, e Estamparia Ypiranga Jafet. I have also kept names as they appear in letters and the historical record, without accents.

Throughout this study I often reference individuals by their first names. This decision is grounded in a Brazilian practice that often privileges first names, meaning that many archival records from the Old Republic are organized by first names rather than surnames. I do use last names when only using first names results in confusion and ambiguity.

NOTE ON CURRENCY UNITS

The Brazilian currency during the Old Republic was the milréis, also written as mil-réis. One milréis was written 1$000, and 500 réis was written 0$500. One thousand milréis was known as a conto and was written as 1:000$000.

Introduction

Living at the Margins

On July 3, 1916, Manoel Teixeira, a Portuguese immigrant living with his young family in the city of São Paulo, resolved to sit down and write his mother to ask for her help. His words were clear: "I ask my dear mother that you sell [your home] and come as quickly as possible because here there is much work for women, but Maria earns little because she has to stay with our little girls."[1] What he was asking was considerable, that his mother sell her house in Portugal and come join his young family across the Atlantic. He did not promise to take care of her in her old age, nor did he speak of his achievements and successes. One day maybe they would return to Portugal, but for right now, the Teixeira family needed another set of hands so they could make ends meet in São Paulo.

The following day, the *Estado de São Paulo*, the largest-circulated newspaper in the state capital, published proceedings from the Brazilian legislature, reported on conflagrations in Europe and major headlines in the Americas, and provided a summary of coffee prices and production. One article reported that the workers at a cigarette factory went on strike because the owners were reducing wages, cutting the piece rate offered by up to 30 percent.[2] This article highlights how city residents were feeling the squeeze brought on by World War I. Manoel's letter demonstrates that the Teixeiras were not immune to the wartime economic hardships.

Manoel's mother did decide to come and help her son, daughter-in-law, and grandchildren in São Paulo. Her arrival meant that Maria could look for work. Wartime shortages made prices high and brought construction to a halt, making many building-trade jobs difficult to find, but women could find jobs in textile factories. Production had increased to fill the cloth shortage, and employing women minimized production costs; women were paid just 65–79 percent of what men were paid in these jobs. Working-class families increasingly saw women's wages as important and even, for many, critical for family survival. Maria's pay was likely crucial to the Teixeiras, as Portuguese immigrants. In addition to highlighting the family wage and gender pay gaps, my research shows how finding a good job for Manoel would have been more difficult. Although he was literate, he undoubtedly faced significant hiring discrimination as a Portuguese immigrant, and many potential employers would have only considered him for unskilled positions.

In *Navigating Life and Work in Old Republic São Paulo* I consider the working lives of Paulistanos, residents of the city of São Paulo, during a period known as the First Republic or Old Republic, 1891–1930. São Paulo refers to the city of São Paulo, the capital of the state of São Paulo. Any references to the state will be explicit. São Paulo had a highly diverse resident population that included immigrants, migrants and established residents, but I use the term "Paulistano" to denote residents in the city for the duration that they lived there regardless of where they were born. Periodically, I use the term "Paulistana" to explicitly reference female residents and their experiences. The term "Paulista" refers to residents of the state; there is no gendered distinction in this term.[3] Identity as Paulistanos or Paulistas did not supersede national identity, so I also consider these categories. Thus, Manoel and Maria Teixeira and their daughters lived in São Paulo and were both Portuguese and Paulistanos.[4] To denote different racial groups, I refer to individuals who appear in the historical record as brown (*pardo*) or black (*preto* or *negro*) as Afro-Brazilian. I do so to avoid the term "nonwhite" but also to recognize that racial discrimination extended to all individuals with darker skin color in São Paulo.[5]

To consider the lives of Paulistanos in a period of rapid and large-scale transition in Brazilian and Latin American history, this book is both a social history using quantitative economic history methodologies and an economic history grounded in qualitative analysis. Only by combining these methods and questions can one appreciate the varied experiences in rank-and-file workers' daily lives and understand how individuals' and families' choices and adaptations affected larger trends. Examining historical experiences, particularly when considering the masses and marginalized groups, has become increasingly restricted to the realm of social and cultural historians. The peripheral role of economic history within this growing scholarship limits the ability to interpret important social and cultural changes.[6] Many economic historians would encounter the Teixeiras, but it would mostly like be at the aggregate level, in official statistics. Their understanding would miss what Manoel's letter reveals about the family wage structure in Old Republic São Paulo and how the working class adapted to World War I hardships.[7] Without a micro-level approach that uses regression analysis, one may understand where the Teixeiras intersected with "modernization" and "whitening" efforts in Brazil's Old Republic but fail to uncover the hiring discrimination they faced as Portuguese immigrants.

In the 1980s and 1990s, a number of labor histories combined social and economic history to examine working-class experiences during Latin America's first industrialization. Scholars of Brazil expanded an understanding of labor organization, the composition of the industrial labor force, and real wages and paid particular attention to questions of racial discrimination and female labor force participation, particularly in São Paulo and Rio de Janeiro.[8] Theirs were vital contributions but still left much room to expand the understanding of Brazil's workforce, particularly for the years 1891–1914.[9] Another group of scholars in the 1980s and 1990s revisited dependency theory assumptions about Latin America's growth and development. Growing out of the tradition of Stanley Engerman, Robert Fogel, and Douglass North, they took a data-grounded approach that combined quantitative history and applied economics. This approach has come to be known as new economic history.[10] Their research has dispelled many dependency theorists' claims while also recognizing that Latin America rarely developed to its full potential.

Cristina Peixoto-Mehrtens has noted in her introduction to *Urban Space and National Identity* a turn among historians away from economic history and a transition toward cultural history. She describes a shift when historians in the 1990s increasingly considered "the city as an economic-political space intertwined with other sociocultural practices."[11] Even here, the studies she references that consider entrepreneurial initiatives and are written by labor historians are vastly outnumbered by those that consider punishment, crime, gender roles, and ethnicity. The turn toward cultural history has only become stronger and economic history more isolated in the twenty-first century.[12] It is time to reencounter and reconsider economic history. Studying working-class families in São Paulo is the perfect place to start.

Economic history's potential analytic power is illustrated by considering recent discussions surrounding silences in the archives and embedded narratives.[13] Careful statistical methodologies provide an ideal starting point for extracting some of these seemingly hidden stories. Labor economists and economic historians have provided key models for investigating questions of discrimination and opportunity often missing from the traditional written record.[14] The Teixeira story proves an illustrative case. Maria may have been relatively silent in Manoel's letter, but my analysis of the hiring, wage, and tenure patterns of more than five thousand workers in São Paulo's Old Republic reveals the expectations Maria most likely had about her work opportunities. She would have looked for a textile job not only because those were positions available but also because the sector concentrated the highest-paying positions available to women. Even though these were the best jobs, they still reflected a notable gender wage gap; even if she gained considerable experience, Maria would receive minimal raises over her lifetime. Hers would not have been an isolated experience; given their participation in the labor force, this was the expectation of one of every five Paulistanas in 1920. Reading these results alongside textile industrialists' circulars, interview transcripts, and worker profiles shows that in addition to pay discrimination, women like Maria faced increasing labor exploitation after the war ended. As imported cloth returned to the Paulistano market, industrialists doubled down with heavy-handed labor practices. For the Teixeira daughters, this would mean that if Manoel was unable to find a good job that offered training, a high wage, and employment opportunities, they too would have joined their mother in the textile labor force. The consequences of that decision would have been considerable in their own lifetimes and would have extended to future generations.[15]

The rapidly growing and diverse urban environment characterizing São Paulo's Old Republic provides the ideal setting to investigate where and how working-class stories, expectations, hopes, and failures intersected with impersonal trends such as unprecedented economic growth, inflation, and wide-scale unemployment. Understanding how race, nationality, and gender influenced those opportunities and workers' choices allows a greater appreciation of working-class motivations and adaptations. In fleshing out the city's remarkable growth from this standpoint, the findings I present here challenge what is known about São Paulo's immigration history, the role of families in the early twentieth century, the use of binaries in Brazilian history, and the complex impact World War I had on the region's working class.

São Paulo functioned as a node of family-centered immigration during the era of European mass immigration in the nineteenth and early twentieth centuries. As such, the family unit played a central role in survival and success. In São Paulo, family-level concerns were strong enough to limit the effectiveness of labor organizing and to shift children out of the classroom and into the workforce. The influence of the family unit spread well beyond the labor market. Research highlighting the prominence of family-centered theater in São Paulo during the era reflects this impact. Investigating the Paulistano working-class family demonstrates that while individual agency, contestation of power structures, and worker movements will remain important lines of inquiry to understanding the working class in general, the family should also be considered as a base collective unit.[16]

In distinguishing between immigrant groups and highlighting the divisions within the working class, my research also demonstrates the limitations of the binary approach that pervades much scholarship on Brazil. In the case of the Teixeiras, many studies would consider Manoel as having more opportunity because he was white or because he was an immigrant.[17] I do not dispute that Manoel fit these classifications, and I likewise find that persistent racism at the hiring level put Afro-Brazilians at a considerable disadvantage during the Old Republic; however, I also find that Portuguese immigrants in São Paulo experienced hiring discrimination. While German and Austrian immigrants were more likely to hold jobs that provided for mobility into the laboring middle class and Italians could hope to find jobs in factories of compatriots, an influx of unskilled Portuguese in the prewar era meant employers expected Portuguese to be unskilled. That was simply not always the case.

This research offers a much richer understanding of how World War I served as an important inflection point for the working class. Many studies of the period either highlight the pre- or postwar era, and those that consider the Old Republic in its entirety often fail to disentangle changes emerging during the war years. While hardships existed prior to the war, many residents became adept at navigating the ebbs and flows accompanying migration and economic cycles. To a certain extent, as the period saw declining real wages, their beliefs were based on marked gains in health and education that demonstrated quality-of-life improvements. But the war tarnished those dreams for many Paulistanos. It may have solidified the role of a woman like Maria in the labor market, but her opportunities were largely restricted to exploitive jobs in the textile or domestic-worker sector. While male laborers with the right skin color who were employed in the construction or transportation industry could gain access to the middle class, wartime shortages and changes in migration cut short important advancements for women and exacerbated the lack of opportunities for Afro-Brazilians. Many of these individuals were forced to find housing that was overpriced, in regions prone to flooding, or on the city's outskirts where infrastructure was scarce. This additional challenge drove an even larger wedge in the laboring class before the presidency and dictatorship of Getúlio Vargas (1930–1945). This finding calls for scholars of Latin America to revisit changes in working-class experiences both before and after World War I. Doing so will reveal the extent of the war's impact on pervasive racial, ethnic, and gender discrimination in the region and the consequent challenge to development.

THE CITY GROWS

At Brazil's independence in 1822, São Paulo was a relatively quiet entrepôt connecting the coastal port of Santos to Brazil's southeastern interior. Founded in 1554 along an Indian route that connected the state's interior to the coastal ports, the city's location on the inland side of the Serra do Mar coastal range offered a hospitable area for settlement. Getting to the city, however, remained complicated. A paved road was constructed between Santos and São Paulo in 1791, but the road often flooded, requiring merchants to transfer goods to canoes for transport.[18] The city's primary economic activities were related to the mule trade and agricultural production catering to local markets. Fewer than 25,000 people lived in the city proper, and almost 80 percent of the population was free. In the late eighteenth century, small, nuclear families predominated among both the freed and enslaved populations. Elizabeth Kuznesof has described the city as a town based on kinship.[19]

Within thirty years of independence, coffee's arrival to the region brought many dramatic changes. Introduced to Brazil in 1727, coffee reached the fertile soils of Rio de Janeiro in the late eighteenth century and by 1835 surpassed sugar and cotton to become Brazil's leading export product.[20] The Paraíba Valley, nestled along the state border between Rio de Janeiro and São Paulo, served as the early center for coffee production, but by 1850, São Paulo's hinterlands became the country's and world's primary coffee-producing region. As the world demand for coffee increased, particularly in the industrializing Germany and United States, the coffee frontier expanded. Rich *massapê* soils in São Paulo state's western plateau were ideal for cultivation, and São Paulo state became the center of Brazil's export economy.[21]

On a plateau and along the Tietê River floodplains, the city's own soils were not suitable for coffee growth, but São Paulo was the state capital and stood at the juncture of railway expansion, coffee growth, and capital market formation. And so, as coffee production expanded, the city grew. The population hovered around 60,000 residents at the end of the Brazilian Empire in 1889, but by 1900, almost 240,000 people called the city home. That number increased to 450,000 on the eve of World War I and reached 579,000 by 1920. Two-thirds of those Paulistanos were either immigrants themselves or children of immigrants. By 1920, establishments in the city employed more industrial workers than those in Rio de Janeiro, the national capital, and events like the São Paulo Modern Art Week in 1922 ensured the city's growing cultural prominence. The city was well on its way to being the megalopolis that it is today.

The city's growth was entangled with coffee expansion during a period of what Luis Bértola and José Antonio Ocampo have described as commodity-export-led growth in Latin America between 1870 and 1929. Whether coffee in São Paulo, rubber in the Amazon, bananas in Central America, wheat in Argentina, guano in Peru, or copper in Chile, Latin America helped supply the rising demand for raw materials in the industrialized and industrializing world. Region-wide, exports accounted for half of national revenues, and the leading export commodity represented half of each Latin American country's total exports between 1870 and 1929. Exports were essential to national revenues, but they only represented 20 percent of national production. This imbalance ensured that the impact of commodity-export-led growth and policies extended well beyond the export sector and economic sphere.[22]

The experience with labor demonstrates how export support intersected with important social changes. Commodity production was labor-intensive, and expanding production often came hand in hand with exploitive labor practices and migration.[23] In Brazil, early coffee production relied heavily on enslaved labor. Elsewhere in the hemisphere, independence movements had brought abolition in Mexico, Central America, and Chile. In Brazil, the heir to the Portuguese throne, Dom Pedro I, proclaimed Brazilian Independence in 1822, creating a situation whereby he was simultaneously heir to the Portuguese throne and the Brazilian emperor.[24] This unique relationship to the old metropolis saw many colonial institutions transition seamlessly into Brazil's imperial era; slavery was one of these institutions. Even when Brazil technically abolished the transatlantic slave trade in 1831, clandestine shipments of slaves from Africa, largely from

Kongo and Angola, continued to arrive through 1850. In certain years, the number of imported slaves even increased.[25] By midcentury, Brazil was the only independent country in Latin America without a free-womb law, and it would be the last to abolish slavery, in 1888.[26]

Abolition in Brazil was a gradual process, and with each step taken, elites embraced alternative labor systems that relied heavily on immigrants. Brazilian independence may not have stopped slavery, but it did open the door for voluntary, non-Portuguese immigration. As early as the 1830s, an immigrant sharecropping program known as *núcleos coloniais* developed. *Núcleos* encouraged distinct immigrant groups to settle semi-autonomous communities on tracts of agricultural land that could be subdivided. At first, the vast majority of immigrants were Germans and Azoreans, but smaller groups such as Chinese "coolies" were also contracted. On a large scale, these early immigrant programs were minimally successful, and planters continued to rely on slave labor, often complaining that immigrant workers were "lazy."[27] It was only after the effective abolition of the slave trade in 1850 that the popularity of these alternative labor forces increased.[28] At the same time, coffee production expanded exponentially in São Paulo, aided by the growth of railroads and capital markets.

The ending of the transatlantic slave trade meant that former financiers of the system looked for alternative investments. Once independence wars and caudillo violence settled down in the latter half of the nineteenth century, Latin America became a region for foreign investment. Brazil's history of repaying loans and its relative political stability attracted investors to the country.[29] Railroads proved to be a particularly enticing venture. Planters needed more reliable and efficient transportation than the time-consuming mule trains used during early years of coffee production. If coffee was to be profitable, the seven-day trek between São Paulo and Jundiaí, an entry city into the state's coffee frontier, was simply not acceptable; the cities were less than forty miles apart. Once railroads connected the two, the same trek could be completed in a day.[30] The key connection, however, came in 1867, when the São Paulo Railway Company linked São Paulo to the Atlantic port city of Santos. Close to fifty miles separated the two cities, but to pass the Serra do Mar required constructing four long inclined stretches of track, a viaduct, twelve bridges, five smaller bridges, and a tunnel more than a quarter of a mile long.[31] Once the rail line was finished, the state's coffee frontier exploded, with São Paulo serving as the linchpin.

Investments went into industrial production as well. The need for jute sacks to carry coffee helped jumpstart Brazil's textile industry, but by the early nineteenth century, coffee was hardly the primary focus of most textile industrialists.[32] The largest number of textile factories quickly concentrated in cities, and other types of factories followed suit. In 1873, São Paulo had just 18 types of industries and counted 31 industrial firms. By the start of the Old Republic, the city already had 45 types of firms and 143 industrial establishments.[33] By 1941, it registered 8,400 factories. Many of these enterprises operated on a small scale, but the growth was still considerable.[34] Building railroads and factories required sizeable investments, and recent studies have demonstrated that important capital market expansion occurred in Brazil during the nineteenth century. Limited liability and a relatively sophisticated credit structure developed, with Rio de Janeiro and São Paulo serving as primary centers of those markets.[35]

Supporting immigration in the transition away from enslaved labor offered another avenue for investment.[36] By the 1870s, Brazil was closer to abolition, but in São Paulo state, 18 percent of the population was still enslaved.[37] Coffee production, capital markets, and railroads continued to expand the state's coffee frontier, and plantation owners needed more *braços para a lavoura*, agricultural workers. Then, in 1871 Brazil finally passed a free-womb law ensuring eventual abolition for more than 1.5 million slaves, 156,612 of whom lived in the state of São Paulo.[38] In the same year, Paulista planters formed the Associação Auxiliadora de Colonização e Imigração (Association to Aid Colonization and Immigration). Planters themselves funded transportation subsidies to bring European agriculturalists and their families to come work in the coffee sector, connecting them directly with employers and providing transportation to those destinations. Earlier *núcleos coloniais* had met with minimal success, but with the impending end of slavery and an expanding coffee frontier, an immigration program was successful, and the state took charge of the association's program. A majority of the millions of immigrants coming to São Paulo came with their families, fundamentally changing the state and the city. By 1920, São Paulo had become a bustling home to more than 579,000 residents, two thirds of whom were either immigrants or first-generation Brazilians.[39]

The immigration program's popularity came not just because it fulfilled an economic need. Politically and socially, it came at an important transition in the country's history. One year after abolition, a coup ended imperial rule in Brazil and ushered in the republican era. Brazil adopted a new constitution in 1891 that marked the start of the Old Republic. Technically a democracy, it is also referred to as the politics of *café com leite*, coffee with milk, because it was functionally an oligarchy with political elites from the states of São Paulo (coffee) and Minas Gerais (milk) wielding disproportionate power. The lifespan of the Old Republic only extended through 1930, when regional disparities and infighting among political elites prompted another successful coup that ushered in the Getúlio Vargas era.[40]

The immigration program established in imperial times survived the transition to the republic because in 1891 the state Department of Agriculture, Commerce, and Public Works took over the immigration subsidies. This change transferred the financial burdens from the coffee elites onto the government and reinforced the state's commitment to agriculture and coffee exports.[41] The end of the Old Republic roughly coincides with the end of state-subsidized immigration. After World War I dramatically altered the stream of immigrants, Brazilian migrants increasingly came to the state of São Paulo. Migration continued to outpace immigration, and by 1928 the state ended the subsidy program. Immigration did not stop altogether, with large numbers of arrivals from Japan, but the era of mass immigration to São Paulo was over.[42]

Socially and culturally, the immigration program coincided with the eugenics movement. Eugenics had a formative impact on Brazilian and Latin American identity and in defining the region's nation-states. Many US and western European eugenicists espoused Mendelism, which emphasized the inheritance of immutable traits. At its extremes, Africans and their descendants were often seen as degenerate. Latin America, whose colonial past contained considerably more miscegenation than the United States or western Europe, struggled to find its footing in these currents, and many embraced neo-Lamarckian eugenics. This perspective held that good traits could be acquired and passed on to later generations. Neo-Lamarckism was particularly popular in Brazil, whose population in 1872 was only 38 percent white. While many elites and politicians rejected the idea that Latin America was destined to degeneracy, the alternative they embraced held that progress and success required whitening the national populations socially, culturally, and physically through miscegenation.[43] For São Paulo state, subsidizing incoming European immigrant families served a dual purpose; it provided cheap labor and "improved" the state's population, making it "whiter" and more "modern."[44] That logic was inherently flawed and untrue, but it did fundamentally change and whiten the city's population.[45]

A Note on (Im)migration Studies

Regionally, as the need for mass labor in commodity production expanded, a distinct tension developed; the interior and rural areas produced export revenues, but the population increasingly settled in urban centers.[46] São Paulo's growth offers a space to investigate opportunity in Latin America because no other country had as diverse a population as Brazil and no other Brazilian city grew to be São Paulo's size. By the end of Brazil's Old Republic, sizeable communities of Afro-Brazilians, migrants from other states, and European, Syrian, and Japanese immigrants all called the city home. Understanding the complexity of the city's population necessitates positioning São Paulo's experience within the broader context of immigration to the Americas and urges scholars to rethink immigration studies in Brazil.

As Paulista planters made the transition toward immigrant labor, they were tapping into a second wave of migration that carried millions of Europeans across the Atlantic to the United States, Canada, Argentina, Uruguay, and Brazil seeking opportunity and success.[47] Between 1870 and 1914, more than 32 million emigrants left Europe. While the majority went to the United States, the relative impact in Latin America's Southern Cone was much larger. Almost 60 percent of Argentina's population in 1914 was either foreign-born or first-generation, and for more than sixty years, more than half of Buenos Aires's population remained foreign-born. Seasonal migration was another feature of Argentine migration that demonstrates how labor mobility marked this period of commodity-export growth. In the extensive literature on world labor markets, however, the city of São Paulo is minimally considered. No study comparing Buenos Aires and São Paulo exists like Baily's study of Buenos Aires and New York City; Rio de Janeiro is often the point of comparison.[48] Anecdotal evidence and summary statistics challenge the argument that São Paulo was weakly linked to Argentina's immigration stream. The state was the primary destination of immigrants to Brazil, and the city's population was predominantly foreign-born or first-generation Brazilian. Its immigrant population makes the omission of São Paulo from empirical studies comparing real wages and work hours in European and American labor markets a considerable oversight.[49]

This lacuna is especially important because São Paulo's immigration program was unique within the Americas. While young, single men dominated immigration streams from Europe to other immigrant destinations, the family continued to be the core of migration to São Paulo state. Second, the immigrant hostel built in the city of São Paulo to support the program, the Hospedaria de Imigrantes de São Paulo (hereafter *hospedaria*), was different because of its location and the services it provided. Most other cities and countries with sizeable migration streams located immigrant hostels in coastal areas, but the capital city of São Paulo state was the logical choice over its main port city, Santos. In terms of services, the hospedaria's official placement agency was designed to directly link workers with employers in the interior coffee economy.[50]

The importance of the state's subsidy program and the hospedaria for the city's growth and development has been vastly underestimated.[51] In addition to immigrants who eventually migrated to the city after meeting their contractual obligations in the interior, some immigrants and migrants settled directly in the city. In Thomas Holloway's detailed study of immigrants' roles in São Paulo's interior (*Immigrants on the Land*), he emphasizes the guards who stood watch at the hospedaria. I have found documentary evidence that disputes this depiction and shows considerable movement from the hospedaria to the city and vice versa. Chiara Vangelista emphasizes the preeminence of coffee plantations in defining the state's labor market through the 1920s, but a more nuanced examination of the hospedaria registrations shows important distinctions between urban and rural immigrants.[52] Today, exhibits and audio tours in São Paulo state's Museu da Imigração, housed at the old hospedaria in the Brás neighborhood of São Paulo, note the program's importance in expanding Brazil's coffee production and growing interior cities like Campinas and Ribeirão Preto. Missing from this interpretation is the fundamental role that the subsidized immigrant program and the hospedaria itself played in the city. Laborers and families relied on the hospedaria during times of extreme duress to find guaranteed jobs, just as industrialists relied on the hospedaria to find workers when their own employees went on strike. This safety net was an important aspect of the city's draw, especially for families, and set São Paulo apart from other immigrant centers. This was particularly true in the pre–World War I years when there is evidence that São Paulo's labor market was more closely linked to Buenos Aires than it was to Rio de Janeiro.[53]

Given the established history of nuclear families in São Paulo's colonial and imperial past, both the city and the state were the logical home for the family-structured immigration system that developed in the nineteenth and early twentieth centuries.[54] While colonial sources lend themselves to a more family- or household-centered approach, the availability of a greater variety of sources for the modern era and a move toward examining societal power structures dominates current understanding of the family unit for this period. In examining how notions of family connect to nationalism, eugenics, identity, and changing gender norms, knowledge of family goals and units is limited.[55] This is an unfortunate omission, for while São Paulo may represent the family unit at its extreme, families were central in other Latin American urban centers and throughout the region.[56] In closely analyzing family motivations among São Paulo's working-class strata, I begin here to fill that void.

I also push against two tendencies in Brazilian scholarship related to immigration. One is a tendency to study specific or select immigrant groups. These studies often focus on questions of identity and national identity, but they fail to provide a full understanding of how and when distinct groups came together.[57] The other and more polemic tendency is a move away from the immigrant/national and white/nonwhite binaries. In an effort to resolve the region's history of miscegenation and the eugenicists who insisted the African and indigenous races were degenerate, many officials espoused another approach. Paulista elites' reference to prospective Japanese immigrants as the "whites of Asia" to gain support for this non-European flux demonstrates their intention to whiten the population. For too long these binaries have been the underlying groups used in scholarly analyses.[58] What resulted from the state's immigration system was much more complex. Holloway's study of São Paulo's coffee-growing interior (*Immigrants on the Land*) demonstrates important differences between national groups in terms of the types of land owned and agricultural products cultivated. Studies investigating the importance of regional identities in defining national identity have noted important differences between Brazilians.[59] There is no reason to think the city of São Paulo was any different.

A Note on Development

An important story of discrimination, racism, and glass ceilings in São Paulo emerges upon investigating the city's rich diversity. Periods of heavy in-migration and economic hardship amplified the challenges, and even rapid growth in an era of relative integration into the global market during the period of commodity-export-led growth was not enough to overcome these problems. By the 1920s, there were decidedly good jobs and bad jobs in São Paulo, but discrimination denied many individuals access to the good jobs. Women often took jobs at lower pay in sectors that offered few opportunities for advancement and less stability and exposed them to more exploitive labor practices. Many Afro-Brazilians were never able to gain access to formal-sector jobs. It was not impossible to move from a bad job to a good job, but workers' expectations about who could make that transition diverged considerably.

Speaking of good and bad jobs invokes the language of dual labor market theorists. The theory gained traction among economists in the 1960s and 1970s to explain persistent underemployment, poverty, and career outcomes in local labor markets of large industrial cities in the United States,[60] and it emerged amid rising racial tensions. Scholars contended that members of minority groups and women were confined to bad jobs in secondary markets, which had different expectations, tenures, and wage structures than good jobs in primary sectors.[61] Findings from my research demonstrate that similar conditions existed in São Paulo in the early twentieth century. The Paulistano reality was more complex than two sectors, but even at the height of market integration in the pre–World War I period, the evidence points to decidedly segmented labor markets across gender and racial lines. Simply put, a combination of nonstatistical discrimination (discrimination not based on statistical evidence) and prejudice played key roles in determining who got the best jobs.[62]

To better understand this nonstatistical discrimination, I embrace a more holistic approach to development by evaluating the Paulistano quality of life and perceptions alongside labor market indicators. Since the 1990s, scholars have increasingly used well-being indicators such as education, political participation, and public health improvements in conjunction with income indicators as a better metric for development than growth indicators used by neoclassical and dependency theorists alike.[63] This approach is key to understanding Latin America's underdevelopment, for while GDP per capita can demonstrate the growth associated with capital markets, railroads, and industrialization, it cannot speak to the distribution of that wealth.[64] In investigating a region with high inequality and pervasive social and cultural imbalances with deep historical roots, scholars must strive to consider how discrimination and expectations restricted or enhanced access to advancements associated with growth.[65] This line of inquiry demonstrates how gender inequality persisted despite educational improvements, and expanding the vote did not limit racial discrimination. Taking this approach will enrich the understanding of why Brazil and Latin America failed to catch up to other industrializing countries in terms of development between 1870 to 1929.[66] Furthermore, it suggests that if the region is to reach its greatest development potential, it must strive to over-come pervasive discrimination and prejudice.[67]

SOURCES AND STRUCTURE

In the six chapters that follow, I bring economic history and social history into conversation. Doing so required integrating a variety of sources and methodologies. To speak of changes in immigration and migration patterns, I draw extensively on immigrant registration records from the Hospedaria de Imigrantes de São Paulo. Livros de registros de matrícula de entrada de imigrantes na Hospedaria de Imigrantes, 1882–1978 (registros), contain records and destinations for 457,811 individuals who arrived at the hospedaria between 1903 and 1927. This time frame starts in the year when detailed individual records began to be kept and ends with the dissolution of large-scale, state-subsidized immigration. In this study I analyze trends among these entries but also create a representative sample of 2,232 immigrants contracted directly to the city during those years. Registros prove instrumental in evaluating changes in contract patterns at the hospedaria during critical moments of São Paulo labor unrest.

To speak to labor market discrimination and opportunity, I draw on individual employee records from four Paulistano firms. There is some variation in the types of records, but to simplify, I often refer to these records by the most common term fichas de funcionários (fichas). Other scholars have consulted these records, but I compiled a representative database of more than five thousand workers hired during the Old Republic by the São Paulo Tramway, Light, and Power Company (Light), the Companhia Paulista de Estradas de Ferro (Paulista Railway), and the Fiação, Tecelagem e Estamparia Ypiranga Jafet textile factory (Jafet). The resulting real wage series was published in Research in Economic History.[68] In the present work I use that series to statistically analyze gender, racial, and national differentials in real wages and hiring patterns.[69] I also used salary and employee evidence from the Lojas Mappin department store to speak to class differentials and understand how women experienced the Paulistano labor market. To further explore racial discrimination, I look to changes in explicit racial preference in help-wanted advertisements published in the Estado de São Paulo.

I use immigration and employee records also to create mini biographies of Paulistanos whose experiences proved representative of general trends identified in the statistical analyses. Their stories are instrumental in bringing statistics and numbers to life, especially for those who may be unfamiliar with regression analysis. Individual stories, however, are not just storytelling tools; they inform an understanding of workers' motivations, dreams, disappointments, and goals. I use immigrant letters, interview transcripts, worker profiles, and newspaper accounts to create this window into rank-and-file Paulistano workers' lives. These include letters sent from Paulistanos to relatives in Europe that are preserved in the Memória do Imigrante archival records in the Arquivo Público do Estado de São Paulo (APESP); they are among 157 *chamadas* (calls to immigrate) that I researched. Other letters accompany Portuguese passport applications housed at the Arquivo Distrital do Porto. Many of these letters have been digitized and offer a treasure trove for future studies. In the calls to immigrate, there are 430 letters available online. I complemented these letters with insights workers provided in interview transcripts, both published and archival, and in profiles published in General Motors' *Panorama* and *GMWorld* employee publications. As most Paulistanos did not leave written records, I also looked to reports of labor unrest, life, and civil strife as reported in the labor press and in the "Capital" section of the *Estado de São Paulo*. These stories, together with the trends and workers identified in the statistical analyses, demonstrate where new economic history and social history meet.

Chapters 1 and 4, in particular, build on the new economic history tradition in evaluating changes in immigration to the city of São Paulo and in the city's labor market, respectively, during the Old Republic. Immigration records show noteworthy shifts in immigrant and migrant profiles, the shares of groups coming to the city, and important distinctions between urban and rural migrants. Factory-level employment evidence reveals the degree of hiring discrimination that Afro-Brazilians, Portuguese immigrants, and women had to overcome. Observable changes in job advertisements complement new research on the *Boletins de Ocorrências,* incident reports from public safety's medical outposts, to highlight reduced opportunities for Afro-Brazilian advancement as the city's rate of growth slowed and as waves of migrants arrived in the city. Effectively, World War I accentuated a cleavage within the working class, creating subsets of winners and losers. Scholars interested in how the hospedaria sample database was constructed and the results of the statistical regression and logit analyses used as evidence will be particularly interested in the appendices that complement chapters 1 and 4.[70]

Unexplored immigrant letters, interview transcripts, and newspaper articles are essential to providing the human voices that all too often prove elusive in these processes. These sources reveal the pressure of contributing to the family wage that compelled Justina de Carvalho to become a strikebreaker at the Villela hat factory in 1908 despite the ridicule and physical danger she faced. They show how João André Macedo, a young Brazilian agriculturalist escaping a drought in Rio Grande do Norte and settling in the city in 1915 had a smaller social network than the Augusto family, recently arrived Portuguese immigrants settling with their children in São Paulo's Brás neighborhood. In essence, Justina, João, and the Augustos bring economic history to life for the non-economic historian.

Each chapter demonstrates how Paulistano and potential Paulistano working-class individuals made calculated decisions about moving and settling, taking jobs, and getting an education based on their prior experiences, social networks, and knowledge of the city's opportunities. Family goals and decisions were often at the core of their choices. In making these connections, the importance of the Hospedaria de Imigrantes was undeniable. Thus, in each chapter I consider the hospedaria's impact on the city and its residents. Finally, I consider the extent to which World War I affected workers' lives, opportunities, and decisions. Organizationally, chapters 2 and 3 predominantly focus on the prewar era and chapters 5 and 6 on the postwar era. In chapters 1 and 4, which span the entire period, I examine the changes that came with the wartime economy and pressures.

Chapter 1 provides the context to compare the city of São Paulo with other major migration centers in the Americas. While the great European migration wave coincided with the city's rapid growth and definite parallels can be drawn between São Paulo and other immigrant cities, São Paulo had its own blend of history and culture. This chapter also details the various ways the hospedaria connected workers to the city's labor markets. Evidence on incoming immigrants' and migrants' characteristics including nationality complicates current binary analysis of skills and suggests how expectations about immigrant groups influenced perceptions of those groups. This is not to suggest that there were not important distinctions within groups. Brazilians themselves offer the prime example. The chapter presents how Brazilian migrants to the city tended to be more educated than most other groups. The evidence simply does not support the association of northeastern and northern Brazilian migrants with backwardness and minimal skills.[71] In looking at incoming immigrants, I also mark a rising importance of capital-intensive industries in the city in the 1920s.

In chapter 2 I examine how immigrants and Brazilians responded to the conditions they encountered in the growing city between 1891 and 1918.

Letters to family members shed light on how working-class individuals and families confronted the challenges of employment, increasing cost of living, housing, and quality of life.[72] Digital archives, through letters and digitized newspaper databases,[73] facilitate this investigation and show a decided pattern emerging in the city's development. Rapid construction and growth attracted new arrivals, especially in 1908 and 1911–1914. When housing construction or job opportunities lagged, individuals made their own opportunities, often before the municipal or state government could react. If conditions became too difficult, they used the hospedaria to connect to employers, either within the city or in the state's interior.

The city of São Paulo, relatively speaking, offered residents opportunities and stability until the start of World War I. Records of school attendance, literacy, marriages, and mortality rates show that by many quality-of-life measures, improvements did accompany the city's growth. There was no reason that residents would have expected the downturn in 1914 to be any different than those in 1901 and 1909. The war's prolonged nature, however, did change the nature of working-class life in the city. Wartime scarcities accelerated the cost-of-living increase relative to wages, and a halt in construction dramatically limited job opportunities. Residents often left the city to seek better opportunities. Evidence from the hospedaria shows increased migration to coffee-growing areas by 1915, as many individuals and families could not survive in the city. For those working-class families that remained, most adopted a family wage strategy, choosing to put school-age children, especially girls, to work or to watch their younger siblings while the mothers worked. These strategies survived well past World War I, stifling educational improvements and social mobility in subsequent years. This chapter ends with a discussion of the 1917 general strike as representative of the changes the war precipitated for laborers and the working class. Conditions deteriorated enough to bring about the first successful large-scale strike in the city.

Discussion in chapter 3 complicates the alluring qualities described in chapter 2 as I examine why workers responded differently to strikes and labor organization in the lead-up to the 1917 general strike, by far the most-studied strike in Brazil's early labor organization. The emphasis is well deserved, given the scope, scale, and relative success of the strike; in most ways, however, the general strike was an anomaly. Laborers were rarely so unified in Old Republic São Paulo, and to understand this exceptionalism requires looking to smaller movements. In chapter 3 the focus shifts from strike leaders and labor demands to understand who nonstriking and replacement workers were and what motivated them to cross the picket line. The hospedaria was critical in undermining labor's ability to mobilize prior to the war. The seemingly endless supply of unskilled laborers to the city willing to sign direct contracts allowed factory owners to replace striking employees with new hospedaria arrivals. The state's willingness to ensure the "freedom to work" by increasingly deploying police forces during times of labor unrest was key to minimizing organization. The large number of nuclear family units lessened willingness to join strikes. Portuguese immigrants in particular seemed less willing to join movements. Missing a paycheck detrimentally affected the entire family, not just the individual.

In chapter 4 I utilize new wage evidence to systematically address the discrimination individuals faced in São Paulo's labor market. In essence, employment records reveal that three distinct groups suffered discrimination in the Paulistano formal labor market. Portuguese, Afro-Brazilians, and women all suffered hiring discrimination. The experiences of these groups, however, were not identical, and their decisions in the Paulistano labor market may be understood as reflecting their differences. Faced with significant hiring discrimination, some workers were more willing to stay in positions than to seek out other opportunities. Others were unwilling to put hard-won jobs on the line. Limited access to better-paying positions during the Old Republic proved a major hindrance to social mobility and opportunity where literacy and an education did not necessarily equate to being hired into those jobs.

World War I was an event Paulistanos, industrialists, and middle- and working-class individuals could not control. Economists often refer to these occurrences as exogenous. How sectors, factories, and individuals responded to those events and adapted to constraints was within their control. In chapters 5 and 6 I examine the different ways that sectors, factories, individuals, and families responded to the changes and postwar reality. Good and bad jobs emerged, and those with access to good jobs could aspire to be part of a working middle class that included laborers alongside white-collar workers. Portuguese had reduced access to good jobs, but women and marginalized Afro-Brazilians were rarely included among the ranks at all.

Chapter 5 highlights how São Paulo's textile sector adapted to constraints. Scholarly discussion of the war's impact and the sector's development tend to focus on capital costs, with the approach to labor costs remaining understudied. How employers approached labor costs, however, held the greatest implications for workers themselves. During the war, textile magnates who were used to elastic labor supply turned again to a cheap labor solution by employing more women and children. As pressure on the sector continued and the industry became overstocked, most industrialists added blacklisting and heavy-handed labor control to their repertoire. This environment came at a considerable cost to workers. Looking at the textile industry's failure to adapt during the war and in the postwar era shows how growth could mask significant decline. Other sectors developed more sustainable and innovative responses to wartime scarcities, but in textiles, São Paulo's urbanization was marked by underwhelming development.[74]

Chapter 6 introduces a working middle class that had formed by the 1920s, the world and labor market they confronted in São Paulo, and the values they held. I consider who was excluded, as well. The city's population again began to grow in the postwar era, but many strides toward decreasing inequality from the prewar period disappeared. Nevertheless, profiles of successful individuals demonstrate that Paulistanos employed in mechanical trades and the transportation industry could aspire to upward economic mobility. These positions were not open to everyone, though, and many women and Afro-Brazilians found themselves marginalized not only politically and economically but geographically as well. As the city's population swelled into the surrounding floodplains of rivers, these groups were more susceptible to increasing flooding brought on by expansion. It was this fractured Paulistano working class that would confront Vargas-era reforms and agendas.

A tale of two working-class São Paulos emerged in the 1920s: that of opportunity and success and that of decay and despair. Identifiable trends mark a definable divergence within the working class. Those individuals with greater social connections, the right skin color, and willingness and opportunity to work in growing industries like transportation, cement, and cars found the keys to success. These individuals were part of an emerging middle class. Yet, this left behind most workers in the textile sector, many women, Afro-Brazilians, and most of those in the informal labor market. Differences compounded over time, creating important distinctions not just between São Paulo's elites and the working class but also between workers themselves.

1

Making an Immigrant City

At first glance, São Paulo, Brazil, resembles other American immigrant cities such as New York City and Buenos Aires. All were full of European immigrants, people struggling to negotiate their own regional and national identities alongside other immigrants and native citizens in new homes. The character Beppino in Danton Vampré's popular 1914 play *São Paulo Futuro* symbolized the aspirations of these immigrants when he proclaimed in Italian "Non ha vita migliore Che questa vita mia" (There is no better life than this my life).[1] While hopes and dreams of opportunities drew migrants to these urban centers, the reality was often much harsher. Still, goods and services such as schools enticed them to stay and weather unemployment and sickness. São Paulo was no different in these respects. At second glance, though, São Paulo's development as an immigrant node was destined to be unique. Specific immigration policies made the city a much more attractive destination for families, and exponential growth should have, theoretically, created more opportunities. But hypotheticals do not provide the important piece of the puzzle to understand how São Paulo experienced immigration and its effects in the early twentieth century.

In the 1890 census, the city of São Paulo had just over 65,000 inhabitants, yet on the eve of World War I, there were likely 450,000 individuals living in São Paulo.[2] The population had increased sevenfold in a matter of twenty-three years. For incoming immigrants, especially families, this growing city held more promise and opportunity than established cities.[3] Rio de Janeiro, like New York City and Buenos Aires, was already an established urban center by 1870, and its population was eight times larger than São Paulo's at the start of the Old Republic. Furthermore, Rio de Janeiro and Buenos Aires were national capitals at the seat of bureaucratic structures. São Paulo was a city coming into its own, and new arrivals could make it their own.

In this chapter I clarify how immigrants came to settle in São Paulo in such dramatic numbers; I establish a clearer picture of the national profiles of Paulistano residents. Gilberto Freyre's *Casa grande e senzala* (*Masters and the Slaves*) still looms large in the treatment of cultural and ethnic fusion in existing scholarship. A revision of Freyre's utopian vision began mid-twentieth century when scholars found discrimination and colorism more difficult to ignore, but there was a distinct challenge to understanding the historical underpinnings of racial discrimination. Between 1900 and 1940, there was the near-erasure of race as a category in many official and census documents; that was the same period of mass European immigration to São Paulo. The historian Paulina Alberto asserts, "As African culture moved toward the center of official and popular formulations of national identity in this period [under Vargas], indigenous people faded further from the public view."[4] The indigenous Brazilian was not the only group to be pushed to the research margin in this turn; immigrant groups tended to be either lumped into a singular "foreign" (implying "white") group or to be treated independently.[5] Scholarship has developed along similar lines.[6]

To remove this mystery about the city's development, I examine and analyze a combination of documents related to the individuals who used the city's Hospedaria de Imigrantes, the city's immigrant receiving station. These documents include a database. Livros de registros de matrícula de entrada de imigrantes na Hospedaria de Imigrantes (*registros*) allow for a targeted analysis of families and individuals moving directly to the city of São Paulo rather than to the state's interior, as the program was originally designed.[7] As the Old Republic progressed, immigrants contracted to work in the city became more skilled. The existence of important national differences in skill levels and human capital caution against lumping all immigrants into a singular "immigrant" category. The analysis here thus problematizes the traditional Brazilian/immigrant binary, the assumptions that Brazilians and immigrants had distinct skill sets and that there was a preference for immigrants. The hospedaria evidence shows that the binary is sustainable insofar as the registrations point to a bias against Brazilian migration up until World War I. During and after the war, Brazilians who chose to migrate tended to be individuals with higher levels of human capital. In comparison with other groups, Brazilians proved more literate than some, such as the Portuguese, and less literate and skilled than others, such as German immigrants. Analyzing these differences is key to understanding why employers may have been inclined to hire a qualified German worker over an equally qualified Portuguese worker.

As primary source evidence derives from documentation produced by the hospedaria, the hospedaria, as an institution on a very local level, nurtured the Brás neighborhood's diversity and fundamentally altered the city's labor market for workers and employers. In the expansive literature on the important role institutions play in economic development, little if any attention has been paid to how employment agencies affect development.[8] The hospedaria simultaneously provided a safety net for workers and allowed employers to exploit incoming immigrants and unemployed Paulistanos. Ultimately, the continual cheap supply of labor discouraged investment in technological improvements and training at a critical point in São Paulo's development.

THE ENIGMATIC CITY

Scholars have been unable to delve deeply into what types of immigrants were moving to the city of São Paulo during the Old Republic, 1891–1930.[9] Official demographic statistics make this a difficult question to assess because the documents often fail to distinguish between immigrant groups living in the city. Given the city's characteristics compared to other immigrant centers, it is critical to recover this information to understand the underlying social and cultural fabric of Brazil's and Latin America's largest urban center today. Brazil was the last bastion of slavery in the Americas, and the persistence of the nefarious institution through 1888 made the country a latecomer among immigrant-receiving nations. While race may not have been a binary construction in Brazil, racial prejudice was prevalent, and a policy of whitening, *branqueamento*, was espoused.[10] European immigrants would have been the direct beneficiaries of this prejudice against Afro-Brazilians. That would have been the case throughout Brazil but particularly in the state of São Paulo, which issued immigration subsidies.

Immigration subsidies came as a resolution to the *falta de braços*, literally "lack of arms," that coffee planters feared would come with the abolition of slavery. In 1871, the same year the free-womb law passed, the provincial governor and several planters formed the Associação Auxiliadora de Colonização e Imigração (Association to Aid Colonization and Immigration) to help fund a program to bring in foreign workers. Over the next fifteen years, this private initiative transitioned into the public sector. In 1886, two years before abolition and now supported by the province of São Paulo, the Sociedade Promotora da Imigração printed pamphlets in German, Portuguese, and Italian to attract entire European "agriculturalist" families to work on the coffee plantations. The immigration subsidy offered by the Sociedade Promotora and later the state of São Paulo's Department of Agriculture, Commerce, and Public Works covered oversea and overland transport from the port of departure in Europe to the final destination.[11] It also provided food and lodging until immigrants (and migrants beginning in 1900) signed contracts and arrived at their work destinations. One-year contracts were signed between plantation owners and *colonos* (contract plantation laborers), with conditions based on the number of hoes the family or individual could wield. Housing and plots of land to grow food provided *colonos* and their families with income in kind, and workers could also earn wages as day laborers. In effect, the system combined sharecropping, wage labor, and household production for the *colonos*.[12] By 1888, almost 92,000 immigrants arrived through the program, and between 1886 and 1930, more than 2.25 million immigrants arrived in São Paulo state, 58 percent of them under the state subsidization program. Italian, Spanish, and Portuguese immigrants represented the largest national groups, in that order, but immigrants from Germany, Syria, eastern Europe, and Japan also formed significant immigrant populations in São Paulo.[13]

Europe was in transition, facing production shifts due to mechanization and industrialization as well as demographic pressures. Technological advancements in agriculture led to greater production and efficiency but reduced the need for agricultural workers. Cottage industries also became mechanized, and a similar transition moved production from the home to the factory, as artisans became rank-and-file workers. The period saw a substantial population increase as well. In agricultural communities, the confluence of factors prompted migration to urban centers in Europe. The urban centers, however, did not necessarily have better opportunities, and many Europeans continued their migrations by moving to the Americas. Religious pogroms, armed struggle, agricultural blights, and the 1873 Depression in Europe only exacerbated conditions that led more people to emigrate.[14] By the time São Paulo began offering subsidies, they came as a welcome boon to many poor European families.

While the subsidy program was the most popular immigrant settlement program, *núcleos coloniais*, immigrant colonies, could also be found throughout the state. More prominent in Brazil's southern states and during the nineteenth century, they also supported São Paulo's developing coffee interior. The *núcleo* system set apart significant tracts of land in rural and urban settings that were then subdivided into plots. Families could buy tracts with 10 percent down payments or sign contracts to work in particular communities. Early *núcleos* concentrated immigrants from one nationality and were given a certain degree of autonomy; migrants in later *núcleos* were allowed to buy land with larger down payments. The *núcleos'* activities were consciously integrated into the coffee economy; the urban and rural *núcleos* produced the food, goods, and services that coffee plantations needed.[15] A fair number of *núcleos* were also dedicated to coffee cultivation. As a program, however, the *núcleo* system simply did not draw the same number of laborers as the state's subsidy program.[16]

Plantation owners had a clear preference for families, as they considered it easier to tie an entire family unit to the land.[17] Demand for coffee workers was a primary factor in stimulating immigration and migration to the state of São Paulo, but as coffee production expanded, so too did the need for workers in nonagricultural jobs.[18] Many former coffee workers migrated to urban centers in search of these jobs. Congressional representative Antonio Mercado commented in 1899, "[Congress] cannot stop this phenomenon and cannot quit relying on it." So, by 1906 the state began allowing a portion of subsidies to be granted to nonagricultural workers.[19] Railway companies and a growing number of factories benefited from this change in the legislation.[20] The traditional story is that these nonagricultural workers were essential in developing cities in the interior of the state, but some workers bypassed the interior entirely and signed contracts to work in São Paulo. By nature of the immigration system's design, this meant São Paulo's new residents often navigated the city alongside family members. In this way, the state's subsidized immigration program also expanded the city's population and was crucial to São Paulo's development.

Few details are available about how immigration affected the city's growth, environment, and development during this period. Looking at the population estimates and the number of foreigners compared to Brazilians underscores the important roles immigrants played. In 1872, less than 10 percent of the city's population was foreign-born; among them, Portuguese and Africans, some of whom were enslaved, were the largest groups. Of the city's nine neighborhoods, only one, Brás, could be considered dominated by immigrants.[21] By 1920, the city had almost 580,000 residents, two-thirds of whom were immigrants or first-generation Brazilians.[22] These new Paulistanos moved from the interior or directly from Europe, the Rio de la Plata region, or other areas of Brazil. These new residents quickly populated the city's older working-class neighborhoods such as Bom Retiro and

Santa Ifigênia and expanded into adjacent regions like Brás. The growing importance of immigrants in São Paulo, despite the ten years of continuous residence required for naturalization, demonstrates that with entire family units settling, immigrants were less apt to return to their countries of origin.[23] While studies of individual immigrant communities grant important glimpses into this vibrant community, a systematic understanding of these groups is lacking. Understanding who lived in the city is essential to analyzing how they experienced and responded to the large, impersonal economic forces during the Old Republic. The Hospedaria de Imigrantes provides the path to that knowledge.

THE HOSPEDARIA DE IMIGRANTES

The old Hospedaria de Imigrantes still stands at the end of Rua Visconde de Parnaíba as today's Museu da Imigração do Estado de São Paulo. A part of the working-class Brás neighborhood and a few blocks off the Bresser-Mooca metro stop on São Paulo's red line (*linha* 3), the museum is dedicated to preserving the memories and experiences of immigrants who passed through the hospedaria before settling in São Paulo. As the hospedaria, its doors opened in 1888, the same year slavery was abolished in Brazil, and the building last functioned as an immigrant receiving station in 1978. The Old Republic marked the hospedaria's peak years of bringing immigrants to the state of São Paulo. Before the Brás hospedaria opened, immigrants were processed through a building in the Bom Retiro neighborhood, but it could only house five hundred people at a time.[24] The Brás complex was built to accommodate three to four thousand immigrants, but even then, it was often pushed well beyond that capacity. The walls surrounding the Brás structure still stand, and to enter the museum, visitors and researchers must pass the old guardhouses where officials once patrolled the hospedaria.

The São Paulo hospedaria was built to facilitate connections between subsidized immigrant families arriving in Brazil and coffee plantation owners in the state's interior. Other immigrant-receiving stations developed throughout Brazil, but the city of São Paulo's was by far the most important from the 1890s forward. Immigrants arriving on a boat in Santos were quickly transported by train directly to the hospedaria. The distance by rail between the two cities was just over fifty miles, and the steep inclines of the Serra do Mar dramatically complicated arriving by other means. There was even a train stop at the hospedaria from which disembarking passengers went straight into the fortress-like building (figure 1.1). By the

Figure 1.1. Immigrants arriving in São Paulo, ca. 1908. Arriving by train barely gives passengers time to see the city. Once they enter the train station, they will be inside the walled Hospedaria de Imigrantes. Anonymous photo, ca. 1908. Courtesy of Museu da Imigração, Arquivo Público do Estado de São Paulo.

early 1890s, as many as 10,000 individuals crowded into the building.[25] In contrast to the relatively quick processing of immigrants on New York's Ellis Island, immigrants in São Paulo usually resided at the hospedaria for several days and sometimes up to a week before signing work contracts. To accommodate them, it had female and male dorms, a cafeteria, an infirmary, a hospital, food storehouses, a post and telegraph office, a currency exchange, and administrative buildings.[26] The facilities did not guarantee good living conditions; hygiene was often deplorable, with just one toilet for every other dorm room. But the hospedaria provided adequate shelter and above-average food for its temporary residents.[27]

Beginning in 1900, the state began allowing reentries into the hospedaria. The move expanded the hospedaria's services to individuals and families living in the city and included both immigrants who had already used the hospedaria's services and Brazilians already living in or arriving to the city. Planters insisted that they needed more laborers in the coffee-growing interior. To a certain extent, they did. Despite the declining price of coffee in world markets, Paulista coffee production continued to increase. From 1900 to 1906, the solution to Paulista overproduction was keeping coffee off the market. This was a viable option because of Brazil's virtual monopoly, but in 1906, overproduction prompted a crisis. A coffee valorization known as the Taubaté Agreement went into effect. A critical detail of the agreement was that in order to stabilize world coffee prices, Brazilian states would take out loans to buy back their coffee, removing it from the world market.[28] The impact on laborers was substantial, and more immigrants left São Paulo state than arrived. Already strapped for funds, the state's immigration subsidies came under scrutiny. The Department of Agriculture saw the state as doubly losing money, and hospedaria officials agreed to accept reentries.[29] Planters were one source of that pressure; the growing population right outside the hospedaria's doors was another. The city's population was growing, but so too was competition for jobs, and real wages were declining. For Paulistanos who were experiencing a period of extended unemployment and unable to make ends meet, the hospedaria represented a solution.

While reentries attest to a desire to leave São Paulo, that flux was vastly outnumbered by migration into the city. Opportunities and services were important factors promoting this movement. Wages were higher than in the interior, schools were more accessible, and the city had more resources. In addition, the city offered many of the proclaimed agriculturalists, who were actually tradesmen or daily laborers, more opportunities to practice their crafts.[30] Consular services and offices were also housed in the city of São Paulo, making it easier for immigrants to use these services if they lived in the city. Roughly 17 percent of Italian immigrants working in the *lavoura* between 1884 and 1904 chose to eventually move to the city. While the vast majority of *lavoura* contracts were for coffee plantations, the term also included other agricultural activities.[31] Conditions in the interior were so bad that amid rising complaints, the Italian government sent a representative of the General Emigration Commission, Aldo Rossi, to investigate conditions in São Paulo. His published finding of hunger and an overburdened consular system led to Italy's issuance of the 1902 Prinetti Decree, which banned Italians from accepting subsidized passage to Brazil.[32]

Other individuals bypassed the coffee economy completely and came to settle directly in the city. Immigrants used several strategies to avoid the hinterlands. Whether directly or indirectly, in most cases the hospedaria played an important role in their settlement. Some subsidized immigrants never intended to work in the fields or the interior. In effect, they took advantage of the state's system to get free passage to Brazil. Many scholars have assumed the hospedaria's fortress-like structure, guard patrols, and association with plantation labor gave immigrants little access outside of its walls.[33] As the Moreus and Viola families demonstrate, this was simply not the case. José Nuñez Moreno, a Spanish stoneworker,[34] arrived with his wife and three children in July 1906, but the hospedaria registros note that the family escaped into the city before they embarked for the interior.[35] Guiseppe Viola left Italy in the summer of 1912 with his wife, Carmella Saffiotti, and their two daughters, six-year-old Orsola and three-year-old Rosa.[36] A third party, José Aleixo da Silva Passos, paid for the family's passage, planning to be reimbursed by the state's treasury, to come and work on his farm in the interior. This process was called the *chamada* (call) system; it allowed farmers and other employers to bypass restrictions that some sending countries, notably Italy, imposed on subsidized immigration to Brazil.[37] Immigrants or employers would call a family member, friend, or future employee to Brazil. City residents sent money and the required documentation so their loved ones could get the necessary paperwork to move to or return to Brazil. In the Viola family's chamada, one day they left the hospedaria on a walk and simply never returned.[38] One farmer complained that an extended family of eight adults and three children never intended to accept his chamada and used the system for free passage to the city.[39] Other individuals and families openly rejected chamadas, often to meet up with family already established in the capital.[40]

Other immigrants at the hospedaria signed direct contracts to work in the city. The concept of direct contracts was nothing new and developed from the established practice of companies contracting workers from Europe and other Southern Cone areas. Direct contracts continued to be a common practice throughout the era.[41] The British department store Loja Mappin in São Paulo hired Silvio Ciacrelo Carlini away from the Gath y Chaves department store in Buenos Aires. He left his position as manager there in 1921 and started as Mappin's furniture and decorations department's manager; by 1925 he became Mappin's general manager.[42]

The importance of direct contracts like Silvio Carlini's to the city of São Paulo's development is undeniable, but such upper-level jobs were beyond the reach of most of the working class. More likely was that industrialists or managers would hire workers from their own countries of origin.[43] As the diversity among Paulistano business and factory owners shows, immigrants of many different backgrounds used national networks to secure employment. Records from April–September 1917 show that immigrants controlled 55 percent of the city's incorporated businesses.[44] The share of immigrants coming to the city substantiates this more popular form of direct contracts; in 1911, more than 12 percent of the 44,556 individuals passing through the hospedaria were contracted directly for jobs in the city. Even Italians signed such contracts, although they were less likely to use the hospedaria as an employment office because of the early influx of Italians and the number of Italian industrialists in São Paulo. The share of direct contracts to work in the city doubled, to more than 24 percent, in 1912 and to 23 percent in 1913 before dropping to 5.4 percent in 1914.[45]

The City Calls

Coming to São Paulo to meet up with family members already there was another common route to the city. Many unsubsidized immigrants would have fit into this category, as would have immigrants coming through the chamada system. The range of documents produced for a chamada included official certifications and testaments of residence, declarations of intent, and letters from family members. The hospedaria's surviving *cartas de chamada* (letters of calling) offer a window into the importance of family connections.

Documentation survives for 406 chamadas sent from the city between 1911 and 1927 that called 527 family members.[46] There is no apparent order to the frequency or methodology with which these letters and official documents were preserved. Many descriptions note that even when letters were found in the passenger registers, researchers were unable to link them to arriving immigrants. Other notes reference discrepancies in the name on the chamada and the name that appeared on passenger lists. Nevertheless, these documents serve as a valuable source of information in two contexts. First, even without knowing how and why hospedaria officials preserved this sample of letters, they still indicate the intentions of the city's immigrant population. Second, these letters in the immigrants' own words offer a window into how São Paulo's working class experienced and adapted to the city's growing pains and economic strains.

Of the 406 chamadas originating within the city, almost 35 percent were sent between 1911 and 1914,[47] with twenty-seven to forty documents a year. Italians, who dominated late nineteenth-century migration to the city, represented three out of every four documents sent between 1907 and 1914. Portuguese and Spanish immigrants made the remainder of the chamadas at 14 and 6 percent, respectively. The war years marked a steady decline in the number of chamadas, with just eight available documents for 1917 and 1918. Even then, most of the chamadas were likely destined for Buenos Aires rather than Europe. Italians still dominated, representing 65 percent of the documents, but Portuguese and Spanish remained a significant presence, at 17 and 19 percent, respectively. Once the war ended, more chamadas were sent but never with the frequency of the early period; for 1927, only two chamadas with documents are available. A small shift in immigrant nationality is seen in records for this later period. The Italian share of chamadas continued to drop, to 55 percent for the postwar period, while the Portuguese share rose to 33 percent.

As there was an increase in Portuguese migration to the city right before World War I, the timing of the rise in Portuguese chamadas supports the interpretation that it took immigrants around five to eight years to become rooted as permanent Brazilian residents. As immigrants became established and sometimes successful in the city, they were less likely to return home. At some point, a sense of responsibility for parents' well-being motivated many to ask their parents or in-laws to join them in the city. This responsibility was apparent, as six out of ten requests were directed toward parents or parents-in-law. There was minimal variation across time and nationalities. Opportunities and quality of life declined with the onset of World War I, but the war did not significantly affect immigrants' sense of obligation toward their parents.

For the remaining chamadas, one quarter were directed toward loved ones of the same generation such as spouses, siblings, compadres, brothers-in-law; the largest number was sent to spouses.[48] These spousal chamadas display some national variation. Italians initiated almost 90 percent, and of these, twenty-eight were wives calling their husbands to the city. Even in São Paulo, where family migration was more common than in other immigrant centers, Italians were more inclined to engage in the famed cyclical migration seen in Buenos Aires and New York City.[49] While that migration did not always require returning to Italy and could constitute shorter trips between Argentina and Brazil, it still set the Italian community and its experience apart from other nationalities residing in the city.[50]

Hospedaria Registrations

The number of immigrants arriving to the city on individual contracts and through the chamada system is indeterminable, although it was certainly many more than the 527 individuals documented in the chamadas. The registrations for subsidized and unsubsidized immigrants passing through the hospedaria provide an important and much more systematic glimpse into understanding who constituted São Paulo's newest working-class residents. Between 1903 and 1927 about 45–55 percent of immigrants coming to the state passed through the hospedaria's doors. This was in addition to city residents who arrived at the hospedaria seeking employment, roughly a quarter of the hospedaria's registrations over the period.[51] Even though the registrations do not include all migrants coming to the city and state, the records are still instructive. Given the hospedaria's deplorable conditions, most migrants or immigrants would have preferred to rely on friends and family for jobs or lodging. The historian Thomas Holloway asserts, "The system was clearly aimed at recruiting workers who were indigent or nearly so." He quotes the Italian consul's description in 1908 of subsidized immigrants as "in the condition of have-not."[52] Those passing through the hospedaria generally were the least socially connected or the poorest. Systematically studying these individuals and families at the bottom socioeconomic sector of each immigrant group arriving directly to the city reveals the uniqueness of the city's development and of incoming immigrant groups' relative skill levels.[53] These differences heightened Paulistano employer biases and preferences.

Between 1903 and 1927, a total of 17,789 adult individuals were contracted directly to the city, 9,060 of them heads of household and 8,729 other adults.[54] This number excludes individuals arriving in the earliest years of the Old Republic because consistent record keeping beyond an immigrant's name and arrival date did not begin at the hospedaria until 1903. Immigration officials began to keep better records after Italy's Prinetti Decree restricted Italian emigration to Brazil.[55] The end date, 1927, signifies when São Paulo Governor Júlio Prestes abolished state-subsidized European immigration.

Dividing the registrations into three different periods helps in examining the changing roles the hospedaria played in the city's labor market: 1903–1913, 1914–1918, and 1919–1927. These periods correspond to the years before, during, and after World War I.[56] The average annual number of capital contracts between 1903 and 1913 was 1,483. That average declined to 279 during the war years and continued to fall to 231 contracts per year between 1919 and 1927.[57] The decline of contracts during the war years reflects the economic challenges facing the city's residents at that time. The low number of contracts in the postwar period indicates the hospedaria's waning importance in the city's population growth. This trend in contracts also confirms the state's renewed dedication to coffee production through the immigration program. As direct contracts to the city declined,

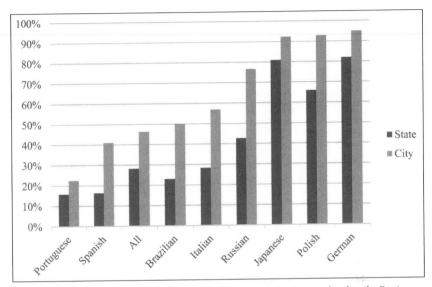

Figure 1.2. Literacy rates in São Paulo, 1903–1927. Appendix A provides details. Registros, Hospedaria de Imigrantes.

an immigration program developed between Japan and Brazil gained traction.[58]

The registrations show that immigrants signing contracts to work in the city were twice as likely to be literate as those who entered coffee production in the interior. This was true not only for the population as a whole but also for each national group. However, there were substantial differences in the literacy rates between national groups (figure 1.2). German, Polish, and Japanese immigrants consistently recorded literacy rates over 90 percent. While the Japanese rates are most likely artificially inflated, the German and Polish rates are genuinely notable.[59] Equally important are the low Portuguese literacy rates, below 35 percent. The differences in national literacy rates are not surprising within the global historiography; however, the evidence on different immigrant groups' literacy rates shows how the tendency in Brazilian historiography to compare the Brazilian literacy rate to the entire immigrant population's literacy has distorted the discussion of human capital by combining dissimilar groups.[60]

Changes in literacy rates for those signing contracts to work in the city can also reflect the trajectory of the city's development. Labor-intensive growth, featuring a labor force with a relatively high share of unskilled workers, often characterizes early industrialization. As the industrialization process matures, there should be a push to expand into capital-intensive

Table 1.1. Adult migration share to São Paulo state and city, 1903–1927, by nationality and period

	1903–1913		1914–1918		1919–1927		1903–1927	
NATIONALITY	STATE	CITY	STATE	CITY	STATE	CITY	STATE	CITY
Brazilian	9.5	1.9	31.5	6.1	51.9	4.3	22.1	2.4
Italian	22.9	15.1	25.9	22.4	7.4	8.3	19.0	14.9
Spanish	41.5	31.6	23.3	28.1	2.5	5.1	30.0	28.6
Portuguese	17.2	40.0	11.7	24.6	7.0	3.9	14.2	35.3
German	1.2	3.1	1.1	3.1	3.9	41.2	2.7	7.0
Russian	1.7	2.8	0.7	3.2	0.2	0.3	1.3	2.5
Polish	0.1	0.2	0.0	0.0	0.5	1.2	0.2	0.3
Japanese	2.4	1.1	3.4	5.9	17.8	3.0	6.5	1.6

Source: Based on 457,812 state observations and 17,789 city observations in registros.
Note: Other immigrant groups were a remainder of the shares.

industries. Whether this transition began in Brazil's Old Republic, prior to the state-led industrialization starting in the 1930s, is debatable.[61] As capital-intensive firms and businesses usually rely more heavily on semi-skilled and skilled workers than on their less skilled counterparts in labor-intensive sectors, the hospedaria registrations shed some light on this debate. The constant supply of agricultural workers through the subsidies presents an opportunity to examine the dynamics of the city's growth. Theoretically, large groups of unskilled workers would be more likely to remain in the city during periods of labor-intensive growth. A shift toward more literate workers later in the period would indicate a demand for more skilled labor in the city and a shift toward more capital-intensive industries.[62] Although evidence on immigrant literacy cannot reveal managerial and technological innovations or improvements in São Paulo's industrial sector, it does indicate that at least some structural change occurred.[63]

Based on increasing literacy rates over time in the hospedaria registrations, the education or at least the literacy levels of immigrants did increase during the Old Republic. In the first period, 1903–1913, the average literacy rate for adult male immigrants settling in the city was just 38.7 percent, with the rate for heads of household 28.9 percent. The war years showed a sharp increase, to 69 percent literacy, and the third period showed a similar jump in literacy, to 93 percent. Literacy gains were not gender-restricted, as adult women recorded similar increases: 20.5 percent in the prewar period, 30.5 percent during the war and 83.7 percent in the postwar period.

Table 1.1 presents the national shares of city contracts as compared to all signed contracts in the state; the breakdown serves to clarify driving factors behind the dramatic increase in literacy rates over the three periods. The two columns on the far right, for city and state during the entire period, show that two groups were more likely to sign contracts to work in the city: Portuguese and Germans. However, the timing of their migrations differed substantially. A large influx of Portuguese occurred during the first period, before World War I. The 1910 Portuguese revolution definitely increased the number of young, male Portuguese immigrants to Brazil in 1911–1913, but it was the demand for unskilled workers in the city's early expansion that brought more of them to the city than to the interior.[64] The considerable migration of Germans in the postwar period shows a transition toward greater demand for skilled work in the city during the 1920s.

THREE STORIES OF PORTUGUESE AND GERMAN DIVERGENCE

A family- and individual-level approach gives a better understanding of how immigrants from these distinctive immigrant streams navigated and encountered the city. Drawing from the hospedaria sample, these stories provide minibiographies of families and individuals whose traits and characteristics typified the prewar Portuguese immigrants and postwar German arrivals.

Julio Augusto and Manuel Joaquim were Portuguese immigrants to the city in the extraordinary influx of 1911 to 1913.[65] Most Portuguese arrivals during that period were young men who were agriculturalists, carpenters, day laborers, or stoneworkers. They left from Leixões, northern Portugal, and traveled with their families. Julio and Manuel largely fit these patterns. They came with their families, left Portugal's interior, and arrived in São Paulo in 1913. Julio, a thirty-two-year-old stoneworker from Mogadouro, in Bragança district, traveled with his wife and four children, ages one to nine years. Manuel, at almost sixty, was older than the typical immigrant, but as a widower, the agriculturalist from Gouveia likely hoped to provide his four children, ages thirteen to twenty-eight, with a new start. Within six months of each other, both men and their families left the homes they had known all their lives, traveled to Porto, made the short trip to Leixões, and left Portugal aboard ships headed to Brazil.[66]

Julio, his wife, Ricardina, and their children arrived at the hospedaria shortly after the start of the new year. Their journey began before the Christmas holidays in Mogadouro, a small city in Portugal's northeast corner. Packing up clothes and essentials, they likely took a train to Porto. Arriving in the city's impressive Estação São Bento, they merely had to walk into the adjoining Praça da Batalha to find immigrant transportation agencies ready to take them to Brazil.[67] As fate would have it, Julio Augusto and several other Portuguese immigrants got passages aboard the *Titian*, which was docked in Leixões and headed for Rio de Janeiro. After a ten-day passage, the family disembarked in Rio de Janeiro, ready for the final leg of their journey. Like many Portuguese immigrants who eventually came to São Paulo, the final stretch was a train ride on the Estrados de Ferro Central from Rio de Janeiro to the Hospedaria de Imigrantes in São Paulo. It was probably a few days after arriving on January 12, 1913, that Julio signed a contract to work in the city of São Paulo. Julio may not have intended to go to the interior to work. He and his family would have understood that his skills as a stoneworker were in high demand in the rapidly growing city when they made the decision to leave Mogadouro.

The Augusto family's first registered address in Brazil, on Rua João Teodoro in the Brás neighborhood, was just a short distance from the hospedaria (figure 1.3). City life was not new to the family, but São Paulo would have been much larger than their hometown of Mogadouro, a city of about 17,000 inhabitants.[68] The family evidently did not travel with friends or family members from their parish, and the Brás neighborhood would become their new community. Most of the 279 immigrants who had been aboard the *Titian* and traveled to the hospedaria with the Augustos also signed contracts to work in the city, and many also settled in Brás. Joaquim Canelles, another stoneworker in his thirties, moved to Rua João Teodoro with his wife, Ernestina, and their eleven-year-old son, Victor. The friendships and camaraderie developed on the passage provided important social networks for the new families. While Julio and Joaquim went to work, perhaps Ricardina and Ernestina navigated the new city together. While not from the same town, both women had just made the journey on the same ship, were married to stoneworkers, were mothers and neighbors, and came from the Bragança district in Portugal. They had much in common and would have had much to talk about.[69]

Manuel Joaquim and his family arrived four months after the Augusto and Canelles families. While Manuel may not have intended to stay in the city when he set out from Gouveia, his experience in getting to São Paulo was similar to that of the Augusto family. Once arriving in Porto, the family boarded a ship headed for Rio de Janeiro. When the family disembarked the *Samara* in Rio they continued the trek to São Paulo. At the hospedaria, on April 11, 1913, Manuel signed a contract to work in the city. Although no address is recorded for the Joaquims after they left the hospedaria, many

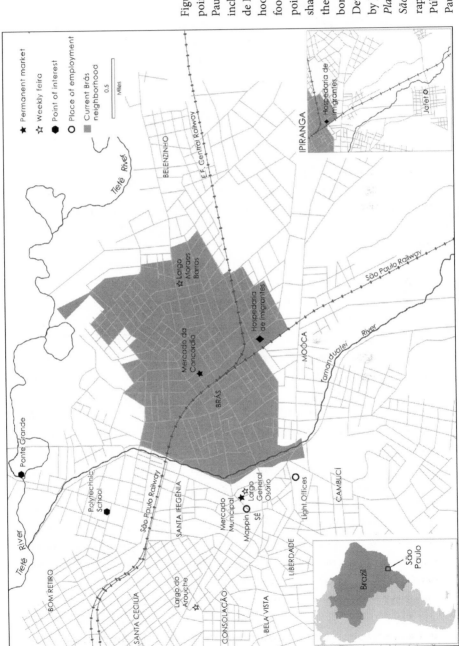

Figure 1.3. Working-class points of interest in São Paulo, 1914. The sites include the Hospedaria de Imigrantes, neighborhoods (*distritos da paz*), food markets, and other points of interest. The shaded area highlights the current Brás neighborhood boundaries. Developed from map by João Pedro Cardoso, *Planta geral da cidade de São Paulo*, 1914, Cartography Division, Arquivo Público do Estado de São Paulo.

of the immigrants signing contracts that day moved to the Brás neighborhood, home to the Augusto and Canelles families and the hospedaria. The Joaquim family likely did the same.[70] The change would have been striking. One hundred years later, the family's hometown of Gouveia, Portugal, as a metropolitan region has just 14,000 inhabitants and the city itself fewer than 4,000 residents. Brás's population alone was larger than the city the Joaquim family had known all their lives. Manuel's ability to read may have made the transition a little easier, but as they were agriculturalists, the shift would have been dramatic.

More than ten years and one world war after the Augusto and Joaquim families came to the city, Heinrich Strauss arrived to try his luck.[71] He was a part of the extraordinary wave of Germans to immigrate to the city after World War I that has been understudied.[72] As most historians concentrate on Italian and Portuguese newcomers, the importance and role of Germans and eastern Europeans is often neglected in the São Paulo immigration story.[73] Heinrich's profile and trajectory conform to those of many Germans arriving during that period; more than 40 percent of individuals contracted to work in the capital between 1919 and 1927 were German, and most of them left from Bremen.[74] There was also a steady stream coming from other Brazilian ports and from Buenos Aires.[75] German importance in the city is remarkable considering that Germans made up less than 7 percent of immigration to the state. Unlike the earlier wave of Portuguese immigrants, Germans to the city were overwhelmingly male (95%), literate (nearly 99%), and usually traveled alone although many were married. Almost half were agriculturalists, but carpenters, stoneworkers, industrial laborers and mechanics also signed contracts in sizeable numbers.

Although much of Heinrich's story will never be known, the hospedaria database and documentation give glimpses into his first moments in São Paulo. These insights demonstrate the uniqueness of the German migration experience to São Paulo in the 1920s. Born in 1895 or 1896, Heinrich would have been around eighteen at the start of World War I. He probably enlisted in the army and would have spent the first years of his adult life as a soldier for the Central Powers. This was probably not the start to adulthood that the young tailor and stoneworker had imagined. In the wake of Germany's defeat, the economic hardships facing Heinrich and much of the population could have made immigrating to Brazil attractive.[76]

The ship Heinrich boarded in Bremen in the winter of 1924, the *Seydlitz*, was full of other individuals like himself, single, semi-skilled and skilled laborers looking for new opportunities. Of more than 190 individuals who disembarked the ship in Santos and arrived at the hospedaria, only 32, among them 5 adult males, were agriculturalists; most of the others claimed professions related to machinery or metalworking. Employers in the city quickly contracted most of the ship's passengers; only 13 percent settled outside the city. In a distinct change from the years immediately preceding the war when unskilled and semi-skilled migrants were quick to find work in the construction sector, employers using the hospedaria in the postwar era preferred skilled laborers familiar with machines and metal trades. Another group of immigrants, mostly Polish agriculturalists who left Amsterdam for São Paulo, were staying at the hospedaria at the same time as the *Seydlitz's* passengers. As agriculturalists, the majority of these immigrants signed contracts for the interior.

Biased Expectations

The profiles of the Augusto and Joaquim families and of Heinrich illustrate the stark differences between the immigrants who arrived in different periods. How might these trends have affected individual experiences? Based on the hospedaria literacy rates, it is reasonable to expect that employers in São Paulo's Old Republic developed implicit biases about certain groups of immigrants. Those biases gave certain groups advantages over other groups arriving in the city. A series of statistical tests highlights how individual characteristics affected the chance that an individual passing through the hospedaria was literate. Although innumerable elements help determine an individual's likelihood of being literate, the information recorded in the registros allows consideration of the impact of certain characteristics on that likelihood; among them are gender, age, nationality, whether the individual arrived with a family, whether the individual had been in Brazil before, the skill level in the person's recorded profession, and the period when the immigrant arrived.[77] Of particular interest are the variables associated with nationality because it is there that one can begin to distinguish what expectations employers and fellow city residents may have had and developed about different national groups in the city.

The determinants shown in table 1.2 indicate how much more or less likely it was that an individual was literate as compared to an unskilled, single, Brazilian male who signed a contract to work in the city between 1903 and 1913. The results are restricted to the five largest nationality groups of immigrants who signed contracts to work in the city: Brazilians, Portuguese, Italians, Spanish, and Germans and Austrians as one group.[78] An

Table 1.2. Impact of individual determinants on Paulistano literacy, 1903–1927

Variable	% Change	Standard error	Z-value	Pr>|z|
Female	-16.0	0.082	-1.95	0.051
Age	-0.8	0.013	-0.62	0.537
Experience	0.0	0.000	0.63	0.529
Family	-10.1	0.053	-1.9	0.057
Brazil prior	7.9	0.068	1.15	0.248
NATIONALITY				
Portuguese	-39.9	0.217	-1.84	0.066
Italian	-15.5	0.216	-0.72	0.472
Spanish	-25.8	0.218	-1.18	0.237
German/Austrian	16.9	0.204	0.83	0.409
SKILL LEVEL				
Semi-skilled	26.4	0.112	2.36	0.018
Skilled	23.1	0.066	3.49	0.000
Highly skilled	8.7	0.146	0.6	0.550
PERIOD				
1914–1918	-7.9	0.088	-0.89	0.371
1919–1927	8.0	0.132	0.61	0.543

Source: Registros head-of-household sample. See Appendix A.
Note: Comparison is an unskilled Brazilian male migrating between 1903 and 1913.
"Brazil prior" is a dummy variable that records previous residence in Brazil.

unskilled, single, Portuguese male was nearly 40 percent more likely to be illiterate than his Brazilian counterpart, while the typical German or Austrian was 17 percent more likely to be literate. City employers paid attention to these differences. This evidence suggests that while the unskilled German immigrant likely benefited from these assumptions, the skilled Portuguese worker probably had to go above and beyond to prove his or her abilities to a potential employer.

One important limit to the literacy evidence is that it privileges literacy over an equally or perhaps more important trait: experience. In the Old Republic, especially during the city's rapid urbanization and labor-intensive growth, many employers preferred an experienced carpenter or stoneworker to a literate office worker. This was especially true in the prewar period, when construction jobs could barely be filled to keep pace with the city's population growth.[79] Incoming professions recorded in the registros, then, may give a better understanding of employer expectations. Analyzing all of the entries is not advisable because so many individuals were mislabeled or purposefully misrepresented themselves as agriculturalists to gain subsidized passage. Considering select professional categories offers a better approach. Textile workers, mechanics and blacksmiths, and businessmen are three professional categories that represent three distinct sectors of the economy and a range of skill levels.[80] Textile workers were largely unskilled or semi-skilled and mechanics and blacksmiths either semi-skilled or skilled tradesmen. Skill level is more difficult to determine with the businessmen category because the category allows for a range from unskilled peddlers to highly skilled business owners, but the nature of the profession offered more opportunities for social mobility.

In all of the registrations, there were 1,135 textile workers, 1,659 mechanics and blacksmiths, and 284 businessmen. Of these 3,078 individuals, 39 percent settled in the city.[81] Looking at the national shares among these three professions again distinguishes Germans, Austrians, and Portuguese from other groups. Germans and Austrians constituted roughly half of the registered businessmen and almost a quarter of metalworkers, even though they represented less than 10 percent of migration to the city between 1903 and 1927. No other nationality was so overrepresented or underrepresented within the categories. In contrast, Portuguese immigrants were underrepresented in each of the three professions considered.[82]

A statistical approach similar to the literacy likelihood addresses whether certain immigrant groups in the registrations sample were more likely to declare unskilled and highly skilled professions when registering in the hospedaria. The results are consistent with the observations except that they show Brazilians the most likely group to declare unskilled professions.[83] Furthermore, Germans and Austrians were as much as 21 percent less likely to be unskilled workers. While the overstatement of agriculturalists must be considered in interpreting the results, the tests show that employers in São Paulo's labor market were reasonable in perceiving Germans as a highly skilled immigrant group.

Brazilian Expectations

New immigrant arrivals were integral to the city's growth and changing character, but what did native Brazilians encounter in São Paulo? Scholars debate Brazilians' skills relative to those of incoming immigrants, but the debates structured around this question have been relatively restricted to the immigrant/Brazilian binary.[84] Brazilians in the city themselves represented a wide range of people, from established Paulistano families to migrants from the state's interior and other Brazilian states. At the time of abolition, roughly 30 percent of the state's population was Afro-Brazilian. Abolition also brought a significant migration of Afro-Brazilians from coffee plantations to urban centers.[85] The hospedaria registrations also prove useful in examining the city's Brazilian population. Even though the hospedaria's original design was for incoming immigrants, its acceptance of reentries and extension of services to city residents in 1900 meant that Brazilians started appearing alongside immigrants. The way Brazilians used the hospedaria would have been different, but the registros still provide a systematic approach to understanding the changing Brazilian population within the city.

The first Brazilians in the hospedaria's registros were a family from Ceará state. Manoel Cordeiro de Souza, his wife, Rosa, and their eight children, ranging in age from seven months to fourteen years, arrived at the hospedaria on May 15, 1884. One day later the family signed a contract to work in the interior, in Rio Claro.[86] While a handful of Brazilians did use the hospedaria in the 1890s, as expected, the number jumped dramatically once reentries were legally permitted in 1900. More than 700 Brazilians registered at the hospedaria that year. In the peak years of migration, 1911–1913, it had 10,449 Brazilians registered, an average of almost 3,500 per year. As shown in table 1.1, these Brazilians were more likely than immigrants to end up in the *lavoura*. Brazilians wanting to move to the city would have used their own means or existing social connections. The discrepancies between the literacy rates of migrants using the hospedaria and registered literacy rates in the 1920 Brazilian census reveal important regional differences in how migrants used the hospedaria. While northeastern migrants lacked the social connections, it was southeastern migrants who lacked the literacy and work experience.

Brazilians who migrated to São Paulo state had higher human capital levels than those who chose not to migrate. The literacy rates for the populations passing through the hospedaria were higher than those registered in the 1920 census for every single state, with the exception of migrants arriving from northern and northeastern states during extreme droughts.[87] This difference was particularly pronounced for Brazil's northern and northeastern states. In a sense, the state of São Paulo gained Brazil's most educated citizens, imposing a drain on the rest of the country.

Brazilian migration patterns also suggest World War I as the period when northeastern migration to the Southeast became ingrained. Most migrants prior to the war were agriculturalists from the interior regions of São Paulo and Rio de Janeiro, often poor farmers from the Paraíba Valley with high illiteracy rates.[88] As immigrant streams waned from Europe to Southern Cone destinations like Buenos Aires and São Paulo, the responses diverged. Argentina's labor market was saturated, but Paulista planters still needed agricultural workers.[89] They increasingly looked to Brazilians within the state and in other regions to fill the labor void. The share of migrants from Minas Gerais increased from 5.9 percent in 1903–1913 to 15.1 percent during the war years. An even more pronounced increase occurred in northeastern migrants to the state, jumping from just 3 percent to 26 percent. In the period after the war, the northeastern share continued to increase, comprising 43 percent of Brazilian registrations at the hospedaria from 1919 to 1927. During the same period, Mineiros, residents of the adjacent state of Minas Gerais, constituted 34.4 percent of entries.

While arriving Mineiros had low literacy rates (35%), northeasterners had higher literacy rates than the traditional historiography suggests; they were more likely to be literate than Portuguese, Spanish, Italian, and Russian immigrants passing through the hospedaria.[90] Here racial prejudice likely funneled many of these northeasterners into the *lavoura* instead of the Paulistano workforce. As João André Macedo's experience shows, the likelihood of moving directly to work in the city from the hospedaria for Brazilians was slim.

João André was born in Caicó, the largest city in Rio Grande do Norte's Seridó region. In the northeastern inland area and on the state's border with Paraíba, by the late nineteenth century traditional cattle ranching and cotton agriculture dominated the economy. Fueled primarily by southeastern textile factory demand, cotton surpassed sugar as the Seridó region's primary product in 1905.[91] Perhaps it was a change in cotton demand associated with World War I that convinced inhabitants to leave for São Paulo. In late June or early July 1915, just before the city's patron saint festival, at least fifty-seven inhabitants started their trek to São Paulo. They first went to Natal, where they boarded a ship named the *Maranhão*. Once aboard, they traveled down the coast to Rio de Janeiro. Some of these migrants may have stayed in Rio, but fifty-seven boarded a train headed for São Paulo's Hospedaria de Imigrantes.[92]

João André, a twenty-six-year-old, unmarried, literate agriculturalist was among the fifty-seven.[93] There is nothing particularly remarkable about his entry except that he was the only individual from the ship contracted to work in the city. While the number of city contracts during the war greatly decreased, on the same date that the Caicó migrants received agricultural contracts, July 19, 1915, a group of five immigrants arriving from Buenos

Aires were all directly contracted to work in the city.[94] It cannot be known for sure if racial prejudice factored into this discrepancy, as registrations did not record race; however, given that many of the Caicoenses aboard the *Maranhão* were literate, race probably played a role in their movement to the interior.[95] As the lone migrant passenger to gain work in the city, João André was as unfamiliar with São Paulo in 1915 as Julio Augusto and his family had been when they arrived two years earlier. The Augustos were fortunate to have each other and a network of friendships established on the passage from Porto to Rio and then onto São Paulo, while João André was thrust into São Paulo alone.

Conclusion

Delving into the depths of São Paulo's period of fastest growth reveals the complexity of the city's population. As a whole, arrivals in the city were more skilled and had higher literacy rates than individuals settling in the state's interior. However, there were important differences between national groups. The stark contrast of unskilled Portuguese immigrants arriving prior to World War I and skilled German immigrants arriving after the war underscore that there was no singular immigrant experience. The changes in these immigrant streams over time also reflect important changes taking place in the city's development. As the Old Republic progressed, there was some movement from labor-intensive to capital-intensive growth.

The hospedaria was instrumental in that process by facilitating connections between employers and potential employees. After 1900, when reentries were allowed, the institution served a pivotal role in recruiting, moving, and connecting migrants and immigrants with available employers. By 1906, of all subsidized immigrants, 5 percent could be nonagricultural laborers, and in 1907, the share rose to 10 percent. A well-oiled machine, the hospedaria also facilitated laborers' ability to move between rural and urban opportunities. By providing free passage to the interior, it allowed laborers and agriculturalists to transition into other jobs without having to put forth expensive moving costs. For employers, it offered direct access to workers looking for jobs.

Just how did the city of São Paulo continue to entice immigrants and migrants alike? How did families like the Joaquims and Augustos and individuals like Heinrich Strauss and João André adapt to their new city? Although the exact fates of these immigrants and migrants remain a mystery and will prove difficult to determine, it is possible to imagine what types of experiences they would have encountered.

Examining the changing daily realities that working-class individuals and families encountered from the onset of São Paulo's Old Republic through World War I shows that city residents were forced to adapt to the hardships imposed on the city's lower classes during the war. As the building trades all but came to a halt by 1915, the stoneworker Julio Augusto would have found new sources of family income if he wanted to stay in the city. Agriculturalists Manuel Joaquim and João André may have returned to the hospedaria with plans of moving into the interior to work on farms. At the end of the day, it was having a job and keeping good health that provided the hope of moving beyond the margins.

2

The City of Opportunity?

Rapid expansion and a swelling population was a double-edged sword for the majority of São Paulo's population. For the first twenty-two years of the Old Republic, from 1891–1913, a natural ebb and flow characterized the expansion, and residents responded and adapted accordingly. As new industries and factories appeared along newly laid transit and railroad lines, more people were drawn to or remained in the city. An oversupply of labor would lead to a temporary increase in unemployment and underemployment. Some immigrants would return to Europe or try their luck in Buenos Aires, other residents would leave for the interior, but others remained in the city waiting on new opportunities to arise. Quick to respond to the increasing demands of the growing population, small shops, impromptu housing, and peddling developed. Independent mechanic shops sprang up to maintain older machinery that was costly to replace. Where factory jobs and steady employment were lacking, Paulistanos made their own opportunities. Ten years into the Old Republic, if individuals and families were still unable to make a living in the city, they could move to the interior for work with relative ease by just reentering the hospedaria.

To understand the world immigrants and migrants encountered in the city, one must investigate how daily challenges facing Paulistanos changed from the start of the Old Republic through the end of World War I. In clarifying how the working-class population as a group experienced uncertainty and hardship, their responses to these challenges also become clearer. This is not to suggest that everyone in São Paulo's working classes experienced the city in the same way. Nationality and discrimination altered opportunities for certain groups, particularly Afro-Brazilians and women. However, the impact of general economic trends on lower economic classes' lives remains understudied for this period.[1] Scholars paint a picture of the city in the early years of the Old Republic that is murky at best, highlighting poor working conditions and inadequate services and housing. Maria Inez Pinto best approximates the working classes' challenges, opportunities, and adaptations, but her analysis stops in 1914 and fails to underscore marked quality-of-life improvements Paulistanos experienced during the city's intense period of growth.[2] As immigrant letters attest, while the cost of living did slowly increase, many of the city's working-class residents benefited from the growing urban economy.[3] These trends underscore how dramatic a change was to come.

Combining a variety of archival, primary, and secondary sources presents a much clearer picture of daily Paulistano life in the pre–World War I era. Official municipal, state, and federal reports show the cyclical nature of the formal labor market. Letters included in passport applications and calls to immigrate provide a window into how the working class perceived the labor market. These letters also provide a window into perceptions about the cost of living, as do hygiene and housing reports and a new price series on the food costs developed for the period.[4] Official vital statistics and marriage rates and school attendance records indicate how workers' quality of life shifted in the prewar era.

For the working class, World War I marked a watershed. External factors completely out of their control had affected them in the earlier period, but the war arguably had the greatest impact on the Paulistano working class during the Old Republic. Distinct migration patterns emerged before and after World War I. The war also adversely affected Paulistanos' quality of life and precipitated an outmigration toward the interior. Families who stayed in the city during the war adapted. Municipal markets became an important source of food to mitigate rising food prices, and most families adapted the family wage strategy honed during the prewar period to survive the economic downturn. This move toward more childhood and female employment made it more difficult to attend school, cutting short earlier advancements in education.[5] In essence, by limiting human capital, the war stunted development. Those individuals who could not find opportunities in the formal labor market often turned to the informal market. The adjustments Paulistanos made to endure the years 1914 through 1918 institutionalized the family wage and informality, making both permanent solutions in the years to follow.

Employment Conditions

Employment opportunities at the dawn of the Old Republic were numerous. They had actually been on the rise since 1882, when a law permitting joint-stock companies to form without government charters led to the expansion of public utilities, urban transportation, insurance companies, and mills in São Paulo.[6] These new business ventures resulted in a steady increase in working-class jobs. In January 1890, reforms loosening credit restrictions and limiting investor liability accelerated business formation in São Paulo. The number of firms grew so dramatically that São Paulo began its own stock exchange in 1890, the São Paulo Bolsa. While just 30 joint-stock companies operated in 1887, within the first six months of the new laws, 222 joint-stock companies and banks were formed. Just as quickly, however, many of these new companies failed, and by April 1892, the Encilhamento had crashed and the Bolsa closed due to minimal trading. This boom-and-bust cycle is referred to as the Encilhamento; the boom spanned the late 1880s to the early 1890s. Growth was not merely speculative, and the companies surviving the euphoria and speculation were arguably stronger and more established by the late 1890s.[7]

For the city's working class, the Encilhamento's crash greatly changed employment opportunities. In the short term, company failures resulted in job loss. Migration to the state as a whole in 1890–1892 reflects the prevailing business climate; approximately 38,000 immigrants arrived through the port of Santos in 1890, and the number grew to 108,000 in 1891 before contracting to 42,000 in 1892.[8] A more important long-term effect of the Encilhamento was an increase in the diversity of sectors and the jobs available to working-class Paulistanos. The post-Encilhamento failures actually did little to slow the city's development. As early as 1892, a variety of new firms opened their doors, and the city's footprint began to grow.[9] When the Bolsa reopened in 1895, most of these new ventures did not trade shares on the market. In 1907, for example, just 1 percent of all industrial firms and 20 percent of industrial capital were traded on the Bolsa. During the 1890s, more than eighty firms formed through the Bolsa, suggesting the substantial growth taking place in the state as a whole in the last decade of the nineteenth century. Growth was diverse and included rudimentary chemical production, machinery and metalworking, textiles, and beer brewing. Even though the Bolsa's growth was substantial, the city's expansion was more impressive in the fifteen years following the Encilhamento.[10] Estimates place the city's population at just under 65,000 residents in 1890, but in just three years, the population nearly doubled, to 129,000. The working-class neighborhoods of Santa Ifigênia and Brás showed the greatest growth.[11] By the 1900 census, the population nearly doubled again, with almost 240,000 individuals calling the city home.

A growing city meant more construction jobs, and job advertisements in the *Estado de São Paulo* newspapers portray a labor market favorable to workers. Local companies posted ads for experienced construction workers, offering as much as 4$000 per day in 1892.[12] While 4$000 was competitive in terms of wages, after buying a chicken and a dozen eggs, a man would only have 0$800 left for all other expenses.[13] To compete, another company offered 4$000 a day plus housing, medical services, and discounted meals.[14] For the four hundred to five hundred workers taking the second offer, these additional benefits would have been substantial.

As the city's population grew, so did residents' demand for goods and services. Accordingly, the number of manufacturing, utility, urban improvement, and real estate companies increased substantially in São Paulo between 1907 and 1913. New migrants to the state and city sought out these products, and prospective and established industrialists responded, harnessing capital and opening new establishments. Their ability to open new businesses was connected to the government's intervention in the coffee economy in 1906. Coffee overplanting had flooded the world market, decreasing coffee prices and thus crippling state revenues. As Brazil produced nearly 85 percent of the world's coffee, planters convinced the São Paulo government to buy the surplus coffee and stabilize domestic prices. These measures, which would be the first in a series of coffee valorization schemes, were unique in the Latin American context, but they had the additional impact of stimulating investment in the city's industrial ventures.[15]

Factories opened in various sectors, but no other sector grew as rapidly as textiles.[16] A creeping protection for the textile industry in the late empire that accelerated into de facto protectionist policies by the early twentieth century stimulated the sector's growth. It was the first wave of globalization in Brazil and Latin America, but most textile factory owners were lobbying for protection.[17] Factory owners in Brazil successfully lobbied to have both higher import tariffs levied on finished textile products and tariff exemptions for imported factory machinery. They justified the move away from laissez-faire policies as a matter of national interest and patriotism.[18] As a result, the number of textile factories in the city was substantial by the start of the twentieth century. In 1900, the Brás neighborhood housed at least nine industrial factories, five of which produced textiles and related products. A report ten years later recorded thirty-one textile operations employing thousands of workers throughout the city.[19]

Constant industrial growth and construction was not uniformly sustainable; they were concentrated in the years 1890–1894 and 1906–1910.[20] Even during these periods of growth, many workers struggled to find steady employment. A masons league noted in 1909 how many stoneworkers in the city only worked 188 days of the year. Most spent almost a quarter of the year unemployed and looking for work.[21] These work hiatuses meant individuals fell well short of earning sufficient income to support their families or even themselves. Workers did become accustomed to the cyclical unemployment patterns and held out hope for future opportunities.

Working extra hours provided São Paulo's working class with one important tool to mitigate the downturns in the volatile labor market. Even if employment was not steady, during stretches of employment, overtime work of sometimes thirteen-hour days was common. Jacob Penteado recalls how most textile and glass factories operated on large orders to prevent stockpiling and overproduction. Factories would even open on Sunday if there was a large enough order to fill.[22] Given these conditions, attendees at the state's second Congresso Operário, held in mid-September 1908, requested that employers compensate employees weekly because on multiple occasions, employers, likely short on capital, simply did not pay monthly wages.[23] In a more stable market, workers would have preferred to receive monthly salaries as a sign of security. Indeed, this was the worker preference in later years of the Old Republic.

In the first three months of 1913 many factories laid off 20 percent to 50 percent of their personnel, all but eliminating an increase in salaries awarded in the previous three months. Other companies failed entirely.[24] Employees in some sectors and companies, such as São Paulo Tramway, Light, and Power's mechanics department, fared better for the first part of 1913; by December, the company reduced its workforce by 35 percent due to a lack of work.[25] These workers were feeling the impact of a worldwide recession precipitated by European monetary restrictions that limited capital inflows and effectively slowed down economies. In contrast to the first twenty-three years of the Old Republic, the 1913 downturn persisted. World War I further disrupted Latin America in the years that followed. The value of the goods and services produced in Argentina dropped by almost 20 percent from 1913 to 1917.[26] For the state of São Paulo, wartime disruption led to a decline in the importance of coffee in state revenues.[27] While domestic production increased, as did trade to other states within Brazil, the fall in imports brought on by the war made serious hardships and led to a period of inflation and a decrease in quality of life.

Letters to family members across the Atlantic provide insights into how city residents, particularly immigrants, understood the city's employment opportunities during this downturn. The letters' characteristically poor spelling and penmanship indicate the working-class background of the writers or of the individuals dictating the letters. Many were day laborers and semi-skilled urban workers hoping to take advantage of the opportunities the growing city provided. Even as work began to wane on the eve of World War I, letters were generally positive about the city's labor opportunities. As one immigrant described the city, "He who is healthy and has work" is happy in the city.[28] Another referenced "a lot of work," and even when the writer's employment situation seemed more tenuous, the tone remained hopeful. José assured his wife, Adelaide, that "living together here [in São Paulo] things will come well to me and my work." He insisted they could be successful opening a laundry business in the heart of São Paulo's downtown.[29] Antonia Moreno counseled her son that São Paulo was like anywhere: "He who wants to work eats and employment is not lacking[.] the rest depends on a person's industry and luck and ability."[30]

The extent to which ability and hard work brought success contracted dramatically with the onset of World War I. Industrialists pointed out that the war years led to "low-cost maintenance and minimal construction."[31] What did this mean for workers themselves? In the first place, it meant lower wages. The impact in the construction industry was immediate, and as early as 1913, workers experienced decreasing nominal wages. Even in a best-case scenario in which nominal wages did not fall, rising inflation during the war years meant those wages could buy fewer products. The 1918 real wage for unskilled, low-skilled and medium-skilled workers was just 56 percent, 50 percent, and 67 percent, respectively, what it had been in 1913.[32] In addition to lower wages, business failures represented another challenge for workers. One failed business was not a problem, but many failed businesses and no new businesses meant substantial job losses. World War I saw many business failures. The number of firms traded on São Paulo's Bolsa decreased from 147 in 1913 to 138 in 1917, and many companies failed that were not publicly traded. Several important railroads, banks, and public utility companies folded, and textile firms registered the highest number of failures on the Bolsa.[33] As textiles made up the largest industrial employment sector in the city, those firms' failures dealt particularly severe blows to the lower classes. When the state again surveyed the city's textile industry in 1919, only twenty factories were recorded as compared to the thirty-one in 1911.[34]

For workers, these business failures signaled a dramatic and long-lasting decrease in available jobs. Over the course of 1914, the workforce in São Paulo Tramway, Light, and Power Company's mechanical department was cut by 35 percent, with the greatest number of layoffs occurring in August. In August and September, eighty-three employees working in the offices, garage, car barns, and shops lost their jobs.[35] It did not take long for Paulistanos to realize that the economic downturn from World War I was distinct. Within the year 1914, residents left the city at a faster rate. Immigrants were unwilling and often unable to return to war-torn Europe. The downturn inspired many city residents to enter the *lavoura* during the war years. The share of urban migration to the interior through the hospedaria jumped up from 15 percent in 1913 to 45 percent in 1914. The rate remained high during the war period, reaching 55 percent in 1915, 45 percent in 1916, and 54 percent in 1917. In the first three months of 1915 alone, more than 6,500 individuals, mostly from the city of São Paulo, entered the hospedaria to find employment.[36] The war also marked a change in whom the hospedaria served in terms of nationality. One of every four people who entered the hospedaria in 1915 was Brazilian, while from 1901 through 1914, Brazilians accounted for just one in twenty entries.[37]

For those Paulistanos who chose to stay in the city, a few found success, but most still struggled to get by despite adapting to less than ideal conditions to the best of their ability. While many companies and ventures failed during the war years, those that survived become more stable. With high and persistent unemployment surrounding them, individuals fortunate enough to have employment at these companies sought to secure their positions with biweekly and then monthly salaries although such a change often meant accepting a lower wage or a salary.[38] In the textile companies that survived, these jobs were increasingly held by women, who received lower wages. For Paulistanos, however, even a lower income was better than no income.

The words residents penned to family members during the war years reflect São Paulo's tarnishing luster and their movement between the city and the interior. Unable to make ends meet in the city meant following a trajectory similar to that of Joaquim Teixeira de Souza. Joaquim left Porto and arrived in Rio on February 5, 1914, but he encountered absolutely no work. By mid-March he arrived in São Paulo and met with similar frustration.

However, in São Paulo, Joaquim went to the hospedaria to inquire as to where some family friends had signed *lavoura* contracts. The immigration officials not only found out where the family was but actually sent Joaquim a telegram telling him the family was working close to Rio Claro. Joaquim joined the family friends about 200 kilometers northwest of the city of São Paulo and worked for two weeks but again was unable to earn sufficient income. It was then that he found work nearby at the Fazenda de Santa Maria in Taquarintinga, São Paulo state. By May, he felt confident enough in his situation to ask his wife back in Portugal to join him.[39]

FOOD AND COST OF LIVING

While employment opportunities were relatively abundant during the early years of the Old Republic, their sporadic nature severely complicated budgeting and planning for daily expenses. Paulistanos could hedge against periods of unemployment by making larger purchases during times of gainful employment, but food purchases and rent were two expenses for which this strategy was not viable. Food prices and rents rose as a whole after the fall-out from the Encilhamento, but until the onset of World War I, these rising costs did little to discourage mass migration to the city. The gradual increases led many Paulistanos into a false sense of security. Minor spending adjustments and a few more work hours made inflation manageable. Even when times were difficult, life back in Europe or in other Latin American urban centers was not much better, and the state's welcoming policy toward families continued to make the city an attractive destination.

Considering changes in food prices and inflation is particularly instructive for understanding how larger economic trends affect the working class. Food was one of the largest expenses for the working class, and individuals' and households' quality of life was particularly susceptible to increases or decreases in food costs. The typical Paulistano five-person, working-class family consumed around 3.8 kilograms of beans, 5.2 of rice, 2.2 of potatoes, 9.2 of meat, 1 of lard and bacon, 14 of bread and 1.8 of sugar weekly.[40] The variations in food prices up until World War I show just how dramatic increases could be. The greatest jump in prices occurred just after the Encilhamento, with prices rising between 1.3 and 1.7 times their 1891 levels. Banks issued paper money in excess during the eighteen-month Encilhamento period, and inflation quickly followed, directly and disproportionately hitting the lower classes. While prices continued to rise until 1896, they did so at a much less dramatic pace. As this increase roughly coincides with the 1890–1894 industrial and construction boom in the city, available job opportunities likely lessened the impact of higher costs.

The changing prices for a dozen eggs and a hen between 1890 and 1898 demonstrate the relatively slow increase in prices, especially relative to wages. Table 2.1 displays these prices alongside an estimate for daily food expenses for a family of five and the hourly nominal wage for the typical day laborer in the city.[41] More practically, in terms of the hours of work required to cover just food expenses, working-class Paulistano families likely budgeted 40–50 percent of earnings for food costs in families with only one working adult male. Table 2.1 also shows that during the last decade of the nineteenth century, nominal wages did not increase as quickly as food prices did. Effectively, food became more expensive. The price increase was modest, though, and did not rise more than 10 percent annually after the first dramatic increase; that slower rise allowed for relatively easy budget modifications.[42]

As 1914 approached, food prices were double to more than triple what they had been at the beginning of the Old Republic. During the same period, nominal wages also rose, meaning that real wages even slightly increased in the first few years of the twentieth century.[43] That food prices did not increase more quickly than workers' wages explains why immigrants rarely mention food prices as a cause for concern in their letters to family members joining them in São Paulo. In fact, although likely exaggerated, sons, daughters, and spouses wrote messages home such as "Here you will not lack in food" and even "There are good onions you can cut in your own corner in peace."[44]

This trend would change dramatically between 1914 and 1918. The state's secretary of justice and public safety, Elói Chaves, described "a situation so distressing in that the majority of the population, deprived of resources for their own subsistence, because of a lack of work."[45] Several options were debated, but a series of price-controlled markets throughout the city formed an important part of the city's plan to address the issue. These *feiras livres* were traveling markets that appeared in different city neighborhoods on a weekly basis. Organized and financed by the city, the traveling markets were intended as a means to better link suppliers to consumers and extend to areas where residents could buy basic necessities beyond the city's three permanent markets. Ultimately, the goal was to control the increasing cost of living by keeping food costs lower. In 1914, three *feiras* began operating, in the Largo do Arouche, Largo General Osório, and Largo Morais de

Table 2.1. Average Paulistano prices and wages, 1890–1898

Year	Dozen eggs	Hen	Family daily food expenses	Hourly nominal wage[a]	Hours/food expenses[b]
1890	0$900	1$100	0$673	0$222	3
1891	1$000	2$750	0$886		
1892	1$700	2$750	1$328	0$344	4
1893	2$100		1$602	0$317	5.25
1894			1$422	0$325	4.5
1895	1$900	2$750	1$736	0$356	5
1896	2$050	2$750	1$656	0$428	4
1897	2$100	2$650	1$705	0$411	4.25
1898	1$700	2$650	1$700	0$423	4.25

Source: Prices from Estado de São Paulo prices database.
[a] Hourly wage for a twenty-five-year-old unskilled Brazilian male worker. Calculated from Ball, "Prices, Wages, and the Cost of Living," 12–13.
[b] Work hours per food expenses rounded up to quarter hours. Estimation technique as described in Ball, "Prices, Wages, and the Cost of Living," 12–15.

Barros (figure 1.3). By 1915, seven of these rotating markets operated in the city.

While the *feiras* may have kept prices from skyrocketing to even greater heights for consumers, food prices still rose considerably during the war years, as shown in table 2.2. The Paulista press in 1917 blamed the city government for being unwilling to institute price ceilings on necessities or to regulate food producers. The grains needed to bring down prices were being grown, but they were sent to the international market, where they fetched higher prices, rather than remaining in Brazil. There was also the important question as to the quality of the food that was being sold at the *feiras*. From the very start, there was the question of spoiled food and products being misrepresented or adulterated. Marketgoers learned to be wary of butter, tomato sauce, salted pork, and sausages. The oversight by the municipal government did not improve these subterfuges, and in 1917 the city had a number of deaths resulting from food poisoning. By 1917, it was clear that the laissez-faire approach was failing the city's lower classes.[46]

Using a cost-of-living survey for the city for 1913 to 1935, I show that while salaries for domestic workers increased 33 percent from 1913 to 1918, most food costs rose more dramatically. The prices Mario Cardim records for the city demonstrate how bread, beans, meat, and rice prices rose more quickly than wages, marking a dramatic shift from the prewar period.[47] Coupled with the scarcity of job opportunities in the city, the increase in

Table 2.2. Percentage Paulistano unit cost increase, 1914–1918

Year	Domestic salary	Rent	Bread	Beans	Meat	Potatoes	Rice	Sugar
1914	0	6.7	16.7	35.4	0.0	-33.3	0.0	-26.4
1915	16.7	6.3	14.3	-26.1	37.4	29.0	9.4	18.3
1916	0	5.9	0.0	-17.7	0.0	0.0	8.6	12.7
1917	0	5.6	12.5	21.5	19.7	16.3	0.0	7.4
1918	14.3	5.3	11.1	35.4	-8.9	19.4	17.1	52.5
1913–18	33.3	33.3	66.7	35.4	49.8	19.4	39.1	60.6

Source: Cardim, *Ensaio de analyse*, 20–25. Increase in percentage is constructed comparing average unit cost with the previous year.

food costs would force many individuals and families out of the city, send more family members to work, and move more people into the informal economy.

Food products were not the only items subject to inflation during the period; coal and clothing costs also increased dramatically, by 80 percent and 67 percent, respectively.[48] Protecting the textile industry did not improve the lives of most workers; rather, it exacerbated a problem residents already faced in the city, of overpriced clothes of poor quality.[49] In the prewar era, immigrants and other residents seemed relatively unconcerned with food costs, but clothing costs and quality were a completely different story. Constant references asking family members to bring clothes and sheets and sometimes even sewing machines demonstrate that it was particularly difficult to acquire quality clothing in the city. As of the late 1880s, the government had increasingly protected the textile industry by raising import tariffs on finished cloth and lowering tariffs on raw materials, textile machinery, and capital goods. Textile tariffs were already high in 1895, at 22 percent, and they effectively reached 50 percent by 1906.[50] Given that the city had at least thirty textile factories by 1912, these complaints attest that amid heavy protection, Brazilian products were still highly inferior to imported products.

Letters from Brazil humanize the impact that protective measures had on individuals. Luiz Moreira Barbosa emphatically instructed his wife, Eugenia, to bring at least two pairs of shoes or boots with her from Portugal because of the high prices in São Paulo. Luiz seemed to have been particularly incensed after buying a pair of new socks for 0$600 that after just three hours' wear already had a big hole in one.[51] Luiz's experience appears to have been common, as requests to bring clothes and sheets crossed class lines.

Agriculturalists requested good hats and farm clothes, and urban laborers asked for work clothes. More refined immigrants sent specific instructions to make sets of clothes.[52] For the city's many poor residents, high clothing costs would have been another burdensome but important portion of the budget. In a society in which a good appearance could open doors for jobs, dressing the part was key. Thus, recent European immigrants who could ask kinsmen and friends to bring extra clothes with them had a distinct advantage over Brazilians and long-established immigrant families.

The number of cost burdens for São Paulo's lower classes grew dramatically with the onset of the war. Letters no longer referred to abundant food and building supplies. Clothing was no longer the only problematic expense; food, housing, and jobs became issues, and immigrants' depictions of the city lacked the wonder and luster of the early years. Families reunited less to pursue chances for success and more from obligation. Carme Escobar Alsar wrote to her mother, "It is my obligation to support you."[53] Senhor Amadeu recalls misery during the era and how many families living in the working-class Brás, Moóca, and Pari neighborhoods, including his own, came to rely on the Cia. Mecânica Importadora's free soup lunches and dinners.[54]

Finding affordable and adequate housing represented another challenge for working-class residents. The city had long struggled to provide the goods and services for its growing populations, but this did little to deter movement to the city. Affordable housing was hardest to come by in the city center, close to affluent neighborhoods. Compounding high demand, municipal projects aimed at making the city modern were concentrated in the city center, and lower-class residents who once called this area home were often forced to find new housing options. Ramatis Jacino notes, "Hygiene initiatives pushed poor nationals, blacks especially, from the center regions of the city."[55] Displaced Paulistanos came to compete with incoming immigrants and migrants for good housing.

In the prewar years as municipal authorities and residents alike grappled with housing shortages, it was workers and entrepreneurs who found the fastest solutions. As the city's population swelled, so did the number of *cortiços* (tenements) in working-class neighborhoods. These popular housing structures, immortalized in Aluísio Azevedo's 1890 novel, *O cortiço*, epitomized the duality of the city as a cesspool for disease and poverty but also a location for congregating among the working class. A typical cortiço crowded families, often of multiple nationalities, into ten-by-twenty-foot housing units lined on either side of a long, ten-foot-wide patio.[56]

Technically, any new cortiços were supposed to meet strict regulations as defined in the municipal planning codes, but in São Paulo, these constructions and other building projects were constructed with little regard for codes. First enacted in 1875 and revised in 1886, the Código de Posturas regulated the city's development and dictated a number of elements from building heights to street widths, but enforcement was concentrated in the established city center, leaving the city's working-class neighborhoods and the peripheries to develop with minimal oversight. By 1893, 72 percent of the city's 11,305 new buildings were constructed without the requisite permit request having been submitted to the municipal government. The greatest concentration was in the Brás neighborhood; just one official building permit request was submitted to the city for every 9,238 residents living in the neighborhood.[57] Brás was the first neighborhood immigrants encountered upon leaving the hospedaria; in the late empire and early Old Republic periods, Italians, especially Puglians, dominated its landscape. One municipal inspector found the cortiços lining Brás's Rua Carneiro Leão in complete violation of municipal standards. He was particularly troubled by the "complete lack of cleanliness," a single entrance to the complex, and significant amounts of stagnant, fetid waters throughout the area.[58] Rio de Janeiro Mayor Fernando Passos's 1904 urbanization and modernization projects destroyed many cortiços in the nation's capital, while São Paulo's unprecedented population growth and geographic and radial expansion ensured that many of these units survived well into the Old Republic.[59]

Even among cortiços in working-class neighborhoods, there were important distinctions; some were built on higher ground, while others were built in areas susceptible to flooding. During the nineteenth century, residents avoided construction near the Tietê River and its two largest tributaries, the Pinheiros and Tamanduateí Rivers. As more factories were built, São Paulo's population swelled, and inhabitants began constructing houses closer and closer to the rivers and into the floodplains. The first ten years of the twentieth century proved exceptionally destructive and challenging in these low-lying areas more susceptible to flooding. In four of the five years 1902 to 1907, the neighborhoods of Brás, Tatuapé, Bom Retiro, Cambucí, and Ponte Pequena experienced substantial flooding. Dam construction downriver likely increased the severity of the floods during these years, but so too did the pressure to build in these low-lying areas. A new reservoir in nearby Santo Amaro in 1908 alleviated some of the flooding threat. The year ushered in a relatively calm period in terms of catastrophic flooding until 1919.[60] The earlier floods, however, would have encouraged residents to look for other options than to build in the floodplains.

Worker villas represented another housing option. Real estate laws emerged that benefited developers and industrialists who designed this new type of popular housing. Located in the immediate vicinity of large industrial factories, the villas offered subsidized housing of varying sizes to many workers and their families. The villas brought workers closer to their jobs but gave industrialists greater control over their employees. Housing availability and subsidized rents were contingent upon working in the factory.[61] While eventually buying one of the units and being freed from the contingent housing restraint was theoretically an option, the reality was that doing so was virtually impossible. Down payments equaled one month's pay and subsequent monthly payments that often were deducted from a worker's wages and continued over the next eight to sixteen years. In the event a payment was missed, the tenant incurred a 20 percent late fee.[62] That these housing arrangements benefited industrialists and were untenable for the Paulistano working class became apparent by 1908. Amid rising population pressure, city residents organized the first rent strike.[63]

Just how many of these villas existed? Were conditions any better than in the cortiços? A census of worker villas of 139 city factories shows that only 15 reported offering worker housing in 1919.[64] As construction nearly came to a halt during World War I because materials were so scarce, this census provides a good idea of extant villas in the pre–World War I era.[65] Some projects were grandiose, but most were much smaller in scale. The Belenzinho textile mill's villa offered very few houses.[66] The conditions described by the state's Serviço Sanitário (sanitation service) in 1914 suggest little hygienic improvement over cortiços; the villas were places "where the sun barely shines, where the dwellings, usually inhabited by numerous families, are cramped areas, where there is a lack of open spaces, guaranteeing heatstroke from the buildings' walls."[67]

The influx of immigrants to the city from 1911 to 1913 only exacerbated the housing shortage in the six years that followed. With the influx, tenant associations appeared that were organized by blocks and neighborhoods and advocated for rent boycotts.[68] Under the established patterns, the housing shortage would have self-regulated in subsequent years, with new units and villas or a new housing option emerging to accommodate the city's growing population.

Brazil and São Paulo heavily depended on imported capital products, durable goods used to produce other goods and services, in many sectors, including construction and transportation. When war broke out in Europe, access to those materials nearly ceased, and urban transportation expansion all but halted, slowing the city's geographic expansion. Construction jobs became scarce, and the housing shortage continued to be acute. The housing shortage was just one more reason some city residents migrated to the interior.[69] As coffee production remained relatively steady during the war, agricultural jobs were available, while standards of living in the city began to decline.[70] The war meant fewer work opportunities, rising food costs, and worsening housing shortages; quality-of-life improvements in the city waned and development was stunted.

Quality of Life

Despite the less than ideal housing arrangements and sporadic employment, between 1891 and 1913 more readily available goods and services and hope drew residents to the state's capital city. Better education was one important advantage. The city also offered a better environment and health services, making São Paulo unique among most developing urban centers of the period. In general, up through the mid-twentieth century, higher densities in urban centers facilitated the spread of diseases, making rural life expectancies higher. This was simply not the case for the state and city of São Paulo. Urban centers like São Paulo, Santos, and Campinas were ahead of national and state trends in the decline of the crude birth and death rates. The state of São Paulo was at the forefront in Brazil in implementing more modern sanitation systems, and city residents benefited from the decision to concentrate efforts in urban areas. Paulistanos had the additional benefit of being more than 2,400 feet higher than coastal Santos; its altitude diminished the threats of yellow fever and other tropical diseases in São Paulo and resulted in less-erratic death rates.[71] Prior to the war, these essentially urban advantages helped convince many residents to remain in São Paulo despite rising food prices, rents, and unemployment. Evidence of improvements in mortality, marriage rates, and education demonstrates advantages that accompanied rapid urbanization.

Quality-of-life indicators shed light on whether improvements and development for the city's working class accompanied this period of rapid urban growth. In Latin America, with notoriously high inequality (most would argue historically high inequality), it is paramount to examine these indicators. Merely using increasing GDP per capita as a measure of growth does not address whether the population at large had access to resources, and that measure could mask persistent or increasing disparities.[72] Since the 1990s, the United Nations Development Programme (UNDP) standard-of-living index has been accepted as an indicator. The UNDP index considers per capita GDP, life expectancy at birth, and level of education equally in assessing quality of life. Based on these standards, vital statistics can be particularly instructive, and mortality rates can show important shifts in historical working-class experiences that GDP growth cannot.[73] For example, if infant mortality rates decline and life expectancies increase during periods of economic growth, these changes are often correlated with greater wealth redistribution. The opposite results can signal increasing and problematic inequality.

Some scholars have begun to estimate this index for areas of Latin America, but most estimations only begin in 1900.[74] Existing measures for Brazil do indicate improvements in standards of living in the first thirty years of the twentieth century, but São Paulo's experience was likely distinct given the rapid influx of immigrants and urbanization and the state's and city's relative wealth. The city provides an ideal setting to examine changes in these areas; although the rising GDP per capita would tip indicators toward development, the city's population density provided an environment conducive to the quick spread of infectious diseases and increased mortality rates that would tip development in the opposite direction. Officials of the state's Serviço Sanitário understood this balance and concentrated hygiene and health efforts in urban areas through 1918; the efforts resulted in lower infant mortality rates and deaths from infectious diseases. Quality-of-life improvements from the early Old Republic did not continue in the latter half of the period and in some cases were even reversed during the war era.

In 1912, Luiz Barbosa advised his wife that she should only come to Brazil if she was in excellent health because he did not have enough money or resources to pay for treating an illness.[75] Letters from other residents also emphasized good health as key to finding success in the city.[76] Their letters demonstrate that despite early improvements in the first ten years of the Old Republic, health continued to be a concern.

Stillbirths are an especially important and understudied indicator; recent scientific research demonstrates that women's increased exposure to stressful events during pregnancy is correlated with an increased rate of stillbirths.[77] Through the end of the nineteenth century, the estimated stillbirth rates per 1,000 births declined dramatically in the city (figure 2.1). That rate was 63 stillbirths of every 1,000 recorded births in 1896 and dropped to

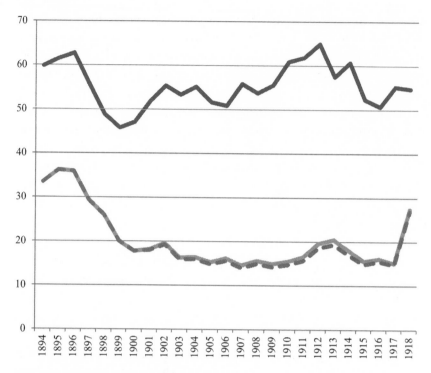

Figure 2.1. Stillbirth and mortality rates in São Paulo, 1894–1919. John Allen Blount III, "A administração da saúde pública no estado de São Paulo o serviço sanitário 189–1918," *Revista de Administração de Empresas 12*, no. 4 (October–December 1972): 40–48.

━━━ Stillbirth rate
━━━ Mortality rate
■ ■ Revised mortality rate

46 just three years later. A number of factors would have contributed to this substantial decline in stillbirths and resulted in a less stressful environment for pregnant women. In the same period, Paulistano gross death rates per 1,000 residents dropped from 36 to 20 deaths.[78] Similarly, infectious disease deaths declined dramatically, accounting for a 5.13 rate between 1894 and 1900 and just 2.9 in 1901–1910.[79] The gains did not persist through the twentieth century, however. Stillbirth rates rose, peaking in 1912 at 65. This increase in stillbirths was likely associated with considerable migration to the city and more crowded housing between 1900 and 1913. Death rates from infectious diseases stagnated between 1910 and 1920.[80]

A word of caution must be noted for the estimated mortality rates, as they are likely overestimated for the 1900–1913 period and underestimated during the war years. The population figures the state provided to estimate these rates were constructed assuming uniform population growth for 1890–1900, 1900–1920, and 1920–1940. However, the hospedaria evidence indicates the city's substantial population growth before 1913, meaning that mortality rates were slightly lower in the prewar period than previously estimated.[81]

Childhood and infant mortality indicate relative poverty levels for the period. In 1905, deaths of children through age three represented more than 58 percent of all registered deaths. The share still represented 49 percent of all deaths in 1927. In working-class neighborhoods of Brás and Belenzinho, the instances of childhood deaths were higher, respectively 72 percent and 66 percent in 1905 and 70 percent and 68 percent in 1910.[82] Manoel da Costa wrote to his mother in July 1919 that he, his wife, and their five-month-old son had all been sick, and their son, who remained unnamed in the letter, died.[83] Perhaps the seeming lack of emotion in Manoel's letter stemmed from the frequency of infant death in the city; about 17 percent of children in the city died before they were a year old. Compared to other Brazilian urban areas, São Paulo's infant mortality rate in 1909 was lower, at 167 per 1,000 children under one year; by 1926 the rate increased to 174.[84]

Comparing São Paulo's mortality records to other immigrant centers in the early twentieth century produces mixed results. The city's gross death rates were similar to those observed for Buenos Aires at the turn of the century but lower than those reported for New York City.[85] Stillbirths paint a different picture. In Buenos Aires, the rate was 44.9 per 1,000 births in 1910 and down to 39.3 by 1920.[86] By 1916, the rate of stillbirths of 1,000 total births was 43.4 in New York City and more than 50 in São Paulo.[87]

Fertility outcomes and marriage rates can shed light on how residents, particularly young women, experienced São Paulo. In general, an increase in the average marrying age speaks to quality-of-life improvements. Although catastrophic events and migration can raise the marrying age, the gains to education that Paulistana girls experienced are more often correlated with later marrying ages and decreasing fertility rates. The choice to delay marriage for more education or as a strategy for family social mobility was certainly one that Paulistana women made.[88] In São Paulo, a combination of these correlations is seen during the Old Republic. At the turn of the century, 55 percent of Paulistanas between the ages of fourteen and twenty were married.[89] The stillbirth and mortality rates suggest relative stagnation in terms of quality-of-life gains between 1900 and the end of World War I, but young women's marriage rates show marked gains during the same period. By 1910, the rate of married teenage girls dropped to 51.7

percent and then 36.1 percent in 1915 and 33.3 percent in 1919, registering similar rates to those in the United States.[90] While this drop could be somewhat attributed economic hardships of the war, the continuing decline, to 30.8 percent in 1927, suggests that women's delayed marriage was part of an established pattern. Teen marriage rates were higher in peripheral and poorer areas of the city, but the delaying of marriage occurred across class lines. In the more established and elite neighborhoods, the share of teenage girls who got married dropped from 34 percent in 1915 to 25 percent in 1927; peripheral areas recorded the same decrease, from 46 percent to 38 percent.[91]

Evidence that educational opportunities influenced an increase in marrying ages reflects in the city's educational improvements in the early part of the Old Republic. Both Paulistanos and Paulistanas benefited from the city's educational opportunities. During the late empire, expenditures on education per capita and per student in São Paulo province, the demarcation that preceded states, were well above the Brazilian average and on par with Rio de Janeiro and Rio Grande de Sul provinces.[92] With the onset of the Old Republic, São Paulo state's commitment to immigration grew, leading to a relative decline in education expenditures.[93] Despite the decelerated investment in education, the state maintained similar per capita expenditures, at least until 1915.[94] While these funds did not fully accommodate the city's rapidly growing school-age population, they indicate a continual investment in education.

The working class's commitment to education can be harder to parse together, but São Paulo's working class was also clearly committed. Renato Colistete's research on parent petitions to the state legislature prove particularly illustrative. Each year some of these petitions were successful, with new schools or school groups being offered to meet some communities' needs. Petitioners included Brazilians and immigrants and literate and illiterate individuals, attesting to education's broad appeal.[95] Many residents understood that social mobility was tenuous at best and few rags-to-riches dreams would become a reality. In São Paulo, education offered a chance for intergenerational upward mobility, especially for boys not confronting racial discrimination, and the city disproportionately received support for its schools.

Building a school, however, is not the same as attending school. Evidence of increasing enrollment and literacy rates demonstrates a level of commitment to use the schools that were provided. The growth of public and private schools and the number of matriculated students attests to the city's continual lure through the first fifteen years of the twentieth century. Young girls especially benefited through schools and compulsory education; until 1920, education was compulsory for children between seven and twelve years old. Among the population born before 1906, males were roughly 20 percent more likely to be literate than females. For the younger population, born between 1906 and 1913, only a few percentage points separated literacy rates between genders, and in the working-class downtown, suburbs (outskirts), and small suburbs (more rural outskirts), girls were even more likely to be literate than boys.[96] The decline in gendered education inequality was one of the clearest markers of development and growth for the working class during the period.[97]

While the increase in public schools and matriculated students between 1900 and 1905 was encouraging, the share of the school-age population that was actually matriculated remained below 25 percent citywide and even lower in most working-class neighborhoods.[98] In essence, two simultaneous and somewhat contradictory movements were at play during these years. When the municipal government simply could not keep pace with the city's rapid population growth, families who could afford to and who benefited most from educational achievement turned to private schools to fill the void. This was particularly true of Italian families who saw the multiple Italian schools in the city as viable alternatives. By 1908, the Italian School Federation, a society organized in the city, controlled most of the city's sixty-three private secondary schools, matriculating more than five thousand boys and girls. Many of these schools had been started during the first or second decade of the Old Republic.[99]

Various factors help explain the dramatic decline in matriculation in 1920 noted in table 2.3. First, the number of private schools had increased, and more than 42,000 foreign and national students were enrolled in the city's 195 private schools by 1923. Most of these private-school students were enrolled in primary schools.[100] Private-school educational quality likely surpassed that of public schools. Strapped for funds and qualified teachers, in 1920 the state reduced the years of compulsory education from five to two. Literacy among working-class children, which was seen as a measurable sign of modernization, could be achieved within two years.[101] Even during the imperial era, parents petitioned for more public schools, but this draconian decision was met with relative silence. The silence is a reflection of the working-class reality and a shift that took place during the war years. The economic downturn made many more Paulistanos rely on children's incomes and labor as an important component of a more general

Table 2.3. Paulistano primary public schools and matriculation, 1898–1920

Year	Grupo escolar	Escola isolada	Escola reunida	Total	Students matriculated
1898	8	66	-	74	43,021
1900	10	85	-	95 (+28)	30,831 (-28)
1905	13	114	-	127 (+33)	49,112 (+59)
1910	25	86	-	111 (-13)	99,203 (+102)
1915	28	182	-	210 (+89)	168,245 (+70)
1920	31	134	-	165 (-21)	38,339 (-77)

Source: Marcílio, Escola, 172, table 6.

Note: Reflects number of schools and students enrolled. Percentage change reported in parentheses.

family wage strategy.[102] Hopes of better opportunity eroded, and parents saw two years' education as enough; the family needed children to be workers, not students.

FAMILY WAGE STRATEGY

Historically, the idea of family income is nothing new, but the industrial hourly wage marked a distinct transition from earlier cottage industry. This shift often has forced reevaluations of gender roles, norms, and family dynamics as labor legislation restricting child and female labor restructured the family income. São Paulo did experience shifting gender norms and structures; however, as labor regulations were very loosely enforced during the Old Republic, the family wage became more important as a go-to strategy to combat temporary economic hardships in the first twenty-five years of the Old Republic. These contributions do not always appear in census records, but letters reveal that by the end of World War I, the family wage was an established practice that persisted throughout the Old Republic and into the Vargas era.[103]

In theory, as early as 1891, child labor was restricted, with children below age eight banned from any form of industrial employment and children under twelve from anything beyond textile jobs. In actuality, these laws were largely ignored and enforcement really only began after the 1930 revolution when judicial regulations and institutions were established to enforce labor laws.[104] In terms of adult female employment, the rhetoric from industrialists and labor leaders alike idealized an adult male's wage as sustaining a household, but this was not feasible for many families. Female employment was an accepted practice among many working-class families in the Old Republic, especially during times of duress.

The rise in food prices, rents, and temporary unemployment led families to turn to multiple or alternative sources of income to cover expenses. Some families in slightly better standing chose to add another income to cover education expenses, to save for a rainy day, or to enjoy a little escape from daily routines. Even in the worst of times, there may have been just enough money to attend a play or movie, join a neighborhood soccer team, host a small dinner with friends and family, or buy a beer or lottery ticket at a local *botequim* (corner bar).[105] São Paulo's extremely weak labor laws meant women and children featured more prominently in the family wage structure than in countries with more effective regulation of female and child labor.[106] Adela Ibañez Moreno from Mazarrón, Spain, was even able to earn and save enough to assure her husband a life of relative leisure. She coaxed him to return to São Paulo, where he "will not work and will have nothing else to do except eat, drink, and stroll around."[107]

Attendance records from the city's public schools convey what the family wage meant for working-class children. Ninety-nine inspector reports on select city schools show that from 1894 to 1914, on any given day an average of one in four students missed school.[108] A school inspector observed in 1898 that chronic absences were explained by a number of factors. He recorded ten girls at a Barra Funda female school leaving during the month of March alone for the following reasons: two never even attended, two moved, two were deemed too old for school, and two left to get jobs.[109] The reality was not quite as bleak as his report suggests. From 1894 to 1913, attendance in working-class neighborhood schools was improving steadily. Gains were modest, and many schools still woefully underprepared students who did attend, but literacy rates show that the city was making improvements.[110]

With the onset of the war, families depended more on the extra income children and women provided the household. Between 1915 and 1920, the city's public school enrollments dropped by 77 percent in total numbers (table 2.3). This dramatic decline reflects both the outflow of the São Paulo population and the greater number of children entering the city's labor force during this period. Three years into World War I and on the eve of the 1917 general strike, one effect of the war on the city's youngest residents was their increased employment in factories throughout the city.[111] While textile growth benefited from creeping protection since the 1860s, Brazilian consumers continued to rely on substantial cloth imports.[112] To fill the void brought on by the war, Brazilian textile factories expanded production. This expansion presented a problem to factory owners who could no longer rely on imported machinery to improve efficiency and production.

Greatly constrained by the economic situation and looking for ways to cut costs, they found that employing women and children, who received a fraction of the adult male wage, was a cost-effective solution. Working-class Paulistanos, facing rising food costs and a housing shortage but also committed to living in the city, looked for ways to keep afloat by accepting those jobs. Seven- and eight-year-old boys like Benedito Caraviele, Francisco Garcia, and Manuel Martinez went to work ten-hour days for miserable wages in the Cristaleria Colombo instead of going to school.[113] Girls and boys ages seven to ten worked more than ten hours a day at the Fábrica Cia. de Tecidos de Juta, sometimes only receiving their first paycheck after three-month apprenticeships.[114] While labor leaders described these children as "vampires" depriving adult men of employment,[115] families saw them as lifelines.

Alfredo Pinto de Queiroz's story represents how most working-class families approached the declining economic situation. A carpenter by trade, Alfredo and his oldest son left Portugal for São Paulo looking for opportunity. Their timing, however, brought them to the city during the economic downturn. Still, in 1915 he wrote his wife, Ignacia, to reunite the family by coming to Brazil with their four other children, Eliza (fifteen years old), Olinda (six), Aventino (six), and José (four). Given the paucity of opportunities available, Alfredo's four younger children were an integral part of his plan to get out of debt. In his own words, he hoped his eldest daughter, Eliza, could "earn money for her and her brothers . . . as a seamstress's assistant." By his calculations, she could earn 60$000 to 70$000 monthly helping a seamstress and the younger children could work as companions in some of the elite Portuguese households to earn 30$00 to 40$000 monthly.[116] Although his two middle children were of school age and should have enrolled in one of the city's public schools, education was never mentioned as part of Alfredo's plan.

The Queirozes' decision to send Eliza, Olinda, Aventino, and even José to work may have been a good short-term solution, but it diminished their children's opportunities in the long run. Patrick Emerson and André Souza document how "people who start work as children end up with lower earnings as adults."[117] For Aventino and José, working as household companions would have minimized their work prospects in the Old Republic labor market. For Eliza and Olinda, the immediate impact may not have been as dramatic, but forgoing their education ultimately could have been more costly for Brazilian development. The consequence of this decision also likely extended into future generations of the Queiroz family, as the children of Eliza, Olinda, Aventino, and José also were more likely to work as children. Although the Queiroz family tree cannot be traced any further through immigration records, research on intergenerational child labor in Brazil supports this interpretation. A three-generational study from the late twentieth century demonstrates that even for people with considerable education and high incomes, if they worked as children, their children and grandchildren were also more likely to work as children.[118] Considering the important role the family played in Paulistano immigration, these practices likely intensified during the Old Republic, and wartime hardships would have accentuated differences between those families whose children worked and those whose children did not.

In the case of the Queiroz family, Ignacia would just as easily have featured into the family wage strategy. Despite social and cultural norms against the practice, female labor was clearly tolerated in the Old Republic. It was an accepted practice among the working class, and in 1916 many working-class women gained the legal right to work.[119] The pivotal role women played in starting the 1917 general strike demonstrates their considerable impact in the city.[120] As an indicator of the wars' impact on female employment beyond the working class, in 1916 the upper-middle-class women's magazine *Revista Feminina* advised its readers to start making chocolates at home for a small income. By 1917, the magazine was lauding the exposition of female work, noting that women should not be ashamed of needing to sell handicrafts. While these middle- and upper-class women may have been embarrassed about having to contribute to the household income, the magazine's frank discussion signifies an important level of acceptance.[121]

We know little about how workers perceived this reality beyond conjecture. Immigrant letters in which family members candidly wrote about female employment as an opportunity during war years suggest its acceptance. Adela Ibañez Moreno's letter to her husband in Spain in 1914 unabashedly speaks to how she worked and saved enough money so that he would not have to work.[122] Manoel Teixeira explicitly asked his mother to leave Portugal and join his family in São Paulo so his wife could go to work. A few sentences later he highlights just how much a young woman could make daily at a factory. The wage he describes, 2$400 a day, was just half what a semi-skilled adult male could earn at the time, but it is clear that any income was a vital contribution during the war years.[123]

When extra income was needed and jobs were not available, Paulistanos made opportunities. They opened small businesses to provide goods and services where the government fell short. They peddled baked goods and lottery tickets such as the popular *jogo do bicho* (animal game) and took in extra washing or piece-rate work to complete from home. They sublet space or beds to other working-class residents. Informality became entrenched with the family wage. Although informality was by no means new to the Old Republic, during São Paulo's first period of rapid urbanization it became a fixture of the city's twentieth-century fabric.[124]

Despite these adaptations, workers and their families faced considerable instability and hardships. The São Paulo reality was bleak and mirrored similar hardships that shortages and inflation brought throughout the region. The years 1916–1925 saw a rise in labor organization in South America, with strikes concentrating in 1917–1919 in cities like Buenos Aires, Montevideo, Santiago, and Lima.[125] São Paulo's breaking point came in May and June 1917 when wages were not increasing but food costs were; in the city's *feiras livres*, adulterated products were being sold at exorbitant prices and led to food-poisoning deaths around the city.[126] By June, female weavers in the Crespi textile mill, whose relatively high earnings were critical to their own survival and their families' strategies, reached the brink. They organized a factory commission to bargain with management, but when they failed to gain pay increases, an end to fines, safer conditions, and respect from supervisors, they went on strike. It was the spark that launched the city into its first wide-scale general strike. São Paulo was a tinderbox, and quickly other textile workers and then workers at Antârctica Paulista brewing company joined the strike. Tensions were beginning to wane, but when police shot and killed Antônio Ineguez Martinez on July 9, the strike's intensity escalated. By July 12, at least 20,000 workers were on strike, a number that would double just two days later.[127] Joel Wolfe has asserted that although anarchist leadership eventually entered the strike and brought a degree of cohesiveness, it was the workers themselves who brought about this watershed moment.[128] The war had exacerbated the conditions and pressures many city residents and particularly women faced beyond the point of adaptability.

Conclusion

That life was difficult for São Paulo's lower classes during the Old Republic is evident. Getting by and getting ahead often meant making great sacrifices, especially during stretches of unemployment. It often required living in overcrowded and miserable housing and sent whole families into the workforce. In this respect, São Paulo was not very different from other urban immigrant centers in the Americas. Although the reality may have been bleak, potential migrants, both Brazilians and foreigners, still hoped for opportunity. The city's growing population during this period attests to the lure of the Paulistano dream.

The key to the city's reputation was that until World War I, many families were able to get by and get ahead. There was hope and there was opportunity. There were important indicators that life was improving for the vast majority of the city's population. More children, boys and girls, were enrolled in and attending school, and women were waiting longer to get married. People were living longer, even in the crowded, working-class neighborhoods. Food costs were relatively stable, and when times were difficult, the city's businesses, government, and residents adapted relatively quickly by creating new opportunities, expanding the city's footprint through new transportation lines, building houses, and providing new jobs. The economic ebb and flow was familiar and somewhat predictable.

The downturn of 1913, which continued through World War I, broke with the established cycle. Food prices continued to rise, jobs did not return, and a housing shortage remained. Amid the pressure, the city established *feiras livres* to try to reduce pressures on the working class, but for many families, the measure was insufficient. For those who were unable to make it in the city, agricultural work in the interior now became a beacon of hope for Brazilians and immigrants alike. Returning to Europe was no longer a viable option for immigrants, and the hospedaria was just a short walk or trolley ride for many city residents. The institution offered job security amid waning opportunity in the city, reflecting once again its capacity to alter the city's development. Paulistanos were forced to adapt their approach to city life and increasingly embraced the family wage strategy and informality as effective survival means. For children, this often meant having jobs instead of going to school. For women, this meant returning to or entering the formal labor market or doing additional work from home. For men, it made having a steady job with an established employer more valuable. Even with these adaptations, pressures became overwhelming, and by the middle of 1917 the city found itself paralyzed in its first wide-scale general strike; the day-to-day instability residents faced finally coalesced into a broad movement.

While glimmers of opportunity appeared in the first half of the Old Republic during this period of rapid expansion, experiences were not alike and opportunities were not equal for all city residents. One of the most reviled and understudied groups within the working class was that of strike-breakers and nonstriking workers in the years before the 1917 general strike. Understanding who these individuals were and the motivations leading them to become strikebreakers in the first half of the Old Republic provides a counterpoint to labor leaders in the historical records and a key understanding of the hospedaria's importance in the city. Social networks, discrimination, and expectations varied depending on a person's background, skin color, and gender. Discrimination and prejudice often greatly affected whether an individual looked for opportunities in the formal labor market or the informal economy and how difficult it could be to escape marginal life in the city.

3

Nonstriking Workers and São Paulo's *Sindicato Amarelo*

Prior to the 1917 general strike, most organized work stoppages in the city were on a smaller scale. These smaller strikes, such as the hatmakers' strike that spanned from late 1907 into March 1908, offer an important window into Paulistano working-class divisions. On December 23, 1907, factory workers in São Paulo's four largest hat factories went on strike.[1] Less than a month later, six strikebreakers tried to enter the Casa Matanó Serrichio and M. Villela hat factories but were beaten by strikers outside. By February the 39 individuals working in the M. Villela factory had undermined the 170 striking workers' demands for an eight-hour workday.[2] Anarchist strike leaders called these individuals "crumiros," an Italian word for "scabs," and written attacks on their character grew more vitriolic as the strike persisted. By mid-March, just ten days after *carnaval* ended, the unfathomable occurred; strike leaders reported that the "crumiros," who they described as "poor devils—donkeys and cowards, unconscious and evil," had joined the vilified hat factory industrialists and created a *sindicato amarelo*, a yellow union.[3] The strikers' disgust is palpable, but just who were these "poor devils, donkeys, cowards," and why were they willing to risk their personal safety for tenuous job security?

Scholars often focus on labor leaders and strikes in an effort to understand the working class in the early twentieth century. Historical records contribute to this focus; there are records from labor congresses, rallying cries in the labor press inciting workers to organize, and articles in other publications that denounce labor organizations. From this line of inquiry, research shows that the first decade of the twentieth century saw a marked increase in labor organization and demonstrations of labor unrest in Latin America's Southern Cone. Urbanization pressures and the arrival of anarcho-syndicalist immigrant leaders led to new worker organizations and labor instability. Notably, there were general strikes in Uruguay and Argentina.[4] While there is much to be learned from this line of investigation, nonstriking and replacement workers were also a considerable minority. In Chile, employers used replacement workers in more than one third of strikes from 1902 to 1908, and the government even helped provide some of those strikebreakers.[5] In the Paulistano hat strike, almost one in five workers did not strike.

To better understand why strike leaders were unable to connect with rank-and-file Paulistanos, a better understanding is needed of who constituted the rank and file and the individuals unwilling to join movements.[6] Striking and nonstriking workers alike were Paulistanos with families, friends, obligations, and dreams. By continuing to marginalize these individuals in the scholarly literature, researchers push their experiences and motivations further to the fringes. Going beyond the traditional sources associated with labor organization and reading periodicals against the grain allows for a window into their reality.

I look into two important questions by studying these individuals. First, why was Paulistano labor organization unsuccessful compared to organizing in other immigrant urban centers? Workers in Argentina organized ten general strikes between 1900 and 1910, and Uruguay's president passed labor legislation and even welcomed "foreign agitators" who had been expelled from other countries for labor organization. Even within Brazil, Rio de Janeiro hosted worker conferences and the creation of eight broader worker unions. In contrast, São Paulo's two dominant labor organizations were severely weakened between 1906 and 1917.[7] The Hospedaria de Imigrantes' ability to make almost immediate connections between incoming workers and employers with striking employees was one key component.[8] So, too, was the willingness of the municipal and state governments to deploy police force by what was deemed "necessary means" to ensure the "freedom to work." To examine the second question, I seek to understand strikebreakers and acknowledge the agency they rightfully exercised. What drove individuals to the brink in São Paulo that they would be willing to cross a picket line? This necessitates exploring why Portuguese workers seemed less willing to strike than workers of other nationalities and how family motivations were of particular importance in the city of São Paulo.[9]

Focusing on the early Old Republic is key because São Paulo's labor movements met minimal success in those years. There is an understanding of how rank-and-file workers contributed to the 1917 general strike, the first true general strike of the period, and to the pivotal female role in the strike.[10] Smaller, less successful labor movements are also informative and essential to understanding the divisions and tensions within the working class. This inquiry builds on studies of the Companhia Docas de Santos dockworker strikes that occurred in the 1890s and in 1908.[11] In the dockworker strikes, Afro-Brazilian workers were largely brought in as strikebreakers, highlighting the racial tensions and discrimination in the period. In the city of São Paulo, immigrant workers often served as strikebreakers. The ready supply of immigrants coupled with the pervasive racial prejudice in the period, then, pushed Afro-Brazilians either further to the city's economic margins or into the interior.

Although there was hope and opportunity in the city during the prewar period, many residents were living day to day in survival mode. Job insecurity and rising food prices made life in the city difficult, and the arrival of new migrants and immigrants exacerbated housing shortages for the working class, many of whom were new transplants themselves. Already navigating a world in which they had no control over coffee prices, textile tariffs, or energy crises, the decision to go to work or not was ultimately their own or at least that of their family. It is, in fact, the family-level decision that distinguishes rank-and-file Paulistanos and their reticence to organize.

The hospedaria immigrant registrations again provide a valuable starting point for this analysis. These records indicate who the rank and file were and the importance of the nuclear family in the city and among different immigrant groups. The hospedaria records can also be read alongside accounts of labor disputes and strikes found in select labor newspapers and the *Estado de São Paulo*. An increase in city work contracts often coincided with heightened labor unrest. Newspaper reports further demonstrate how industrialists often relied on a swift and sizeable police response if strikes occurred. While the newspaper and hospedaria accounts attest to the state's role in suppressing strikes, newspaper reports on arrests and disputes in the city between strikers and strikebreakers also identify individuals by name and shed light on why a sizeable minority of the labor force chose not to join strikes or be replacement workers. The 1907 general strike and the hat factories strike spanning from late December 1907 to March 1908, in particular, provide valuable perspectives into the strikebreaker world. A combination of family concerns and survival help explain why nonstriking and replacement workers were such a large group during labor movements. So too, however, does discrimination.

THE FAMILY EFFECT IN LABOR DECISIONS

The hospedaria was intricately linked into the city's formal labor market. The registros and information on individuals and families signing contracts with employers upon leaving the hospedaria furnish an understudied and remarkable source of information on individuals arriving in the city. Established to funnel immigrant agricultural laborers into the coffee-growing interior, the institution also provided Paulistano employers with a vital and almost instant workforce.[12] Using these valuable records of the city's newest workers provides a means to understand potential strikebreakers and the role family likely played in fostering a reticence to strike.

The matriculation registrations from the hospedaria (appendix A) hold records on immigrant entries from 1882 to 1978 and more detailed data starting in 1903. For these years, across all nationalities, immigrants contracted to work in the city were more literate than their brethren who continued to the interior, although the records indicate variation in national literacy rates and even important differences within nationalities. For example, 41 percent of Spanish heads of household leaving from Gibraltar were literate, while 63 percent and 71 percent of those leaving from Barcelona and Málaga, respectively, were literate. Although the variation is not as large, 86 percent of Genoese heads of household and 60 percent of Neapolitan household heads were literate.[13]

An established story of European mass migration in the late nineteenth and early twentieth centuries was that the process placed an ocean between many nuclear families. Through this migration process, family dynamics shifted and priorities changed. For Argentina, Alan Taylor has found that family dependence diminished the amount that Argentines could save, making individuals ill-prepared to weather wartime scarcities.[14] In Argentina, it was not uncommon for married men to travel to the Americas alone, trying to establish themselves and then call their families to join them. Equally acceptable were single men who migrated, established themselves, and then found brides back at home who would meet them in the Americas.[15] By the early twentieth century, approximately 60 percent of Italian men in New York City and Buenos Aires were married.

São Paulo, however, was remarkable in that its subsidized immigration program and related chamadas facilitated and encouraged entire family units to move to the state. Trying to find laborers for the coffee plantations, owners lobbied the state to subsidize entire family passages. The coffee elite hoped that contracting entire families would diminish worker's willingness to move on to the next farm, back to Europe, or to the city. This system was adapted over the Old Republic, but one key feature did remain: nuclear families were much more likely to migrate to São Paulo than they were to other immigrant cities. In the 20 percent hospedaria sample (appendix A), 283 individuals came into the city as heads of household and with family members, and 127 arrived independently. Immigrants arriving in the city were also highly likely to be traveling with their spouses; three of every four married household heads traveled with a spouse.

The hospedaria sample reveals that although there were differences by nationality, the nuclear family was the core of migration to the city. Among Portuguese married households, three out of four arrived in Brazil with their spouses.[16] Among Italian families, 60 percent fit this model, and almost 83 percent of Spanish families did.[17] Portuguese, Spanish, and Italian families also traveled with two children on average.[18] A closer look at all Portuguese immigrants arriving between 1903 and 1913 shows that despite the immigration system's design to channel immigrant families into the state's interior, family settlement was much more common in the city than it was in the state as a whole. The share of unmarried Portuguese household heads in the state was about equal, but in the city, married household heads outnumbered their unmarried counterparts five to two.[19]

There were other national differences when it came to the likelihood of arriving with a family in the city. Similar to patterns for Buenos Aires and New York City, single Italian males passing through the hospedaria into São Paulo slightly outnumbered their married counterparts.[20] Portuguese and Spanish married men outnumbered their single compatriots by factors of 2.9 and 3.4, respectively, and were a large portion of the immigration stream after the start of the twentieth century. As Portuguese and Spanish migrants outnumbered Italian migrants settling in the city through the hospedaria by more than four to one, much of the city was being settled by newly arrived married couples and their children.[21] The city's high proportion of married Spanish immigrant arrivals contrasts with the rates José Moya records for Buenos Aires in similar periods.[22] The distinction further strengthens the argument that São Paulo was a desired destination for nuclear families and that pressures in making labor decisions would have reflected accordingly.

The Portuguese arriving in the city in the period 1903–1913 represented the ideal strikebreakers. They came with families to support, and just two of every ten adults who passed through the hospedaria were literate.[23] These rates parallel those registered in Portuguese records, where just one in four people over the age of six could read in 1900.[24] Portuguese were also under-represented in more skilled positions, like those of businessmen, mechanics, and blacksmiths.[25] It is within the context of the rapidly growing and cyclical labor market that the anomalous stream of Portuguese immigrants to the city of São Paulo registered from 1903 to 1913 is understandable. The city needed cheap, unskilled labor, and these men and women needed jobs to support their families.[26]

Hospedaria registrations mark differences within the Portuguese community regarding family migration patterns that merit attention. There was about an equal number of individuals coming from Leixões in northern Portugal and from Lisbon. Both groups registered about the same low literacy rates and unskilled positions, but heads of household or individuals departing from the northern region were more likely to come with families and were on average six years older than those departing from Lisbon.[27] This characteristic would have made northern Portuguese immigrants and families even more mindful of family when deciding whether to strike. A low literacy rate among Spanish immigrants departing from Gibraltar would have put those households in similar circumstances.

Scholarship has often failed to distinguish these Portuguese immigrant experiences in São Paulo for two main reasons: the exaltation of the country's Portuguese ancestry and the erasure of ethnicity and national origins from most official documentation. The first reason can be understood as a conflation of racial prejudice and the rise of eugenics in the late nineteenth and early twentieth centuries. Many eugenicists argued that racial mixing led to degenerate populations, but this concept was highly problematic for elite Latin Americans.[28] The region's colonial history was often defined by miscegenation between indigenous, African, and European populations. The success of Brazil and other nations in the region, thus, was dependent upon a largely mixed population. Even the elite often had at least some degree of racial mixing in their lineage. Latin American nations turned to Lamarkian eugenics in embracing the idea that the populous could "improve" with racial mixing.[29]

As a result, many policies and practices, both official and de facto, made concerted efforts to whiten the national populations. Brazil perhaps grappled with this inferiority complex more than most other nation-states. The country had been the largest importer of African slaves during the transatlantic slave trade, and its national boundaries had largely been forged by *bandeirantes* (explorers who expanded the borders through slaving raids and mining ventures) of mixed Tupí-Portuguese heritage.[30] São Paulo's immigrant subsidization program, although economic in terms of providing coffee laborers, was also part of the regional whitening effort. Jeffrey Lesser has shown that the arrival of Japanese and other nonwhite immigrant groups complicated the traditional story of whitening, but overall, it was European immigrants whom employers sought to hire.[31]

In January 1918, a group of the city's elite men, most of whom were medical doctors, formed the São Paulo Eugenics Society. Nancy Stepan holds that the debates surrounding the role of miscegenation and whitening did not begin at this time, but an official program dedicated to implementing practices "required concrete institutional mediations."[32] The timing in the city's history is understandable, as a shift was taking place toward more national migration. Eager to deemphasize the African and indigenous ancestry that they considered so problematic, elite Brazilians celebrated their Portuguese, ostensibly civilized heritage. Stereotypes from the period exalted Portuguese as "hardworking" and brave workers and noted Portuguese as important dry-goods grocers and community leaders.[33] To a certain extent, the Portuguese immigrants arriving in Rio de Janeiro and Santos conformed to these idealized stereotypes. In these port cities, Portuguese often became prominent merchants. In contrast, the city and interior of São Paulo largely drew agriculturalists and unskilled laborers.[34] In a notable irony, at the same time that a large number of poorly educated Portuguese immigrants were in the city struggling to find jobs and make ends meet, most official writings celebrated all things Portuguese as the font of Brazilian civility and progress.

A turning point in this dialogue could have come with Gilberto Freyre's *Casa grande e senzala* in 1933 (*The Masters and the Slaves* in translation). However, his understanding of racial mixing as strengthening the country's national character rather than weakening it again privileged the imagined colonial Portuguese immigrant experience.[35] As interpretations of Freyre's writings evolved, Portuguese preeminence in Brazil's supposed racial democracy and Brazilian identity solidified, making it even more difficult to distinguish the unskilled Portuguese immigrants arriving in the early twentieth century from the colonizers whom the poet Olegário Mariano Carneiro da Cunha called "the strong and generous race that the blood of the Portuguese molded in this favored region, transmitting to [São Paulo] the enterprising impulse and the civilizing instinct."[36]

Marriage and births were central to the rhetoric of improving the Brazilian population through racial mixing. In the state's annual demographic reports, immigrants were present in almost 60 percent of all marriages in the city from 1895 to 1929. What was problematic for eugenicists was that many immigrants tended to marry other immigrants.[37] Furthermore, most of those marriages were between immigrants of the same national background. Endogamy rates reported for Brazilians, Portuguese, Italian, and Spanish men in 1916 and 1917 were 85, 62, 45, and 59 percent, respectively. Endogamy rates for women were even higher except for Brazilian women, who only married Brazilian men in 64 percent of registered marriages.[38] Given that Italians dominated migration to the city between 1871 and 1902, the relatively low endogamy rates for Italians are likely reflective of Italians marrying first-generation Brazilians of Italian backgrounds.[39] These marriage patterns and the births resulting from the unions increased the city's so-called white population, but most of the new population was still part of the lower class. The location of city marriages, with the largest number occurring in the Brás neighborhood, confirms the growing working-class population.[40]

For workers, marriage increased the nuclear family pressure's role in defining the decision to strike, not to strike, or to be a strikebreaker. The birth of a child would have exponentially increased the pressure.[41] In addition to the children moving to the city with their parents, babies were born in the city every day, most of them first-generation Brazilians. In 1901, two thirds of the city's registered births were to immigrant families. Although their share had declined by the end of the Old Republic, in 1929, six of every ten children were born to immigrant parents.[42] The state's *Annuario estatistico* of 1901 provides further information on these patterns. The city registered almost 8,600 births in 1901. Of these youngest Paulistanos, 2,234 were born to Brazilian mothers and 1,150 to Portuguese mothers. The largest group of newborns, however, were born into Italian families; those 4,396 births represented more than 50 percent of the city's registered births.[43] The majority of these surviving first-generation children would have lived with their families in the Brás, Consolação, and Santa Ifigênia neighborhoods.[44] Unable to get by, some of these families would have turned to the hospedaria to find employment. City residents arrived at the hospedaria on a daily basis. Reentries were allowed starting in 1900, and more than seven hundred Brazilians registered in that year alone. Between 1908 and 1927, reentries represented about 25 percent of all hospedaria registrations.[45]

STATE INTERVENTION IN LABOR STRIKES

By the start of the twentieth century the hospedaria funneled workers to the interior, but it was also a de facto employment office for the city. As Paulistanos entered the hospedaria, they would have encountered recent arrivals to the country. At least every couple of days passengers from ships docked in Santos and Rio de Janeiro arrived in the building. Simultaneously, resident and immigrant groups turned to the hospedaria for guaranteed jobs and offered industrialists a seemingly endless supply of cheap labor.[46] With limited opportunities, unskilled immigrants, particularly Portuguese, often were ideal workers for Paulistano employers trying to whiten the labor force and keep the cost of labor as low as possible.

The Hospedaria and the Replacements

An account in *Lucta Proletária*, an anarchist labor periodical, confirms that Paulistano employers used the hospedaria to contract strikebreakers. In January 1908, workers at several of the city's hat factories were on strike. By February, workers and industrialists had failed to reach an agreement. By late February, strike leaders complained that industrialists had replaced many of the strikers with unskilled laborers. The striking workers noted industrialists hired shoeshine boys, box carriers, banana vendors, and vagabonds to take their places.[47] In the following week, however, the strikers learned that one of the top hat factory owners, Catani, was contracting replacement workers directly from the hospedaria. A hatmaker who had reentered the hospedaria named Giovanni Sironi reported this back to the strikers, as Catani had tried to get him to sign a contract to work.[48]

The registrations from the hospedaria offer names of other workers Catani might have tried to contract. On February 28, forty-nine of the fifty-seven individuals signing contracts at the hospedaria came to reside directly in the city. This share of movement to the city was noticeably high, as the preceding and following entries showed almost exclusively agricultural contracts. Illiterate Portuguese families comprised the contracted group, and many were laborers from Lagoaça, a small town on Portugal's northeastern border. They included the Amaral family: Francisco Augusto, a thirty-one-year-old stone cutter, who was at the hospedaria with his wife, Amelia Augusta, age thirty, and their two children, Laurentina Jesus and Manoel Augusto, ages four and one. The cart driver José Joaquim Paulo and his wife, Maria Rodrigues, also signed contracts and moved to the city with their three sons, ages ten, six, and two. Young children would not have signed contracts, but factory owners would have understood their potential as workers. These families left Leixões aboard the steamship *Argentina* three weeks earlier, on February 5.[49] Men like Francisco and José Joaquim would have been just the ones industrialists like Catani were seeking: new arrivals with minimal connections and families of young children to feed.

The spike in contracts awarded directly to employers in the city during this period of labor unrest was not isolated. While the immigrant registries rarely record exact city employers, examining spikes in city contracts alongside newspaper accounts of strikes and disputes helps make this connection. In the prewar years, an increase in workers hired directly to the capital accompanied periods of labor unrest on at least two other notable occasions. On July 19, 1905, the workers at the Coelha da Rocha shoe factory went on strike. New machines had been installed, resulting in fewer jobs and reduced salaries for the workforce. On the same day, eight Spanish heads of household were contracted to work in the city, one of whom was a shoemaker. Four days into the strike, Coelha da Rocha had arranged for police presence at the factory, and the *Estado de São Paulo* reported that the workers' factory commission was ready to negotiate with the owners.[50] This was the last mention of the striking shoemakers in the newspaper; left here, it would seem as if the factory commission and owners came to an agreement. The hospedaria registries tell a very different story. On July 27 and 28, six shoemakers, nine adults with experience in the textile and garment industries, and twelve adults from a variety of professions also signed contracts to work in the city. It is not just the spike in employment that is telling but the heavy concentration of shoemakers. As with the hatmakers strike, the recently arrived Celestino Campos, Candido Gago, and Rosa Raiz Alvarez made ideal replacement workers.[51] While there is no further mention of the shoemaker strike, Aldrighetti factory hat workers went on strike at the end of the month because they were not receiving consistent paychecks. Once again, a group of newly arrived immigrants signed contracts to work in the city on August 5.[52] The emerging *posto zootécnico* (livestock research station) hired some of these individuals, but the rest just have "capital" listed as their destination. The hospedaria's presence and services, once again, provided arriving workers with jobs while it limited the power of striking workers.[53]

The following July, Paulista Railway workers went on strike, and a number of city establishments joined in solidarity. On July 17, 1906, hospedaria registrations showed a larger group of Spanish laborers hired in the capital than in the interior. Predominantly arriving with their families from Barcelona, these carpenters, weavers, and stoneworkers were the perfect replacement workers.[54] Records cannot confirm that Francisco Freixas, Felix Bartolome Perez, Enrique Font, and the other men were the strikebreakers Paulista Railway brought in, but the timing of their contracts would have coincided with weakening the growing labor movement.[55]

There were limits to the hospedaria providing industrialists with replacement workers. A large enough labor movement effectively curtailed using the state institution for this purpose. This, in fact, was what happened throughout May 1907, when a large-scale strike permeated the city.[56] The strike began on May 5, but the movement grew; as bricklayers, machinists, weavers, and even sanitation workers joined the strike, much work stopped throughout the city. During this period, the hospedaria largely kept new arrivals moving to the interior. Save for some German and Austrian metal and machine workers and a few Spanish families, less than 5 percent of the 1,241 individuals contracted in the month following the start of the strike signed city contracts.[57] While the breadth of the strike limited the hospedaria's ability to provide industrialists with replacement workers, the movement was not strong enough to gain the eight-hour workday that strikers sought, largely because most disputes were handled at the factory level. Industrialists had another key strategy to cripple the movement: the ability to call on state intervention in the form of police protection and violence.

The Police

When strikes and labor movements threatened the city's order and productivity, industrialists could count on police intervention and protection. The state was willing to ensure the freedom to work through positioning, violence, and intimidation. There were some boundaries such as a stigma against attacking female workers, but in general the relation between striking workers and the police was one of conflict and a looming threat of violence. Police protection was often the first state resource that industrialists used. Prior to 1906, the police presence was identifiable, but once Washington Luís became the state's secretary of justice and public safety, factory owners more often turned to this resource.[58] Police intervention was apparent in the Coelha da Rocha shoe factory and Catani hat factory strikes in 1906 and 1908, respectively. In both cases factory owners had already reached out for and been provided police protection before going to the hospedaria. By combining police protection and the hospedaria, the state played a considerable role in minimizing the impact of smaller labor movements in São Paulo. The 1907 strike, however, was a different case. As more workers joined, the strike's breadth grew enough to limit the hospedaria's role, leading employers to increasingly rely on police interventions. An evaluation of the methods and tactics the police used throughout May 1907 indicates that the state's willingness to provide protection for nonstriking workers' freedom to work expanded to using violent intervention to help industrialists and prevent worker mobilization.

As early as May 7, Washington Luís met with Paulistano industrialists to preemptively talk about the support the state would provide to avert disorder during the strike. He promised that the cavalry of the First Battalion of the state police would help industrialists and stand guard throughout the city. During the month, police presence was key in ensuring that nonstriking or returning workers safely made it to their jobs and that workers whose jobs required deliveries or working on the streets could do so safely.[59] The day after Luís granted protection, the cavalry apprehended strikers who were reported to be threatening nonstriking workers on Rua João Teodoro.

The police did not stop at protection and violently intervened on a number of occasions. By May 12, the city was divided by police into four sections, and the First Battalion's cavalry charge was to provide the resources "to ensure the freedom to work," guaranteed with force.[60] That force included a sizeable presence of troops who broke up worker meetings, stood guard to prevent gatherings, and exercised an unprecedented display of violence. When the sanitation workers went on strike to protest their miserable monthly incomes of 70$000–80$000, the First Battalion sent in twenty cavalry officers and then thirty reinforcements who attacked the two hundred workers with blows from their swords.[61] By mid-May, cavalry stood at many factory entrances, and sixty extra troops stood guard in the city center. Their aim was to prevent workers from congregating, but if workers were successful in meeting, the police and cavalry swiftly stepped in and arrested participants.[62] May 14–16 marked the most forceful displays of police intervention, but the police presence continued through the end of the month, posing a threat for workers on strike or considering going on strike.

When the Bonilha factory seamstresses went on strike in the last week of May, their bosses called the police, who immediately came to intimidate the striking workers. Intimidation marks an important deviation from the more physical approach police took toward other workers throughout the month. The unwillingness to break up the workers stemmed from the heavy female presence among the Bonilha strikers.[63] By and large, even when the city was under police order, official violence toward women was not tolerated. After the police beat striking sanitation workers with their swords, the strikers reorganized the following day in Praça Roberto Penteado. This time, however, the workers made sure to bring their wives and carried their small children in their arms. The demonstrators were not attacked.[64] A similar phenomenon occurred ten years later during the 1917 general strike at a public funeral that strikers organized for Antônio Ineguez Martinez, a young shoemaker shot and killed by police.[65] This is not to say that women were exempt from violence during times of labor unrest. To the contrary, in the tensions that developed between workers, women both precipitated initiated and were on the receiving end of violence, but the state was less likely to become physically involved in these altercations.

The police presence and violence did minimize the effectiveness of labor organization, but so too did the substantial number of workers who chose not to go on strike. In the May 1907 general strike, they were the laundry and bakery workers the police escorted, the seamstresses and seamsters who wanted to return to jobs at the Mariangela and Penteado factories, the street cleaners sweeping the streets at night. In effect, industrialists, the police, and the hospedaria cannot bear the full responsibility of labor's failure to coalesce and form effective movements in São Paulo. Nor can anarchist and labor leaders, whom scholars have highlighted as unable to connect to rank-and-file workers. Alongside industrialists, the hospedaria and labor leaders were nonstriking workers themselves. Knowing the social consequences of their actions, they made the decision to break strikes. The city's reality made many willing to bear those costs: survival above camaraderie.

THE STRIKEBREAKERS

Newspaper articles and reports provide an additional window into strikebreaker identities and motivations. The hatmakers strike from late December 1907 to mid-March 1908 is a particularly instructive episode for under-standing these individuals. Some reports directly identify what compelled individuals to cross the picket line, and other accounts provide workers' names. The labor press identified key strikebreakers in an effort to shame them into joining the cause or to make the offenders into pariahs to dis-courage others from joining their ranks. Their vilification of these indi-viduals should not be taken at face value. Police incident reports in the *Estado de São Paulo* also provide names in articles on physical disturbances between strikebreakers and strikers. Both kinds of reports reveal significant tension and lack of solidarity within the working class across genders and nationalities.

On December 23, 1907, workers presented a list of demands to owners of the city's four largest hat factories: Matanó Serrichio & Cia., M. Villela and Cia., J. Bosisio & Filho, and the Dante Ramenzoni & Irmão hat fac-tories. Less than eight months after the 1907 general strike began on May Day, workers again demanded an eight-hour workday. Leaders behind the demands made particular note that Dante Ramenzoni, one of the offending owners, was a member of the Socialist Party.[66] The decision to put forth the demands and go on strike, however, was not uniform among the factories' workforces. On the same day the demands were submitted, Camillo Aure-lio tried to return to work, João Ignacio da Silva stood in his way, and a fight between the two ensued. João Ignacio was arrested.[67]

As Christmas passed and 1908 began, the strike continued, but the fac-tories kept up production, albeit on a limited basis. On January 9, strikers threatened Marz Spozbront, Carlos, Antonio, João dos Santos, and Firmino Silva, all *contramestres* (supervisors) who continued to work.[68] On the same day, the striking workers would have received news that two thirds of the *gráphicos* (printers) at Werszflog & Irmãos also decided to walk out to demand improved workday schedules.[69] A few days later, workers at the Henrique San Marino bakery went on a ministrike. Workers at other firms and in other sectors also went on strike.[70] Although 1908 has been presented as a lull in labor activity in São Paulo, the first half of January told a different story.[71] For labor leaders in the hatmakers strike, these days represented the high point of labor unrest. The movements failed to unify workers, however, as the printers and bakery workers resolved their griev-ances with management,[72] and workers on strike at the hat factories had gone three weeks without paychecks.

As days passed without pay, workers increasingly turned to violence against those who continued to work in the hat factories. Justina de Carvalho tried to return to her job on January 15. On her way to work, she encountered Lulalia de Amorim on Rua Martim Francisco. Clearly frustrated by how her coworker's actions were undermining the movement, Lulalia began taunting and yelling at Justina. The two women began to physically fight. Justina's mother, Rosa, must have been close by and entered the fight and hit Lulalia several times in the head. Lulalia was hurt badly enough that Justina and her mother were arrested.[73] On the same day, Paulo Chiavegetti was attacked by a striking worker while going to his job at the Irmãos Lozazatti.[74] At least six strikebreakers were beaten up on Friday, January 17, as they returned to their jobs at the Matanó Serrichio and M. Villela hat factories.[75] Not all organizing efforts led to violence, but desperation was palpable. Eduardo Rezski went door to door trying to convince people to join or remain in the strike effort. His presence must have been formidable or his effectiveness palpable because he was also arrested for his efforts.[76]

As tensions led to more violence, factory owners called on police to restore order. When more than two hundred striking workers tried to get their tools from the Villela factory, the company fired those individuals and called the police in anticipation of the violence that would erupt. The police became a constant presence after the mid-January incidents. Matanó Serrichio owners reached out personally to thank Secretary of Justice Luís for repressing the strike enough that its operation could continue, even if on a diminished schedule.[77] At another of the large factories, 38 of the 168 workers continued to work. This was nearly a quarter of the workforce.[78] By this point, striking workers had endured almost two months without paychecks.

By the second month of the strike, owners began looking for full-time replacement labor. This is when strike leaders accused the Matanó Serrichio factory of hiring untrained workers such as shoeshine boys, box carriers, banana vendors, and vagabonds.[79] These jobs were stereotypically associated with Afro-Brazilians, but the names of strikebreakers show that European immigrants were just as likely to cross the picket line in São Paulo.[80] Anywhere from one fourth to one third of the workforce was willing to risk serious social consequences and physical harm or had not joined the organized workers. These individuals' willingness to work coupled with active recruitment at the hospedaria and police interventions effectively undermined the labor movement.

The factories' new workforce moved to protect their own interests and began to form a union that labor organizers called a *sindicato amarelo*. That union became a reality, and on March 13, 1908, strike leaders had to accept defeat.[81] Most of these replacement and hat factory workers were not the "donkeys," "cowards," and "butchers" strike leaders claimed them to be; they were working-class men and women in the city, new arrivals and established residents, trying to survive in a rapidly changing urban environment. They were navigating sporadic work and rising food prices and rents and just trying to stay healthy and take care of their families. They were one quarter of the original hat factory workforce. They were one third of the Werszflog printers. They were one fifth of the city's ceramic factory workforce. They were Paulo Chiavegetti and Justina and Rosa de Carvalho, and most were desperate.

Nonstriking and replacement workers' reluctance to strike was not unique to the 1908 hat factory strikes. Nor was the uptick in violence associated with strikes. In the early Old Republic and in May 1907, despite strikes and threats of violence, work continued to varying degrees around the city.[82] Strikers did attack businesses that remained open, and workers wanting to return had legitimate fears of retribution and violence from their coworkers. Workers returning to factories under police protection were actively threatened by strikers with tools, and in general, reports of violence in the city increased during periods of labor unrest.[83] These trends were also notable in hat-worker strikes of 1905 and 1906.[84]

Females often featured less prominently in newspaper reports on labor organization and strikebreakers and in reports of urban unrest, but there is clear evidence that divisions on striking crossed gender lines and that violence emerged between female workers. The example of Justina, Lulalia, and Rosa highlights these tensions but was not an isolated occurrence. One particularly damning and gendered method of intimidation was the threat of cutting nonstriking workers' hair. Such an action would have marked the women throughout the city as strikebreakers and scabs.[85] Reports on textile industry strikes in the first two years of the twentieth century also expose these tensions. Thirteen women returned to work only four days after the Anhaia textile factory strike began in October 1902. Despite needing armed protection, at least some workers continued to try to work in the week prior to management and striking workers reaching an agreement.[86] Scholars emphasize women's willingness to strike, but the women willing to cross the picket line were in some ways braver. It is helpful to imagine the desperation that gave five workers enough courage to confront the six hundred striking women standing guard outside the Sant'Anna factory in February 1901.[87] Perhaps Assumpta Crescencio was one of the women willing to face the hundreds of strikers. One week earlier, she had physically fought to try and return to work.[88] She would have come up against coworkers like Guiseppina Cutolo and her brother, Guiseppe, who assaulted strikebreakers on February 22.[89]

When studied collectively, strikebreaker names demonstrate a strong immigrant presence. In addition to Justina and Rosa de Carvalho, Paulo Chiavegetti, and Assumpta Crescencio are the names Cesare Pacini, Ferruccio Pedrezzoli, Basile Maraon, Francisco Sarno, and the Morellis;[90] others were Narciso Zani, Paolo Gatti, Ludovico Finardi, and the Mangiamorti brothers.[91] The prominence of Italian surnames may exaggerate their proportion of nonstriking and replacement workers. As Italians were important labor organizers, the relative frequency of Italian surnames in the labor press may be understood as reflecting tensions within this national group. Even strike leaders were willing to show some of their Italian brethren compassion. This was especially true of new arrivals and the poorest among them.[92] Labor organizers did not deny that surviving and thriving in São Paulo was difficult, and they understood that for some workers, the costs of striking were exceptionally high. Real vitriol was reserved for repeat strikebreakers, especially those who could get jobs elsewhere. Ferruccio Pedrezzoli, for example, was criticized because he could find work in other factories and Francisco Sarno for being a strikebreaker on three separate occasions.[93]

Portuguese workers especially were unconvinced to join the cause and willing to "do anything to preserve their jobs."[94] During the May 1907 general strike, fifty striking workers forced the state's water and sewage department to stop work on Rua Ana Cintra in the city's center by threatening workers on the project.[95] Striking workers also intimidated nonstriking workers at worksites on Avenida Paulista and Rua Müller.[96] Most of the state's water and sewage company workers were Brazilian, Italian, and Portuguese. Collectively they represented more than 90 percent of the water and sewage company employees, at 42, 26, and 24 percent, respectively.[97] The large Portuguese presence in the water and sewage department is representative of the role official jobs played for the Portuguese in the city's labor market. As state and city employees rarely joined in labor movements during the early Old Republic, taking official positions effectively meant workers were deciding to distance themselves from labor organization.

One of the most abominable official positions was that of police officer. It was police who shot and killed the shoemaker whose public funeral intensified the 1917 general strike. It was police who were called to protect nonstriking and replacement workers, intimidate and control striking workers, and arrest those deemed threatening.[98] Even when it came to less repressive involvement, the state called on firemen, a division of the public safety department, to be replacement workers.[99] Afro-Brazilians were over-represented in these positions; they constituted less than a quarter of the city's population, but in Ramatis Jacino's study of racialized job opportunities, they represented all registered police agents, 38 percent of rank-and-file soldiers, and 52 percent of soldier firemen.[100] Portuguese more than any other immigrant group, were willing to take "vile" policemen jobs and in general were a significant part of the state's unskilled labor force.[101] Even when they did not become policemen, there was the question of collaboration. One anarcho-syndicalist writer in 1907 said of the Portuguese, "The poor 'Maneis' . . . run to the police headquarters in order to become puppets ready to kill strikers."[102] Racial prejudice likely funneled Afro-Brazilians into these positions, but what made Portuguese workers willing to take jobs that others would not?

The importance of family survival was a critical motivator for residents. By the numbers and across national lines, the nuclear family's hold on Paulistano workers was stronger than it was in Buenos Aires and Rio de Janeiro. Choosing to join a strike meant not only going hungry oneself but also watching the family go hungry. Just as families worked together to earn a livable wage, like the Carvalho and Cutolo families, they made decisions to join or eschew labor organization. If need be, families were willing to risk jail time to come to their loved ones' defense. The stakes were higher for Portuguese immigrants, women, and Afro-Brazilians. It is within this context that threats to family survival could convince workers to break with national, regional, and personal ties and cross the picket line. Their decisions to put family first ultimately contributed to failed labor organization in the prewar era.

Conclusion

To understand why labor organization was not more successful in the city of São Paulo during the Old Republic requires pushing beyond the explanation that strike leaders were unable to connect to rank-and-file workers and that industrialists exploited labor. Here I posit three equally important elements at play: the Hospedaria de Imigrantes' ability to connect replacement workers with industrialists, the state's willingness to forcefully intervene on behalf of industrialists, and working-class Paulistanos' willingness to remain on the job as nonstriking workers or to serve as replacement workers. The pressure to survive in the city was high; São Paulo was not just a city of immigrants and migrants, it was a city of family immigrants and migrants. This distinction meant that time and again, significant shares of workers remained on their jobs despite picket lines and threats of violence.

When there were not enough workers willing to remain, industrialists had other options; they could call on the state's public safety division, and they could contract replacement workers directly from the hospedaria. On more than one occasion, the city contracts for hospedaria registrations spiked in days after labor unrest. A particularly damning report of how industrialists recruited workers from the hospedaria confirms that this was a viable practice. While family was an important factor in a worker's willingness to cross the picket line, so too was his or her expectation about job prospects. São Paulo was not a land of equal opportunity. Italian strikebreakers were criticized because they had other work opportunities, but this does not seem to have been the case for everyone. The large presence of Afro-Brazilians and Portuguese among the police force's ranks suggests that for these groups in particular, opportunity often meant significant social sacrifices. The discrimination these individuals had to overcome may have made them less willing to connect with labor leaders.

4

Discrimination in
the Paulistano Labor Market

Being a strikebreaker held serious, long-term consequences; neighbors, acquaintances, and fellow workers remembered these transgressions. In essence, being a nonstriking worker, a replacement worker, or a police officer meant compromising the social network that many Paulistanos depended on in times of need. What, then, compelled some individuals to make this decision? Were some groups more inclined to do so than others?

A key to answering these questions lies in understanding employers' expectations of employees and workers' expectations about available opportunities. Going on strike, looking for new work, or filling in as a replacement was a calculated decision. While no individual had the exact same circumstances as another, different groups of people had shared expectations based on gender, racial, and national identities. In addition to prejudice, employers also held expectations about work performance that had significant impact on opportunities in the labor market over the course of the Old Republic. More succinctly, as employers discriminated, workers adapted their strategies to navigate the discrimination they faced. Workers facing the most extreme prejudice had greater incentive to look for opportunities outside of the formal labor market.

That there was, and still is, discrimination and inequality in Brazil's labor market is no secret. The São Paulo School of Sociology long ago dispelled the myth of Brazil's racial democracy. Since the 1950s, estimates of socioeconomic disparities in Brazil registered among some of the highest in the Western Hemisphere.[1] The country's late abolition of slavery, in 1888, indicates the extent of an earlier era of inequality. The Old Republic, 1891–1930, is often understood as the natural bridge between the two periods, and some recent research on racial discrimination supports this interpretation.[2] This reasoning, however, does not fully consider the opportunities for improvement the Old Republic should have provided. The city of São Paulo grew quickly and appealed to many immigrants and migrants. While there were few rags-to-riches realities, such a dynamic environment did provide opportunities for advancement and social mobility, especially in the prewar era. For new residents arriving on a daily basis in the rapidly growing city, social mobility should have been a tenable goal. Should-haves, though, do not always constitute reality.

Discrimination and prejudice cut short dreams for several groups of people. I delve into just how large the obstacles were for Afro-Brazilians and women. Both groups faced significant hiring discrimination throughout the period, albeit through different channels. Women also had to overcome sizeable and persistent wage disparities. Scholars have paid particular attention to the discrimination facing Afro-Brazilians, but the lack of racial categories on most official documents makes it difficult to address the importance of that discrimination.[3] I examine company-level hiring records and help-wanted advertisements in the *Estado de São Paulo* to understand the prejudice Afro-Brazilians faced.

The absence of racial categories has also meant that much scholarship reduces the non-Brazilian population to a uniform group of foreigners. This effectively ignores the immigrant population's complexity. In the city of São Paulo, there was a distinct movement of unskilled Portuguese immigrants who arrived between 1903 and 1913 and a movement of skilled German and Austrian immigrants who arrived in the years following World War I. Equating these two groups has distorted the understanding of the foreign experience in the São Paulo labor market.

Looking at different national groups' experiences in the formal labor market reveals that Portuguese workers also faced discrimination in São Paulo. Even in the postwar period, qualified workers had trouble finding jobs. This made the Portuguese experience distinct from the Afro-Brazilian experience. Because Portuguese immigrants, as a group, were the least skilled in the city's population, employers expected Portuguese workers to be less skilled, and they were disproportionately hired into unskilled positions. Economists term this type of discrimination based on rational expectations "statistical discrimination." Overcoming statistical discrimination was easier than overcoming racial prejudice, because at the end of the day, Portuguese workers had jobs through which they could advance.

Historians will find the statistical discrimination facing women of child-bearing age more familiar. While Brazilian labor laws in the Old Republic did not exclude these women from the workforce, employers often avoided hiring or promoting women into positions that required more extensive training.[4] Employers based their hiring practices on the expectation that women would leave the workforce upon getting married or having children. Many women did exit the labor force, but many Paulistano working-class households accepted and encouraged wives to work during the Old Republic, and evidence from department store employees confirms this trend. Over a lifetime, the reduced opportunities and wages these women received amounted to considerable sums.

How did these competing factors affect individual decisions to remain, exit, and stay in the workforce or to strike? For individuals facing the great-est hiring discrimination, Afro-Brazilians and Afro-Brazilian women in particular, the cost of striking once a good job was found would have meant giving up hard-won employment. If employers did not forgive strikers, striking for Afro-Brazilians likely meant leaving the formal labor market.[5] Discrimination's impact on Portuguese workers was different. Although they also faced hiring discrimination, opportunities for unskilled employ-ment were readily available. As strikebreakers, they would still have been able to find future employment, and if they had trouble in the industrial sector, there was always the option to join the police force or other official jobs.

METHODOLOGY AND SOURCES

To reveal the impact that discriminatory practices had on workers requires a systematic examination of hiring and promotion practices. Individual stories provide valuable insight and document the existence of discrimina-tion, but a statistical approach helps distinguish more persistent trends. Measuring just how much individual characteristics affected an individ-ual's wage or opportunity to get a skilled job accentuates discrimination's sizeable lifelong impact. While there are several avenues to explore formal labor market discrimination, as discrimination often appears in wage dif-ferentials and hiring practices, these are two logical areas to investigate.

Economic historians often use census data to explore these themes, but Brazil's censuses from the Old Republic simply do not provide enough evidence to fully address the complexity of the Paulistano labor mar-ket.[6] To address these questions in this critical and understudied period, it is necessary to explore alternative sources. Help-wanted ads and company hiring records provide other avenues for exploring labor market discrimination.[7]

I use this evidence to evaluate discrimination in three ways. First, a new wage series developed for the city of São Paulo allows for analysis of how much a worker's nationality, race, and gender affected the wage received and the probability of being hired into a good job or an unskilled position. Analyzing this evidence from a statistical framework highlights the degree of hiring discrimination and helps quantify the obstacles certain groups had to overcome.[8] In addition to looking at persistent hiring and wage inequalities for the entirety of the Old Republic, I also investigate how practices changed after the start of World War I. Second, I take a more nuanced approach and evaluate the opportunities for individuals at four companies in the city. Hiring evidence from the São Paulo Tramway, Light, and Power, the Estamparia Ypiranga Jafet textile factory, the Companhia Estadas de Ferro Paulista, and the Mappin department store helps explore how worker job experiences varied across sectors. Both these analyses demonstrate sizeable exclusion of Afro-Brazilians from the formal labor market.

These approaches to the labor market are restricted because racial prejudice and discrimination often kept Afro-Brazilians out of the labor market and thus out of company records. Understanding discrimination is further limited because employers often did not keep records on race, just as race is absent in most state and national records. In 1872, more than 72 percent of the state population was black or *pardo*, but by 1940, just 12 percent of the state's population was considered Afro-Brazilian. To understand the degree of Afro-Brazilian underrepresentation in the formal labor market, I contend that 20 to 25 percent of the city's working-class population was Afro-Brazilian.[9] In theory, one in every four or five hires should have been an Afro-Brazilian. This was not the case.

To address this shortcoming in the company records, the third alternative approach is to analyze help-wanted ads in the *Estado de São Paulo* to supplement an understanding of the prejudice facing Afro-Brazilians. Systematically, Afro-Brazilians were excluded from many opportunities and even faced substantial obstacles in finding service-level positions.[10] Domestic and service workers already had minimal opportunity for advancement. The written preferences for white, black, immigrant, or national applicants in unskilled positions reveal even larger obstacles for Afro-Brazilian women. Building on scholarship examining Afro-Brazilian workers' exclusion in the Brazilian labor market, my research shows how a subtle "boa aparência" (good appearance) preference grew alongside the wide-scale migration from the Brazilian Northeast to the city in the postwar era.[11]

There are limits to this statistical approach. It does not speak directly to the growing informal labor market. It does not fully take into account cultural and social norms that affected workers' decisions, and it cannot analyze individual experiences in depth. It does, however, shed light on just how much individuals were pushed further to the Paulistano margins and who those individuals were likely to be. This information is critical to understanding who would be more likely to join the informal labor market, who would benefit from more education, who might be more likely to strike or be a strikebreaker, and who would be willing to stay in a low-paying job.

SÃO PAULO, LAND OF UNEQUAL OPPORTUNITY

The Paulistano working class used creative strategies and methods to adapt to the city's dramatic changes. Immigrants and Brazilians alike rented out spare rooms, built new housing, embraced the family wage, and used the hospedaria as an employment agency and a safety net. Paulistanos, native and immigrant, were enterprising and clearly aware of opportunities. Day-to-day experiences and conversations with family, friends, acquaintances, coworkers, and neighbors helped them understand just how much their national, racial, and gender identity affected their available schooling and job opportunities. These working-class individuals innately understood their reality, but as the records they left behind are often slim, social scientists continue to look for insight into their world.

Individual experiences are important to understanding that world, but systematic favoritism or discrimination toward specific groups of people also had profound impacts on individual decisions. This would have been especially true in the formal labor market. Although many historians shy away from statistical analysis, when used carefully, this tool can provide a window into working-class lives. I use this approach with a new wage series based on 6,642 wage and work observations for 5,051 individuals from the São Paulo Old Republic to measure just how important nationality, gender, and race were in determining a worker's wages and his or her job opportunities.[12] Although the series is imperfect, it offers the best understanding of the city's working-class formal labor market during this critical period.

Appendix B provides the detailed results of the statistical analysis, and here I offer a short introduction. To evaluate the labor market, I rely on two statistical tests, the standard linear regression and the logit analysis. These analyses do not claim to determine outcomes but rather record correlations between two factors. A standard linear regression helps explain how certain variables (x-factors) affected a particular outcome (the y-factor). A number of elements should have affected an individual's wage. First was the type of job; unskilled day laborers were not paid the same starting wages as mechanics, and apprentices were not paid what master craftsmen were. A worker's age, experience, and year he or she got the job also affected wages. In addition, some companies paid more than other companies. What should not have affected a worker's wage in the Paulistano labor market was his or her nationality, race, or gender. The standard linear regression, by accounting for all the factors that affected wages, shows that when there are still substantial differences between wages based on nationality, gender, or race, those results are not due to random chance. These types of results point to evidence of discrimination.

In an equation form, the standard linear regression I use to evaluate wage differences is the following: $\ln(wage_i) = xN_i + yR_i + zF_i + u_i + e$. In this analysis, the natural log of the real wage is used as the dependent variable (y-factor) because it facilitates comparing an engineer's salary to a bobbin worker's wage. In the equation, x, y, and z are coefficients that represent the degree to which nationality (N), race (R), and gender (F), independent variables, affected those wages.[13] The term u is purely notational and combines all the other variables into one coefficient.[14] Finally, e refers to the residual, which can be understood as a combination of factors affecting wages that are not accounted for in the statistical analysis. This term, then, captures how social and cultural norms, a worker's civil status, or the number of children affected wages.[15]

In interpreting the results, the concerns are largely whether there is a negative or positive correlation between certain worker characteristics and whether that result is statistically significant. The following hypothetical in which the coefficient for German workers is positive and statistically significant to the 10 percent level helps explain these concepts. In this hypothetical, the positive correlation means that if two workers were identical in every way except that one was German and one was Brazilian, the German worker's wage would be higher than the Brazilian's. The significance means that when a random German worker is pulled from the sample, nine times out of ten that wage will be higher than that of a Brazilian worker with the same variables. Knowing that there was a steady influx of skilled German workers to the city, one can infer that the German worker likely benefited from statistical favoritism.

Analyzing the real wages São Paulo workers made in the formal labor market points to some persistent wage differentials. Many jobs were closed to women, but even in positions filled by workers of both sexes, women received just 65–79 percent of the pay men got for the same jobs.[16] While this result could be expected, it does allow for transnational comparisons and shows that even though Brazilian women were receiving less than their male counterparts, gendered wage disparities were lower than they were in the United States. Women working full-time in the United States in 1914 made just 59.2 percent weekly and 62.2 percent hourly of what men did. By 1929, there was little improvement, as women made just 57 and 63 percent, respectively, of what men made overall, and women in manufacturing were making just 57.5 percent of what men in manufacturing were making.[17]

In terms of national preference, the wage analysis first seems to support the interpretation that foreigners received higher pay than Brazilians. In just considering the impact that nationality and gender had on wages for the duration of the Old Republic, Italian, German, Russian, and Polish immigrants all received statistically higher wages than their Brazilian counterparts. However, further investigation shows this largely was a factor of age; foreign workers tended to be older and working in their prime. Once age is accounted for, most differences in wages between nationalities are not significant.[18] For the period as a whole, there is some evidence that companies paid Portuguese workers less and German workers more, but it is difficult to determine if this was a product of ability or of biases. Dividing the analysis into two time periods does show that the war represented a changing point, as some national wage differences began to emerge after 1913. Between 1914 and 1930, Portuguese workers' wages were 7–16 percent lower, and German workers' wages were 10 percent higher than Brazilian workers' hourly wages.[19] These wage differences suggest that the influx of unskilled Portuguese workers continued to affect the Portuguese labor experience well into the Old Republic. Again, the lower wages could have been a result of ability but were also likely evidence of statistical discrimination.

The wage analysis also shows that white Brazilians were not paid significantly more than Afro-Brazilians. In fact, there is even a negative, although statistically insignificant, correlation between white workers and wages. Furthermore, no substantial changes came about as a result of World War

I; studies of racial discrimination have found similar patterns in Rio de Janeiro and in the United States. Effectively, if Afro-Brazilians could get jobs, they were likely more than qualified and would have deserved a higher wage.[20] To understand the degree of systemic racial discrimination in São Paulo's Old Republic, then, one must look to discrimination at the hiring level within the wage series and at help-wanted ads during the period.

The typical working-class city resident did not need statistical analysis to understand how unfair prejudices and advantages played out in the job market. Very simply, if a male worker could actually get a job in the formal labor market, he was going to be compensated approximately the same as other men were for the same work. The only sizeable and persistent wage differences at individual firms were based on the worker's gender. The key to opportunity and mobility, then, was getting a good job. It is with job opportunities that Afro-Brazilian, women, and Portuguese workers faced discrimination and Italian and German workers received preferential treatment.

A series of logistic analyses helps investigate hiring practice discrimination. The logit analysis varies from the linear regression because the y-factor outcome of interest is a yes or no answer (Could a worker get a job?) rather than a continuous number (What was a worker's wage?).[21] In the Paulistano case, I wanted to see how an individual's nationality, race, and gender affected his or her ability to be hired as a mechanic or to be hired as an unskilled worker. The mechanic position represents a good job in the Paulistano labor market. There was significant gender discrimination, as there were no female mechanics in the sample. Day laborers and ring spinners represent unskilled work, as the many workers holding these jobs could be easily replaced.[22] Whether certain groups had advantages in getting better positions or were pigeonholed into unskilled positions is important in understanding worker motivations to stay in jobs with little room for advancement or to look for better employment.

Portuguese workers consistently received fewer opportunities to be mechanics and were more likely to be unskilled workers. Even when accounting for the impacts that age, experience, the year, and literacy had on wages, Portuguese workers were 6–14 percent less likely to be hired into mechanical positions than Brazilian workers and 22–23 percent more likely to be to be hired into unskilled positions.[23] The impact was accentuated in the prewar period, when Portuguese workers were roughly 40 percent more likely to be hired as unskilled workers and statistically less likely to be mechanics.

Although the impact diminished after the start of the war, Portuguese were still 19 percent more likely to be unskilled workers in the postwar period.[24] As with the hourly wage differences, the influx of unskilled Portuguese to the city of São Paulo in the prewar era had a long-standing impact on the worker opportunities throughout the Old Republic.

As to whether any one national group received preferential treatment for the entire period, the logit analysis does not consistently demonstrate that one national group was more likely to be hired as mechanics or less likely to be hired as day laborers. There is some evidence, however, that after the start of the war, Italian and German workers received preferential hiring treatment. German workers were less likely to be hired into unskilled positions, and Italians were 11–14 percent more likely to be hired as mechanics.[25]

This logistic analysis does reveal significant evidence of racial preference. For the entire period, white workers were not overrepresented as mechanics, but they were statistically less likely to be in unskilled positions. As mechanics, nonwhite workers would have had minimal contact with outside customers, making physiognomy less important in terms of hiring. That whites were less likely than an Afro-Brazilian with the same characteristics to be hired as day laborers or ring spinners shows how white Brazilians in the Old Republic received quantifiable advantages in job placement.[26] Recent research on accident reports submitted to the state confirms the dramatic effects of this hiring discrimination. A conservative estimate of the impact of such discrimination shows that due to different job opportunities, the average Afro-Brazilian could expect to make just 82 percent of what the average white worker received.[27] Even these approaches yield an underestimate of the discrimination facing Afro-Brazilians. The steepest uphill battle was getting hired into the formal labor market in the first place. A closer look into four Paulistano companies shows how many Afro-Brazilians would not be able to overcome the sizeable labor market barriers they faced. Just like women, they would be pushed into the marginal and often informal economy.

FOUR FIRMS AND THEIR EMPLOYEES

São Paulo was an extremely diverse city, and in certain ways, employers could choose their employees. The state's subsidization of immigration and the city's Hospedaria de Imigrantes serve as just two examples of the institutional frameworks that facilitated employers' choosing workers. They should have chosen the best workers, but in practice, they did not. To study how workers responded to labor market discrimination and insecurity, scholars have traditionally used labor newspapers and industrialists' publications and circulars. These approaches are valuable because they demonstrate general concerns affecting the industrial labor force and highlight labor organization leaders.[28] Yet they fail to seriously consider the vast majority of the city's formal labor market, rank-and-file workers. Employee entry data on individual workers in four distinct sectors help demonstrate the barriers facing certain groups in the Paulistano formal labor market: the railroad, transportation, textile, and commercial sectors. Re-creating the profiles of employees reveals more industry-specific nuances.[29]

Paulista Railway

São Paulo state's rise to prominence was intricately connected to coffee, but it was just as connected to the expansion of railroads and the extension of the coffee frontier.[30] Early on, railroad companies were key employers during the Old Republic. When the state allowed a portion of subsidized immigrants to be nonagriculturalists in the early twentieth century, many of these artisans or laborers found jobs on railroads.[31] In 1912, one railroad company sent a direct request to the state secretary of agriculture asking for 500 Portuguese workers. The company needed 20 carpenters, 50 stoneworkers, and, presumably, 430 unskilled workers. This type of request was not unique.[32] One of the city and state's premier railway companies, the Companhia Paulista de Estradas de Ferro (Paulista Railway) employed thousands of people within the greater metropolitan region during the Old Republic. Working for the company was not ideal, as evidenced by the 1906 Paulista Railway strike, but in general its workers could aspire to long careers and upward mobility within the company.[33]

Most workers hired by the company came in at entry-level positions. These jobs were often unskilled, unspecified labor positions, and the workers taking them were men in their early twenties. Pay was above average, and workers could earn around 3$700 per day. Ana Lucia Lanna reports on Theodulo de Macedo, a good representative of a typical hire: young, Brazilian, and entering into an unskilled position in 1913. He was not originally from São Paulo but had migrated from Sapucaia, Minas Gerais state, 375 miles from the city of São Paulo. He was hired as a cleaner at the age of twenty-three. Five years later he became a stoker, and by 1924 he had received several promotions and was working as a machinist. Theodulo would remain at Paulista Railway until September 1941, when he retired at the age of fifty-one.[34]

A closer analysis of incoming workers reveals the impact race had on work opportunities and the hiring discrimination that nonwhite workers had to overcome. More than 85 percent of entering workers for whom Paulista Railway recorded racial categories were considered white, 10 percent were considered black, and the remaining workers were considered *pardo*.[35] This aggregate share, 15 percent, was well below the share of the city's Afro-Brazilian population. As in Rio de Janeiro, white workers were more likely to be hired into medium-skilled positions, representing nine out of every ten workers hired into these jobs. Nonwhite workers were more likely to be hired into unskilled positions, representing 19 percent of these hires.[36]

Not all black and *pardo* workers were Brazilian. Attilio Nicoletti was Italian and António dos Santos was Portuguese, but both men were considered *pardo*. Several Portuguese workers at Paulista Railway were black.[37] Did Afro-Brazilians' experiences diverge from those of nonwhite foreigners? The simple answer is yes. Afro-Brazilians were even more likely to be hired into unskilled labor positions. While only one quarter of Brazilian workers hired were nonwhite, these individuals represented 44 percent of workers hired into unskilled positions (table 4.1).[38] Paulista Railway effectively relegated Afro-Brazilians into unskilled positions. Arguably, white workers did register a slightly higher level of educational achievement, but schooling was a poor judge of competency for many of the low- and medium-skilled positions at Paulista Railway.[39] Clearly, Afro-Brazilians, even compared to other nonwhites, faced considerable hiring discrimination.

Afro-Brazilians were not the only group of individuals who found it difficult to get good jobs at Paulista Railway. Women were completely excluded. While it is not surprising that the company was overwhelmingly male, the absence of female workers is glaring. When General Motors came to Brazil in the 1920s, women were at least hired into secretarial positions.[40] Portuguese men were also hired disproportionately into unskilled positions at Paulista Railway. Almost nine out of ten Portuguese employees were hired into unskilled positions, double the rate for Brazilian workers as a whole, although there were important racial distinctions between Brazilians. This concentration in unskilled positions can be understood as employer expectations that Portuguese workers were unskilled. The incoming Portuguese population to the city was decidedly unskilled. Paulista Railway's Portuguese workforce, for the most part, conformed to these

Table 4.1. Entry-level jobs at Paulista Railway, by race and skill level

Race	Unskilled	Low	Medium	Total
White	170	69	78	317
White Brazilian	44	47	50	141
Nonwhite	39	7	6	52
Nonwhite Brazilian	35	7	6	48

Source: Paulista Railway portion of wage series in Ball, "Prices, Wages, and the Cost of Living," derived from Lanna, Ferrovia, cidade e trabalhadores.

expectations, with 43 percent being either illiterate or with poor education, making them more likely to be illiterate and with less schooling than Afro-Brazilians. This hiring bias made it difficult for Portuguese workers like Joaquim Pereira and David de Campos Ribeiro who had some schooling but had to start their careers in unskilled day laborer positions. This discrimination also helps explain why it was Portuguese men more than other national groups who turned to municipal and state jobs. Whether as sewage workers, maintenance employees, or even as "the ultimate betrayal of their fellow workers," police officers,[41] Portuguese simply could not find jobs as easily as other immigrant groups.

Light

The Portuguese experience was not isolated to the Paulista Railway company. Worker employment patterns at the São Paulo Tramway, Light, and Power Company also demonstrate that Portuguese workers were treated differently, and this often translated into discriminatory practices. Light is a particularly telling example for two reasons. Tramway conductors had to speak Portuguese, so this immigrant group, theoretically, should have had increased access to jobs with the company.[42] And Light employment evidence only began consistently registering nationality in 1924. Thus, discriminatory hiring practices registered in the latter half of the 1920s meant that practices persisted past the initial influx of unskilled Portuguese coming to the city in the prewar era. This provides further evidence that employer expectations from an earlier period were transferred to a new generation of Portuguese immigrants.

A 20 percent sample of workers hired by the company during the Old Republic shows how these prejudices persisted. For the 877 workers with known nationalities in the sample, 45 percent were Brazilian, but Portuguese and Italian workers also represented 16 and 14 percent of hires, respectively.[43] Records from the 1920s did not have any information on race;

Table 4.2. Light hires, 1923–1929, by skill level and nationality

Skill level	Brazilian	Portuguese	Italian	Spanish	German	Other	Total
Unskilled	72	61	17	18	3	18	189
	38.1	32.28	8.99	9.52	1.59	9.52	100
Low	133	40	40	15	7	51	286
	46.5	13.99	13.99	5.24	2.45	17.83	100
Medium	188	37	65	12	44	56	402
	46.77	9.2	16.17	2.99	10.95	13.93	100
Total	393	138	122	45	54	125	877
	44.81	15.74	13.91	5.13	6.16	14.25	100

Sources: Light portion of wage series as constructed from Light *fichas*, São Paulo Tramway, Light, and Power Company; FESESP as elaborated in Ball, "Prices, Wages, and the Cost of Living."

Note: Most of the workers were hired between 1924 and 1929. German workers also include Austrian workers. Number of workers and percentage of skill level are represented by national group.

based on George Reid Andrews's analysis of records from the 1930s that inferred race from photographic evidence,[44] Afro-Brazilians at Light likely faced similar hiring discrimination as described for Paulista Railway. Nationality observations show Portuguese workers disproportionately hired into unskilled positions. These men represented 32 percent of unskilled laborers despite being just 16 percent of the incoming workforce. Furthermore, as shown in table 4.2, they were the only national group to be over-represented in unskilled positions.

Examining why workers left Light offers another window into workplace discrimination facing Portuguese workers. Scholarly studies of individual firms in the 1930s demonstrate relatively long employment tenures, but this was simply not the case for most companies in São Paulo during the 1920s, and Light registered a particularly high worker turnover. The sample worker records (*fichas*) show the reasons 491 workers left during the decade. The most common reason given was "livre vontade," a worker's free will, but the ambiguity of the term complicates interpreting these individuals' opportunities. More instructive is examining those workers who left involuntarily or who sought out better opportunities. In the sample of 491, only 12 workers were fired outright. Four of those men were Portuguese, but this number was proportional to the share of Portuguese workers at Light and only a slightly higher proportion than the share for all workers.[45] Spanish workers were targeted to a greater degree; 11 percent of Spanish employees were fired from the company.[46]

The reasons for leaving also demonstrate the advantages German and Austrian workers had in the Paulistano formal labor market. Low wages and other opportunities compelled 14 percent of workers in the sample to leave Light. The share was almost 15 percentage points higher for German and Austrian workers; 23 percent left because of low wages, and an additional 5 percent went to other jobs, presumably with higher pay. While qualified Portuguese applicants would face greater difficulty in finding new jobs, unqualified or untrained German and Austrian workers benefited from employers' assumptions that they would be more skilled.

German men may have had an unfair advantage at Light, but the same could not be said for German women. Just as at Paulista Railway, women were completely excluded from the company's workforce. These companies were by no means unique. Exclusion began among child workers, defined as children and adolescents between the ages of seven and fourteen. Girls were restricted to specific areas of the labor market and tended to concentrate in the few high-paying positions available to them.[47] Textile and food preparation were the most likely sectors to employ girls, but the relatively high-paying positions available to girls within these industries offered minimal opportunities for advancement. Boys, on the other hand, could find jobs in glass and pottery factories, as trade apprentices, and in cafés around town.[48]

Boys had almost double the job opportunity that girls did in terms of variety; the 1920 census registers girls in just 63 jobs throughout the state, while boys were employed in 120.[49] Working conditions were no better for boys, but pay was often significantly more in sectors that were closed to girls. A busboy in a local café earned as much as 150$000 per month (5$371 per day), more than twice what a child working in a textile factory could expect to earn.[50] Even within the textile sector, boys had more opportunities than girls did. Most children would be employed in the bobbin and rings positions, but only boys held higher-earning apprentice positions with greater promotional opportunities in the bleaching and mechanics departments.[51] Antonio Stocco's labor market experience highlights this reality. He worked in the dyeing section of a textile factory at age fourteen, earning 5$940 réis per day at the end of the 1920s.[52] Such a position would not have been available to a girl.

Given this reality, girls were concentrated in the highest-paying positions available to them. The top four were hemmers (textiles), sausage makers (food), coat liners (textiles), and sergers (textiles), and competition for these jobs was stiff. Most girls sought more readily available jobs in the textile industry, particularly as spinners, bobbin workers, and folders, positions for which girls received higher hourly wages than boys.[53]

The occupational limitations a girl faced extended into adulthood. Women also were concentrated in positions where they received the highest pay relative to men, in particular as weavers, spinners, bobbin workers, folders, and floral seamstresses.[54] To understand why females were concentrated in so few positions, it is helpful to imagine an alternate 1920 Paulistano reality. In this version women and men receive the same average wages for their jobs as recorded in the 1920 census, but occupational distribution is switched. In other words, females occupy the share of positions reported for men and vice versa. In this reality, the average female wage drops dramatically, more than 40 percent. The result is likely even more dramatic, as this exercise only considers jobs for which both men and women were employed. This exercise demonstrates that in these few positions women could best confront the city's high cost of living.[55] Understanding the female experience is critical because approximately one in five females in the city worked for pay by 1920. Two key sectors offering opportunity for formal female employment were textiles and commerce.

Jafet

In July 1916, Manoel Teixeira wrote his mother, asking her to sell her house in Portugal and join him and his family in São Paulo to take charge of the grandchildren to facilitate his wife's working outside the home. In the letter he describes how his compadre's daughter earned 2$400 per day in a factory.[56] As the textile sector paid some of the highest wages to girls and women, the Teixeira family likely planned on Maria entering a cotton or wool textile factory once Manoel's mother arrived. By 1913 there were more than eighteen textile firms in the city. The sector was the largest industrial employer in both the city and state, employing more than 40 percent of the state's industrial workforce in 1920. As almost 60 percent of textile workers in 1920 were female, analyzing available opportunities in textiles is key to understanding female labor experiences.[57] Looking at the hiring practices provides a window into lives of working women and the degree to which national and racial discrimination was gendered.

The Fiação, Tecelagem e Estamparia Ypiranga Jafet textile factory (Jafet) in the city's Ipiranga neighborhood was just one of many large establishments in the city. It was founded in 1906 by Lebanese brothers. While the factory was by no means the city's largest or smallest, its workforce and hiring tactics provide a good representation of what workers could expect in the textile sector.[58] Average wages at Jafet fit within the norm reported for other Paulistano textile factories, and the division of labor by gender was consistent with shares reported in the textile industry.[59]

For boys and girls, there was minimal difference in the wages they made. At Jafet, there was a negligible gender wage gap for children under fourteen, and for those under fifteen, girls made 90 percent of what boys made.[60] As additional schooling provided more opportunities for boys in São Paulo's Old Republic, girls frequently took textile jobs and became important contributors to the family income.[61] This was Alfredo Pinto de Queiroz's rationale when he wrote to his wife, Ignacia, in 1915 to join him and one of their sons in Brazil along with their other four children. The eldest daughter could earn as much as 70$000 monthly as a seamstress assistant.[62] Men and women, however, did not receive equal pay for similar work. The 1912 *Boletim do Departamento do Estado de Trabalho (BDET)* report on textile wages for men and women in the state of São Paulo stated that in positions where both men and women were employed, men receive 1.6 times greater pay than women.[63]

Just how much was the gender discrepancy, and how did it affect worker expectations? The Jafet company *fichas* highlight the lower wages for women and the age at which expectations diverged. Dividing adult workers into five-year cohorts and evaluating how the male real wages compared to female real wages demonstrate that wage differentials appeared when women reached childbearing age. For males and females ages fifteen through nineteen working at Jafet, there were still minimal differences in their wages. This is true when considering pay differences for all positions and only low-skilled positions. For adults ages twenty and older, men at Jafet received between 1.19 and 1.89 the pay that their female counterparts did. Although including managerial and mechanical positions exaggerates these results, the discrepancies persist even for low-skilled positions such as spinning and warping. Columns 4 and 9 in table 4.3 present these discrepancies. Lower compensation for women persisted for weavers, who were paid piece rates rather than hourly wages. At Jafet, a handful of records from 1919 to 1921 report how many looms weavers tended. Five of the six individuals tending four looms were male, one female tended three looms, and only one of the twenty-four individuals tending two looms was male. Although the 1912 *BDET* recorded a mere 1.125 male-to-female wage ratio among weavers, the Jafet reality was that female weavers expected to take home about half the income of their male counterparts.

Why did employers like Jafet consistently pay women lower wages? That

Table 4.3. Gender pay differences at Jafet, by age cohort, 1913–1929

Age	Wages and ratios, all positions					Wages and ratios, low-skilled positions				
	M	F	M:F	M Δ%	F Δ%	M	F	M:F	M Δ%	F Δ%
15–19	53.96	53.37	1.01			51.3	53.23	0.96		
	(95)	(124)				(83)	(107)			
20–24	85.06	59.82	1.42	58%	12%	81.26	61.29	1.33	58%	15%
	(55)	(43)				(36)	(31)			
25–29	83.41	62.02	1.34	-2%	4%	79.5	63.8	1.25	-2%	4%
	(24)	(28)				(15)	(17)			
30–34	97.1	62	1.57	16%	0%	87.29	62.14	1.40	10%	-3%
	(13)	(18)				(9)	(12)			
35–39	114.32	60.37	1.89	18%	-3%	75.64	63.77	1.19	-13%	3%
	(11)	(12)				(3)	(7)			
40+	87.49	57.53	1.52	-23%	-5%	91.71	56.4	1.63	21%	-12%
	(34)	(14)				(19)	(8)			

Sources: Jafet portion of wage series as constructed from "fichas e holerits," Fiação, Tecelagem e Estamparia Ypiranga. Centro de Documentação de Informação Científica, as elaborated in Ball, "Prices, Wages, and the Cost of Living."

Note: Low-skilled positions are based on HISCO analysis and do not include weavers. Reporting average hourly wages/(n). Percentage change is calculated by dividing change in average wage ($\overline{W}_e - \overline{W}_{e-1}$) for cohort by average wage for cohort $_{(t-1)}$.

discrepancies persisted in positions where strength did not increase efficiency discounts the argument that male workers were more productive.[64] The cohort evidence points to statistical discrimination as the best explanation for these differences. The employer expectation that women would exit the workforce upon getting married or having children resulted in lower wages for tasks that women were equally capable of completing. Women would have been slower to speak out against lower wages for several reasons. They did not have many formal job opportunities; they were already fighting societal norms and general prejudice against their presence in the labor force; labor leaders saw women as weak and as taking away men's jobs; businessmen claimed that women had no training or aspiration and it was unnatural for them to work.[65] In effect, women did not have the privilege that white male workers did in their ability to look for better jobs and higher wages within the textile sector.[66]

This prejudice against female workers from labor leaders, businessmen, and a number of other sources was ironic, given that women could receive support on an individual, family, and even institutional level to actively participate in the labor force. Families depended on women and girls to contribute to the family income. This corresponds with the marked increase in the number of advertisements for female workers during the late nineteenth and early twentieth centuries.[67] São Paulo's female professional school also provided avenues into the labor force, and there was even legal support from one unlikely source, Brazil's 1916 Civil Code.[68] Most Latin American nations adopted civil codes in the nineteenth century. When Brazil finally adopted a civil code in 1916, it was highly patriarchal in nature. On family rights, the code "brought little innovation to Brazilian law" and reinforced traditional Catholic values and definition of family, distinguishing between legitimate and illegitimate children and prohibiting divorce.[69] This control extended to the labor market; article 242 prohibited a woman from holding a profession without her husband's permission, but article 245 made one important distinction; it legally allowed a woman to work without her husband's permission if "the husband does not provide livelihood for his wife and children."[70] Effectively, this was a class distinction that gave women the right to enter the workforce and recognized their economic role in working-class families.[71]

Upon entering the workforce, Paulistanas confronted lower wages as only part of the discrimination story. The Jafet company evidence shows that women received lower rewards for experience. The changes in real wages by cohort highlight this discrimination. Age has a dual impact on a worker's wage. On the one hand, age is often equated with experience, and more experience is often associated with higher wages. On the other hand, the value of each additional year of experience declines over time. This means that wages grow more slowly over time or sometimes even decline if an individual is no longer able to perform the assigned tasks.[72] At Jafet, the gains for experience were much more modest for women than for men. In table 4.3, columns 5, 6, 10, and 11 show how working-class men and women could have understood their chances for higher wages in the textile sector. While men could expect their wages to increase over their lifetimes and to make at least 47 percent more per hour when they left the company, women, at the most, could expect to make just 20 percent more.

Women's lower wages and minimal returns for experience suggest that it was not just societal pressures, motherhood, and marriage compelling them to leave the Paulistano workforce. Female expectations for work opportunities after the age of twenty declined so dramatically that many women would have left the textile sector to explore alternative ways of making an income. As women were excluded from so many formal-sector jobs, they were pushed further into the marginal and informal economies. Their entry into piece-rate work, washing clothes, making soap, and growing gardens leaves minimal historical records.[73] While renting out rooms or being a laundress could provide higher incomes, these ventures lacked the stability a formal sector job provided.[74] These wage and job discrepancies meant substantial losses over a woman's lifetime.

The Jafet evidence also allows for evaluating the degree to which national and racial prejudice extended into the textile sector. In terms of how nationality affected the Jafet worker experience, no distinct patterns of discrimination emerged, but Syrians and Italians had more opportunities at the hiring level. The Jafet factory was owned by four Lebanese brothers, and the considerable share of Syrian workers and the long tenures of those employees were related. Additional Syrian opportunities should be understood as a product of the social networks between owners and rank-and-file workers. Yet Italian men also displayed disproportionate advantages at the firm. Their presence in medium-skilled jobs was higher than their overall presence in the sample, making them overrepresented in these higher-paying positions.[75] Italian women registered distinctive work patterns as well; married women remained at the firm for longer periods and were much more likely to return to work as wives and mothers than women of other nationalities.[76]

These Italian work patterns support scholarship on Italians' overrepresentation at the industrialist and worker levels in the textile sector. Just as Syrians were overrepresented at Jafet, Italians would have had substantially more opportunities in the textile sector because of the prominence of Italian textile factory owners.[77] While Italian workers were more likely to be hired into medium-skilled positions at Light and Paulista Railway, their representation in those jobs was proportional. At Jafet, they were overrepresented, providing further support that Italian men were more likely to be hired into more skilled positions and at a higher proportional rate in the textile sector than in the transportation sector. The textile sector provided Italians with greater opportunities for mobility than it did for workers of other nationalities.

Clearly the opportunities for Italian males outweighed the stigmas attached to working in the textile sector. Jacob Penteado recalls how glassworkers "treated textile weavers with contempt. They told me:—You don't ever want to be a weaver. That's women's work. Our jobs are for men!" Wage evidence supports Penteado's statements; a mechanic working at Jafet received a lower wage than one working at Light or Paulista Railway.[78]

Unlike Italians, Afro-Brazilians had a minimal presence in the Jafet sample; more than 93 percent of individuals in the Jafet sample for whom race was recorded were considered white.[79] By comparison, the 15 percent share of *pardo* and *preto* workers at Paulista Railway seems substantial. An Afro-Brazilian man had twice the opportunity of being hired there than he did at Jafet. Given that the textile sector represented 40 percent of industrial employment in the city, the near exclusion of Afro-Brazilians was particularly problematic in terms of job opportunities. The reality was even bleaker for Afro-Brazilian women, who faced substantial racial discrimination in hiring and gender discrimination in job opportunities and wages.

Mappin

The same discriminations and prejudices were amplified in the working middle class. While they constituted a significantly smaller proportion of the female labor force, more than 21,000 women worked in commercial retail in the state in 1920.[80] Some of these women would have worked at the Mappin stores. The Mappin store was one of the city's first when it opened in 1913. Being a sales associate at Mappin was a coveted position.[81] Single women and married women with their husband's permission to work not only earned sizeable monthly salaries, but they also worked a reasonable work week, could buy merchandise at a discount, received eight days paid vacation a year, and had a right to sick days. Despite the benefits, employment and interview records from the Mappin department store highlight the consistencies of gender and racial discrimination across class lines.

Even though women were the store's target clientele, women's opportunities were limited compared to their male counterparts. Of the company's 253 employees hired between 1914 and 1930, only 61 were female. Nine out of ten of these women were seamsters, vendors, or department heads. Men had decidedly more opportunities; only half of Mappin's male employees fit into these categories, and men exclusively arranged windows and worked as advertisers.[82] Men also had a greater chance of being hired as office personnel or department heads. In fact, male employees were three times more likely than female employees to be in one of these upper-level positions. Finally, there was a decided age discrepancy between male and female upper-level employees at Mappin. The average starting age for department

Table 4.4. Gender employment patterns at Mappin, 1914–1930

Males					Females				
Tenure (years)	Entry age	Salary	Number	Position	Number	Salary	Entry age	Tenure (years)	M:F
9.3	26.5	192.23	2	Seamstress/tailor[a]	19	94.38	17.8	8	2.04
9	19.9	248.83	19	Vendor	12	181.21	21.5	7.1	1.37
7.5	21.4	620.64	29	Department head/office	4	280.92	27.5	8	2.21
9	21.6	340.28	99	All positions	39	175.56	20.3	7.6	1.94

Source: "Folha de pagamento," box 2, Mappin Collection, Museu Paulista.
Note: Wages are real hourly wages reported in mil-reis. M:F reports the male-to-female salary ratio.
[a] The 1920 Brazilian census reports male tailors (cortador de roupa) made 1.87 more than female tailors, and male seamsters made 1.24 more than female seamsters. Male tailors made 2.63 more than female seamsters.

heads and office personnel was 21.4 for men and 27.5 for women. Table 4.4 presents the gendered differences among Mappin employees hired between 1914 and 1930.

Expectations help explain these discrepancies. While store managers hoped male employees would have long tenures, Mappin required women hired into the same positions to already have experience and to be well into their childbearing years. Again, the expectation was that younger women would leave if they got married or had children, but interview evidence shows how these expectations were not always realized. Several women broke with expectations and enjoyed long-standing careers at Mappin.[83] Furthermore, the typical tenures reveal no major differences between male and female employees at the department store. Both groups stayed over seven years with the firm, a considerable time, and while women stayed 1.4 years less than men, female department heads actually stayed on average eight years, a half year longer than their male counterparts.[84]

Hiring discrimination was not the only issue facing female employees at Mappin. Despite working for a good employer, women consistently received lower wages than their male counterparts in all levels of positions at the department store. Starting salaries for tailors were double those of seamstresses, and male department heads and office personnel made more than double what their female counterparts did.[85] While salespeople's salaries were the closest, saleswomen's starting salaries were still 70 percent of salesmen's starting salaries. As a whole, the gender wage discrepancies at

Mappin were larger than those registered among Jafet's working-class labor force.

Afro-Brazilians also experienced greater discrimination at Mappin than they did at Jafet. The Mappin company stipulated that department heads speak two languages. Leonor Perrone, a former female department head and lifetime Mappin employee, explained, "The girls who worked [in sales and as department heads] at Mappin had to be very clean, very attentive to hygiene and to their health. They had to be recommended by good families, and they had to come from good families."[86] These subjective requirements favored white foreigners and discriminated against Afro-Brazilians, isolating them into service positions.[87] The employee national profiles confirm this hiring practice and a preference for foreign workers. The largest shares of workers at Paulista Railway, Light, and Jafet were Brazilian, while three out of four Mappin employees were foreign. Italians, Portuguese and British employees made up more than 70 percent of Mappin's workforce.[88]

The detrimental and exclusionary results of the state's whitening policy are most visible in the Mappin company and the commercial sector. The requirement for salespeople to be from good families was a less than subtle exclusion of Afro-Brazilians and representative of the commercial sector as a whole.[89] Even if she graduated from the city's professional school for girls, an Afro-Brazilian woman would find substantial barriers to entering the commercial sector. Images of restaurants serving lunches to upper-lower-class and middle-class working women confirm a profound absence of Afro-Brazilians in this sector.[90] Already excluded from jobs at companies like Light and Paulista Railway because of their gender, Afro-Brazilian women faced exclusion from the best opportunities available to white Brazilians and foreign women.

The types of Mappin jobs available to Afro-Brazilians were limited. Alfredo José dos Santos, the lone Afro-Brazilian whom every customer met, was the doorman at the store. His tenure was long, just like that of the company's legendary manager, Silvio Carlini. Carlini was contracted away from a competing firm in Buenos Aires and found considerable success rising in the rank to become the general manager; he was even able to secure jobs for individuals within his social network.[91] In contrast, dos Santos knew when he took the doorman job that there was little room for advancement.[92] The service sector in general allowed for minimal social mobility, but these were the jobs most readily available to Afro-Brazilians, especially Afro-Brazilian women.[93] The need to help provide for their families led them into other lines of work, often in the service sector. More than 12,700 individuals reported being domestic workers in the city in 1920, and more than 80 percent of these workers were women, largely Afro-Brazilian women.[94]

An elder whom Ecléa Bosi interviewed was Dona Risoleta, who had been a domestic worker. She was born in 1900 outside of Campinas, about sixty miles northwest of the city of São Paulo. Risoleta's father was a formerly enslaved house servant (*mucamo*) of mixed race who became self-employed, and her mother, Teodora Maria da Conceição, did everything from making manioc flour to selling sweets and washing clothes. By age eight Risoleta was working as a domestic and by thirteen had become a cook, waking up at four in the morning and working all day. Her parents depended on her wages, as her father collected her earnings at the end of the month until she was twenty-two.[95] After moving to São Paulo, she continued to work as a domestic. When she could not afford housing and food, she sublet rooms in her house, providing housing and meals and washing clothes for her renters. She preferred this added burden to asking for a raise, even when food costs increased considerably. In certain ways, she had a good domestic job, as she did not have to endure the "most revolting punishments" and abuses that many domestics did.[96] Mappin workers made relatively high salaries, and Jafet female workers could band together and organize for safer work conditions and better wages, while Risoleta could be fired at a moment's notice.[97] This was the tenuous reality of domestic work, the reality of almost 10,500 Paulistana domestics, many of whom would have been Afro-Brazilian women like Risoleta.[98]

RACIAL DISCRIMINATION

These company realities confirm research on racial discrimination in São Paulo's labor market between 1912 and 1920 based on *Boletins de Ocorrências*. While these reports do not necessarily reflect the true composition of the workforce, they have particular value in demonstrating sectors in which Afro-Brazilian workers were concentrated.[99] In these records, Ramatis Jacino demonstrates how Afro-Brazilians were concentrated in jobs as domestic workers, firemen, carpenters, tailors, cobblers, policemen, and soldiers.[100] The absence from the records of Afro-Brazilians as mechanics, weavers, itinerant vendors, and bakers is striking, particularly given that Afro-Brazilians, enslaved and free, occupied the latter two of these positions in the late empire. Jacino argues that the 1886 imperial law restricting Afro-Brazilian access to some of these positions was key to explaining their exclusion from these positions during the Old Republic. Equally

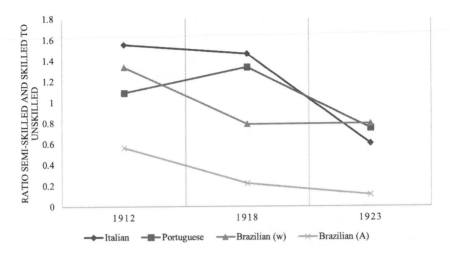

Figure 4.1. Paulistano labor structure changes, 1912–1923. "Domestics" are excluded from the unskilled jobs count because of ambiguity between domestic service and women who were homemakers or who worked from their homes. *Boletins de Ocorrências*, Arquivo Público do Estado de São Paulo.

problematic and puzzling is the absence of Afro-Brazilians as day laborers and errand boys and an underrepresentation of general laborers.[101]

Extending the analysis of these records to consider change over time and differences between nationalities supports the interpretation that job opportunities deteriorated for Afro-Brazilians between 1912 and 1920. In figure 4.1 a set of *Boletin de Ocorrência* records shows this decline and other important changes in the Paulistano labor market.[102] The records demonstrate an overall increase in unskilled jobs relative to semi-skilled and skilled jobs. The skills ratio shows a conversion of Italian, Portuguese, and white Brazilian labor market expectations; white Brazilians saw their opportunities drop between 1912 and 1918, but by 1923, they were in similar positions as Portuguese and Italian immigrants. The figure also shows the dramatic advantage each of these groups held compared to Afro-Brazilians; already facing a restricted labor market in 1912, Afro-Brazilians' opportunities continued to decline. By 1923, nine of every ten Afro-Brazilians registering jobs were unskilled workers.[103] These trends continued through the decade, with Afro-Brazilians constituting just 3 percent of industrial workers but 27 percent of the lowest-paying jobs in 1927.[104]

By 1920, Afro-Brazilians were increasingly excluded from positions in which they once maintained a sizeable presence. Even as domestic service workers, they encountered a troubling transition; while cooks were over-whelming Afro-Brazilian males, their helpers tended to be white.[105] It is unclear if this transition was a continuation of an earlier trend or World War I and migration to the city from the Paraíba Valley and the Northeast further diminished opportunities for Afro-Brazilians already in the city. A systematic study of help-wanted advertisements can help illuminate the dynamic behind the changes.

In a letter written in July 1920 to call her mother to migrate to Brazil from Portugal and join the family in São Paulo, a woman asks her mother to also bring along two to three servants. She specifies that one should be a "serious, quiet, and hardworking young girl," and one or two should be young boys or men in their thirties or forties who "are serious, respectful, and hardworking, and if they do not know how to read or write, that isn't a problem either." She had a clear preference for newly arrived Portuguese immigrants to be in her service at her home, and it seems like the less literate, the better.[106] A help-wanted advertisement in the *Estado de São Paulo* from almost thirty years earlier showed a similar preference: "Couple needs a couple, without children, the wife as a cook and the husband as a *copeiro* [kitchen servant]. Portuguese preferred."[107] These cases were not unique, and over the course of the Old Republic, it was not uncommon for help-wanted ads for unskilled positions to specifically ask for white or European workers. Only a few kitchen positions specified a preference for Afro-Brazilians, and in these cases, the ads were specific about preferences for men.[108] In ads specifying female cooks or domestic servants, the prefer-ence was often for white or European applicants.[109]

Given the explicit and implicit discrimination in these ads, it is perplex-ing that the historian Kim Butler describes hope as "perhaps the most com-mon reason for migration echoed by the São Paulo families" among those whom she interviewed for her research.[110] Samuel Adamo has found that for Rio de Janeiro, Afro-Brazilian migrants outnumbered white migrants by two to one. The myth of opportunity in the two cities held elements of truth. There is some evidence in the newspaper advertisements that during periods of rapid growth in São Paulo, Afro-Brazilians experienced slightly less discrimination.

Wanted advertisements cannot account for how everyone got jobs; word of mouth would have been the most common way for individuals to post and find out about positions, especially in domestic work. A systematic col-lection of newspaper ads can be used to reflect broader tendencies in the Paulistano labor market. Examining preferential language in a sample of advertisements for unskilled positions shows years in which there seemed to be a greater preference for European or white workers. The *Estado de São Paulo* sample counts help-wanted advertisements for unskilled positions on the second Sundays of January and July of each year during the Old Republic.[111] In six of the first ten years of the Old Republic, at least some portion of advertisements in the sample mentions explicit preference for white or European employees. From 1901 to 1909, there was a decrease in the number of unskilled jobs being advertised, and just one advertisement in the sample explicitly stated a preference for a white or European worker. During these years, the city was expanding, and construction jobs would have been readily available. The decline in explicit preferences for whites or Europeans suggests that the accompanying increase in labor demand was strong enough to diminish some of the discrimination facing Afro-Brazilians.

In the years that followed, there was a marked increase in immigrants arriving directly to the capital, and the prejudicial language in advertisements increased. This shift coincided with the large influx of unskilled Portuguese immigrants from 1911 to 1913. In 1912 and 1913, when almost one in five immigrants passing through the hospedaria remained in São Paulo, there was an oversupply of labor. Under these conditions, employers could include racial or ethnic preferences in their advertisements and still receive many applicants to their liking. For Afro-Brazilians, this meant getting jobs was more difficult during years with more immigration and little construction.

It was during the prewar era and with the large influx of European immigrants that São Paulo's black press emerged. These elites often found themselves excluded from the social mobility that white Brazilians and foreigners enjoyed in the city, and while their focus was on elite exclusion, their complaint clearly extended to other socioeconomic sectors.[112] It was only in years of high labor demand that the hopes drawing Afro-Brazilians to the city were realized.[113] World War I's impact on migration streams to the city greatly exacerbated existing prejudicial tendencies. As fewer European immigrants arrived and more Brazilian migrants took their place, "boa aparência" (good appearance) became a distinguishable phrase with specific racial undertones; the implicit understanding was that it meant "white."[114] Starting after World War I, a number of wanted ads mentioned "boa aparência" or "boa apresentação" (good presentation) as a requirement for unskilled positions.[115] It was in the postwar era, especially in the mid-1920s, when black writers began writing about immigrant favoritism in the labor market, and denunciations grew even stronger by the end of the decade.[116] Even Afro-Brazilians' presence in law enforcement was cut short when the new Civic Guard, instituted in 1926, excluded them. In addition to being of good moral and civil character, guards were to be at least 1.75 meters tall, literate, twenty-one to forty-five years old, and white.[117] The traces of hope from the prewar era had all but disappeared, and Afro-Brazilians found access to social mobility increasingly limited.[118] Afro-Brazilians faced continued and increasing discrimination, even with a shift toward Brazilian migration in the city's history and as some elites were debating the fallacies of eugenics in Brazilian society.

Lifetime Consequences

The substantial and consistent hiring discrimination facing both women and Afro-Brazilians and the lower wages women received compared to men had lifetime consequences. For working-class women, the accumulation over even a month was substantial, 20$000 to 39$000. For working-class families, this was the equivalent of 5–10 percent of the total family budget and the equivalent of a child entering the labor market.[119] For middle-class women, the difference over eight years, the average tenure at Mappin, could total 6:491$520. This sum could buy a respectable house in the city and an entire *chácara* (country home) on the city's outskirts.[120] The reduced opportunities for working women especially diminished families' incentives to send girls to school. In households where only one child attended school, the reward for a boy's education was higher, so it was often girls who went to work first. For Brazil as a whole, this tendency represented a missed opportunity for development.[121]

These labor market differences are exaggerated where race and gender intersect; while an education may result in greater opportunities for white individuals, the odds for Afro-Brazilians of securing a good position were extremely limited. Estimating the loss the prejudice and discrimination meant for Brazil as a whole goes beyond the scope of this analysis, but suffice it to say that the loss was considerable. The Old Republic did not provide sufficient opportunities for many of the city's marginalized populations. Periods of rapid growth offered the greatest chances for these individuals to get ahead, but when there was an oversupply of labor and growth slowed, the opportunities withered away. World War I brought a considerable slowdown in most of the city's economy. Textiles were the one sector in which production increased, but the opportunities that growth created were not equal. Women working in that industry benefited during the war years in finding work, but being employed came at a considerable cost in terms of labor exploitation.

CLASS DIFFERENCES

Given the substantial and sustained gender, racial, and national prejudices and discrimination facing workers in the Paulistano labor market, there was minimal worker unrest. The hospedaria's role in mitigating labor dissent and strikes was important, as were family concerns; however, family and the hospedaria were far from the only factors. Large, persistent income disparities between the middle and working classes and even within the working class were also critical factors. In essence, the difference between middle-class and lower-class workers' opportunities and incomes dwarfed gender, national, and racial wage and hiring disparities.

Schooling and wage disparities were two areas in which these class differences manifested. Among young Paulistanos, more privileged children went to school, while lower-class children often entered the workforce. This was especially true of working-class children as the Paulistano economy tightened during World War I and in the postwar era.[122] Within the working class there was some gender variation, as vocational training was mostly a male privilege.[123] In general, however, Paulistano working-class boys and girls were much more likely to leave school for work than their middle-class counterparts were.

Neighborhood literacy rates from the 1920 census displayed in figure 4.2 highlight these class differences. While literacy rates for boys and girls are approximately the same within neighborhoods, there is substantial variation across neighborhoods. The established downtown (*centro*), middle-class neighborhoods showed the highest literacy rates, reaching almost 80 percent for children ages seven to fourteen. Small, peripheral neighborhoods had children with the lowest literacy rates, falling below 50 percent, and the subset of the three largest working-class neighborhoods—Brás, Móoca, and Belenzinho—registered rates below 60 percent.[124]

The wage evidence makes class differences among adults easier to quantify. Comparing middle-class to lower-class wages reveals considerable disparities. Even within Mappin records, upper-level employees recorded salaries 2.5 to 1.6 times higher than those of middling employees and more than three times the salaries of lower-level seamstresses and tailors. The differences between Mappin workers and Jafet workers was even more dramatic. The top 25 percent of Mappin's female earners made three and a half

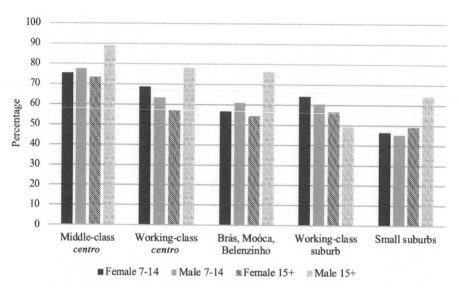

Figure 4.2. Paulistano literacy rates, by gender and region, 1920. Brazil, *Recenseamento 1920*, vol. 4.4, 803–804.

times what their counterparts at Jafet were making. The contrast for male employees was even more stark, with Mappin male employees making nine times what Jafet's top male wage earners made. Even for the bottom earners, Mappin female employees still made 1.77 times what their Jafet counterparts made.[125] In almost all cases, class wage disparities were greater than gender wage disparities.

Conclusion

Considering the relative scale of gender and class wage differentials in Old Republic São Paulo, it is understandable that gender differentials remain understudied. Although women of all socioeconomic levels may have felt similar pressures and responsibilities that came with the gender stigmas of the times, class affiliations and concerns were much more prevalent for the Paulistano working class. Getting ahead, especially in the postwar years, meant getting a better job to move up the ranks of social class.

Making this step was more difficult for some individuals than it was for others. Scholars have debated the Brazilian/immigrant binary for years, but in looking at how worker experiences varied by nationalities, it can be seen that Portuguese immigrants also faced considerable barriers to getting hired into more skilled positions. The large influx of unskilled workers in the prewar period set an expectation that Portuguese workers were less skilled and would accept low wages. This bias persisted through the Old Republic era. If success was the top of a ladder, Portuguese workers started a rung behind but at least had their feet on the ladder.

Afro-Brazilians were often excluded from the formal labor market altogether, a situation exacerbated by the arrival of unskilled Portuguese just prior to World War I. Their small presence in company records indicates the prejudice they faced, as does the language in help-wanted ads and their recorded jobs. Ads consistently specified white or European applicants, and it was only during peak periods of rapid urbanization that these prejudicial barriers began to break down. A transition during and after World War I expanded the barriers. Now, a "boa aparência" and being from "good families" were also requirements for getting a job, further disqualifying most Afro-Brazilians. This shift in language would make combating racial discrimination more difficult in the 1920s and beyond. The subtlety allowed for just enough interpretation and the technical possibility for Afro-Brazilian mobility that these terms survived the pro-Brazilian policies of the Vargas era. Ultimately, Afro-Brazilian workers were unable to successfully challenge the systemic racism in the Old Republic labor market. As the intersection of race magnified gender and class inequalities, Afro-Brazilian women would have the least access to good jobs in the Old Republic.

5

The Textile Response

Labor Exploitation in the Postwar Era

Despite the discrimination and prejudice in the city's labor market, São Paulo loomed large in the imagination of migrants prior to World War I. Construction and expansion were the norm, and when opportunities proved elusive, there was always the possibility of going to work in the interior of the state. Success stories allowed working-class residents who were often just subsisting to dream big. Experiences during World War I, however, dramatically tarnished the city's luster; wonder and hope eroded as the economy in the municipality, state, and country became more constrained. Businesses and Paulistanos of all social classes entered into survival mode. How survival mode manifested was intrinsically linked to past experiences and institutional frameworks. I unpack Paulistano responses in the wake of World War I and the structural changes precipitated by this outside event. I detail how textile industrialists responded as compared to industrialists in other sectors and how those reactions impacted workers.

Prior to 1914, São Paulo already had an established industrial elite.[1] The city's industrial sector expanded rapidly in this period because monetary policies aimed to benefit coffee production as well as changes in incorporation laws and credit provided opportunities for investing outside of coffee. An 1882 law facilitated incorporation, and early in the Old Republic the Encilhamento speculation loosened credit, spurring the creation of industrial firms with limited liability.[2] Despite firm failures with the Encilhamento crash, São Paulo's population continued to expand domestic demand, further incentivizing nonagricultural investment.[3]

While this growing industrial sector provided mobility into the elite classes for only a limited number of people, the new elites made their importance felt. They lobbied for government intervention in industrial sectors, sometimes even to the detriment of the agricultural sector.[4] Duties were low on most raw materials and intermediate and capital good inputs needed to produce finished products, but some firms received exemptions altogether and imported these materials duty-free. Industrialists also lobbied for high tariffs on consumer goods like textiles. Producers reasoned that Brazil no longer needed to import these products cheaply; with favorable exchange rates and tariff policies, they could be produced domestically and profitably.

Steven Topik notes, "State direct and indirect aid, coffee's woes, together with foreign investments spurred the most rapid industrialization of the First Republic between 1906 and 1914."[5] Textile production led the way; by 1907, national industry was supplying two thirds of the domestic market, and by 1913, taxes on internal consumption of cotton and wool textiles came to represent 15 percent of Brazilian revenues,[6] making the textile sector the most developed in the state on the eve of World War I. Coffee's prominence in the Paulista economy remained the major source of the state's revenue during the Old Republic, but other sectors were clearly growing, and in the city, the power of industry was particularly important. That relative textile success was contingent upon government intervention and foreign capital investments. In the postwar period, when state intervention shifted toward sectors connected to national security, textile industrialists had to find new ways to keep their businesses profitable.

In this constrained economy, textile industrialists' strategies toward labor were often rooted in the prewar practices and expectations based on constant immigrant arrivals keeping labor costs low and the government intervening on their behalf during times of labor unrest. But the workers' economic reality had changed. Inflation increased labor instability, and workers had successfully organized the 1917 general strike. As a result, industrialists adapted their labor practices.[7] Similar popular unrest and labor escalations in other Southern Cone urban centers underscores that the war's impact extended well beyond São Paulo and Brazil.[8]

Existing scholarship provides the foundation for this analysis. Barbara Weinstein has detailed how the industrialists' response to these changes involved transitioning toward rationalization, a restructuring and reorganization to increase efficiency. Joel Wolfe contends that workers shifted from factory-level organization toward a more unified labor front. The historian Maria Alice Rosa Ribeiro outlines the distinct changes in the industry's gender and demographic composition.[9] Scholars have also gone to great lengths to evaluate workers' lives outside of the factory, where they confronted social control measures and made room for leisure activities.[10] I build on these studies by singling out the degree to which Paulistano textile industrialists were reluctant to adapt technologies and at the forefront of labor repression. I draw on changes in hospedaria reentries and workers contracted to the city in the 1920s to show that textile industrialists could no longer rely on that institution to provide an endless labor supply. Evidence from industry circulars and a case-study analysis of the Jafet textile factory demonstrate how in the face of wartime and postwar shortages and the city's new labor demands, textile industrialists often doubled down on repressive labor practices to the detriment of workers.

The timing of World War I was a pivotal reason many textile industrialists sought to control labor rather than invest in rationalization and innovation. The labor-intensive textile industry was at a disadvantage as production in the postwar era shifted toward sectors that required larger capital investments.[11] This shift also put women at a disadvantage; to solve cost and overstock problems, industrialists not only employed more women but also embraced a heavy-handed approach to labor. Ultimately, for the firms, this approach perpetuated inefficiencies, making the companies more susceptible to political and economic crises. As the textile sector employed the largest share of São Paulo's industrial labor force, these approaches had substantial ramifications for workers and their families.[12] Workers experienced weakened bargaining power, and female workers in particular were restricted to the bottom rungs of the industrial labor hierarchy.

As a counterpoint to the textile response, I investigate how other companies modified their approaches to wartime shortages, overstocks, and labor. There were important limitations to innovation facing textile industrialists, but the scarcity-driven experimentation occurring in some sectors and innovative solutions to overstocks that some companies embraced were remarkably lacking in textiles. The workers in more successful sectors became part of a privileged group within the working class. This created a wedge within the Paulistano working class and a definable laboring middle class well before Getúlio Vargas took office in 1930.[13]

Hospedaria Changes

The hospedaria records provide insight into the changing labor dynamics facing industrialists in the 1920s. The war had effectively cut off immigration to the state, but many officials hoped that a dramatic immigration flux would return after the war. The state's official economic priority remained returning laborers to coffee production, but urban industrialists were also eager for a return to their golden era. It was, after all, the dramatic influx of unskilled, low-wage labor in 1911–1913 that facilitated expansion. The characteristics of immigrants signing contracts to work in the city during the war and in the postwar period demonstrate an important change in the city's labor supply in the last decade of the Old Republic and a transition toward more capital-intensive industries.

Subsidized immigration to the state and city would never again reach the prewar levels. Nevertheless, migration from other parts of Brazil became more common and supplied much of the needed labor. The city almost doubled in size between 1920 and 1934 and broke the one million inhabitant mark in 1933.[14] The hospedaria, in terms of sheer numbers, did not feature as prominently during this period, but the institution still served an important function. After the war, it continued to provide a safety net for the city's working class and began providing more skilled immigrant laborers to the city's industrialists.

During the 1920s, about 60,000 city residents returned to the hospedaria to find employment.[15] This represented 10 percent of the city's 1920 population and 6 percent of its 1934 population. In the prewar era, city residents were more inclined to use the hospedaria as reentries, but even in the 1920s, one out of every ten individuals living in the city turned to the hospedaria. The safety-net strategy may have waned in popularity, but it was still viable. There are several possible ways to understand the hospedaria reentry policy's decline in popularity. One that merits particular attention was the increased likelihood of being contracted into the interior over another job in the city. In 1920, just 5 percent of immigrants registering with the hospedaria signed contracts to work in the city. For city residents hoping to find viable city employers, this meant that in a best-case scenario, they had less than a one-in-five chance of remaining in the city.[16] The odds would have been even lower for workers in the textile sector, which was plagued by energy crises and overstocks. Paulistanos returning to the hospedaria in the 1920s would have understood that this choice most likely meant accepting a move to the state's interior.

Even though there was a decline in the number of hospedaria registrants signing direct contracts to work in the city during the 1920s, the share of skilled German and Austrian workers selected for work in the city was significant. Although there might not have been outright employer preference for these individuals, the demands from the growing mechanical and transportation sectors accounted for an increase in contracts awarded to Germans and Austrians. These immigrant groups also endured violent attacks in southern Brazilian states during World War I, which would have encouraged these national groups to move to São Paulo.[17] They found a more welcoming environment and more job opportunities in the city.

There was a demand for semi-skilled and skilled workers, as signified by companies struggling to get these workers to remain at their companies.[18] On average, Light could only get employees to remain in its mechanics department for slightly over three months.[19] While there is no evidence to show that Light directly used the hospedaria to contract employees, given the relatively competitive market for skilled workers and the high share of German workers in the mechanical trades contracted directly to the city, some employers with particularly tight finances would have seen the hospedaria as a viable option to diminish excess costs. In essence, the receiving station continued to provide cheap and readily available labor to the Paulistano labor market, but workers were more skilled and did not provide the type of labor that textile industrialists most needed. No longer able to rely on the hospedaria for a wealth of unskilled labor, industrialists had to look to other strategies to keep costs low and increase profitability.

SLOW TO INNOVATE, RELUCTANT TO CHANGE

The timing and the early success of the textile industry discouraged industrialists from embracing more efficient methods and adaptable approaches. Slavery was still a viable institution in Brazil and São Paulo in the 1880s, when the American engineer Frederick Winslow Taylor was conducting "'time and motion' studies which broke down workplace activities into their most efficient constituent parts" and would become the basis of Taylorism.[20] As the abolitionist debate raged, the state's and city's nascent textile industry expanded. Most textile firms started in the nineteenth century opened in the interior, but Diogo Antônio de Barros opened the first textile factory in the city in 1874, fourteen years before slavery was abolished.[21]

Even after abolition, Paulistano industry held onto paternalistic attitudes and was slow to adopt the scientific approach to labor and industry espoused in much of the United States and Europe.[22] The city's remarkable growth prior to World War I did not encourage any fundamental structural changes to labor, which would have been costly to implement. Immigration and migration ensured that there was no shortage of labor, and the relatively high share of nuclear families and the hospedaria's ability to be an employment service and provider of replacement workers during labor unrest continued to keep labor costs low in the city.

World War I shortages tested these established patterns and required industrialists to consider different ways to keep costs low and profits high while also navigating worker discontent. It was starting in 1916 that one of São Paulo's most influential industrialists, Roberto Simonsen, began "pioneering attempts at scientific organization and management."[23] His experimentation was occurring at about the same time that Henry Ford began constructing the River Rouge plant in Michigan that included an assembly line and organization embodying Ford's principles regarding transforming workers.[24] In Brazil and São Paulo, factories established before World War I were often hesitant to incorporate Taylorist and Fordist principles. This hesitation is most apparent in textile industrialists' minimal capital improvements and continued exploitation of employees.

Ribeiro has observed that "evaluating the level of technical development in [São Paulo] cotton textile spinning and weaving factories . . . is a difficult task," but the evidence that does exist points to minimal innovation in the sector during the 1920s.[25] Among textile firms that survived into the 1940s, half of the machinery was installed before 1915, and Stephen Haber's evaluation of Brazil's textile industry demonstrates a decline in productivity in the 1920s.[26] Through 1913 there was a seemingly endless labor supply to the city of São Paulo and high protection in place for Brazilian textiles. With minimal incentive to innovate, textile industrialists often reduced costs by employing cheap labor rather than restructuring, training workers, or investing in new machinery. This dynamic was distinct from what occurred in the United States, Canada, and Britain; it made Brazil similar to other lower-wage countries in the world that employed more workers per machine.[27]

Had Brazilian industrialists been interested in making capital improvements, there would have been an increase in worker output over the duration of the Old Republic. That was not the case, though, and each textile worker was producing less cloth at the end of the period than at the beginning. In 1905, each worker in São Paulo produced on average 5.81 meters of cloth. Slight efficiency gains that were registered prior to World War I all but eroded with the economic downturn during the war. Twenty years later, the ratio had dropped to 5.41 meters per worker and by the end of the Old Republic was down to 5.09. A temporary efficiency gain in the early 1920s was not accompanied by a dramatic investment in looms or spindles. Even when investments in machinery were made, industrialists failed to hire foremen who could make sure the machines operated at capacity.[28] In fact, while the state's textile industry averaged 17.62 spindles per worker in 1905, the ratio increased only slightly to 19.85 in 1920 before falling to 17.41 in 1925. These ratios were similar to the spindle-to-worker ratios reported for Mexico during the 1920s.[29] Recovering from the Mexican Revolution undoubtedly contributed to Mexico's low ratio, but São Paulo textile industry's failure to improve could not be blamed on civil strife.

In sheer production measures, during the war years and until 1923, output grew and the textile industry expanded, but that growth often masked the sector's underlying problems.[30] Scholars have emphasized that firms that survived the wartime conditions did so by increasing production for domestic consumption.[31] To keep costs low, industrialists employed women and children over adult men, especially in times of greatest financial duress. Most textile magnates showed little interest in technological experimentation or restructuring.[32] Industrialists also overestimated enthusiasm for Brazilian cloth, and once imports returned, factories were left with unsellable stocks that would plague them for the rest of the decade.[33] They insisted that "the war came to save our textile industries from almost certain ruin: imports disappeared, and European stocks quickly sold out and our people [consumers] were obligated to recognize that national textiles were just as good as similar foreign products."[34] But consumers knew otherwise; Paulista products were notorious for their poor quality. Nevertheless, textile industrialists continued to simultaneously lobby for increased import duties on nonluxury textiles and lower rates on the machines needed to produce their own textiles.[35]

These policies made life for the everyday consumer more difficult. One politician from northeastern Brazil implored Paulista textile producers to reconsider their stance on nonluxury cloth import tariffs. The industry's approach, he wrote in 1924, meant that "the poor man can no longer buy clothes, shoes, and much less food." Although he was writing on behalf of his fellow northeasterners, many a Paulistano faced similar circumstances and could not rely on family members responding to chamadas to bring clothes from other countries. Unfortunately for those individuals, his plea fell on deaf ears; instead of the 20 percent duty he proposed, industrialists placed their support behind an 80 percent import tax.[36]

Increased government interest and intervention in select agricultural sectors and those industrial sectors deemed of national interest compounded the plight of Brazilian textile magnates. Coffee, iron, steel, transportation, and petroleum made the cut, but cotton and textiles did not. There was no revision of cloth tariffs immediately after the war, so imported cloth returned to the Brazilian market even cheaper than it had before the war.[37] In 1922 industrialists continued to ask for government intervention, through cotton production regulation, but to minimal avail. The government seemed to be doing everything in its power to help coffee producers to the detriment of the cotton industry.[38] As the decade continued, local and global events brought the Paulistano textile industry closer to crisis. An extreme energy shortage plagued production from February through September 1925, forcing factories to cut operation days and production hours. Effectively, the Paulista energy grid could not support the growing population and industrial consumption of electricity.[39] Less than a year after the crisis abated, in June 1926 most factories again returned to reduced schedules, but this time the aim was to reduce domestic textile overstocks. Funds and warehouses were being used to store excess coffee for the defense of coffee, and there was no room for extra cloth. Owners of struggling factories contended that restricting production and implementing new import duties on finished textiles "to the extreme limit of protectionism" would drive up domestic prices and save the industry.[40] The push for increased protection continued through 1927, but it was only with the threat of the entire textile sector's failure in 1928 that duties were revised to effectively eliminate imported cloth from the Brazilian market.[41]

Faced with stiff import competition, industrialists had spent most of the 1920s lobbying for more protection and fighting tax increases.[42] What they rarely discussed was increased innovation within the sector. A lone circular mentions how lowering import duties on machines could also aid in explorations for using cotton residuals in other industrial practices. Even when it came to agricultural innovation, investment was minimal; only one cotton mill had established a scientific plantation to supply it in 1921, and a publication on worldwide cotton production was one of the first expenses sacrificed to offset financial pressures of the 1925 energy crisis.[43]

In contrast to the textile industry, World War I scarcities inspired innovations and a more concerted move toward rationalization in the mechanical and construction industries.[44] The decrease in imports brought on by the war immediately resulted in machinery and construction material scarcities. Building in the city all but came to a halt, but small repair shops proliferated. After the war, several of these smaller shops would grow to become factories.[45] The duration of the slowdown also proved enough to incite experimentation in larger, newer firms. It is fitting that one of the state's most ardent and vocal proponents of rationalization, Roberto Simonsen, owned a construction company that opened in Santos in 1912, just two years before the war started and brought wartime shortages.[46]

Simonsen was not alone in applying scientific principles to industry. Barbara Weinstein highlights his role alongside those of other prominent figures such as Roberto Mange and Asprígio de Almeida Gonzaga.[47] The 1918 annual report from Light declared, "Due to the absolute impossibility of getting poles, we began some time last year experimenting with a concrete pole, and after many tests finally developed one that was satisfactory, and established a yard for building some."[48] Wartime shortages effectively stimulated investment in backward linkages, products or services needed to create other products and services.[49] The cost of building the concrete poles was less than half the cost of the 26$000 iron equivalents. The company deemed the experiment so successful that it anticipated continuing concrete pole production even when and if iron prices dropped.[50]

This push continued past the end of the war, although in a muted fashion. As a key ingredient in concrete and construction, cement's importance to São Paulo was apparent by 1921. Some industrialists called for its increased domestic production. Brazil had to overcome specific disadvantages including insufficient natural coal deposits and an untrained workforce, but proponents' argument was that with high cement import costs, the 1920s were an ideal time to develop this infant industry.[51] The potential forward linkages, industries and sectors that would use the domestic cement, were considerable. The state of São Paulo and Light rose to the occasion; in 1926, the state opened a laboratory dedicated to cement research and Light opened the Companhia Brasileira de Cimento Portland, with seven hundred employees.[52] Discussions fell into familiar tropes for production techniques such as relying on Brazil's ample supply of firewood rather than experimentation with more sustainable models that would have required further backward linkages. Nevertheless, the early investment paid off; Brazil only produced 13 tons of cement in 1926, but 605 tons of cement were produced in the country in 1938. Cement was on its way to becoming a Brazilian industry.[53]

Experimentation with sugar by-products represents an underdevelopment of backward linkages in the Old Republic. Businessmen were aware of sugarcane's ethanol capabilities, but state and federal support for these initiatives was limited, and the substantial investment required to develop such innovation to scale was directed toward other industries of national importance. Had the state invested and linked into explorations of using sugarcane ethanol as an alternative fuel source, the story of Paulistano industry could have been dramatically different.[54] Returning to earlier practices extended beyond production choices. Companies also returned to the practice of contracting skilled personnel from outside of Brazil to jump-start production rather than using skilled Brazilians or foreigners already living in Brazil. The available workforce may have needed more training, but only select companies began to develop schools and training programs for workers.[55]

Labor Control versus Worker Training

In hindsight it is easy to advocate for investing in new machines, ideas, and equipment, but this type of investment was impossible for many Paulistano employers. Even after the war ended and machine imports resumed, the cost of bringing in new machinery was often prohibitively high. Factory owners also felt the squeeze of the 1920s credit and capital constraints. They simply could not afford to buy new, cutting-edge machinery in the years directly after the war.[56] Many of the Taylorist and Fordist principles that were more readily discussed and implemented related to how employers interacted with employees and labor organization.

In this discussion of the relations between employers and employees, it is critical not to conflate industrialists' intentions with the effects restructuring had on employees. For example, industrialists promoted technical schools and worker training programs because they understood that these programs could increase profits and efficiency. Simply put, workers were often seen as "'good and simple souls' who needed to be bought off with better wages in order to avoid the introduction into Brazil of the class struggle."[57] Sometimes workers objected to implementing rationalization methods toward labor, but this was not always the case.[58] Rationalization was at times tenable with workers' own goals.

Industrialists did not completely ignore the scientific approach to manufacturing; however, most textile industrialists struggled to implement these labor rationalization schemes and opted for more forceful control of labor to keep production costs low. This often placed textile industrialists and workers alike on the losing end of the restructuring tug of war. Even vanguard industrialists like textile magnate Jorge Street provided schools and worker villages out of a paternalistic model rather than a labor rationalization model.[59] Both approaches produced similar institutions in terms of schools and worker benefits, but rationalization placed a higher value on working-class individuals' capabilities.[60] São Paulo's working class was largely poor and lacked opportunities, but the workers were not incapable; they were innovative, determined, and driven.

The 1917 general strike elicited an immediate response from textile industrialists. Laborers seen as instigators or agitators were often fired, and although industrialists made some concessions, the long-term result was increased and institutionalized control over labor. Another general strike in 1919, albeit a less dramatic one, asked for many of the same concessions, illustrating the failure to enforce labor legislation in São Paulo's Old Republic.[61] In October 1919, on the heels of the second general strike, the state's leading textile industrialists formed the Centro dos Industriaes de Fiação e Tecelagem de São Paulo (CIFTSP, Center for Spinning and Weaving Industries of São Paulo).[62] This organization allowed a unified approach to sectoral and labor concerns. Within the group, industrialists discussed a number of issues directly related to labor including prevailing wages, changes to workdays, and troublesome employees.

In reading the circulars it does not take long to determine that most CIFTSP members cared little about employees, who were called "the social escumalha [throwaways] rejected by the old European civilizations."[63] Ironically, factory owners had extraordinary expectations of these "throwaways." A survey asking for minimum and maximum wages for specific positions pinpoints burdensome workloads as well as remarkable differences in pay. In addition to an intense ten-hour workday, workers at Kowarick, the largest wool factory in the Paulistano region, finished the day by cleaning their assigned machines without any further compensation. Considering that other factories paid upward of 0$850 an hour for this task, Kowarick employees were grossly undercompensated.[64] The disparity in standards and wages across factories confirms the fragmentation among textile laborers in the 1920s.[65] In the prewar era, the large number of immigrant families arriving in the city had discouraged such organization. Under the pressure of wartime shortages and growing labor movements during and after the war, industrialists ramped up their control efforts rather than pursuing negotiations.

The heavy-handed approach toward labor in São Paulo is most apparent in the blacklists industrialists developed in conjunction with Rio's similar organization to prevent possible labor movements. These blacklists began in 1921, but March 1923 marked an important escalation. Concerned that weavers would quickly join the ongoing printers strike, the CIFTSP asked members to provide names, addresses, and distinguishing characteristics of workers seen as leading labor organizers. They assured members that they would use this information "to make it so that the designated worker *disappear* for some time, until the atmosphere of agitation had passed."[66] The Capturas e Investigações division of the police force played a central role, as its directors agreed to apprehend the workers in question. An industry-wide collaboration with the official police force and the use of "disappear" as a transitive rather than intransitive concept escalated labor repression. Textile industrialists were discussing "disappearing" workers before the Departamento Estadual de Ordem Política e Social, São Paulo (DEOPS-SP, São Paulo State Department of Political and Social Order) was established in 1924, before Vargas took office in 1930 and forty years before Brazil's military seized power in 1964.

Drawing on their pre–World War I reliance on police intervention during periods of labor unrest and decades of oppressive labor control, most CIFTSP members applied similar approaches to their workforces in the 1920s.[67] They championed the state Justice Tribunal's rejection of Benjamin Motta's mandate of habeas corpus for arrested labor organizers during a 1924 textile strike, and many industrialists readily added names to the growing blacklist distributed among factory owners.[68] One name on the list was Lucio Lopes, described as a short, fat, Portuguese man with blue eyes and a small, light-brown mustache.[69] While many laborers appeared on the lists for reasons related to labor organization, just as many appeared because of petty theft and disciplinary complaints.[70] Rather than offering higher wages that might deter such thefts, industrialists advocated that the state help the working class "expunge from its breast the bad elements that make them [the workers] miserable."[71]

The CIFTSP did dialogue at times with rationalization, but discussions of improving efficiency by encouraging good worker health and providing schooling opportunities were greatly outnumbered by those related to outright repression, expulsion, and the "scum" of the Paulistano workforce.[72] Members often flouted laws and decrees that afforded workers more rights, and the CIFTSP begrudgingly offered minimal concessions to combat extraordinary cost-of-living increases during the 1920s.[73] Opposition, which spanned from ignoring to lobbying for changing laws, was particularly aimed toward laws regulating child employment and the *lei de férias*, a law providing for time off.[74] Industrialists reiterated that child labor was essential to the efficiency of their enterprises but also minimized delinquency.[75] When federal decree 17.496 instituted the *lei de férias* in July 1926, the CIFTSP blatantly told its members to ignore the law as the organization was lobbying for its repeal. This directive remained protocol for three years. It was only in July 1929 that the CIFTSP finally instructed its members to begin implementing the law.[76]

One component of the *lei de férias* loosely supported by the CIFTSP addressed new mothers. The industrialist stance on breastfeeding demonstrates just how complicated the textile sector's relations with female labor could be. In 1928 the CIFTSP advocated for allowing lactating mothers breaks every three hours to breastfeed. Industrialists were even willing to extend this right to all female employees, not just those women with eleven to twelve months' service to the factory as the law stipulated.[77] The CIFTSP leadership recognized that its position incentivized breastfeeding, despite logistical challenges, over artificial lactation. The proposal also preserved women's jobs for the month before and after they gave birth, and if a woman became widowed during her pregnancy, it allowed for a continued paycheck during her maternity absence.[78] Support for the lactating mothers portion of the *lei de férias* derived from industrialists' reliance on female labor in the absence of enforced labor laws. During the 1926–1927 textile industry crisis, there had been a shift toward greater female employment. Operating on part-time schedules, married and single women filled available positions, lowering labor costs for industrialists and providing the women with employment that was tenable with household responsibilities.[79] It is within this context that Paulista industrialist support of working mothers makes sense.

As was often the case, theoretical support was not put into practice. Factories failed to facilitate breastfeeding breaks throughout the workday, and very few CIFTSP members complied with a 1924 state law requiring that nurseries and schools be built next to factories to support working parents. The CIFTSP presented the law as optional.[80] Just where breastfeeding mothers were supposed to keep their infants so they could feed them every three hours was not addressed. Faced with this predicament, some mothers worked with infants on their laps.[81]

Textile industrialists were slow to offer training or any concessions to laborers. Worker training was a notable problem in the 1920s, and new employees usually learned by observing more experienced workers, not through official apprenticeships.[82] Opportunities for advancement were limited, meaning that few workers counted on promotions to help combat the city's high cost of living. Despite inflation plaguing the city's working class in the early 1920s,[83] many industrialists fought against offering 10 percent wage increases. Only the threat of strikes convinced CIFTSP members to accept a sector-wide increase in November 1924.[84] The sad irony for workers was that just three months later, the energy crisis struck the city, forcing employers to operate on reduced hours.[85] The reduction in hours effectively lowered the incomes workers had just fought so hard to increase. The only reform textile industrialists seemed to somewhat adopt was the construction and expansion of *vilas operárias*, worker housing compounds. These substandard houses boosted factory profits.[86] Workers paid rents and steep late penalties, and they often agreed to have multiple household members work for the same employer in order to gain access to housing. In the event of labor unrest, there was precedent for employers to evict tenants living in company *vilas*.[87] Finding housing close to work was difficult, so workers made these sacrifices, knowing the chance of ever owning their homes was beyond remote.[88]

Nontextile industrialists seem to have placed a higher value on technical education, and many owners themselves graduated as engineers from the São Paulo Polytechnic School.[89] Through their own edification, Polytechnic students also came to understand the importance of worker training programs as a means to increase productivity and to create a pool of highly skilled workers in Brazil. Coursework at Polytechnic School required students to participate in practical laboratories, and the school operated five distinct research laboratories by 1926, one dedicated to concrete, two to metalwork, and two to wood.[90] During the 1920s, between 160 and 180 students matriculated into the Polytechnic School in any given year, the majority of whom were from the state of São Paulo. They entered either a one-year preliminary program, a two-year general program, or a more specialized three-year program. The three-year programs trained civil, industrial, electrical, chemical, and architectural engineers as well as chemists and industrial chemists. The one-year program was by far the most popular, followed by the general program, but the civil engineering program was also fairly popular.[91]

A diploma from the Polytechnic School meant an almost certain job upon graduation. The Paulista and Mogiana railway companies along with the port at Santos offered competitive, one-year, paid internships to students upon graduation throughout the 1920s. Three students accepted the positions at the companies in 1920 and 1921 and two in 1922, each earning a 300$000 monthly salary. As a testament to the success of this investment in education and the need for qualified graduates, from 1923 to 1927 not a single student took one of the internships. All graduating students had secured guaranteed, full-time positions.[92]

Assistance from industrialists did not stop at internships; they also provided financial resources to the school on several occasions. The Paulista, Mogiana, and Sorocabana railway companies contributed significant funds toward buying expensive laboratory equipment when state funds proved insufficient.[93] Very few textile industrialists were willing to make monetary investments toward the Polytechnic School's commitment to education and technological research. When a research division, the Institute of Technological Research, needed extra funding to become its own entity in 1934, only one of the eight contributing companies was purely dedicated to textiles, the Cotonifício Rodolfo Crespi. Light, two cement companies, two ceramic companies, a paper company, Fábrica Votorantim, and Indústrias Reunidos de F. Matarazzo provided the vast majority of the funding needed to form the research institute. Votorantim's substantial investment of 33:333$200 is particularly intriguing, given that the business was about to expand from textiles to cement production in 1936.[94]

Votorantim's ability to change sectors and thrive when other textile companies failed depended on several factors, among them a distinct approach to labor. Antonio Pereira Ignácio, its owner, acquired the factory in São Paulo state's interior at auction after the Banco União failed. He was a Portuguese immigrant, the son of a shoemaker who immigrated to the state when Antonio was ten. The son began working with his father, but then moved to Rio de Janeiro and found work with a textile importer before opening his own businesses in the São Paulo interior. During his lifetime, he went from cobbling to saving textile factories. Antonio Pereira Ignácio and two other men acquired three textile mills in the city.[95] In 1918, Pereira Ignácio reopened the Votorantim factory in Sorocabana, the interior center of textile production.[96] The factory's new start and its owner's interests made it less entrenched in the older labor control system of the prewar era.

True to form, in the 1920s, Votorantim distinguished itself as more moderate in its approach to labor. In 1924, with the rising cost of living, Votorantim offered housing, water, and electricity to its employees at highly subsidized rates. The factory could offer these benefits because of the factory's importance and interior location in the state.[97] The CIFTSP decried this rogue decision, fearing it would bring massive strikes to the industry. The industrialists' fears were indeed realized when an industry-wide strike took place and wage increases followed.[98] Pereira Ignácio again went against the CIFTSP in 1927. While other companies strongly resisted the *lei de férias*, Votorantim was the only member of the organization to provide information facilitating the law's implementation.[99]

Important changes in Votorantim's management help explain the diversification toward cement. When Votorantim reopened in 1918, a young man, José Ermírio Albuquerque de Moraes, left the sugar plantation system he knew in Pernambuco state in northeastern Brazil to attend the Colorado School of Mines. He studied there for the next three years, never losing sight of Brazil in his pursuit of higher education.[100] After graduating in 1923, he returned to work for his family in Pernambuco, but a trip to Portugal would change his trajectory. While there he met the Pereira Ignácio family, and after taking a particular interest in Antonio's daughter, Helena, the two married in 1925. José then moved to São Paulo state to become Votorantim's manager.[101] His metallurgy training at the Colorado School of Mines and experience as an engineer in Minas Gerais undoubtedly facilitated Votorantim's transition away from textiles.

THE JAFET CASE

The most complete picture of a textile factory during the period, Jorge Street's company, is not representative of the typical Paulistano textile factory experience.[102] The Belenzinho factory and its surrounding Vila Maria Zélia worker housing were part of Street's Companhia Nacional Tecidos de Juta textile enterprises, and the paternalistic model he espoused truly made working at Belenzinho distinct.[103] The trajectory of the Jafet factory is a much better case study. The experiences and changes in the Fiação, Tecelagem, e Estamparia Ypiranga Jafet textile factory diverge from the Votorantim model and demonstrate how the patterns and practices played out in a more typical textile firm. The evidence provides specific examples of factory owners and management relying on labor control rather than structural changes to adapt to the prevailing economic climate and labor market changes. General Motors do Brasil and Ford provide a counterpoint for Jafet, showing the viability of alternative approaches to solving overstock and market inefficiency problems.

Like many textile industrialists, the four Jafet brothers began as importers. They arrived from Lebanon at the beginning of the Old Republic;

thinking about future opportunities, they purchased land on São Paulo's periphery. The brothers waited to enter the textile market. Tapping into credit sources, they finally opened the Jafet factory in 1906.[104] Just five years later, Jafet was already firmly established in the Ipiranga neighborhood, employing 257 men, 270 women, 158 boys, and 100 girls.[105] The population influx to the city between 1911 and 1914 led to the company's further success, and a new tram line connecting the Ipiranga neighborhood to the city center facilitated movement of workers and goods.[106] Success inspired juridical reorganization, and on 20 January 1912, the factory officially incorporated as the Fiação, Tecelagem, e Estamparia Ypiranga Jafet.[107]

An ample supply of cheap labor was fundamental to Jafet's success. As the company's owners were Lebanese, Jafet benefited from a pipeline of Syrian, Lebanese, and Turkish immigrants to the Ipiranga neighborhood; Syrians especially made up a notable proportion of Jafet employees. The brothers "displayed their strong sentimental ties to the homeland by, among other works, registering the local immigrant community for the Lebanese government."[108] In the wake of World War I and the dismantling of the Ottoman Empire, emigrants became crucial supporters of the independence movements of Greater Syria and increasingly, Greater Lebanon.[109] The Jafets' list contributed to global lists of potential nationals. They would have registered Ida Dias, Nadina Faralk, and Wadika Sabel, among others. Wadika, who was called Wady, was born in Syria in 1892. She migrated to Brazil at some point in the first thirty years of her life. In 1923, when she was hired as a weaver at Jafet, she was married to Salamão Sabel, another member of what was loosely called the city's "Syrian" community. Wadika worked full time at the factory and stayed almost ten years, a considerable time compared to many other adult women.[110] Ida and Nadina would also remain at the firm through the 1930s. Their employment records and those of many other so-called Syrian workers show how the Jafet family's efforts to register compatriots did create a valuable social network that likely provided a convenient list of potential employees.[111]

Evidence on the factory's structure and loom and spool efficiency also indicate that management preferred to cut costs by manipulating labor rather than by investing in new machinery or techniques. By 1911, the factory employed 785 individuals and had 444 looms and 13,000 spools. The ratio of spools per worker was 17.83, placing Jafet right around the city's average. The labor force increased to 1,200 employees by 1917, but changes in the company's labor force relative to machinery during World War I suggest conditions were not improved. To increase production, Jafet increasingly relied on cheap labor. The factory's capital-to-labor ratio actually declined to 15 in 1917.[112] Cheap labor, which meant employing women and children over men, cut costs with minimal efficiency loss. On the one hand, more women in the labor force could strengthen women's bargaining power, especially after the momentum built during the 1917 general strike. In September of the same year, Jafet female employees went on strike protesting sexual harassment. In this instance, organization was somewhat successful, as Jafet allowed strike organizers to return and ceded shorter work hours.[113] This success, however, was an exception; Jafet's strategy tended toward labor manipulation rather than improving efficiency.

Once the war ended and machinery could again be imported, Jafet submitted a request to acquire new machinery.[114] Just what machines were imported is unknown, but at least through 1922, most Jafet weavers tended just two looms, and the maximum number tended was four. This was well below the eight looms that weavers in the competing Mariangela factory would command by the end of the decade.[115] The immediate impact of any investments Jafet made in new machinery was minimal, and there is little evidence to suggest that the company increased investment later in the decade. The industry was in decline by 1923, and the only factories forced into upgrading were those whose machinery was destroyed in 1924 during a series of army revolts known as the Tenente Revolt.[116] Little destruction occurred in the Ipiranga neighborhood, and Jafet was not forced to make these investments.

Circulars and meeting minutes from the CIFTSP provide further examples of the company's oppressive approach to labor. Amid the city's rising cost of living, a number of factory-level strikes occurred in the early 1920s; Jafet workers went on strike in November 1923.[117] The factory ceded a 10 percent wage increase to workers one month later, but the raise was only reflected in wages starting in January 1924.[118] Considering a conservative estimate of a cost-of-living increase of 30 percent between the 1917 general strike and 1923, the raise workers received would have just scratched the surface of their needs.[119]

Tensions in São Paulo related to city's rising cost of living became so apparent that in October 1924 the CIFTSP called an extraordinary assembly to discuss preventing further strikes. Members debated several proposals, including a one-time payout to workers and opening factory stores with subsidized prices. Ultimately, members chose an industry-wide 10 percent wage increase to start in November 1924 as the best strategy. Nami Jafet voiced considerable opposition to the increase. Annoyed that he had granted workers a 10 percent raise just eleven months prior, he inquired as to whether he could be exempt from the CIFTSP's decision. He reluctantly supported the measure but stated that he would only implement a wage increase if his employees asked for it. He kept his word, and Jafet granted another wage increase starting January 1, 1925.[120]

Employees felt some added security asking for the increase because it was a sector-wide movement, but a fear of restructuring or getting black-listed often discouraged workers from advocating for higher wages or improved conditions. The Jafet *ficha* evidence shows only one other factory-wide wage increase, in the amount of 0$020 per hour, occurring during the decade. The date of the increase is remarkably close to May Day, pointing to labor discontent as a motivator behind the raise.[121] The reality was that starting in 1923, complaining easily led to termination and even blacklist-ing. Jafet embraced and contributed to the CIFTSP's growing list of "un-desirable" workers. The factory fired and blacklisted Dolores Fernandes, a twenty-six-year-old Spanish woman; Rosa dos Santos, an eighteen-year-old Brazilian woman; José Campaner, a forty-one-year-old Italian man; and Maximiliano Vieira, a thirty-nine-year-old Brazilian man. They were accused of the unfathomable crime of stealing cloth.[122]

The fear of not being able to find another job was real and would have been heightened among women and Afro-Brazilians because of their ex-clusion from so many other sectors and jobs. Crisis years also would have exacerbated these fears because textile jobs were becoming scarce. Like Jafet, most factories operated on reduced schedules during these periods.[123] Already faced with limited opportunities, any appearance on a blacklist further complicated the odds of getting a different or better job.

The Jafet fichas show two additional structural changes in the factory's hiring practices that made workers more vulnerable to unwanted termina-tions. First, as the Paulistano economy contracted in the early 1920s, Jafet workers saw shorter tenures. Of the 912 employees in a 20 percent sample of Jafet workers with specified termination dates in the 1920s, more than 60 percent left between 1923 and 1926.[124] Starting in 1923, adult men and women working at Jafet had remarkably short work tenures.[125] A man hired at Jafet in 1922 could anticipate working at the factory for at least fourteen months (median 428 days) and a woman for the better part of two years (median 646 days). Male and female workers hired at Jafet in the follow-ing year stayed 59 percent and 48 percent less time than those hired in 1922. The average tenure continued to decrease substantially through 1925, when the typical man and woman remained employed for just 117 and 150 days, respectively.[126] As workers anticipated shorter employment tenures, families would have adapted accordingly. Some wives and mothers found shorter and part-time employment attractive and better suited for their responsibilities at home, and more of these women entered the formal labor market.[127] However, for those individuals relying on the full day's wage for survival, the income drop would have been catastrophic. Any woman or Afro-Brazilian who lost income and had to find work elsewhere was effectively pushed toward the marginal and informal economy.

The other structural change entailed Jafet increasingly hiring women over men. Between 1922 and 1925, the ratio of adult men to women hired at Jafet was 1.1, but between 1926 and 1929, that share dropped to 0.36. Nami Jafet adapted to the sector's crisis not just by supporting production restrictions but also by taking advantage of gendered wage differentials.[128] Hiring women dramatically reduced production costs. This change persisted after the 1926–1927 industrial crisis, and women continued to be hired more frequently than men. For Jafet employees, these wages simply did not provide the necessary income to cover daily expenses.

Some evidence suggests that management offered few incentives to workers. Prior to World War I, the Jafets claimed to help with schooling costs, but other evidence challenges this commitment. Before the war, children made up a considerable share of Jafet's workforce. The company blatantly ignored the state and federal restrictions on child labor under twelve years and nighttime employment for children.[129] School-age children often enrolled in the state-funded isolated school near Jafet and worked morning or night shifts; it cannot be ascertained how many of the factory's child workers were actually working in violation of the code. When it came to working mothers, as the share of working women increased over the 1920s, Jafet failed to provide any child care facilities, and mothers worked with breastfeeding infants on their laps.[130]

The factory did offer a 10 percent rent discount on houses that the Jafet family owned in the vicinity as early as 1911. By 1925, the surrounding area was known as Vila Jafet, and a worker apartment building known as the Pombal had been built. Management tried to recruit workers with the cheaper rent, but housing came at a cost; reduced rents were only offered when more than one family member worked at the factory. The subsidized rates did not make up for the low wages or the loss of mobility and freedom that came with jobs at Jafet. When they could find higher-paying jobs, every family member but one would leave Jafet.[131] In this way, the family retained access to company housing, but only one member of the family was subject to the low wages, job uncertainty, and threat of being blacklisted that came with being a Jafet employee. Conditions were also problematic, and on at least one occasion a typhus epidemic broke out among workers and their families because they were forced to use contaminated water.[132]

The choices Jafet owners and management made in the 1920s did not ultimately doom the factory to failure. Unlike many textile enterprises, Jafet survived the economic downturn accompanying the Great Depression. The factory appears in the 1942 census of the city's industrial establishments, along with the David Jafet Fábrica de Sedas Ipiranga. The names of these establishments and their concentration in the Ipiranga neighborhood show that the Jafet family relied on family connections and social capital to survive the hardships of the 1930s. Their firms, like others, turned to greater ownership concentration in the 1930s.[133] Only state-mandated labor laws and their enforcement changed the Jafet approach to labor.[134]

With increased government support and interest in the postwar era, industrialists, entrepreneurs, and managers in the transportation sector were much more willing to accept and implement innovative methods and training than their textile counterparts. A glimpse at Ford and General Motors' overstock problems in the 1920s demonstrates the difference emerging between the two sectors. It was shortly after the end of World War I that Ford Motor Company in the United States decided to open an international branch in São Paulo. The company already had established a branch in Argentina and recently expanded to Montevideo, Uruguay. The company rented out a skating rink where the Ford assembly line consisted of the 800 to 1,000 workers using the push method to assemble thirty cars per day. São Paulo's version barely resembled its American counterpart. Even though production was minimal, demand for cars was so low that Ford found itself in a similar situation as textile factories, overstocked, by 1921.[135]

Management in Ford's São Paulo branch took a dramatically different approach to this problem than their textile counterparts did. As one of Ford's three South American branches, Ford in São Paulo benefited from being able to pull on international capital and having a fair degree of autonomy in day-to-day decisions. Kristian Orberg, São Paulo's Ford manager starting in 1921, approached the car overstock issue by establishing dealerships. Orberg and Ford fully capitalized on the commitment by São Paulo's governor from 1920 to 1924, Washington Luís, to expanding the state's road system through the São Paulo Good Roads Program. Under his direction, the company actively participated and received an award for signing up the most members for the movement. Enthusiasm from a high-ranking politician was a key component to Ford's expansion, but so too was Ford management's willingness and ability to take risks and to make large investments in innovative ideas.[136] In contrast, the CIFTSP continually lobbied for more protectionism for Brazilian cloth to address overstocks in the 1920s.

Ford's investments continued to expand; confident in the Model T it was selling and the opportunity in Brazil, Ford opened a proper assembly plant in 1925. The three-story building on Rua Solón finally incorporated Ford's mass-production principle. Including a proper assembly line was costly, but the investment paid off. The company sold 25,000 to 30,000 cars in 1925. The increased production required further innovation to stimulate demand, but that was something Orberg and his employees embraced. This change did not come at the expense of employees, who were paid relatively high salaries.[137] Just as the São Paulo branch was flourishing, the assembly plant moved toward building Model A's. While the new model worked well on smooth roads, the Model T still worked better on rudimentary roads. Unfortunately for Orberg and Ford do Brasil, São Paulo and Brazilian roads still needed substantial improvements, and customers preferred the Model T to the Model A.[138]

It was in 1925 and during the transition to the Model A that General Motors arrived in São Paulo and established what Orberg called "an advanced business" that proved stiff competition.[139] In a rented warehouse on Avenida Wilson in the Ipiranga neighborhood, General Motors workers assembled cars for the market Ford had helped grow. Elite individuals, taxi companies, and delivery services in São Paulo were early customers. As at Ford, General Motors management embraced the innovative advertising and promotion necessary to grow the demand for automobiles and trucks. By 1929, on the eve the of the US stock market crash, General Motors had put together more than 50,000 cars, sold 17,700 cars in 1929 alone and employed 1,500 individuals. The company had outgrown the Ipiranga warehouse and planned to open a new assembly plant on the outskirts of São Paulo in São Caetano in 1929.[140] Even though the Great Depression interrupted the expansion and resulted in dramatic layoffs, once production returned to normal, many loyal former employees returned to General Motors do Brasil, some for more than twenty-five years. Emerging in a postwar economy of rising prices and growing labor instability, the automobile industry and General Motors leaders understood that cultivating rank-and-file worker loyalty was a key to long-term success.

Conclusion

As the 1920s drew to an end, most textile workers at Jafet textile factory were part of a backward system that paid low wages and provided few opportunities for advancement. World War I had disrupted the flow of immigrants and imports of both machinery and finished cloth. In response, textile industrialists increased production by employing more individuals at lower wages. This meant employing more women and children. The constant inflow of possible employees in the prewar era made the industrialists inclined to choose this strategy in an effort to keep production costs low. In the postwar period, imports returned, but the labor supply to the city and the state's support for industrialists broadened to include other industries. Textile magnates, instead of experimenting with labor rationalization and innovation, doubled down on oppressive labor practices such as using blacklists and even disappearing workers as strategies. They increasingly employed women over men as childhood labor became scrutinized and energy strikes and a sectoral crisis challenged the sector's profitability. These decisions were not only a detriment to the city's textile industry as a whole but also to its workers and to workers' families, who numbered in the tens of thousands.[141] Working women were especially affected adversely by industrialists' approach to labor, as they had few opportunities in other sectors. Forced to remain in low-paying positions with little advancement, many were drawn outside of the city's formal labor market.

While textile industrialists did not have the foreign credit reserves or government support that the metal, construction, and transportation sectors did, the sector's reluctance to restructure and continued reliance on labor control and protection during multiple crises in the 1920s underscore the sector's lack of innovation. Companies like Ford and General Motors looked to innovative advertising and training during the decade. As a result, their employees demonstrated a sense of dedication to these firms. In contrast to textile workers, some employees at the automobile companies experienced considerable advancements in the postwar era. As a result of having good jobs in capital-intensive sectors, they could aspire to become part of a growing laboring middle class. What they considered to be good jobs, what they demanded of their employers, and who had access to these opportunities were questions that reveal the complex divisions within the working class that had emerged well before the Vargas era.

6

The Middle-Class Glass Ceiling in the Postwar Era

The 1920s were difficult years for the majority of the Paulistano population; men and women and boys and girls working in textile factories were not alone in their quest to survive in the city. A substantial increase in the cost of living and energy crises limiting industrial production complicated the lives of most working-class individuals. Nevertheless, new migrants expanded the city's limits. New Paulistanos arrived from other Southern Cone destinations and from Russia, Germany, Hungary, and Japan, but it was internal migration that drove the city's population boom during the decade.[1] Both new and established residents understood that having a good job was key to survival and could lead to success and access to the middle class. For workers, a good job usually contained three elements: family connections, high salaries, and opportunities for worker training and advancement. As many of these jobs were in the city's commercial sector and in the mechanical and transportation trades, the key was often getting a job in the right sector.[2]

Access to these good jobs was not equal, and for the Paulistano population, the 1920s divided the working class. Those individuals fortunate to work in thriving industries and have the right gender, skin color, or social connections could align their personal goals with those of their employers; they represented an emerging working middle class. This middle class included both commercial workers and laborers. The goals and interests of laborers were distinct from those of liberal professionals, and it is important to distinguish a laboring middle class.[3] Doing so demonstrates divisions within the Paulistano working class that developed before the Vargas era. Many members of this emerging middle class were immigrants or sons and daughters of immigrants. Some came during the prewar immigration wave; others were part of the new influx to the city. For Paulistanos unable to access these opportunities, notably Afro-Brazilians and textile workers, the 1920s represented a period when they had fewer opportunities to break through the middle-class glass ceiling.[4] As the vote was restricted to literate Brazilian men, many others were politically marginalized. With few job opportunities, they were economically marginalized, and with so many avenues to success closed, they often found themselves living at the city's literal margins. These marginalizations left a sizeable population highly vulnerable not only to the threat of unemployment and sickness but also to flooding along the city's rivers.

I draw on a variety of published and unpublished sources to complement an understanding of the period and demonstrate the complexity of the 1920s Paulistano working class.[5] Letters, interview transcripts, *ficha* evidence, and official reports show that the changes in migration patterns brought on by World War I persisted and expanded once the city's population again began to grow. Wage and salary differences, worker profiles, and interview transcripts reveal the types of jobs workers hoped to find. This evidence also shows the distinctions emerging within the working class between white- and blue-collar workers but also between laborers in different sectors. Resident perspectives demonstrate how access to clothing, transportation, and housing were especially important to workers in the 1920s and complement the understanding of the city's expanding horizontal footprint. The Great Flood of 1929 and the hospedaria's role as a refuge center during that event demonstrate just how catastrophic those divisions could be.

RETURN TO THE CITY

In the first fifteen years of the twentieth century, the city of São Paulo drew immigrants and migrants in a definable pattern. New inhabitants came, the existing housing and job opportunities became overburdened, the city expanded to accommodate for new needs, tastes, and preferences, and then the process repeated. The city's growth was spectacular, partially due to the fluidity between the urban and rural labor markets, that is, until the start of World War I, when many of the city's 450,000 residents were burdened with rising prices, fewer jobs, and even scarcer housing. The war all but stopped imports and transatlantic immigration. There were few materials to physically grow the city, and although production continued and even thrived in some city factories that were trying to compensate for the drop in imports, jobs were scarce. To adapt, many Paulistanos moved to the hinterlands and took up agricultural work.

As the war came to an end, industrialists were not alone in their excitement about a return to a prewar economy. The prospect of renewed industrial production enticed many workers to return or move to the city of São Paulo. As the hospedaria had stopped serving as a consistent labor supplier for the city's factories, it was this internal and Southern Cone migration that fueled the city's population increase. The 1918 Spanish flu epidemic temporarily dampened this enthusiasm; residents recalled the panic in the city's public schools and at the hospedaria when the flu arrived, and some wrote of family members who fell victim to the pandemic.[6] Just two years later, though, the city's population had recovered, and by 1920 the Brazilian census counted 579,000 inhabitants. All was not ideal, but the city regained some of its earlier reputation as a place for opportunity and success. By the start of the 1930s, roughly one million people called the city home.

Migrants to the city included individuals from the Southeast and other areas of Brazil, but it was those living in São Paulo state's interior who had the easiest path to return or move to the city. Antonio Carvalho's 1919 letter to his father explains why many individuals migrated from the *lavoura* to the city. The Carvalhos were Spanish immigrants who left the *fazenda* (farm) where they were *colonos*, contract laborers, because the owner only wanted them to plant coffee. Planting and maintaining subsistence food plots was essential to *colono* survival and success, but the *fazenda* owner where the family lived prohibited this practice.[7] The Carvalho family was not alone, and almost all of their fellow *colonos* made the same move. A letter Carvalho dictated was written by one of those *colonos*. Carvalho tells his father, "Excuse that this letter is in Portuguese, Joaquim's Delfina did it, who was part of the group that also came here[,] we are neighbors."[8] For Carvalho, his family lived more comfortably in the city on his 5$500 daily wage than they did as *colonos*. Considering his illiteracy and wage, he was likely employed as an unskilled or possibly an entry-level, semi-skilled worker, but as the city offered "muitos geitos de viver" (many ways to make a living),[9] his preference was the urban center.[10]

Roque Mestrieri also felt called to the city. One of fourteen children and a son of immigrant parents, Roque was itching to leave Itajobi, a town deep in São Paulo's interior. In 1921, at the age of nineteen, he left for the big city. He came with drive but also with connections, as his father was the overseer of a coffee plantation. While Roque described his entry into an enviable position at Mappin department store as lucky, his privilege and social connections played a much larger role. Roque had spent years admiring the Mappin store's catalogues, so he went to visit the store's headquarters upon arriving in São Paulo. There he encountered an acquaintance who was leaving his position at the store. After meeting the influential general manager, Silvio Carlini, Roque took over the open administrative position in the store's furniture section.[11]

The ficha evidence from Jafet and Light attests to a mobility between rural and urban work but also calls for caution against overestimating that mobility or of using Roque as a standard. Roque was likely of a higher social class than most migrants. His easy access to a Mappin job stands in stark contrast to the low literacy rates and unskilled jobs of Jafet and Light employees.[12] His ability to enter directly into a formal-sector job was also anomalous for most lower-class individuals. Just over 3 percent of Jafet workers who reported having prior employers came from the rural interior; that is the same share documented in the Light *fichas*.[13] It seems most new migrants did not enter directly into established firms.

While direct mobility was minimal, there were some years of more movement. The year 1927 stands out in both the Jafet and Light employment records. For Jafet, 30 percent of individuals coming from rural areas during the 1920s were contracted in 1927. At Light, the share of those workers moved slightly higher, from 3 percent in 1927 to 8 percent in 1928. This slight uptick likely represented a lagged response to the increase in migrants arriving in the state during 1926 and 1927 alongside relatively stagnant coffee production.[14] In the same years, planters were able to fill most of the agricultural contracts in the state's interior. All of these indicators point to a competitive labor market in the interior.[15] When contracts came up for renewal during 1927, then, there was a larger number of individuals and families willing to move to the city. Still, the fichas do not record extraordinarily high mobility between the interior and formal labor market jobs in the city of São Paulo.

As for moving away from the city to the interior, Jafet does not provide any evidence on successive employers. Light's records show that a slightly higher share left for jobs in the interior. Still, the movement was minimal, much lower than 10 percent.[16] Many individuals preferred to stay where they already had established social connections. The minimal mobility complicates the cyclical employment argument that individuals would work on farms during peak months and then come to work in the city when agricultural work waned.[17] Nationality and race may help explain this apparent contradiction.

Roque Mestrieri's socioeconomic background was atypical among individuals who moved from the interior and worked at Jafet, but his Italian background fit the norm. Demographic evidence on textile employees suggests that Italians and Afro-Brazilians were the most likely to migrate from the interior to the city. Italians represented 14 percent of employees coming from the interior but just 9 percent of all workers in the sample. The more striking difference was in the racial categorization among Brazilians migrating from the interior; only 7 percent of the sample Jafet workforce was Afro-Brazilian, but 17 percent of workers migrating from the interior were Afro-Brazilian.[18] The ficha evidence alone cannot illuminate how more opportunities in the city or fewer opportunities in the interior affected Afro-Brazilians' willingness to move to São Paulo in the 1920s, but it is probable that even if both were in play, Afro-Brazilians were likely disappointed with the opportunities they encountered in the city.

Migration from other areas of Brazil to the city also increased in the postwar era, especially from the central and Northeast regions. The northeastern outmigration in the 1920s was foundational in setting up more wide-scale migration beginning in the 1930s during the Vargas years.[19] Many Paulistas, preoccupied with whitening Brazil and more specifically the Paulista population, supported the European immigration that dominated the early years of the Old Republic. However, the economic reality and the lack of available workers softened state leaders' views on northeastern, often darker-skinned Brazilians. Just one year after the war's end, São Paulo's governor lobbied his counterpart in Ceará to establish a joint labor venture between the two states.[20] This type of agreement had been established before, and the governor contended that unemployed agricultural workers escaping drought in coastal Ceará cities could fill São Paulo's vacant agricultural jobs. The proposal would have allowed workers to stay in São Paulo or, if that was not amenable to the governor of Ceará, those workers could return to the Northeast after a year.

This instance marks a change from earlier programs when northeastern governors looked to São Paulo for assistance when droughts plagued their dry region. On this occasion, the Ceará governor backed out of the collaboration, and the São Paulo commission returned without northeastern workers.[21] The lack of established programs did not preclude northeasterners with means from making their way to the state and city of São Paulo, fleeing droughts and underemployment and looking for opportunity. Had

Table 6.1. Brazilian migration to São Paulo state, 1923–1928

Year	National migrants	Fluvial migrants[a]
1923	14,558	
1924	12,076	3,992
1925	15,906	7,157
1926	19,366	6,239
1927	30,806	7,435
1928	55,431	12,029

Source: São Paulo, *Relatório do Secretário da Agricultura, Comércio e Obras Públicas*, 1928, 338.

[a] Not all migrants embarked from Brazilian ports. In 1928, of the 55,985 migrants arriving, 53,985 arrived from Brazilian ports. Others arrived from the Rio de la Plata region and from Europe. Given Brazil's geography and railroad network, fluvial migrants were more likely to be from northeastern Brazil than from central Brazil, as hospedaria registros indicate.

the undernourished and impoverished been the main northeastern migrants to the city, the secretary of agriculture's annual reports would have raised distinct concerns. Instead, the 1927 report clearly notes that literacy rates of arriving Brazilians "were not, in fact, a shameful ulcer."[22] By 1926, in addition to migrants arriving by boat, northeastern migrants composed a large share of people arriving to the state and city by train. As shown in table 6.1, even before Washington Luís suspended subsidized immigration from Europe in 1927, migration from other areas of Brazil was already sizeable.[23]

The influx of Brazilian migrants to the state and city did not temper Paulista and Paulistano interest in renewed European immigration after World War I.[24] The immigration trickle of the war years grew decidedly during the 1920s. Between 20,000 and 50,000 immigrants passed through the hospedaria annually through 1928, the year immigration subsidies stopped.[25] Although prices in the city continued to rise and certain jobs were hard to come by, chamada letters indicate that life in São Paulo was better than in much of Europe, renewing some of the city's popularity.[26] This seems particularly true in 1924–1925. A large number of hospedaria residents signed contracts to remain in the city, and Jafet contracted more employees directly from Europe in 1924.[27]

Fortunate immigrants like Antonio Marcelino Pedro found relatively good jobs shortly after arriving in Brazil. Light contracted the Portuguese immigrant in 1924 as a mechanic soon after his arrival at a 1$000 hourly wage.[28] Light was slightly more likely to contract immigrants directly from

Europe than it was to contract workers from the interior.[29] This fits with the explanation that immigrants came with more skills, particularly in mechanic and metalworking jobs. The same was not true in the textile sector. The city's resident population easily filled low-skilled and unskilled textile mill work. Indeed, if Syrian and Lebanese workers are not considered, only one out of every hundred workers hired at Jafet were recently arrived from Europe.[30]

Other Southern Cone cities also represented a potential source for European immigrants. Larita Gorkin wrote to her parents in Buenos Aires in April 1921 asking them to join her and her husband, Máximo, in São Paulo. Her letter gives explicit directions to take a steamship to Santos, as taking a train from Buenos Aires would be too costly. Her parents would be charged for any bags, and their luggage could take up to three months to arrive if it arrived at all. The ship would only take four days, transporting luggage would be free, and Larita and Máximo would be able to accompany her parents on the two-hour train ride back to their house in São Paulo.[31]

The movement Larita describes between Buenos Aires and São Paulo was nothing new.[32] As early as 1902, more than 5 percent of immigrants arriving in the state left from the Rio de la Plata region; in 1907 and 1908, this movement represented roughly 15 percent of all immigrant entries in the state.[33] As subsidized immigrants could not arrive from Europe during World War I, immigrant companies looked to fulfill their quotas by bringing European immigrants to the state who already lived in the Southern Cone. The state secretary of agriculture's 1916 annual report declares, "The Government has used every force possible to get enough immigrants to meet the coffee *lavoura*'s demand."[34] These efforts included contracting Japanese immigrants and facilitating the movement of workers from Argentina and Uruguay.[35] In the first half of the 1920s, Rio de la Plata cities still held the upper hand in attracting immigrants; by 1926, however, the flow between the two areas evened out as São Paulo expanded.[36]

While Larita's parents' movement was not particularly unusual,[37] her explicit directions shed light on shifting immigrant regulations in the city. She is explicit that her parents should arrive using their Russian rather than their Argentine passports. Her instructions are clear: "Put your [Argentine] passport away and say that you are Russian."[38] Her directive addresses how tightened immigration restrictions affected residents and future residents. As the United States implemented quotas restricting Asian and European migration, Brazil and São Paulo opened their doors to these individuals.[39] It is no coincidence that the first Japanese immigrant subsidizations in 1908 occurred the same year that Japanese immigration to the United States all but halted.[40] Similarly, as the US Emergency Quota Act in 1921 severely restricted European migration and the National Origins Act further limited eastern European immigration in 1924,[41] Japanese, Syrian, Russian, and eastern European migrants were relatively welcome in São Paulo and began arriving in the city in discernible numbers.[42] The notable increase in the share of Hungarian, Romanian, and Russian immigrants working at firms in the 1920s also points to this movement.[43] In 1921, more than 1,200 Russian immigrants arrived in the state, a considerable increase over previous years.[44] Larita's parents, Russian Argentines, would have been a part of this count. How many other Russians came along with them is a question beyond this study but well worth consideration.

Larita's instructions also allude to stricter immigration enforcement in the city and residents' knowledge of that enforcement. There was a clear preference for immigrants, but the term "European" was loosely interpreted. Larita was not alone in mentioning heightened restrictions. Edgard Castro explained the subterfuge necessary to submit a chamada for Eliza Maggi to join him in Brazil in February 1922. The exact relationship between the two is unclear, but it seems there was some romantic interest. Edgard convinced a friend to put in a false chamada to have his "aunt" Eliza join him in São Paulo. As the police began asking questions, his friend quickly invented an entire and somewhat complicated family tree. As a result, Edgard wrote Eliza the details she now had to know about her invented parents, sister, and brother-in-law, her own age, and that the São Paulo police considered her a widow.[45] The presence of the letter in the Memória do Imigrante records calls into question the oversight of the laws but also marks an important shift toward quotas and regulations. While immigration, to some degree, had been restricted, earlier letters did not mention lying and fictitious personalities as part of the immigration process.[46] Many Portuguese passports from the prewar era erroneously identified immigrants' final destinations.[47] The transition toward more immigration oversight by the state would be amplified in the decade following the Old Republic with the 1934 Constitution, Vargas's implementation of quotas, and enactment of pro-Brazilian labor laws in 1937 with the Estado Novo.[48]

THE FAMILY AND THE GOOD JOB

The lure of factory jobs pulled in many residents, and for those in the city fortunate to have consistent jobs, the pay they brought home was relatively stable in the 1920s. There were annual fluctuations, but in general, unskilled, low- and semi-skilled workers who had found ways to make a living in the city could build expectations as to what their wages could buy. Still, wages in the postwar era did not come close to buying what they had before the war. Furthermore, job stability could be tenuous. Textile employees worked less during energy crises, and by the end of the decade, real wages were close to the lowest they had been over the duration of the Old Republic.[49]

The right social connections and background allowed some Paulistanos, both migrants and immigrants, to find success in the metropolis and join a working middle class. A good job was often key to that success, but what was a good job in the Old Republic? What can the salary and wage evidence reveal, and how did workers themselves evaluate their employers? In answering these questions, three highly valued characteristics emerged. Good pay and opportunity for training and advancement were expected. These proved important factors for the Paulistano working class in the commercial and labor sectors of the formal economy and inspired long tenures. The third characteristic, family employment, jobs for family members as well as connections for finding jobs, was also highly valued among Paulistano laborers. Its importance reflects the family wage mechanism's strength among the working class during the Old Republic. It was through family work that Paulistanos gained access to the middle class, and this practice did not disappear overnight.

Although higher wages did not necessarily mean access to the middle class, they certainly facilitated entry. Similarly, being employed in the commercial sector did not necessarily mean being part of the middle class, but it provided a greater chance for earning higher wages. Employees at the Mappin department store made between 1.77 and 3.5 times what employees in the Jafet textile factory made. However, there was also considerable wage variation among Mappin employees. Upper-level vendors and department heads who held arguably white-collar positions made approximately double what middling employees made and triple what low-level seamstresses and tailors made. These differences reflect a considerable range in compensation for work in the city.

The city adapted to accommodate these new working-class hierarchies. A number of restaurants opened to provide respectable lunches to women working in the city's commercial establishments. The Women's Restaurant catered to women of a higher economic status and would have counted Mappin vendors among their clientele. Mappin's 110 seamstresses and 20 embroiderers,[50] however, would have been more likely to dine in the

Table 6.2. Sectoral differences in Paulistano hourly entry wages, 1920–1929

Year	Light	Jafet	L:J
1920	600	430	1.40
	(99)	(5)	
1921	600	500	1.20
	(63)	(3)	
1922	650	550	1.18
	(117)	(28)	
1923	650	550	1.18
	(189)	(28)	
1924	800	660	1.21
	(151)	(47)	
1925	900	750	1.20
	(209)	(36)	
1926	1,100	750	1.47
	(139)	(5)	
1927	1,200	850	1.41
	(163)	(17)	
1928	1,014	750	1.35
	(141)	(17)	
1929	1,000	800	1.25
	(198)	(17)	

Source: Light and Jafet portion of wage series, Ball "Prices, Wages, and the Cost of Living."
Note: Median hourly wages are reported. Calculations include apprentices and helpers and consider an adult male over the age of nineteen. Number of observations reported is in parentheses. Column 3 is a ratio between column 1 and 2.

Affordable Soup Room, which provided lunches to women with fewer resources.[51] Neither would have served the store's piece-rate workers toiling long hours in poorly lit rooms at the corner of Rua Lavapés and Rua Espírita in the city's Cambucí neighborhood.[52] Nor would the restaurants have served the city's textile factory workers. These individuals would have quickly eaten small lunches brought from home.[53]

Median entry wages for adult male employees at Light and Jafet displayed in table 6.2 demonstrate that a similar divergence occurred among laborers themselves during the 1920s. Table 6.2 shows that wages did not differ dramatically between the two firms at the beginning of the decade but quickly diverged as the textile sector became burdened. While there was some recovery in the last two years of the 1920s, very few jobs were being offered to adult males at Jafet. The impact of the differences multiplies when considered at the daily or monthly level. At the lowest point of difference, in 1922 and 1923, the typical Light worker made 0$900 more daily and 22$500 more monthly than his counterpart at Jafet. At the greatest difference, in 1926, the difference increased to 3$150 daily and 58$750 monthly. Light's high turnover due to low wages and anecdotal evidence show that nontextile workers at other companies could make even higher wages.[54] The importance of the differences in wages was substantial; Light employees' higher wages were enough to cover a quarter of the monthly housing budget or could keep another child from having to enter the labor market. The generational impact of keeping children out of the labor force would have been even more dramatic.

Those families with enough social and economic privilege could look to send children to professional schools, knowing that training might lead to future opportunities. Bernardo and Rosa Mellado, for example, had enrolled two of their children, Sebastian and Rosa, in the professional school, likely hoping they could find similar jobs to that of their oldest son, Bernardo, who was employed in commerce and on the verge of receiving a raise.[55] This practice was beyond the means of many families.[56] Children were a critical component of the family wage strategy established in the prewar era and continued to serve as such in the 1920s. Labor laws, although technically supposed to protect minors from exploitive employment, were often ignored by employers and parents alike. Antonio Stocco's reflection on his experience as a child worker reveal the widespread dismissal of the law by working-class families. He was employed in the dye section of a textile factory in the 1920s; he lightheartedly explained in an interview that when inspectors arrived to make sure there were no child labor abuses, the floor managers merely directed all the minors onto the factory soccer field to play until the inspectors left.[57] It is uncertain how many children were employed, but there were enough to field a good game of soccer.

As a boy, Stocco had better future job prospects than young girls in São Paulo had. While most jobs and apprenticeships for boys and girls paid similar rates, in the long run, boys worked in almost twice as many positions as girls and could aspire to higher-paying positions that could grant them entry into the laboring middle class. Stocco hoped to one day have a good job. Families in dire situations often resorted to having girls forgo or compromise their two years of schooling to assist the family.[58] Elvira Massari, by the age of eleven, found herself working at Jafet. Hers was effectively a job without a future, but girls were twice as likely to work at Jafet than boys.[59] Elvira was technically too old to attend school and too young to legally work at Jafet, so she did both, going to school during the day and working the night shift, from 6 p.m. to midnight.[60]

The higher wages offered in other sectors were enough to keep some workers loyal to companies. Antonio Marcelino Pedro's work history suggests that this was the case for him. As a recently arrived Portuguese immigrant in 1924, he would have faced hiring discrimination in the city, so he was fortunate to be hired as a mechanic at Light. What is remarkable is that he remained at the firm through 1928, a relatively long tenure, despite never receiving a raise. Knowing that the Paulistano labor market was not the most open to Portuguese laborers, he was likely more interested in keeping his job than in looking for another one. One can only imagine the hardships he would have come up against after he was let go in 1928 because of a lack of work.[61] Many Light employees left for higher-paying positions while he was employed there, suggesting that other individuals had more opportunity.[62]

For workers, good and consistent wages were important, but they were not the only factor to consider when choosing an employer. The Sgarro and Specchio family's experience reflects how important family employment was during the Old Republic in getting and holding positions. Vicente Sgarro moved to São Paulo along with his mother and grandmother to escape a wave of strikes in southern Italy.[63] In the city, he became involved in the transportation sector and came to specialize in *carroços*, animal-drawn vehicles. By the early 1920s, Sgarro had found considerable success; the family owned a large house in the Bexiga neighborhood and employed a number of individuals. The business was a family affair; carts and animals were kept in a back courtyard. Additional income came from renting out spare stables to visitors.[64]

Being Italian opened a door for Sgarro to join Mappin, as he was closely connected to the store's general manager, Silvio Carlini. Sgarro began making Mappin department store deliveries early in the store's history and kept working for the company his entire adult life. He became head of the deliveries division. His transition to work for the department store was not a solitary move. His three daughters, Ripalda, Laura, and Angela, also began working at the store. Angela started working as a seamstress assistant when she was only twelve years old, the minimum age under the Código de Menores. Her older sisters worked in the hat section and in sales. Angela likely met her husband, Paschoal Specchio, in the four years she worked at

Mappin. Paschoal was a cabinetmaker by trade and helped make the Mappin window displays.[65] He remained at Mappin for forty-three years.

The next generation of the Sgarro and Specchio family also remained loyal to the store, as Angela and Paschoal's two children and their nephew became store employees. Just like his mother, Vicente Specchio started working at the store at the age of twelve. In a sign of social mobility, however, the son began working in the store offices. In two generations, the family had gone from cart driver to office worker, a notable jump from blue-collar to white-collar positions.

The Sgarro and Specchio family remained loyal to the Mappin department store in part because of the store management's willingness to employ the entire family. Gainful employment with relatively good pay during the early 1920s put the family in a fortunate group. Although they would not have been immune to labor unrest, the 1924 Tenente Revolt, and rising prices, jobs at Mappin provided them many benefits. Even when Mappin fired her son Vicente, Angela's loyalty to her employer did not sway. She explained that he had worked in the Mappin offices. She said, "Later he left when he was fired because he had another job. But today he has a degree in business and is doing very well."[66]

The Sgarros and Specchios were not alone in their loyalty to the store; many employees worked for Mappin for more than seven years, and other employees stayed their entire working lives.[67] Luis Sequeira was a Portuguese immigrant who arrived in São Paulo at the age of twenty, before World War I. He probably tried a variety of jobs during the difficult war years, but afterward he landed a permanent position in 1921 mounting displays and designing advertisements for a store in São Paulo. Three years and three job offers later, he was drawn by Mappin's higher salary and better working conditions to change employers once again. This time, he stayed for twenty-seven years![68] The benefits the store offered were critical to the good working conditions Luis described: paid vacation starting in 1920, long before the government mandated vacations, significant discounts on store merchandise, and company picnics.[69]

While family and compensation were important, employees also valued chances for mobility. Mappin, a British firm, could have easily brought in British personnel to lead the different sections of the department store, but management sometimes chose to promote from within. Vicente Sgarro became head of deliveries. Bartolomeu Perrota, whose godfather got him a position at the store, started as an entry-level tailor and worked his way up to department head in the administrative offices over his seventeen-year tenure at the firm. Roque Mestrieri began in an entry-level position in 1921 and became the head of the furniture division four year later.[70]

Both men and women experienced mobility from blue- to white-collar positions over a lifetime. João Batista Masetti, a son of Italian immigrants, started working as a Mappin delivery boy in 1924 when he was nineteen. Quickly he was promoted to work with packaging logistics, and before 1925, he was already the assistant to Mappin's head buyer of foreign products. In more than twenty years working for the company, Masetti became a buyer himself.[71] Nelly Colson, daughter of American immigrants, was working in the store when a Mappin executive invited her to complete a training course in beauty treatments in England. After her course, Nelly led the beauty salon at Mappin, the first department store in the city to open such an enterprise.[72]

Workers at General Motors do Brasil held similar values in evaluating employers. Luis Paulo and Laerte Pereira Ribeiro were some of General Motors' first employees in the city. Luis Paulo was hired as a master painter on April 20, 1925, just two months after the company opened in São Paulo. He even helped assemble the first car ever produced by the company in Brazil. Working his way through the ranks, he became a superintendent for painting and finishing and worked at the company for more than forty years before retiring in the late 1960s.[73] General Motors hired Laerte in May 1925 to stock the parts that would be used to assemble the cars. He was just twenty-one years old but already had three years of experience working in the Antârctica brewing company's engineering department. Laerte considered staying at Antârctica, but after three years of service, his salary was still just 120$000, a relatively low salary in comparison to similar companies.[74]

It was family and higher pay that incentivized Laerte to leave the stability of Antarctica for the uncertainty of General Motors. His brother, Joaquim, had been hired a couple of months earlier and was optimistic about the company's future.[75] Perhaps more importantly, he was offered a 300$000 monthly salary, more than double what Antarctica paid.[76] At that time, when a five-person family's weekly budget for food alone was around 135$000, workers greatly valued higher pay.[77] Laerte was among the unfortunate employees who lost their jobs in 1929. However, his loyalty to General Motors was already established, and in 1934, when the company had recovered, Laerte signed on again and worked off and on at the company until 1966.[78]

The incentives General Motors offered new employees help explain why so many became lifelong employees or returned, like Laerte, even after losing their jobs in the 1930s. General Motors do Brasil management was willing to transport workers to the new factory in the São Caetano area on the city's periphery and set up a service school for training mechanics and factory personnel well before the federal Serviço Nacional de Aprendizagem Industrial (SENAI) and Serviço Social da Indústria (SESI) training programs were implemented in the 1930s.[79] Employees were willing to make the trek. Before the company provided transportation, Ettore Fioretto walked five miles from Ipiranga to São Caetano every day.[80] Lifetime employees cited the ability to advance and receive training within General Motors, family connections, and elevated pay as important reasons for their long tenures.[81] Starting in the 1950s, employees began receiving gold watches in recognition of twenty-five years of service to the company. They would come to be known affectionately as the *velha guarda*, the old guard of the company. One of the first employees to receive this watch was Jose Menchini, who was hired to work in the parts warehouse in January 1927. He received his award in 1952 en route to a total of forty-one years' service to the company.[82] A selection of employees receiving watches in the 1960s included supervisors as well as service employees, indicating that employees proved loyal to General Motors do Brasil across different skill levels.[83]

To suggest that these jobs were open to everyone would be misleading. A 1925 photograph of the General Motors employees outside of the Avenida Wilson warehouse does not show a single Afro-Brazilian and shows only seven women.[84] Examining the pictures of those employees who received the *relógios de ouro* (gold watches) reflects this trend. Women and Afro-Brazilians together represented just 5 percent of individuals receiving the award although they were a much larger share of the Paulistano working population.[85] At Mappin, employees in the well-paying sales positions could be women, but as vendors had to speak two languages and have a "good appearance and be recommended by good families," racial discrimination persisted.[86]

Social connections and education could help laborers establish recommendations. For working-class immigrant families, the amount of time they lived in the city helped create those connections. It was only after five to eight years that immigrants seemed to be considerably rooted in the city. Letters written in the early 1920s promised aging parents abroad that they would not have to work if they moved to São Paulo, but these letters came from immigrants who had endured the wartime years in the city, not from the newly arriving immigrants.[87] Education could also be an equalizer, but Afro-Brazilians and Portuguese, who faced hiring discrimination in the city, would have been less likely to make these choices. Getting a good job was still a dream for many of these individuals. Meeting the "good appearance" requirement was more complex. The coded language effectively closed the door for Afro-Brazilians and only left a small crack for laborers. Dressing the part was often prohibitively expensive, and being able to live close enough to the store became more difficult.

SHELTER AND CLOTHING

In late June 1920, João Partaloli wrote to his father-in-law complaining of unpredictability in São Paulo and that "business does not go as you wish." He continues, "What is certain is that there is a great lack of money and a terrible increase in living and clothing, and only harder work makes life bearable."[88] The hope detected in letters from the prewar era luring immigrants to the city had disappeared. While João Partaloli's father-in-law returned to the city and counted in the new migratory wave, it was without fanfare: "We [the family] cannot get any better." He laments that even selling property in Italy would not yield enough income for the family to open a banana stand in São Paulo.[89] Another letter asks for prayers: "There are many unemployed people [in the city,] pray to God for me."[90] Letters like this reveal just how difficult it could be to acquire the wardrobe necessary for a good appearance. Finding good housing was not much easier. Living in São Paulo was still cheaper than in other immigrant destinations, but by the end of the 1920s, the housing market's limitations were painfully apparent.

When imported textiles all but disappeared at the onset of World War I, São Paulo's textile factories increased production to fill the void. Just as increased production did not lead to better management, it also did not resolve the problem of inferior but still expensive products. Virginia Joaquina Ferreira's husband wrote her in Portugal in June 1917 asking her to bring clothes not only for herself and her daughter but also for him, as clothes were more expensive in São Paulo. He even went as far as asking her to buy another suitcase to fit all the clothes.[91] In the same month, Maria de Deus Barbosa told her mother to make sure to send her son with clothes "because they have to be cheaper there than they are here."[92] In October of the same year, Andrés, Petra, and Nicolai Bonilla tried to make the best of the expensive clothing situation. The siblings asked their friend Juan Antonio Gonsales to bring extra suit jackets to São Paulo. The jackets were so expensive in the city that they planned on selling the extra ones he brought for a significant profit.[93] Even though it reflects a middle-class background, Larita Gorkin's letter in 1921 directly addresses the high cost of clothes in the city. She told her mother to buy any clothes she might need in Buenos Aires, saying, "Here everything is very expensive." This instruction is especially illuminating as it was sent on stationery from the Brás clothing store owned by her husband, Máximo Gorkin. One would expect that at least clothing store owners would buy clothes in Brazil, but clearly, this was not the case.[94]

The high clothing costs the letters describe disproportionately disadvantaged the working class, who had little disposable income to allocate to clothing after meeting rent and food costs.[95] In a society where a good appearance could open doors for jobs, dressing the part was key to having these opportunities. What Paulistanos wore often reflected distinctions developing within the working class; immigrants who could ask kinspeople and friends to bring extra clothes had a distinct advantage over Brazilians or long-established immigrant families who could not.

Letters demonstrate how the high rents Paulistanos faced were burdensome but were better than in Buenos Aires and Europe. Gorkin's letter notes that finding a house in São Paulo was easier than it was in Buenos Aires. She was particularly delighted that her family's new residence had a nice yard and room to receive guests for what would have been the equivalent of 500 pesos in Buenos Aires.[96] To a certain degree, the working class also had more options. Workers living in more densely populated areas and working in factories sometimes turned to factory commissions to bargain with factory owners to combat inflation.[97] Many women, Afro-Brazilians, Portuguese immigrants, and textile workers simply did not have these opportunities and had to be more creative if they wanted to succeed. Renting out extra rooms or spaces, thus, was practiced by individuals throughout the economic spectrum. A chamada letter specifically references renting out rooms to tenants, showing how the family valued these payments to supplement the family income.[98] At the economic margins, the combined extra income contributed by three renters and boarders could equal one and a half times a female domestic's salary and provided enough income to cover rent and other expenses.[99]

More densely populated housing, however, increased the likelihood of infectious disease. During the 1920s, pneumonia, tuberculosis, and dysentery were frequent causes of death. Yellow fever and malaria were no longer major killers, and the number of deaths from diarrhea and enteritis dropped dramatically, but childhood mortality was high.[100] Stillbirth rates and infant mortality remained extremely high; more than 50 of every 1,000 births was a stillbirth in the city, and infant mortality reached more than 200 deaths per 1,000 live births in the 1920s.[101] More space, access to clean air, plots of land, and better housing could greatly improve quality of life; between 1914 and 1920, São Paulo's population density was effectively halved. In addition to those workers moving to the interior, the Paulistano working class was moving to the urban periphery.[102]

São Paulo's geography and urban planning decisions allowed residents to move to peripheral areas more easily than they could in established cities like Rio de Janeiro and Buenos Aires. São Paulo's city center became more vertical; in 1920, a building's maximum height could be three stories, but in 1929, three stories became the minimum height. Old Republic vertical growth was restricted to the city center and roughly correlated to the city's small footprint in the nineteenth century.[103] The regulations allowed for the city's boundaries to expand radially to accommodate rapid population growth. By the end of the decade the limits of that expansion were being tested as housing proved insufficient.

Workers able to accrue more resources could look to more permanent solutions to solve the problem of housing shortages. One frequent approach in the 1920s was to buy a little piece of land on the city outskirts. Unrestricted by development regulations, this ad hoc horizontal expansion became the norm of popular housing in the postwar era. When not working in factories, families would construct their own houses. *Autoconstrução* (personal homebuilding) became a common weekend activity among the city's working class, and this solution was often more economical than trying to meet rising rents in more established areas of the city.[104] As many families often hired one or two bricklayers to help with construction, the building of worker houses had the added benefit of providing informal construction jobs to unemployed and underemployed individuals in the city.[105] Most of these houses would have been unregulated, but they demonstrate that for housing, Paulistanos found many ways to get by.[106] Building unregulated houses was not a new practice, but its growing popularity saw the city's footprint expand substantially in the 1920s.[107]

Access to public transportation correlated to the city's expanding footprint, but these services lagged behind housing construction in the peripheral neighborhoods. Transportation was more established in center regions and established working-class neighborhoods. Even when lines did open up in more peripheral neighborhoods such as Penha, demand far exceeded supply (figure 6.1). Like clothing costs, high transportation costs and long

Figure 6.1. Crowded cars on the Penha trolley line, 1916. Paulistanos living in working-class neighborhoods could use public transportation for a prorated fee, but supply did not keep up with demand, and many workers ended up walking. Photo by Guilherme Gaensly, July 1916. Courtesy of the Acervo Fundação Energia e Saneamento.

commutes disproportionately burdened the working class and served as constant sources of complaints.[108]

Challenges to the political status quo and the rise of the Partido Democrático (Democratic Party) in the 1920s provided an avenue for a select group of laborers to finally address the transportation issue through a political framework. In July 1924, the Tenente Revolt brought upheaval to São Paulo.[109] Contingents of young army lieutenants in Rio de Janeiro and São Paulo led the revolt to challenge the established military hierarchy and contest their inability to rise in the ranks. Volunteers and civilians also joined the rebellion, as many Brazilians were discontented with the Old Republic status quo. The Tenente Revolt became a moment to challenge the established political oligarchy.[110] In the aftermath, the Partido Democrático emerged to challenge the coffee-driven Partido Republicano Paulista that had dominated state and national politics throughout the Old Republic. Supporters of the Partido Democrático included middle-class liberal professionals, and about one fourth of the party's followers were laborers and railway workers.[111] Women and illiterate men were still excluded from voting, but literacy advancements in the prewar era and the growing population of first-generation Brazilians made this new group of voters who were laborers a sizeable voice in politics. They were the voters to whom more municipal leaders were paying attention, and their presence was large enough to have an impact on the Light transportation monopoly.

The privately owned São Paulo Tramway, Light, and Power had been the sole provider of trolley transportation since 1907, but it faced stiff competition in 1924 when buses began operating in the city. Buses had the distinct advantage of being able to quickly adapt or add routes. In 1928, Light proposed an overhaul of its public transportation contract with the city to include more trolleys, trolley lanes, and a bus monopoly. However, the plan also included a 0$100 réis fare increase. The Partido Democrático's claim that the hike was abusive led the municipal government to create a commission to study Light's proposal. Ultimately, the city government rejected the proposal and instead moved toward the Plano de Avenidas that would connect peripheral working-class neighborhoods through radial, grid-system roads. Planners hoped these larger avenues would accommodate the city's growing traffic and workers' needs to get to jobs and allow for continual expansion into the periphery.[112] The new avenues also brought new challenges, exacerbating another geographic barrier the city's working class confronted, its rivers.

The Flood of 1929

A propensity for flooding along the Tietê River and its two large tributaries, the Pinheiros and Tamanduateí Rivers, plagued the working class, particularly those living in the Bom Retiro and Barra Funda neighborhoods. In the city's early history, the threat of flooding along these rivers and an insalubrious disease environment kept these regions largely agricultural and sparsely inhabited.[113] The first population boom in the late nineteenth century saw a transition of these floodplains and lower-lying regions into areas for working-class families to settle. Buildings on most land in the two largest working-class neighborhoods, Brás and Moóca, were slightly above the floodplain, but intense flooding could also impact these areas, as it did several times between 1902 and 1907. Between 1907 and 1919, however, there were no major floods in the city.

Renewed population and industrial production pressure in the postwar era brought this period of relative calm to an end, and sporadic flooding became more frequent. The city's horizontal expansion of working-class suburbs increased the number of unregulated houses built along flood-plains. Population growth also led to heightened demand for electricity, and Light, the monopoly power provider, increasingly relied on dams and reservoirs to harness hydroelectric energy. In order to avoid an energy shortage, profit loss, and complaints from industrialists in the dry season, Light opted to keep the reservoir levels high. Raquel Rolnik notes that by 1919, "any intense summer rain resulted in floods that inundated the river banks which were exactly the areas of land with the lowest rent and pur-chase prices, and as such the location of the *popular* settlements."[114] Heavy rainfalls from January through March increased the chance of flooding in Bom Retiro, Cambucí, Brás, Tatuapé, and Ponte Pequena neighborhoods, and large floods occurred in working-class neighborhoods in 1919, 1923, 1926, and 1929.[115]

The pressure for more energy, as highlighted during the 1925 energy shortage, proved more powerful than the pressure to ameliorate flooding in working-class neighborhoods. In 1927, Light was granted permission to commence Project Serra, a plan to expand hydroelectric production that entailed rerouting and widening the Pinheiros River. In January 1929, when rains began, the water levels at Light's reservoirs were again high, but this time, Light held control over the widened Pinheiros River and held conces-sions around the surrounding floodplains. By allowing parts of the city to flood, the company could acquire flooded land through concessions. With the 1929 flood, there is evidence that Light's management made a conscious decision to keep reservoirs high, increasing the likelihood of flooding and effectively passing much land over to Light.[116] While the company's profit-making decisions likely worsened earlier floods in the 1920s, the 1929 flood stands out because flooding reached previously unaffected areas, including the newly constructed, elite Cidade Jardim neighborhood.[117]

By February 19, 1929, less than a week after *carnaval* festivities ended, Paulistano police and civic guards were operating in emergency mode. Wa-ters reached city trash deposits and left many Paulistanos stranded. The po-lice rescued 170 families in Bom Retiro, 78 in Barra Funda, and 46 in Ponte Pequena "without leg warmers, without boots, and with their pants pinned up, [civic guardsmen] walked through the neighborhood, looking for those in need of help from the public authorities."[118] Rising water completely cut off residents in Vila Anastácio, and the municipal government offered free barge transport for individuals in flooded neighborhoods. Many other families fled in their own or borrowed boats to stay with relatives who lived in higher elevations. Some evacuees were brought to the Hospedaria de Imigrantes for temporary refuge.[119]

In 1927, the hospedaria's role had effectively transitioned into funneling internal Brazilian migrants, Japanese immigrants, and a handful of other immigrants to work on coffee plantations. Immigration subsidies from the state had been suspended, bringing an effective end not just to the contracts but to the dynamic relation between the hospedaria and the city's labor market.[120] In the days surrounding the intense flooding in mid-February 1929, however, the hospedaria once again functioned as an escape valve. The 450 displaced Paulistanos staying at the hospedaria slept alongside 498 immigrants and 655 other individuals who had arrived from Rio de Janeiro. The *Estado de São Paulo* reports, "Among the crowd, one could note several types of *caboclos* [Brazilians of mixed indigenous descent] from the North, with the hats and their 'families' on their lap."[121]

In an article about flood victims, the multiple distinct references to Cearenses and other northern and northeastern migrants belie the reporter's fascination with this new migration. These new migrants did not have the same freedom of mobility as the displaced Paulistanos. While "dozens of [displaced] families entered and left daily" to stay with relatives, the hospedaria director notes that "many of the families displaced because of the floodwaters had continued on to the interior to work in the fields, accepting work offers." He writes, "They were, in the majority, families of previous *colonos* who came to [the city of] São Paulo to work in the factories," but they easily could have been first- or second-generation Paulistanos who did not have the fortune of having a good appearance or the right social connections.[122] The hospedaria registrations provide the names of the Cearenses, Bahians, and Mineiros who signed contracts but not the names of the evacuees who chose to leave the city behind. Pushed to live at the margins of the rivers and subsisting at the economic margins of the city, they disappeared from the register.

CONCLUSION

Nelly Colson, Luis Paulo, Roque Mestrieri, Luis Sequeira, and the Sgarro and Specchio family were all part of a working middle class that emerged in the city in the 1920s. Despite the city's hardships, high mortality rates, and stagnant wages, these individuals persisted, found the recipe for success, and demonstrated that there was room for economic mobility after World War I and before the 1930 revolution. Mobility into the middle class was also open to laborers. High wages, family connections, and opportunities for advancement facilitated movement in income and from blue-collar to white-collar positions. The war may have brought more hardships for the majority of the working class, but some of the city's laborers benefited. The family wage was often a key to their success, but so too was finding good jobs in one of the city's growing sectors such as the commercial sector or the nontextile, mechanical sector. These individuals and families consti-tuted a laboring middle class with distinct goals and voting interests.

However, there was not equal access into this middle class. Countless Paulistanos, many of whom lived along the margins of the city's rivers, struggled to make ends meet. A series of floods in the 1920s accentuated the divisions within São Paulo's working class and demonstrated the pre-cariousness residents navigated daily. *Colonos* moved to the city seeking factory employment, but these new arrivals rarely appear in factory re-cords. Faced with a tight job market, saving enough money, having clothes that presented a good appearance, and getting jobs in the commercial sec-tor were close to impossible. Migrants from other states also began to ar-rive, but the *caboclos* migrating from northern and northeastern Brazil had distinctive hats and darker skin and did not fit the elite Paulistano concept of a good appearance. They were largely excluded from the commercial sector. Women, who still could not vote, were excluded from most nontex-tile industrial jobs and had to make headway in smaller ventures or in the commercial sector. In such a complex hierarchy, where did this leave single mothers who needed a reliable income that would also allow them to care for their children? Where did this leave Afro-Brazilian women? All too of-ten, it left them beyond the economic periphery, on the outside looking in.

Conclusion

As the Old Republic drew to an end, it was impossible to speak of a singular working class in the city of São Paulo. People's experiences varied dramatically based on gender and race but were equally shaped by nationality and family expectations. The intersection of these traits affected not just a Paulistano's chances for getting jobs but also how he or she behaved and made labor choices once having a job. The decision to organize, to leave the formal labor market, to look for a new job, and to strike or not to strike were intricately linked to past experiences and future expectations. Unveiling the nuances behind labor decisions gives a better understanding of the importance of worker agency. Considered collectively, workers' actions had great impact on the Paulistano labor market and the city's development.

Worker expectations developed and shifted over the course of the Old Republic, but important patterns developed in three distinct periods, the years before, during, and after World War I. Before the war, rapid urbanization and industrialization attracted tens of thousands of immigrants and migrants to the city; it grew from 65,000 residents in 1890 to almost a half million just twenty-three years later. The city was seen as a land of opportunity, especially for families. São Paulo's was a highly prejudiced labor market, but during this period, when the demand for workers was high enough, even racial prejudice began to break down.

The city these new arrivals encountered and helped to build had all the traditional problems associated with rapid growth: poor hygiene, stagnant air, and poor working conditions. But São Paulo also offered great opportunities. There were improvements in education, mortality rates, and marriage ages. Jobs could be abundant, and having a house was a possibility. Immigrants wrote of these opportunities in letters sent back to family members in their home countries. Life was not perfect, but in general, hopes were high for better futures.

The Hospedaria de Imigrantes greatly facilitated São Paulo's growth by adapting to meet urban labor market demands. For Paulistano workers, the institution provided a safety net, as guaranteed employment was just a walk through its doors into the Brás neighborhood. For employers, the hospedaria offered a quick source of cheap labor. The institution was originally structured to funnel agricultural immigrant workers into the state's interior coffee plantations, but by the early twentieth century, it accepted Brazilians, reentries from the city, and nonagricultural workers. City employers could contract workers directly from the hospedaria and used the institution, along with police intervention, to minimize labor movements and end strikes.

In the city's prewar growth period between 1903 and 1913, a particularly large group of Portuguese immigrants was signing contracts to work in the city. Most were illiterate, from Portugal's interior agricultural regions and arrived in nuclear family units. As a group, these Portuguese arrivals served two key roles in the city's history; they were ideal workers for employers needing cheap labor, and they furthered efforts aimed at whitening the Brazilian population. That many Portuguese workers were unskilled and illiterate in this early period led Paulistano employers to assume that all Portuguese immigrants held these traits. Thus, Portuguese immigrants as a group experienced labor market discrimination throughout the Old Republic and were disproportionately hired into unskilled positions. They were, in fact, four times more likely to be hired into unskilled positions than Brazilians were. Facing these barriers and needing to provide for their families, they were ideal strikebreakers, replacement workers, and police officers. Their unwillingness to strike contributed to keeping São Paulo's labor organization to a minimum during the Old Republic.

World War I brought dramatic and permanent changes to the city. European arrivals all but disappeared from 1914 to 1918. In response, migration from elsewhere in Brazil and the Rio de la Plata region increased. The city's size remained relatively static, as there was an outmigration to the state's interior. For people who stayed in the city, survival often meant embracing a family wage strategy. Husbands, wives, and children all went to work for family survival, and some educational achievements from the earlier period were reversed. In the postwar period, immigration and migration returned to the city, but the newest residents were distinct from those arriving in the earlier period. In addition to Southern Cone and Brazilian migration, eastern European and Japanese immigration increased in relative importance. In the city, a disproportionately large group of skilled German immigrants arrived in the 1920s. Their arrival was tied to an increase in capital-intensive industries that began developing during the war. The war virtually stopped imports to Brazil of machinery, finished products, and capital goods such as iron and concrete. Companies related to the mechanical trades grew out of these scarcities. So too, did jobs, and the influx of German and other skilled immigrants in the postwar period helped fill the demand for semi-skilled and skilled workers.

A good mechanical job in a company like General Motors do Brasil, Paulista Railway, or Ford facilitated access to the middle class. As expected, these good jobs offered relatively high wages and opportunities for advancement and training. Perhaps less intuitively, good jobs also accommodated for worker families. With a good job, a worker and his or her family could aspire to move from blue-collar to white-collar work or could think about that mobility for future generations. The rise of a blue- and white-collar middle class in the 1920s is notable and points to important divisions among laborers prior to the Vargas era.

Many Paulistanos did not have access to these good jobs. Workers in the textile sector had to contend with low wages, heavy-handed labor repression, and job insecurity. As the Paulistano textile sector offered the best jobs for women in the Old Republic, working-class women were at a particular disadvantage in gaining access to the middle class. The hiring and wage discrimination most women faced kept them vital to the family wage strategy, but as individuals they remained on the economic margins. The commercial sector offered women the greatest opportunity for access into the Paulistano middle class, but many of these jobs were reserved for individuals with a *boa aparência*, and there was a distinct preference for immigrants or first-generation Brazilians.

The *boa aparência* requirement effectively excluded many Afro-Brazilians from the commercial sector. While technically not excluded from most other sectors, Afro-Brazilians were significantly underrepresented in the formal labor market, pointing to substantial hiring discrimination. There was an increase in labor market racial prejudice in the postwar era. As migration from other areas of Brazil increased, a good appearance became a specified requirement for applying for even unskilled jobs in the city. In the prewar era, periods of high labor demand had been able to open some opportunities for Afro-Brazilians, but the city just did not grow fast enough in the postwar period to offer similar effects. The war, then, can be understood as a turning point that halted growth in opportunities for Afro-Brazilians and for Afro-Brazilian women in particular. In the aftermath of the war, most would find themselves further behind economically.

Considering the sizeable barriers to entry for so many individuals in São Paulo's working class, it is understandable that so many turned to the informal labor market to combat rising costs in the city. It is also understandable that workers may have been unwilling to join labor organizers. The answer was not just leaders' inability to understand rank-and-file concerns but also systemic discrimination that created a privileged group within the working class. Unless these prejudices were addressed, workers knew that they would not benefit from better wages or conditions. They simply did not have access to those jobs and would continue to be on the economic periphery or on the outside looking in.

FUTURE QUESTIONS

In an effort to understand the city of São Paulo's changing complexity and development during its most rapid period of industrialization and urbanization, this study, in some ways, raises more questions than it answers. Scholars may find their own lines of future inquiry, in addition to the two I provide. First, how did existing Paulistano working-class diversity affect workers and their response to the labor reforms implemented in the Vargas era? Binaries do not address the Brazilian response to provisions in the 1934 Constitution and measures implemented during the Estado Novo. All immigrants did not have the same experiences, and all laborers were not the same. The move of northeastern migrants to São Paulo, as Barbara Weinstein has pointed out in *The Color of Modernity*, further complicated the Afro-Brazilian/white binary that studies tend to fall back on. A logical starting place for understanding responses would be with Afro-Brazilian women. As the most marginalized group in the Old Republic, their decisions regarding work, education, and political support must be understood and how race, gender and family factored into those decisions.

Second, in the quest to understand marginalized individuals and their agency, a concerted effort is needed to understand family agency. Two examples demonstrate the importance of doing so. In terms of real wages and the cost of living, scholars, myself included, tend to focus on adult male wages. Old Republic São Paulo, however, did not grow and develop on adult male wages; it did so on a collective family wage. With a large number of nuclear family units migrating to the city, São Paulo perhaps offers an extreme of this case, but families' wages were critical to working-class survival in most large cities at the turn of the twentieth century. Perhaps the family wage relative to the cost of living will lead to understanding the point at which Paulistano strikebreakers and those in other cities could be convinced or willing to cross the picket line. In connecting the Old Republic to the Vargas era, we researchers must revisit how families adapted to labor legislation that prevented childhood employment and further restricted female employment. Did they give up on the family wage easily, sending children to school, or was there a shift toward an informal family wage? Whether structural changes and laws were enough to precipitate cultural change and how families strategized moving into the middle class should be considered.

THE BIG PICTURE

While we are left with a series of questions, this study does provide some key insights. The dive into the prewar period of the city's history reveals that the early twentieth century could have marked a turning point for São Paulo's working class. Several indicators show that the 1891–1913 period provided more opportunities for advancement to individuals with limited resources or social capital. This shows that Brazilians, immigrants, and first-generation Brazilians living in the city did benefit from rapid growth in terms of available opportunities and quality of life. The benefits varied based on race and nationality, but in comparison to the years that followed, the prewar years filled the working class with hope and the promise of development. The implications of these findings for Brazil and Latin America are substantial. As the region of the world to experience the greatest move toward urbanization in the twentieth century, inequality continues to be pervasive in urban centers.

In the case of São Paulo, two important factors limited the opportunities accompanying the rapid growth: World War I and the Hospedaria de Imigrantes. The war was a factor outside the control of Brazilian residents, the working class, the middle class, and elites. However, the scholarship debating the war's impact on Latin American development has largely ignored its immediate effects on the largest portion of the Latin American population, the working class. The Paulistano case indicates heavy-handed labor tactics for labor-intensive industries during the war years as well as fewer opportunities for some of the city's and Brazil's most marginalized populations. Much of Latin America's industrial workforce was employed in labor-intensive industries when the war began; further study could focus more attention on the war itself in terms of its impact at a critical point in Latin America's history. Other cities may have experienced similar periods of promise before World War I.

The hospedaria's complicated role in the city's development is more instructive of institutional hindrances in overcoming inequality. The hospedaria was designed to connect incoming immigrant families with coffee planters who needed workers in the state's interior. For the city of São Paulo, it also facilitated connections between labor demand and labor supply. For workers and especially for families, the hospedaria provided a sense of security. In doing so, however, the institution incentivized employers to look for cheap labor rather than for long-term solutions that would lead to greater development. By facilitating exploitive labor practices, the hospedaria fostered a segmented labor market in the city. Ultimately, the institution helped preserve inequalities and discrimination from the city's imperial era, when slavery was a viable institution. There are likely similar institutions and practices embedded in the fabric of other cities and countries that must be investigated in order to understand Latin America's failure to overcome these issues.

Finally, we must continue to strive to include marginalized voices as we reevaluate our understanding of the past. They are the largest group of actors, when considered collectively, and their decisions and adaptations have critically affected the course of history. Studying these individuals can prove challenging, but historians and social scientists of Latin America have made great strides in using marriage, baptism, military, and criminal records. It is time to add company records and economic history methodologies to this concert of voices.

Appendix A

Livros de registros de matrícula de entrada de imigrantes na Hospedaria de Imigrantes

The Arquivo Público do Estado de São Paulo maintains the Livros de registros de entrada de imigrantes na hospedaria, 1882–1978, referenced in this work as "registros." The hospedaria's original entry books were compiled into a database that is searchable online, at http://www.inci.org.br/acervodigital/, and at the Museu da Imigração do Estado de São Paulo. Searching the database is generally restricted to basic searches using individuals' last names and origins, but much more information is available within the database for each individual. A link to the digitized registros also allows access to the wealth of information contained in the database.[1] After gaining access to do simple query searches within the database, I isolated individuals arriving between 1889 and 1930, the years between the fall of the empire and end of the Old Republic. This search returned 1,329,918 individuals, but the data for individuals before 1902 contained minimal information beyond arrival date, name, and origin. Limiting the parameters to the 1903–1927 period yielded a population size of 457,811 individuals. These dates capture the post–Prinetti Decree period and stop right before Julio Prestes ended subsidized immigration.

I isolated my search to individuals listing "capital," São Paulo city, as their final destination. I filtered for individuals ages fifteen and older (in order to keep consistent with the *BDET* annual reports), but this only included heads of household. As a result, it would include individuals coming into the hospedaria without a family but leave out all spouses and adult children.[2] The search revealed 8,887 true heads of household and 8,741 individuals coming into the city between 1903 and 1927.

As my access was restricted to simple queries, a random 20 percent sample of the database was manually re-created. First, each group (heads of household and individual) was sorted alphabetically by first name. Using the first name was preferable because most Brazilian documents, including employee records, are filed alphabetically by an individual's first name. Then, every twentieth individual's record locator was recorded; each individual was assigned a book, page, and family number in the hospedaria records. Next, the record locators were used as filters to find and input all relevant information. This included civil status, age, port of embarkation, previous time in Brazil, profession, and more. I was very fortunate to have the invaluable help of Roberta Veiga, an undergraduate student in the Universidade de São Paulo economics department, inputting this portion of the data. For those individuals who were heads of household, we input the information for each member of the family, coding for most of the fields including nationality, port of embarkation, gender, literacy, and family status. Unless otherwise noted, we assumed that all individuals in a family were destined for the capital. We noticed that although literacy was recorded for each individual, professions were not. We also coded differently for family members under age fifteen. The resulting registros sample database included 435 individuals who came to the city as individuals and 1,797 individuals coming over as part of a family, a total of 2,232 individuals, of them 1,404 adults. This sample allowed me to answer some important questions.

The registros provided numerous other search opportunities beyond the sample to answer important questions about the population settling in the city. Guided by the debate as to whether immigrants were more skilled than Brazilians, I paid particular attention to national literacy rates for individuals over age fifteen. One advantage was that literacy was also recorded for non-heads of household, so this search would include wives and children. A great challenge, however, was making sure to include all immigrants, as multiple variations in spelling appeared in the database. Both "aleman" and "alleman" had to be used to search for Germans, "espanhol" and "hespanhol" for Spaniards. Under the literacy column, "nao" and "não" were used. After applying these basic filters, I could look further into literacy by profession as well as differences between immigrants to the entire state and immigrants just coming to the city.

To verify the representativeness of the sample, I compared the 850 adult (considering anyone aged fifteen or older as an adult) males in our sample to the entire adult male population coming to the city between 1903 and 1927 (table A.1). By comparing the shares of the immigrant flow and the

Table A.1. Nationality representativeness of registros sample, 1903–1927

Nationality	Sample share	Population share	Sample literacy	Population literacy
Brazilian	2.1	2.4	61.1	63.4
Portuguese	33.4	35.3	24.3	19.5
Italian	13.6	15.1	58.6	68.9
Spanish	33.9	31.6	34.7	41.2
German	8.1	7.0	95.7	98.5

Source: Registros heads of household 20% sample and entire registros database.

literacy rates by nationality, although literacy rates varied a bit more than we wanted, the random sample correlates well with the entire population.

Further evidence that the sample is representative comes from comparing the share of the sample arriving during each period to the whole adult population coming to the city. For the entire population, 83.4 percent of the data comes from the 1903 to 1913 period, 6.3 percent from the World War I years, and 10.4 percent from the 1919 to 1927 period. In our sample, 86 percent of individuals arrived between 1903 and 1913, 4.2 percent between 1914 and 1918, and 9.8 percent after 1919.[3]

To filter by professions, I applied the same basic principles and allowed for spelling variations. Textile workers included weavers (*tecelões*), seamstresses (*costureiras*), and tailors (*alfaiates*) but left out twenty-seven dyers (*tintoreiros*) because they were arguably more skilled. For the mechanics and blacksmiths category, mechanics (*mecanicos, technicos*), tin workers (*funileiros*), and blacksmiths (*ferreiros, fundidores*) were included. For the businessman category, *negociantes* were included. Chapter 1 has a discussion of this analysis.

Finally, I used the registros to look at the Brazilian population passing through the hospedaria. This was one of the most nuanced portions of data accumulation due to the multiple ways in which Brazilian origins were recorded. In some years, information was recorded in the observation field, while in others it was recorded in a combination of the observation, local residence, reason for entry into the hospedaria, country of residence, departure point, and boat of entry fields. The years 1908 to 1913 offered a particular challenge because origin information for individuals entering to "collocar-se por intermedio da Hospedaria" was available in the local residence section. This required tabulating individuals on a town-by-town basis. Time constraints restricted a full evaluation of the population, but

Table A.2. Migrant Brazilian heads-of-household literacy, 1903–1927, by state

Region, state	Total	Unknown literacy	Literate (%)	1920 15+ literate (%)	Agriculturalists (%)
NORTH					
AC	1	0	100.0	40.0	100.0
AM	11	0	72.7	38.5	100.0
PA	46	1	54.3	41.8	97.8
NORTHEAST					
MA	3	1	33.3	22.8	66.7
PI	6	0	66.7	18.7	100.0
CE[a]	171	5	53.8	27.2	83.0
CE	1,781	5	31.8	27.2	90.6
RN[a]	253	0	48.6	25.3	85.0
RN	673	420	18.3	26.4	86.9
PE	751	6	52.2	25.3	85.0
AL	1,644	0	47.7	21.2	98.8
PB[a]	107	0	72.0	19.8	89.7
PB	179	72	43.0	19.8	85.5
SE	158	0	53.8	22.8	99.4
BA	4,910	8	41.7	27.0	96.7
CENTER WEST					
MT	6	0	50.0	41.5	100.0
SOUTHEAST					
MG	8,521	73	35.4	31.2	98.5
ES	93	23	43.0	35.4	93.4
RJ	4,863	531	31.8	35.5	93.4
SP	804	0	45.3	41.4	61.2
RJ/SP border	5,701	20	18.4		81.2
SOUTH					
PR	49	13	51.0	50.0	77.6
SC	76	1	59.2	41.6	86.8
RS	95	5	65.3	55.5	86.3
CAPITAL (SP)	2,971	1	35.2	67.1	45.8
CAPITAL (FEDERAL)	960	0	67.0	74.2	86.8
FOREIGNER	304	20	63.2		69.1
Total	35,137	1,205	35.4		87.6

Sources: All data are from registros except for the 1920 15+ literacy, which is based on literacy rates reported in Brazil, *Recenseamento 1920*, vol. 4.4, x–xi, 803–804.

Note: Registros literacy rates are calculated assuming all migrants for whom no literacy information was provided were illiterate. State abbreviations are used. Capital (SP) is the city of São Paulo, and Capital (federal) is the city of Rio de Janeiro. "Foreigner" refers to immigrants moving from other states to São Paulo.

[a] Excludes migrants arriving during drought years as a part of a refugee effort. These years are 1915, 1916, and 1920 for CE and 1904 for both RN and PB.

for the 85 percent of these individuals when the town was analyzed, most came from the Paraíba Valley region near the São Paulo and Rio de Janeiro state border. This demonstrates a weakness in the Brazilian data in how to interpret Rio de Janeiro. In many years, individuals labeled as coming from Rio de Janeiro could actually be coming from the federal capital city or from the Paraíba Valley or from other parts of the state of Rio de Janeiro. As the literacy results show in table A.2, since individuals from the city had the highest rate of all Brazilian migrants and those from the Paraíba Valley had the lowest, the registered Southeast literacy rates could be either overestimates or underestimates.[4] All in all, the results demonstrate that São Paulo's immigration program drew more highly skilled Brazilians to the city and state.

STATISTICAL ANALYSIS RESULTS

Once the 20 percent registros sample was created, I used it to statistically analyze determinants of literacy rates and the probability of recording an unskilled profession. Tables A.3 through A.5 show logistic regression results. Chapter 1 provides further discussion of the results listed in tables A.3–A.5 on the following pages.

Table A.3. Paulistano literacy determinants, 1903–1927

Variable	(1)	(2)	(3)	(4)	(5)	(6)
NATIONALITY						
Portuguese	-1.421**	-1.078*	-0.627	-0.603	-0.667	-1.371*
	(0.48)	(0.52)	(0.57)	(0.59)	(0.59)	(0.54)
Italian	0.436	0.691	0.955	0.848	0.735	-0.080
	(0.51)	(0.54)	(0.56)	(0.58)	(0.59)	(0.58)
Spanish	-0.488	-0.175	0.266	0.213	0.151	-0.759
	(0.48)	(0.51)	(0.57)	(0.59)	(0.59)	(0.55)
German/Austrian	4.019***	3.926***	4.323***	4.135***	4.032***	2.967*
	(1.10)	(1.11)	(1.12)	(1.13)	(1.14)	(1.18)
FEMALE	-1.226**	-1.222**	-1.177**	-1.003*	-0.837*	-0.863*
	(0.39)	(0.38)	(0.39)	(0.41)	(0.39)	(0.38)
MARRIED	-0.303	-0.308	-0.258	-0.307		
	(0.22)	(0.22)	(0.23)	(0.23)		
FAMILY					-0.434	-0.548*
					(0.59)	(0.54)
BRAZIL PRIOR			0.546*	0.680*	0.609*	
			(0.26)	(0.27)	(0.27)	
SKILL LEVEL						
Semi-skilled				0.887*	0.873*	1.897*
				(0.42)	(0.42)	(0.77)
Skilled				1.047***	1.050***	1.203***
				(0.23)	(0.23)	(0.33)
Highly skilled				0.147	0.169*	-0.010*
				(0.46)	(0.47)	(0.92)
TIME PERIOD						
1914–1918		0.418	0.377	0.408	0.277	
		(0.43)	(0.44)	(0.48)	(0.47)	
1919–1927		0.979	0.950	1.080	1.151	
		(0.67)	(0.66)	(0.64)	(0.66)	
AGE EFFECTS	Y	Y	Y	Y	Y	Y
CONSTANT	-0.045	-0.280	-0.615	-0.604	-0.500	0.248
	(0.79)	(0.81)	(0.84)	(0.87)	(0.87)	(0.85)
OBS	673	672	662	651	651	608
PSEUDO R-SQ	0.22	0.22	0.22	0.25	0.25	0.18
AIC	741.0	741.2	726.6	697.6	695.6	700.3
BIC	781.6	790.8	780.6	764.7	762.7	775.2

Source: Data from the registros head of household 20 percent sample.

Note: Dependent variable is literacy. Comparison group is an unskilled Brazilian male arriving between 1903 and 1913. "Brazil prior" is a dummy variable that records an individual having already lived in Brazil, effectively a reentry to the hospedaria. Reporting b/(se).

* $p<0.05$.

** $p<0.01$.

*** $p<0.001$.

Table A.4. Impact of port of embarkation on literacy, 1903–1927

Variable	(1)	(2)	(3)	(4)
REGION/COUNTRY OF PORT				
Netherlands/Germany	3.297**	3.060**	2.454	2.784*
	(1.11)	(1.17)	(1.30)	(1.27)
France	0.465	0.489	0.487	0.156
	(1.42)	(1.45)	(1.48)	(2.07)
Rio de la Plata	0.717	0.758	0.716	0.299
	(0.44)	(0.45)	(0.49)	(0.55)
Italy	0.858*	0.778	0.927	0.627
	(0.43)	(0.43)	(0.48)	(0.55)
Portugal	-0.556	-0.516	-0.554	-0.127
	(0.36)	(0.36)	(0.38)	(0.42)
Brazil	0.446	0.419	-0.217	1.038
	(0.69)	(0.74)	(0.85)	(0.93)
Canaries/Azores	-0.704	-0.681	-0.670	Omit
	(1.04)	(1.04)	(1.05)	
Northern Spain	0.164	0.182	0.151	0.638
	(0.73)	(0.72)	(0.74)	(0.81)
FEMALE	-1.333**	-1.266**	-1.289**	-0.983*
	(0.45)	(0.46)	(0.49)	(0.47)
FAMILY	-0.292	-0.334	-0.419	-0.527
	(0.31)	(0.31)	(0.32)	(0.34)
BRAZIL PRIOR	0.501	0.530	0.521	0.544
	(0.42)	(0.41)	(0.42)	(0.45)
PERIOD				
1914–1918		-0.167	-0.820	-0.283
		(0.46)	(1.07)	(0.50)
1919–1927		0.788	0.826	0.851
		(0.71)	(1.21)	(0.75)
PERIOD X PORT			Y	
SKILL LEVEL X PORT				Y
AGE EFFECTS	Y	Y	Y	Y
CONSTANT	1.453	1.460	1.186	0.807
	(1.19)	(1.20)	(1.22)	(1.39)
OBS	305	305	287	259
PSEUDO R-SQ	0.15	0.16	0.12	0.18
AIC	382.6	385.0	389.5	334.1
BIC	434.7	444.5	466.4	408.8

Source: Data from the registros head of household 20 percent sample.

Note: Dependent variable is literacy. Comparison is an unskilled male arriving from a southern Spanish port between 1903 and 1913. "Brazil prior" is a dummy variable that records previous residence in Brazil. Reporting b/(se).

* $p<0.05$.

** $p<0.01$.

*** $p<0.001$.

Table A.5. Impact of nationality on probability of unskilled profession, 1903–1927

Variable	(1)	(2)	(3)	(4)	(5)
NATIONALITY					
Portuguese	0.684	0.974	0.902	1.019	0.888
	(0.93)	(1.00)	(1.05)	(1.10)	(1.26)
Italian	-0.477	-0.243	-0.585	-0.600	-0.381
	(0.90)	(0.95)	(1.01)	(1.03)	(1.31)
Spanish	-0.373	-0.110	-0.331	-0.291	-0.673
	(0.90)	(0.96)	(1.01)	(1.06)	(1.09)
German/Austrian	-0.745	-0.658	-0.980	-1.028	-1.545
	(0.91)	(0.94)	(1.00)	(1.03)	(1.06)
LITERATE	-1.060***	-1.063***	-1.146***	-1.082***	-0.835
	(0.31)	(0.31)	(0.31)	(0.32)	(0.45)
FEMALE	2.916**	2.961**	3.239**	3.192*	3.143*
	(1.03)	(1.04)	(1.05)	(1.06)	(1.07)
FAMILY			-0.771*	-0.704*	-0.700*
			(0.32)	(0.32)	(0.32)
BRAZIL PRIOR				-0.097	-0.038
				(0.37)	(0.38)
PERIOD					
1914–1918		0.242	0.067	0.085	0.115
		(0.45)	(0.46)	(0.47)	(0.48)
1919–1927		0.398	0.557	0.723	0.696
		(0.48)	(0.53)	(0.55)	(0.57)
AGE EFFECTS	Y	Y	Y	Y	Y
Constant	1.199	1.038	0.973	0.621	0.954
	(1.59)	(1.61)	(1.64)	(1.64)	(1.72)
OBS	311	311	311	305	303
PSEUDO R-SQ	0.17	0.17	0.18	0.19	0.19
AIC	352.5	355.8	351.7	342.2	341.0
BIC	386.2	397.0	396.6	390.6	396.7

Source: Data from the registros head of household 20 percent sample.
Note: Dependent variable is if worker is unskilled. Comparison group is an illiterate Brazilian male arriving between 1903 and 1913. "Brazil prior" is a dummy variable that records previous residence in Brazil. Reporting b/(se).
* p<0.05.
** p<0.01.
*** p<0.001.

Appendix B

Chapter 4 Data

A substantial portion of the labor market analysis in chapter 4 focuses on company-level wage and hiring data from three firms (table B.1).[1] Basic characteristics of workers at each firm are described below.

Table B.1. Paulistano firm-level statistics

Worker characteristic	Paulista	Light	Jafet
AVERAGE AGE	23 (569)	29 (855)	21 (1,339)
MEDIAN AGE	22 (569)	26 (855)	18 (1,339)
FEMALE	0% (0)	0% (0)	64.6% (1340)
LITERATE	87.3% (197)	89.8% (205)	52.8% (892)
APPRENTICE	18.6% (569)	26.5% (1892)	23.9% (323)
SKILL LEVEL			
Unskilled	56.41%	21.25%	13.71%
Low skilled	19.51%	38.74%	83.69%
Medium skilled	24.08%	40.01%	24.38%
MECHANICS	20.83%	46.00%	1.70%
BOBBIN WORKERS OR DAY LABORERS	52.00%	15.50%	31.90%
NATIONALITY SHARES			
Brazilian	55.77%	44.81%	66.57%
Portuguese	25.40%	15.74%	4.11%
Italian	12.08%	13.91%	8.45%
Spanish	4.80%	5.13%	11.44%
German/Austrian	0.18%	6.16%	1.20%

Source: Wage series as described in Ball, "Prices, Wages, and the Cost of Living."
Note: Numbers in parentheses reflect number of observations.

Variables and Explanations for OLS and Logit Regression Results in Tables B.2 to B.9

Female: Dummy variable for gender. Female is equal to 1.

Nationality variables: Dummy variables for select nationalities. Where a Portuguese worker will have Portuguese equal to 1 and German, Brazilian, Spanish, Italian, and Other equal to 0. German and Austrian workers are combined into one dummy variable.

Literacy: Dummy variable for literacy where a literate worker is equal to 1. When there is no literacy variable, the dummy variable is coded as missing. When any level of school is listed above literacy, the dummy variable is coded as 1 (see *Education* variable below).

White: Race variable where white workers are coded as 1 and *pardo* and *preto* workers are coded as 0. When there is no racial observation, the dummy variable is coded as missing.

Year fixed effects: Dummy variable for each year in the series.

Age: Continuous variable reflecting the worker's age.

Age^2: Continuous variable to reflect experience based on the worker's age squared.

Cia fixed effects: Dummy variable for Jafet, Light, and Paulista.

Education level: Ordinal variable that measures schooling level reflecting excellent, good, average, poor schooling or illiteracy as defined for some Paulista employees.

Skill level: Four dummy variables for skill level assigned for each worker based on HISCO and HISCLASS classification scheme.

Observation: Continuous variable to reflect wage increases or promotions.

Experience: Continuous variable reflecting the number of days working with the company.

$Experience^2$: Continuous variable to capture the u-shaped return to experience, based on the days of experience squared.

Statistical Analysis Results

Table B.2. Determinants of Paulistano real wages, 1891–1930

Variable	(1)	(2)	(3)	(4)	(5)	(6)
NATIONALITY						
Portuguese	-0.0533***	0.117***	-0.0932***	-0.139***		-0.0207
	(0.02)	(0.02	(0.03)	(0.02)		(0.02)
Italian	0.0460*	-0.0416*	-0.0514	-0.0423		0.059
	(0.02)	(0.02)	(0.04)	(0.03)		(0.03)
Spanish	0.0135	-0.0439	-0.0278	-0.0525		0.0524
	(0.03)	(0.04)	(0.12)	(0.11)		(0.06)
German	0.172***	0.101*	0.161	0.443***		0.105
	(0.03)	(0.04)	(0.12)	(0.11)		(0.06)
Russian	0.328***	0.128	-0.0875	0.108		0.185***
	(0.07)	(0.09)	(0.09)	(0.09)		(0.09)
Polish	0.199	0.0227	-0.174	-0.00283		0.0118
	(0.11)	(0.09)	(0.09)	(0.09)		(0.09)
British	-0.239	-0.191		-0.177		
	(0.21)	(0.19)		(0.19)		
Other	0.132***	0.0491	0.688***	0.485***		0.118
	(0.03)	(0.03)	(0.19)	(0.09)		(0.09)
FEMALE	-0.354***	-0.233***	-0.427***	-0.425***	-0.393***	-0.318***
	(0.05)	(0.04)	(0.12)	(0.10)	(0.10)	(0.05)
AGE		0.0619***	0.0758***	0.0671***	0.0635***	
		(0.00)	(0.01)	(0.01)	(0.01)	
AGE^2		-0.000733***	-0.000962***	-0.000787***	-0.000752***	
		(0.00)	(0.00)	(0.00)	(0.00)	
WHITE			0.0518	-0.0247	-0.0405*	
			(0.03)	(0.02)	(0.02)	
LITERATE			0.146***			0.0503
			(0.04)			(0.03)
OBSERVATION	Y	Y	Y	Y	Y	Y
YEAR EFFECTS	Y	Y	Y	Y	Y	Y
CIA EFFECT	Y	Y	Y	Y	Y	Y
APPRENTICE	Y	Y	Y	Y	Y	Y
CONSTANT	6.068***	5.004***	4.688***	4.933***	4.987***	6.056***
	(0.05)	(0.09)	(0.16)	(0.10)	(0.10)	(0.10)
OBS.	4,457	4,433	1,263	3,393	3,435	1,641
R2	0.42	0.47	0.43	0.39	0.37	0.55

Source: Wages as reported in Ball, "Prices, Wages, and the Cost of Living."
Note: Dependent variable is natural log of real wage. Base is an entering unskilled Brazilian male worker at Paulista in 1920. Cia effect reflects whether a series of dummy variables for each company was included in the calculation. Reporting b/(se).
* p<0.05.
** p<0.01.
*** p<0.001.

Table B.3. Determinants of Paulistano real wage, 1891–1913

Variable	(1)	(2)	(3)	(4)	(5)	(6)
NATIONALITY						
Portuguese	0.0442	-0.041	-0.0415	-0.0347		
	(0.03)	(0.03)	(0.04)	(0.03		
Italian	0.135**	-0.00227	-0.0164	0.0075		
	(0.05)	(0.04)	(0.06)	(0.05)		
Spanish	0.00654	-0.0829	-0.0209	-0.067		
	(0.07)	(0.06)	(0.12)	(0.06)		
German	0.482**	0.0959		0.108		
	(0.17)	(0.15)		(0.15)		
Russian	0.438***	0.259**		0.269**		
	(0.09)	(0.08)		(0.08)		
Polish	0.464***	0.149	-0.121	0.151		
	(0.14)	(0.13)	(0.15)	(0.13)		
British	-0.424	-0.295		-0.284		
	(0.35)	(0.32)		(0.32)		
Other	0.302	0.546***		0.549***		
	(0.26)	(0.07)		(0.06)		
FEMALE						
Age		0.118***	0.125***	0.118***		
		(0.01)	(0.02)	(0.01)		
AGE²		-0.00164***	-0.00176***	-0.00165***		
		(0.00)	(0.00)	(0.00)		
WHITE				-0.0218		-0.0496
				(0.03)		(0.03)
LITERATE			0.0779			
			(0.07)			
OBSERVATION	Y	Y	Y	Y	Y	Y
YEAR EFFECTS	Y	Y	Y	Y	Y	Y
CIA EFFECT	Y	Y	Y	Y	Y	Y
APPRENTICE	Y	Y	Y	Y	Y	Y
SKILL-LEVEL	Y	Y	Y	Y	Y	Y
CONSTANT	6.915***	5.221***	5.456***	5.227***	6.931***	6.971***
	(0.11)	(0.17)	(0.31)	(0.18)	(0.11)	(0.11)
N	1,211	1,197	402	1,195	1,554	1,211
R2	0.4	0.49	0.61	0.5	0.35	0.38

Source: Wages as reported in Ball, "Prices, Wages, and the Cost of Living."
Note: Dependent variable is natural log of real wage. Base is an entering unskilled Brazilian male worker at Paulista in 1920. Cia effect reflects whether a series of dummy variables for each company was included in the calculation. Reporting b/(se).
* $p < 0.05$.
** $p < 0.01$.
*** $p < 0.001$.

Table B.4. Determinants of Paulistano real wage, 1914–1930

Variable	(1)	(2)	(3)	(4)	(5)	(6)
NATIONALITY						
Portuguese	-0.106***	-0.160***	-0.0709**	-0.200***		
	(0.02)	(0.02)	(0.02	(0.02)		
Italian	0.0128	-0.0600**	-0.0256	-0.0852**		
	(0.02)	(0.02)	(0.04)	(0.03)		
Spanish	0.0128	-0.0354	-0.00708	-0.0569		
	(0.03)	(0.03)	(0.04)	(0.04)		
German	0.159***	0.0957*	0.0176	0.428***		
	(0.03)	(0.04)	(0.07)	(0.05)		
Russian	0.293***	0.0982*	0.061	0.0996*		
	(0.06)	(0.07)	(0.05)	(0.05)		
Polish	-0.128*	-0.210**	-0.198***	-0.193**		
	(0.06)	(0.07)	(0.05)	(0.07)		
British	0.132	0.142		0.132		
	(0.12)	(0.11)		(0.10)		
Other	0.0993***	0.0361	0.0676	0.323**		
	(0.03)	(0.03)	(0.08)	(0.11)		
FEMALE	-0.346***	-0.256***	-0.227***	-0.496***	-0.340***	
	(0.05)	(0.04)	(0.04)	(0.11)	(0.05)	
AGE		0.0443***	0.0556***	0.0434***		
		(0.01)	(0.01)	(0.01)		
AGE^2		-0.000498***	-0.000708***	-0.000475***		
		(0.00)	(0.00)	(0.00)		
WHITE				-0.0266		-0.0626**
				(0.02)		(0.02)
LITERATE			0.0739**			
			(0.03)			
OBSERVATION	Y	Y	Y	Y	Y	Y
YEAR EFFECTS	Y	Y	Y	Y	Y	Y
CIA EFFECT	Y	Y	Y	Y	Y	Y
APPRENTICE	Y	Y	Y	Y	Y	Y
SKILL-LEVEL	Y	Y	Y	Y	Y	Y
CONSTANT	5.997***	5.226***	5.102***	5.238***	5.982***	5.985***
	(0.08)	(0.11)	(0.16)	(0.14)	(0.07)	(0.08)
N	3,246	3,236	1,237	2,198	3,962	2,224
R2	0.47	0.5	0.64	0.36	0.45	0.31

Source: Wages as reported in Ball, "Prices, Wages, and the Cost of Living."
Note: Dependent variable is natural log of real wage. Base is an entering unskilled Brazilian male worker at Paulista in 1920. Cia effect reflects whether a series of dummy variables for each company was included in the calculation. Reporting b/(se).
* p<0.05.
** p<0.01.
*** p<0.001.

Table B.5. Likelihood Paulistano worker is a mechanic or unskilled worker, 1891–1930

Dependent variable	Mechanic				Unskilled			
Independent variable	(1)	(2)	(3)	(4)	(1)	(2)	(3)	(4)
NATIONALITY								
Portuguese	-0.287*	-0.655**			1.262***	1.238***	1.351***	1.455***
	(0.14)	(0.25)			(0.13)	(0.20)	(0.16)	(0.26)
Italian	0.354*	0.804**			-0.0341	-0.526*	0.386	-0.133
	(0.16)	(0.26)			(0.17)	(0.25)	(0.20)	(0.33)
Spanish	0.151	0.662			0.294	-0.21	0.36	-0.28
	(0.23)	(0.38)			(0.15)	(0.22)	(0.20)	(0.44)
German	0.698**	0.635			-0.72	-0.967	0.287	0
	(0.26)	(0.68)			(0.42)	(0.89)	(0.55)	(.)
Other	0.257	0.0719			-0.499*	-0.417	-0.683	-0.516
	(0.21)	(0.61)			(0.21)	(0.28)	(0.38)	(0.89)
FEMALE					-0.347**	-0.535***	-0.544**	-0.669
					(0.12)	(0.15)	(0.20)	(0.37)
AGE	-0.0164	0.0774	-0.0214	0.00754	-0.123***	-0.292***	-0.0521*	-0.0577
	(0.02)	(0.05)	(0.03)	(0.05)	(0.02)	(0.03)	(0.02)	(0.04)
AGE^2	-0.000105	-0.00154*	-0.0000302	-0.000703	0.00149***	0.00377***	0.000563	0.000561
	(0.00)	(0.00)	(0.00)	(0.00)	(0.00)	(0.00)	(0.00)	(0.00)

	(1)	(2)	(3)	(4)	(5)	(6)	(7)
WHITE		-0.213	-0.0286			-0.362**	-0.401
		(0.14)	(.25)			(0.13)	(0.22)
LITERATE	1.166***		0.742		-0.798***		-1.020***
	(0.35)		(0.49)		(0.14)		(0.26)
OBSERVATION	Y	Y	Y	Y	Y	Y	Y
YEAR EFFECTS	Y	Y	Y	Y	Y	Y	Y
CIA EFFECT	Y	Y	Y	Y	Y	Y	Y
SKILL LEVEL	Y	Y	Y	Y	Y	Y	Y
CONSTANT	-3.516***	-0.864	-1.921	1.538***	5.415***	0.626	1.977*
	(0.90)	(0.56)	(1.09)	(0.40)	(0.72)	(0.48)	(0.90)
N	2,173	3,742	1,362	5,494	2,199	3,938	1,322
PSEUDO R2	0.21	0.1	0.14	0.13	0.21	0.15	0.23
AIC	1,567.2	3,280.9	1,201.5	5,336	2,079.3	3,764.6	1,128.1
BIC	1,896.8	3,667	1,472.7	5,765.8	2,375.5	4,172.7	1,392.6

Source: Wages as reported in Ball, "Prices, Wages, and the Cost of Living."

Note: Base is a Brazilian male hired at Paulista in 1920. Reporting b/(se). Mechanics include workers coded by HISCO spanning from 72000 and 72999 and 83000 and 87999. Unskilled workers include day laborers and spinners coded as HISCO 99910 and 75220. Results for Russian, Polish, and British workers were included but not reported due to small sample size and statistical insignificance. Cia effect reflects whether a series of dummy variables for each company was included in the calculation. Reporting coefficients and standard errors.

* p<0.05.

** p<0.01.

*** p<0.001.

Table B.6. Determinants of Paulistano worker likelihood of being a mechanic, wartime changes

Variable	1891–1913			1914–1930			
	(1)	(2)	(3)	(1)	(2)	(3)	(4)
NATIONALITY							
Portuguese		-2.018**	-0.727**		-0.449	0.233	-0.266
		(0.63)	(0.22)		(0.26)	(0.20)	(0.34)
Italian		0.544	0.598*		0.957***	0.455	0.998*
		(0.50)	(0.29)		(0.29)	(0.27)	(0.40)
Spanish		1.013	0.191		0.34	0.626*	0.485
		(0.76)	(0.39)		(0.38)	(0.31)	(0.46)
German					0.537	0.823	
					(0.68)	(0.57)	
Polish		2.249	3.749**				
		(1.95)	(1.23)				
British			2.905**			-0.0658	
			(1.06)			(1.37)	
Other			3.183***		0.00162	0.904	2.261**
			(0.82)		(0.59)	(0.83)	(0.86)
AGE	-0.207*	-0.214*	-0.196***	0.226*	0.253***	0.0722	0.224*
	(0.09)	(0.09)	(0.06)	-2.39	(0.06)	(0.05)	(0.10)
AGE²	0.00227	0.00222	0.00272**	-0.00369**	-0.00396***	-0.00131	-0.00372**
	(0.00)	(0.00)	(0.00)	(0.00)	(0.00)	(0.00)	(0.00)

WHITE	-0.241		-0.306	-0.0333		-0.366*	-0.171
	(0.37)		(0.22)	(0.29)		(0.17)	(0.31)
LITERATE	0.389	0.282		0.894	1.332***		1.034
	(0.66)	(0.66)		(0.54)	(0.35)		(0.59)
OBSERVATION	Y	Y	Y	Y	Y	Y	Y
YEAR EFFECTS	Y	Y	Y	Y	Y	Y	Y
CIA EFFECT	Y	Y	Y	Y	Y	Y	Y
CONSTANT	2.16	2.601	0.961	-5.457**	-6.621***	-1.802*	-5.634**
	(1.50)	(1.47)	(0.96)	(1.90)	(1.31)	(0.87)	(1.92)
N	373	365	1,120	986	1,798	2,565	963
PSEUDO R2	0.13	0.19	0.1	0.17	0.24	0.14	0.19
AIC	398.3	376.4	1,105.5	794.4	1,160.6	2,079.8	773.7
BIC	504.2	493.4	1,306.3	970.6	1,385.8	2,348.9	968.5

Source: Wages as reported in Ball, "Prices, Wages, and the Cost of Living."

Note: Dependent variable is whether worker is a mechanic. Mechanics include workers coded by HISCO spanning from 72000 and 72999 and 83000 and 87999. Base is a Brazilian male hired at Paulista in 1900 for pre-war period and 1920 for 1914–1930 period. Reporting b/(se). Results for Russian workers not reported due to small sample size and statistical insignificance. Cia effect reflects whether a series of dummy variables for each company was included in the calculation. Reporting coefficients and standard errors.

* $p<0.05$.
** $p<0.01$.
*** $p<0.001$.

Table B.7. Determinants of Paulistano worker likelihood of being an unskilled worker, wartime changes

Variable	1891–1913			1914–1930			
	(1)	(2)	(3)	(1)	(2)	(3)	(4)
NATIONALITY							
Portuguese		2.548***	1.523***		0.874***	1.260***	0.818**
		(0.48)	(0.23)		(0.23)	(0.21)	(0.31)
Italian		0.0895	0.544		-0.803**	0.247	-0.549
		(0.49)	(0.28)		(0.29)	(0.28)	(0.44)
Spanish		1.368	0.841**		-0.234	0.0992	-0.661
		(0.79)	(0.32)		(0.23)	(0.28)	(0.57)
German			0.574		-1.031	0.105	
			(1.18)		(0.94)	(0.54)	
Other					-0.386	-0.549	-0.593
					(0.29)	(0.37)	(0.85)
AGE	0.136	0.123	0.173**	-0.148***	-0.389***	-0.148***	-0.154***
	(0.11)	(0.11)	(0.06)	(0.04)	(0.03)	(0.03)	(0.05)
AGE^2	-0.00188	-0.00153	-0.00269*	0.00177***	0.00502***	0.00172***	0.00180**
	(0.00)	(0.00)	(0.00)	(0.00)	(0.00)	(0.00)	(0.00)
FEMALE				-0.65	-0.597***	-0.587**	-0.653
				(0.35)	(0.15)	(0.19)	(0.35)

	(1)	(2)	(3)	(4)	(5)	(6)	(7)
WHITE	0.0272		-0.383*	-0.00995		-0.305	-0.15
	(0.31)		(0.18)	(0.27)		(0.17)	(0.28)
LITERATE	-1.818***	-1.814**		-0.980***	-0.809***		-0.954**
	(0.53)	(0.67)		(0.28)	(0.15)		(0.29)
OBSERVATION	Y	Y	Y	Y	Y	Y	Y
YEAR EFFECTS	Y	Y	Y	Y	Y	Y	Y
CIA EFFECT	Y	Y	Y	Y	Y	Y	Y
CONSTANT	-0.392	-1.886	-2.116*	3.541***	7.223***	2.095***	3.589***
	(1.87)	(1.81)	(0.90)	(1.04)	(0.91)	(0.57)	(1.03)
N	369	356	1,159	975	1,821	2,754	949
PSEUDO R2	0.2	0.32	0.19	0.17	0.23	0.12	0.19
AIC	417.5	358	1,280.3	766.1	1,634.9	2,427.2	747.6
BIC	515.3	462.6	1,467.4	917.4	1,833.1	2,675.9	917.6

Source: Wages as reported in Ball, "Prices, Wages, and the Cost of Living."

Note: Dependent variables is whether worker is an unskilled worker. Unskilled workers include day laborers and spinners coded as HISCO 99910 and 75220. Base is a Brazilian male hired at Paulista in 1900 for the prewar period and in 1920 for the 1914–1930 period. Reporting b/(se). Results for Russian, Polish, and British workers were included but not reported due to small sample size and statistical insignificance. Cia effect reflects whether a series of dummy variables for each company was included in the calculation. Reporting coefficients and standard errors.

* p<0.05.

** p<0.01.

*** p<0.001.

Table B.8. Determinants of likelihood of being hired as mechanic by company, São Paulo Old Republic

Variable	Paulista			Light		Jafet	
	(1)	(2)	(3)	(1)	(2)	(1)	(2)
NATIONALITY							
Portuguese	-0.0776	-0.618	-0.545	-0.820***	-0.983*	0.671	1.231
	(0.16)	(0.33)	(0.34)	(0.24)	(0.42)	(0.82)	(1.03)
Italian	0.526*	0.818*	0.904**	0.0877	0.592	0.133	1.073
	(0.22)	(0.33)	(0.35)	(0.23)	(0.50)	(0.57)	(0.70)
Spanish	0.482	0.960*	1.005*	-0.678	-0.684	-0.35	0.555
	(0.27)	(0.43)	(0.43)	(0.40)	(0.74)	(0.64)	(0.6)
German	0.00548			0.630*	1.163		
	(0.41)			(0.32)	(0.95)		
Polish	2.413	0.661	0.768				
	(1.36)	(1.53)	(1.49)				
British	1.152						
	(0.99)						
Other	3.174***	3.169***	3.330***	0.0232	-0.259	-0.76	0.579
	(0.51)	(0.63)	(0.68)	(0.24)	(0.83)	(1.11)	(1.25)
AGE	-0.0909**	-0.0834	-0.0902	-0.0256	0.273	0.348**	0.304*
	(0.03)	(0.06)	(0.06)	(0.05)	(0.15)	(0.11)	(0.12)
AGE^2	0.000553	0.0003	0.000347	-0.000149	-0.00477*	-0.00433*	-0.00348
	(0.00)	(0.00)	(0.00)	(0.00)	(0.00)	(0.00)	(0.00)

	(1)	(2)	(3)	(4)	(5)	(6)	(7)
EXPERIENCE	0.000372***	0.000472***	0.000484***				
	(0.00)	(0.00)	(0.00)				
EXPERIENCE^2	-1.73e-08*	-3.67e-08***	-3.73e-08***				
	(0.00)	(0.00)	(0.00)				
EDUCATION LEVEL		-0.0495	-0.0321				
		(0.12)	(0.12)				
WHITE			-0.241				
			(0.27)				
LITERATE					0.882		2.676***
					(0.52)		(0.69)
YEAR EFFECT	Y	Y	Y	Y	Y	Y	Y
CONSTANT	-0.519	-0.633	-0.38	-0.0395	-5.492*	-10.41***	-10.84***
	(0.57)	(1.01)	(1.05)	(0.76)	(2.15)	(1.57)	(1.83)
N	3,118	1,160	1,160	821	188	1,163	702
PSEUDO R2	0.06	0.12	0.12	0.07	0.12	0.14	0.25
AIC	3,098.6	1,125.5	1,125.9	1,047.6	245.5	212.8	150.1
BIC	3,400.8	1,337.9	1,343.3	1,108.8	287.5	293.7	218.5

Source: Wages as reported in Ball, "Prices, Wages, and the Cost of Living."

Note: Dependent variable is whether worker is a mechanic. Mechanics include workers coded by HISCO spanning from 72000 and 72999 and 83000 and 87999. Base is a Brazilian male hired in 1920. Results for Russian workers were included but not reported due to small sample size and statistical insignificance. Reporting coefficients and standard errors.

* p<0.05.

** p<0.01.

*** p<0.001.

Table B.9. Determinants of likelihood of being hired as unskilled worker by company, São Paulo Old Republic

Variable	Paulista			Light		Jafet		
	(1)	(2)	(3)	(1)	(2)	(1)	(2)	(3)
NATIONALITY								
Portuguese	1.153***	1.176***	1.278***	1.408***	1.450***	0.268	-0.0394	0.597
	(0.16)	(0.24)	(0.26)	(0.24)	(0.41)	(0.36)	(0.42)	(0.55)
Italian	0.232	-0.329	-0.205	-0.925*	-0.595	-0.340	-0.825	0.534
	(0.21)	(0.33)	(0.34)	(0.42)	(0.59)	(0.41)	(0.50)	(0.58)
Spanish	0.538*	0.174	0.196	1.428***	1.263	0.136	-0.0909	0.276
	(0.23)	(0.59)	(0.61)	(0.37)	(0.68)	(0.25)	(0.31)	(0.39)
German	0.516	0	0	-2.191*	-1.548	0.274	-0.0381	0.553
	(0.97)	(.)	(.)	(1.04)	(1.40)	(0.62)	(1.15)	(0.71)
Other	0	0	0	-0.286	1.117	-0.497	-0.655	-0.336
	(.)	(.)	(.)	(0.34)	(0.70)	(0.29)	(0.40)	(0.43)
AGE	0.0889**	0.141**	0.138*	0.130	-0.122	-0.703***	-0.770***	-0.741***
	(0.03)	(0.05)	(0.05)	(0.09)	(0.13)	(0.07)	(0.09)	(0.10)
AGE^2	-0.000573	-0.00180*	-0.00183*	-0.00189	0.00218	0.00909***	0.00965***	0.0101***
	(0.00)	(0.00)	(0.00)	(0.00)	(0.00)	(0.00)	(0.00)	(0.00)
EXPERIENCE	-0.000664***	-0.000807***	-0.000797***					
	(0.00)	(0.00)	(0.00)					
EXPERIENCE^2	2.57e-08***	6.28e-08***	6.28e-08***					
	(0.00)	(0.00)	(0.00)					

	(1)	(2)	(3)	(4)	(5)	(6)	(7)
Education Level	-0.865***	-0.838***					
	(0.13)	(0.13)					
Female					-0.745***	-0.884***	-0.824***
					(0.16)	(0.20)	(.24)
White		-0.320					-0.865
		(0.21)					(0.49)
Literate				-1.705**		-0.815***	
				(0.53)		(0.19)	
Year	Y	Y	Y	Y	Y	Y	Y
Constant	-2.573***	-1.201	-3.264*	2.903	7.482***	9.457***	10.89***
	(0.54)	(1.06)	(1.31)	(1.90)	(1.04)	(1.31)	(1.45)
N	3,323	1,215	850	190	1,304	856	594
PseudoR2	0.18	0.27	0.15	0.17	0.3	0.36	0.29
AIC	2,991.4	919.6	704.9	239.3	1,155.3	721.7	539.3
BIC	3,284.6	1,128.8	766.6	281.5	1,258.8	821.5	609.5

Source: Wages as reported in Ball, "Prices, Wages, and the Cost of Living."

Note: Dependent variable is whether worker is an unskilled worker. Unskilled workers include day laborers and spinners coded as HISCO 99910 and 75220. Base is a Brazilian male hired in 1920. Results for Russian, Polish, and British workers were included but not reported due to small sample size and statistical insignificance. Reporting coefficients and standard errors.

* p<0.05.

** p<0.01.

*** p<0.001.

Table B.10. Adult male and female Jafet employees, 1913–1929, by skill level and nationality

Gender	Worker	Skill level			
	Nationality	Unskilled	Low	Medium	Total
Men					
	Brazilian	27	139	18	184
		14.67	75.54	9.78	100
	Portuguese	2	8	2	12
		16.67	66.67	16.67	100
	Italian	6	29	6	41
		14.63	70.73	14.63	100
	Spanish	7	38	4	49
		14.29	77.55	8.16	100
	German	1	3	0	4
		25.00	75.00	0	100
	Other	6	29	2	37
		16.22	78.38	5.41	100
	Total	49	246	32	327
		14.98	75.23	9.79	100
Women					
	Brazilian	38	317	1	356
		10.67	89.04	0.28	100
	Portuguese	5	25	0	30
		16.67	83.33	0	100
	Italian	12	49	0	61
		19.67	80.33	0	100
	Spanish	5	71	0	76
		6.58	93.42	0	100
	German	1	7	0	8
		12.50	87.50	0	100
	Other	4	45	0	49
		8.16	91.84	0	100
	Total	65	514	1	580
		11.21	88.62	0.17	100

Source: Jafet portion of wage database outlined in Ball, "Prices, Wages, and the Cost of Living."
Note: Considers workers ages sixteen and older. Most records recorded from the 1921–1929. Numbers and shares are reported.

Table B.11. Newspaper help-wanted ads for unskilled jobs, 1890–1925

Year	Number	Discriminatory	Boa aparência
1890	10	1	
1891	9	2	
1892	12	0	
1893	6	1	
1894	4	0	
1895	3	0	
1896	6	2	
1897	8	2	
1898	2	0	
1899	7	3	
1900	2	0	
1901	3	0	
1902	4	0	
1903	4	1	
1904	1	0	
1905	0	0	
1906	2	0	
1907	1	0	
1908	1	0	
1909	2	0	
1910	6	2	
1911	4	1	
1912	4	1	
1913	14	1	
1914	17	2	
1915	5	1	
1916	9	1	
1917	12	3	
1918	6	0	
1919	10	1	
1920	9	2	
1921	8	1	1
1922	3	0	
1923	8	2	1
1924	3	1	
1925	12	1	

Source: Wanted advertisement counts from the *Estado de São Paulo* on the second Sundays of January and July, 1890–1925. Only 14 July 1918 is missing from the archives, possibly due to the Spanish flu. Even the 13 July 1924 issued during the Tenente Revolt includes an ad. "Discriminatory" refers to advertisements for white or immigrant applicants. Boa aparência also includes ads specifying "boa apresentação." Boa aparência and apresentação are considered in the counts of preferences for white or European workers.

Notes

Introduction. Living at the Margins

1. Translations are mine unless otherwise indicated. A *carta de chamada* is a letter requesting someone to come to Brazil, as part of the immigration process. Many chamadas, such as this one from Manoel Teixeira to his mother, remain in the state archive. His letter was found with a list of arriving passengers; the date his mother arrived in Brazil is not shown. She likely passed through the main immigrant receiving station, the Hospedaria de Imigrantes de São Paulo, although she might have arrived in the city directly. Chamada A0000776, Cartas de Chamada, Memória do Imigrante, Arquivo Público do Estado de São Paulo (APESP), São Paulo (hereafter cited as chamada and number). The number provides a unique identifier for the digitized image of each letter in the archive (http://www.org.br/acervodigital/upload/cartas/MI_CC[chamadanumber]X.pdf).

2. "A situação europea," "Senado Federal," "O café," "Notícias diversas," *Estado de São Paulo* 4 July 1916, 1–6.

3. The use of "Paulistano" and "Paulistana" draws on the gendered nature of Portuguese, in which all nouns have a gender. Most adjectives, thus, likewise end in "a," "as," "o," or "os" in accordance with the gender of the noun.

4. These terms were constructed identities, and individuals may not have seen themselves as Paulistas or Paulistanos at the time. However, I consider these terms useful in distinguishing the process by which migrants and immigrants became or worked to become successful in the city.

5. In a few cases immigrants are described as "pardo," but given the social networks of the times, their experiences more likely conformed to national group expectations than to racial expectations. Paulina Alberto prefers "black" to refer to the collective *pardo* and *preto* experience (*Terms of Inclusion*, 22).

6. For examples of scholars achieving this concert, see Hanley, *Public Good and the Brazilian State*; Lamounier, *Ferrovias e mercado de trabalho no Brasil*; Lurtz, "Insecure Labor, Insecure Debt"; Zimmerman, "As Pertaining to the Female Sex."

7. See Luna and Klein, *Economic and Demographic History of São Paulo*, for a recent compendium and excellent aggregate approach.

8. Adamo, "Broken Promise"; Andrews, *Blacks and Whites in São Paulo*; Blay, *Eu não tenho onde morar*; Decca, *A vida fora das fábricas*; Ribeiro, *Condições de trabalho*; Veccia, "Family and Factory"; Weinstein, *For Social Peace*; Wolfe, *Working Women, Working Men*.

Some precursors include Cano, *Raízes da concentração industrial em São Paulo*; Fausto, *Trabalho urbano e conflito social*; Hall, "Origins of Mass Immigration to Brazil"; Lobo et al., "Evolução dos preços"; Maram, *Anarquistas, imigrantes*. Scholarship outside of Brazilian history has followed a similar trajectory: DeShazo, *Urban Workers and Labor Unions in Chile*; Mallon, *Defense of Community in Peru's Central Highland*; Winn, *Weavers of Revolution*; and Daniel James, *Resistance and Integration*.

9. Even outside of labor and economic history, scholarship is often divided by World War I. For predominantly postwar studies, see Americano, *São Paulo nesse tempo*; Besse, *Restructuring Patriarchy*; Blay, *Eu não tenho onde morar*; Dávila, *Diploma of Whiteness*; Maram, *Anarquistas, imigrantes*; Wolfe, *Working Women, Working Men*. Studies of the earlier period include Fausto, *Crime e cotidiano* and *Trabalho urbano e conflito social*; Greenfield, "Challenge of Growth"; Hanley, *Native Capital*; M. Pinto, *Cotidiano e sobrevivência*.

10. Fogel's *Railroads and American Economic Growth* and Fogel and Engerman's *Time on the Cross* serve as good examples of the new economic history approach. Fogel and North won the 1993 Nobel Prize in economics for their work in economic history, in particular Fogel's application of new economic history, North's "Institutions," and North and Weingast's "Constitutions and Commitment." Nathaniel Leff was one of the first to embrace a new economic history approach for Brazil in his 1980 book, *Underdevelopment and Development in Brazil*, approaching sweeping macroeconomic claims espoused by Werner Baer, E. Bradford Burns, Gunder Frank, Celso Furtado, and Caio Prado Júnior. For a succinct introduction to dependency theory and new economic history as well as a strong critique of dependency theorists, see Stephen Haber's introduction to *How Latin America Fell Behind*. Edited volumes typifying a data-driven and new economic history approach include Bértola and Ocampo, *Economic Development of Latin America since Independence*; Coatsworth and Taylor, *Latin America and the World Economy since 1800*; Haber, *How Latin America Fell Behind*; Hatton and Williamson, *Migration and the International Labor Market*. Some recent Latin American scholarship that espouses this approach can be found in proceedings of the sixth annual Latin American Congress of Economic History, http://www.cladhe6.usach.cl/.

11. Peixoto-Mehrtens, *Urban Space and National Identity*, 3.

12. Alberto, *Terms of Inclusion*; Bocketti, *Invention of the Wonderful Game*; Chazkel, *Laws of Chance*; Guzmán, *Native and National in Brazil*; Miller, *The Street Is Ours*; Roth, *Miscarriage of Justice*; Weinstein, *Color of Modernity*. Ramatis Jacino's *Transição e exclusão* continues in the tradition of George Reid Andrews (*Blacks and Whites in São Paulo*) but also falls into a black/white binary. Economic histories include works by Aldo Musacchio (*Experiments in Financial Democracy*), William Summerhill (*Inglorious Revolution*), and Gail Triner (*Mining and the State*). The trend away from economic history extends beyond Brazilian history and is consistent for the region as a whole. Leon Fink's edited volume, *Workers across the Americas*, demonstrates how labor history is evolving, but new economic history methods are absent from its bibliography despite the contributors' similar questions of transnational migration and labor markets.

13. On silences, see Fuentes, *Dispossessed Lives*.

14. Wage inequality research is particularly instructive in this book, such as Boustan, *Competition in the Promised Land*; Goldin, *Understanding the Gender Gap*; Margo and Villaflor, "Growth of Wages in Antebellum America."

15. Various chapters in *Gender Inequalities and Development in Latin America*, edited by Camou, Maubrigades, and Thorp, address the link between education, fertility, and development for women in Latin America. Most research in the volume, however, concentrates on the post–1930 period.

16. In "Forging an Urban Public," Aiala Teresa Levy notes a particular appeal to family in Paulistano theater: "Families were on many occasions welcomed as audiences of performances explicitly deemed appropriate for all children, women and men" (192–193). São Paulo concentrated family migration, but even in other urban centers with more single, male immigrants, the nuclear family continued to constitute an important institution during this early urbanization phase.

17. Documentary evidence from Brazil during this period lends itself to the foreigner/Brazilian binary, as few records distinguish between immigrant groups. Holloway, in *Immigrants on the Land*, and to a certain extent Francisco Luna and Herbert Klein, in *Economic and Demographic History of São Paulo*, distinguish between groups but largely for the state's agricultural hinterlands or the state as a whole, not the capital itself. The relative absence of race information in official statistics has led to increased interest in recapturing these differences. Andrews's *Blacks and Whites in São Paulo* provides a good overview of these trends through the 1980s, and Alberto, in *Terms of Inclusion*, highlights important shifts in scholarship since the 1980s. Both scholars, although they differentiate between *pardo* and *preto*, would lump Teixeira into a "white" category.

18. Luna and Klein, *Slavery and the Economy of São Paulo*, 16–21. The authors describe the city's location as offering "good, open grazing lands in an otherwise dense and inhospitable forest, and [the city] enjoyed a temperate climate, good rivers that penetrated into the backlands, and high grounds that permitted a defensive settlement" (15).

19. Kuznesof, "Role of Merchants in the Economic Development," 575–576. For more on the city's early history, see also Morse, *From Community to Metropolis*, 2–19; Kuznesof, *Household Economic and Urban Development*; Slenes, *Na senzala, uma flor*. The population of the capital region was larger, reaching 58,083 in 1817 and 72,248 in 1836. The male-to-female ratio of the enslaved population was 1.1 (Luna and Klein, *Slavery and the Economy of São Paulo*, 108–109, 111, 143).

20. Bethell and Carvalho, "1822–1850," 85. Coffee accounted for 40 percent of Brazilian export earnings by 1840 and more than half by 1850.

21. Holloway, *Immigrants on the Land*, chapter 2.

22. Bértola and Ocampo, *Economic Development of Latin America*, chapter 3. The authors note some variation by region; in the Southern Cone, World War I largely marked a slowdown in the export-led growth period.

23. For an introduction to labor organization in the region, see Greenfield and Maram, *Latin American Labor Organizations*. In movement to commodity centers, the United Fruit Company provides another clear example of a convergence of migration and exploitive labor practices.

24. Dom Pedro I would abdicate the Brazilian throne in 1831, leaving his five-year-old son, Dom Pedro II, as emperor of Brazil.

25. R. Ferreira, "Suppression of the Slave Trade," 313. Even in Cuba, where historically the enslaved came from diverse ethnic origins, the share from Portuguese Africa represented almost 69 percent of slave purchases after 1850 (Grandío Moraguez, "African

Origins of Slaves Arriving in Cuba," 184). Those estimations are based on the *Transatlantic Slave Trade Database 2*, now part of the larger Slave Voyages website, which includes both the transatlantic and inter-American slave trade databases (https://www.slavevoyages.org/).

26. Slavery persisted in Puerto Rico and Cuba, which were Spanish colonies, until 1873 and 1886, respectively. Even countries with relatively late abolition, Paraguay (1869) and Bolivia (1861), had Afro-descended populations below 10 percent of their national totals.

27. E. Costa, *Brazilian Empire*, chapter 5, and *Da senzala à colônia*, chapter 2; Lesser, *Negotiating National Identity*, chapter 2; Luebke, *Germans in the New World*; chapters 6, 7, 8; Siriani, *Uma São Paulo alemã*, chapters 3, 4. Other immigrant groups, such as Swiss and Russians, came during this period, but their immigrant share was not large enough to constitute an ethnic group.

28. Emilia da Costa, in *Da senzala à colônia*, sees the timing of São Paulo's rise while slavery's viability waned as integral to the state leading Brazil's transition into industrialization and capitalism.

29. Brazil was relatively stable compared to other Latin American countries and did not default on its sovereign debts (Summerhill, *Inglorious Revolution*, 20–25). Abolishing the slave trade also facilitated foreign loans.

30. Holloway *Immigrants on the Land*, 15–25; Summerhill, *Order against Progress*, 60. Railways were also less susceptible to spills and robberies. As in Mexico and Argentina, Brazil's transition from mule to rail transport was a key step toward world market integration. On Mexico, see Coatsworth, "Indispensable Railroads in a Backward Economy." Alfonso Herranz-Locán, in "Role of Railways in Export-Led Growth," shows minimal impact in Uruguay.

31. Lamounier, *Ferrovías e mercado de trabalho no Brasil*, 80.

32. Stein, *Brazilian Cotton Manufacture*.

33. Hanley, *Native Capital*, 46.

34. Morse, *From Community to Metropolis*, 230.

35. Work on credible financial commitments pulls from North and Weingast, "Constitutions and Commitment." In addition, Brazil developed shareholder protections and limited liability to continue to attract investors. On capital markets see Hanley, *Native Capital*; Musacchio, *Experiments in Financial Democracy*; Summerhill, *Inglorious Revolution*; Triner, *Banking and Economic Development*. Warren Dean, in *Industrialization of São Paulo*, also points to the importance of capital markets in Brazil.

36. On immigration investment, see Pérez Meléndez, "Business of Peopling."

37. Shares were highest for the Comarcas of Bananal and Campinas, 41 and 38 percent, respectively. In the capital, 11 percent of the population was enslaved (Luna and Klein, *Economic and Demographic History of São Paulo*, 262–263).

38. Luna and Klein, *Slavery and the Economy of São Paulo*, 109–113.

39. The state came to support the immigration program, so it passed from private hands into the public sphere. Between 1882 and 1934, 2.3 million immigrants came to São Paulo. Argentina tried a similar program to bring in entire families, but it was largely unsuccessful (Baily, *Immigrants in the Lands of Promise*, 77–79).

40. On the cleavage between traditional agriculture and new industrial elites, see Font, *Coffee, Contention, and Change*; Woodard, *Place in Politics*.

41. Holloway, *Immigrants on the Land,* 36–45.

42. The Hospedaria processed arriving immigrants and migrants through 1978.

43. Francisco José de Oliveira Viana, an influential Brazilian intellectual and eugenicist, espoused a more pessimist view of Brazil's mixed past. For Latin America, Mexican intellectual writings such as Vasconcelos's *Raza cósmica* and Manuel Gamio's *Forjando patria* were some of the most influential.

44. Stepan, *Hour of Eugenics.*

45. In 1872, 35 percent of the city's population was registered as either *pardo* or *preto,* and 70 percent of the city's Afro-Brazilian population was free (Luna and Klein, *Economic and Demographic History of São Paulo,* 263).

46. In addition to large-scale European immigration to Argentina and Uruguay, this trend included migration to mining centers in Mexico. Migrant labor was also a key feature of United Fruit Company operations throughout the Caribbean and Central America.

47. See Nugent, *Crossings,* part 1, for discussion of continental effects and an explanation of the fertility transition. See his part 2 on European senders for country-specific effects.

48. See Nugent, *Crossings,* 110–114, for summary statistics on immigration to Argentina and 12–14 on European outmigration. Samuel Baily, in *Immigrants in the Lands of Promise,* offers a good comparison of Italians in New York City and Buenos Aires. Baily does mention São Paulo, San Francisco, and Toronto in his last chapter, but few international labor market studies include São Paulo.

49. Nugent, *Crossings,* 114. On the international labor market, see Lindert and Williamson's *Globalization and Inequality* and Hatton and Williamson's *Migration and the International Labor Market,* chapters 2–5. See Huberman's "Working Hours of the World Unite?" for a related paper on work hour convergence.

50. From 1906 to 1911 the name was the Official Agency of Colonization and Work (Holloway, *Immigrants on the Land,* 45–55). Immigrant disembarking stations existed in Kobe, Hamburg, and Genoa. Notable immigrant receiving stations in the Americas outside of Brazil included the Hotel de Imigrantes in Buenos Aires and Ellis Island in New York City. For a description of Argentina's less successful placement agency, see Baily, *Immigrants in the Lands of Promise,* 77–79. In Brazil, immigrant receiving stations included the Hospedaria da Ilha das Flores and Hospedaria dos Pinheiros in Rio de Janeiro; the Hospedaria da Pedra d'Água in Vitória, Espírito Santo; the Hospedaria de Imigrantes Pensador in Manaus; the Hospedaria Oficia de Rio Branco, Acre; the Hospedaria do Saco do Padre Inácio in Florianópolis, Santa Catarina; and the Hospedaria de Belo Horizonte, Minas Gerais (Paiva and Moura, *Hospedaria de Imigrantes de São Paulo,* 13–15).

51. Leff, in *Underdevelopment and Development in Brazil,* hypothesizes that the immigration system provided the elastic labor supply to São Paulo necessary for industrial and agricultural expansion. He does not, however, speak to a direct connection between the system and the urban labor market.

52. Vangelista, *Os braços da lavoura.* Additional evidence of a lack of transition to capitalism is that few technological changes occurred in coffee production through 1930.

53. Ball, "Prices, Wages, and the Cost of Living," 25–26.

54. Scholars have identified the importance of family organization in the city's early and late colonial history and in the imperial era (Metcalf, *Go-Betweens and the Coloniza-*

tion of Brazil). On the eighteenth and nineteenth centuries, see Dantas, "Picturing Families between Black and White"; Kuznesof, *Household Economic and Urban Development*; Slenes, *Na senzala, uma flor.*

55. See Premo, "Familiar: Thinking beyond Lineage," for colonial Spanish America. On colonial childhood see *Raising an Empire*, edited by González and Premo. Donna Guy, in *Sex and Danger in Buenos Aires*, highlights well the theoretical impact of Michel Foucault, Jacques Donzelot, and Benedict Anderson in her treatment of family (2–4).

56. An 1895–1896 study finds that "the nuclear social unit of Lima's society . . . was the extended family, which might range across all the class strata" (Joaquín Capelo, *Sociologia de Lima*, 3:258–264, quoted in Morse, "Latin American Cities," 483).

57. Moya takes this approach in *Cousins and Strangers*, his comprehensive study of Spaniards in Argentina. For immigrant-specific studies, see Freitas, *Presença portuguesa em São Paulo*; Lesser, *Negotiating National Identity*; Menezes, "A 'onda' emigratória de 1912"; Trento, *Do outro lado do Atlântico*. It is perhaps Penteado's *Belènzinho* that best provides an appreciation of immigrant diversity during the period.

58. Alberto, in *Terms of Inclusion*, provides a good overview of the tendency to focus on the black Brazilian experience in scholarship. Studies that focus on Afro-Brazilian opportunities often lump all immigrants together. Miki, in *Frontiers of Citizenship*, demonstrates how this focus has marginalized an understanding of Brazil's indigenous peoples.

59. Barbara Weinstein, in *Color of Modernity*, provides a good overview of this scholarship.

60. Bales, "Dual Labor Market of the Criminal Economy," 141.

61. Michael Wachter provides both a summary and critique of the debates in "Primary and Secondary Labor Markets" (637–680); R. A. Gordon, Michael J. Piore, and Robert Hall then provide comments and discussion (681–690). As Piore is a proponent of dual labor markets, his response is particularly insightful. On discrimination and dual labor markets, also see Piore, "Jobs and Training."

62. The persistence of nonstatistical discrimination in the prewar period, a time of relatively free trade, challenges Gary Becker's neoclassical theory (*Economics of Discrimination*) that free trade and deregulation will reduce discrimination. The divergence between the Portuguese and Afro-Brazilian experiences demonstrates that statistical discrimination cannot fully explain differences in labor-market opportunities (Figart, "Discrimination," 91–92). One key difference between the Paulistano experience and the theory is that some individuals, even Afro-Brazilians, were able to transition into good jobs.

63. For a summary of the different philosophical approaches economists take toward discrimination, see Figart, "Discrimination," 91–98. Of principal importance is the work by Martha Nussbaum and Amartya Sen. Within economics, Nussbaum and Sen pioneered "the capabilities approach" to labor markets and discrimination (*Quality of Life*). The Human Development Index (HDI), which considers life expectancy, education, and income indicators, has become an important measure of development.

64. The continual reliance on GDP per capita as a primary indicator can be attributed to both scant data and the persistent theoretical connection between GDP per capita and development. While often linked, there are clear limitations to a connection. Research presented in Camou, Maubrigades, and Thorp's *Gender Inequalities and Development in Latin America* pushes against this tendency.

65. In their introduction to *Gender Inequalities and Development in Latin America*, María Magdalena Camou, Silvana Maubrigades, and Rosemary Thorp call this a period of growth "aided by the retaining of an unequal and discriminatory culture in all its dimensions" (11). Stanley Engerman and Kenneth Sokoloff, in "Factor Endowments, Institutions, and Differential Paths," theorize that factor endowments played a key role in developing colonial inequalities that persisted to the modern period. So too have Darin Acemoglu, Simon Johnson, and James Robinson, in "Colonial Origins of Comparative Development," but in both works, GDP per capita is seen as a sign of development. Furthermore, if education and voting are two institutions requiring reforms to overcome historical inequality, the Paulistano case suggests exploration of alternative avenues.

66. See Bértola and Ocampo, *Economic Development of Latin America*, 32–43. For Latin America, where historical records are often scanty, existing historical human development indexes still rely more heavily on GDP per capita and demonstrate the period 1870–1929 as one of minimal advancement.

67. This is true in terms of ethnicity and race as well as gender. In race and ethnicity, there is a general colorism for the region as a whole where darker individuals (indigenous, Afro-descended, or mixed) face discrimination. In terms of gender, research on the later period shows that advancements in education did not necessarily translate into greater labor-market participation. One possible explanation is the persistent cultural pressure for women not to enter the formal labor market. In Brazil, this pressure became more prevalent after 1929.

68. Ball, "Prices, Wages, and the Cost of Living."

69. For additional description of the records see Andrews, *Blacks and Whites in São Paulo*, appendix C; Lanna, *Ferrovía, cidade e trabalhadores*. In addition to the wages, I matched workers' jobs to the Van Leeuwen, Maas, and Miles *HISCO* and Van Leeuwen and Maas *HISCLASS* classification schemes to facilitate comparing skill levels.

70. Scholars wanting to see the process behind the wage and price series formation may consult Ball, "Prices, Wages, and the Cost of Living."

71. This argument furthers one made Andrews, *Blacks and Whites in São Paulo*, refuting the Fernandes thesis.

72. Cardim's 1936 study (*Ensaio de analyse de factores económicos e financeiros*) offers prices for the period from 1913 through the end of the Old Republic, but there is no study of the earlier period. Roberto Simonsen, in *Brazil's Industrial Evolution*, also begins at 1914 (in Dean, *Industrialization of São Paulo*, 92).

73. Particularly useful are the Latin American Newspapers Database, the digitized *Estado de São Paulo* archive, and the multitude of newspapers available through Brazil's Biblioteca Nacional online *hermeroteca* (newspaper and periodical library).

74. Fay and Opal, *Urbanization without Growth*; Jedwab and Vollrath, "Urbanization without Growth in Historical Perspective." This finding conforms to a trend in new economic history in which development and growth occur in Brazil but fail to reach their full potential.

Chapter 1. Making an Immigrant City

1. Vampré, *São Paulo Futuro*, act 2, scene 1, lines 99–100.
2. US Department of Commerce, *Trade Directory of South America*, 1914, 210.

3. Samuel Baily draws parallels between São Paulo and San Francisco (*Immigrants in the Lands of Promise*, 222–231).

4. Alberto, *Terms of Inclusion*, 11; for historiographical discussion related to racial democracy, also see 13–17.

5. Freitas, *Presença portuguesa em São Paulo*; Klein, *Inmigración española en Brasil*; Lesser, *Negotiating National Identity*; Trento, *Do outro lado do Atlântico*; Sánchez-Alonso, "Those Who Left and Those Who Stayed Behind."

6. Studies that do consider immigrant differences within the state of São Paulo are largely restricted to the interior (Holloway, *Immigrants on the Land*; Luna and Klein, *Economic and Demographic History of São Paulo*).

7. Livros de registros de matrícula de entrada de imigrantes na Hospedaria de Imigrantes, Memória do Imigrante, online archive, Museu da Imigración do Estado de São Paulo, APESP, São Paulo, http://inci.org.br/acervodigital/livros.php (hereafter cited as registros). See appendix A.

8. Work on flexible labor markets and the impact on low-skilled workers supports this reading of the hospedaria (Autor and Houseman, "Do Temporary-Help Jobs Improve Labor Market Outcome").

9. Even a thorough 2018 examination of official statistics for the state leaves much to explore about the city's development (Luna and Klein, *Economic and Demographic History of São Paulo*, 192, 244, 245, 282).

10. Alberto, *Terms of Inclusion*, 9–13, 24–30; Skidmore, *Black into White*.

11. Full compensation for their voyages was provided for individuals over the age of eleven, half for children between the ages of seven and eleven, and a quarter for children between three and six, and passage was free for children younger than three (Holloway, *Immigrants on the Land*, 36–45).

12. Thomas Holloway describes the complexities of the system and its many transformations and nuances (*Immigrants on the Land*, 32–38, 74–77).

13. Spanish and Portuguese comprised 11 and 10 percent of immigrants, respectively, between 1887 and 1900 but 22 and 23 percent between 1901 and 1930 (Holloway, *Immigrants on the Land*, 43). In the registros, eastern Europeans included Lithuanians, Hungarians, and Russians.

14. Walter Nugent discusses continental effects and the fertility transition, which led to a demographic bulge (*Crossings*, 19–40).

15. Holloway notes how the *núcleo colonial* largely became a *viveiro* system, a ready labor supply for coffee plantation owners (*Immigrants on the Land*, 122–134).

16. In the first decade of the Old Republic, four of every five immigrants arriving in the state of São Paulo were subsidized. Holloway notes small populations of *colonos* compared to subsidized immigrants (*Immigrants on the Land*, 127). The share of unsubsidized immigrants increased, but the lavoura's importance remained. On *falta de braços*, see Holloway, *Immigrants on the Land*, 35; Vangelista, *Os braços da lavoura*, 125–139.

17. Stolcke, "Exploitation of Family Morality," 265–274.

18. Vangelista, *Os braços da lavoura*, chapter 3.

19. Discussion of project 107, *Camara de Deputados Annaes da Sessão Ordinaria de 1899*, 646, ALESP. State law 1045-C in 1906 allowed day laborers and workers.

20. See Lamounier, *Ferrovias e mercado de trabalho*, 40–45, on the transition from slave

to wage labor in railroad companies; 160–168, on contracts to bring in railway labor in the nineteenth century.

21. Luna and Klein, *Economic and Demographic History of São Paulo*, 264. On the neighborhood shares, see Brazil, *Recenseamento 1872*, 12:1–27. In Matosinhos Braz (Brás), 88 percent of the registered adult population was foreign-born, 47 percent of the neighborhood from Portugal (11).

22. Dean, *Industrialization of São Paulo*, 51; Morse, *From Community to Metropolis*, 175–177.

23. Villela and Suzigan, *Política do governo e crescimento da economia brasileira*, 259.

24. The Bom Retiro hospedaria operated from 1881 to 1888. Before it, the old Núcleo Colonial de Sant'Anna was a provisional hospedaria from 1877 to 1880 (Paiva and Moura, *Hospedaria de Imigrantes*, 20–21). In the Old Republic, the Bom Retiro hospedaria street name was Rua dos Imigrantes; today it is Rua José Paulino (Penteado, *Belènzinho*, 30). The original Bom Retiro building was torn down during the Old Republic.

25. A hygiene report stated that the new hospedaria's capacity was 4,000 individuals but that it often housed as many as 10,000 (Ernesto Tolle, Hygiene Report, 19 November 1912, box C07392, number 344, fol. 11, SA, APESP.)

26. Hospedaria de Imigrantes do Estado de São Paulo, plat no. MI_ICO_AMP_038 _001_001_001 (1908), Memória do Imigrante, APESP.

27. Holloway, *Immigrants on the Land*, 51–59.

28. Luna and Klein, *Economic and Demographic History of São Paulo*, 95–96.

29. *Relatório da Secretaria da Agricultura, Comércio e Obras Públicas*, São Paulo state (hereafter *RSA*), 1902, 166–167; 1904, 116–117. The "Movimento migratório" sections later appear in the "Departamento Estadual do Trabalho" portion of the annual report. State decrees 834 of 1900 and 1.227 of 1904, extend and affirm reentries.

30. A petition supporting the immigration of industrial workers passed the state legislature in 1906, allowing 5 percent of subsidized immigrants to be laborers, machine workers, and artisans (state law 1.045-C). State decree 1.458 of 1907 increased the share to 10 percent. By 1910, decree 1.921 extended the list of eligible trades to include carpenters, stoneworkers, and blacksmiths, although it returned the share to 5 percent.

31. Italians were estimated at 62 percent of incoming immigrants in the state, totaling 654,000 arrivals between 1894 and 1904. Holloway estimates that 310,000 workers were needed for coffee cultivation by 1909, creating a labor surplus ("Creating the Reserve Army?," 202). This leaves a surplus of labor. Roughly 510,000 Italians likely departed from Brazil, 26,195 stayed and became landowners, and about 32,600 remained in agricultural contracts; that leaves 84,857 arriving in São Paulo, a city whose 1900 population totaled 240,000 (Ball, "Inequality in São Paulo's Old Republic," 169–171).

32. The Prinetti Decree was absorbed into Italy's 1919 Immigration Law (Trento, *Do outro lado do Atlântico*, 52–53). The Crispi Decree stopped emigration from March 1889 to July 1891 (35–36; Cometti, "Italian Emigration," 821–824). Other countries instituted and considered emigration bans to Brazil (Lesser, *Immigration, Ethnicity, and National Identity*, 110).

33. Holloway, *Immigrants on the Land*, 54.

34. I translate *pedreiro* as "stoneworker" to reflect the multitude of skill levels the term

encompassed: cutting stones in a quarry, making bricks, working as a skilled mason, and being a *servente*, an assistant.

35. The family arrived on 18 July 1893 aboard the *José Gallant* steamship. His wife's name was Maria Bandera Sanchez (registros, book 077, p. 227).

36. The Viola family likely came from Palmi, a small city in Calabria, southern Italy (registros, book 02B, p. 013, family 31140). The document relating their departure from the hospedaria, however, states that they were from Naples (20 August 1912, box C07393, no. 1776, p. 5, SA, APESP).

37. Holloway, *Immigrants on the Land*, 42–43.

38. The original document reads, "sahiram nest Capital, a passeio, não voltando, para tomar o destino da chamada" (20 August 1912, C07393, no. 1776, p. 5, SA, APESP). Other examples of immigrants eluding the chamada are on page 6 of the record for August 20, 1912, and a month later, September 20 (box C07395, no. 1867, no. 1866, SA, APESP).

39. "Requerimento por Amador de Cunha Bueno (Dr.)," 29 August 1912, box C07395, SA, APESP.

40. Maria da Luz Encarnação, September 1912, C07395, no. 2095, SA, APESP; Josepha Albiere to Dr. Inspector da Imigração, 12 December 1914, C0958, SA, APESP; C07393, no. 1776, 28, SA, APESP; C07395, no. 1866, 1–6, SA, APESP. A petition from October 1912 even includes a letter from the immigrants (C07396, no. 2070, 11–13, SA, APESP). The case of Maria Antonio Fernandes Anes and her family (chamada no. 1148) shows how the chamada system was manipulated (Requerimento 29 August 1912, C07395, 1–3, SA, APESP).

41. Dean, *Industrialization of São Paulo*, 51; Penteado, *Belènzinho*, 63, 109, 117.

42. Typescript interviews, ca. 1980, box 2, documents 42, 43, 65, Mappin Collection, Documentação Histórica e Iconografia do Museu do Ipiranga, Museu Paulista, São Paulo.

43. Angela Sgarro, interview, box 2, document 66, Mappin Collection, explains her father, Vicente, was hired by Mappin because of Italian social connections to Carlini. Family connections were one of the biggest reasons people went to work at General Motors. Minchini and Dal Pogetto family interviews appear in *Panorama* 34, no. 2 (February 1996), and *Panorama* (January 2005), 49. On the prevalence of North American and British engineers and technicians in railways see Lamounier, *Ferrovias e mercado de trabalho*, 186–196; on immigrant prevalence among laborers see 197–203. For the São Paulo Railway, Lamounier notes 1.3 percent of expenditures went toward contracting European workers, with the largest group coming from Portugal (202).

44. Klein, *Inmigración española en Brasil*, 123, table 4.6.

45. São Paulo state Department of Labor bulletin, *Boletim do Departamento Estadual do Trabalho* (hereafter *BDET*), nos. 1–2 (1911–1912), 196; no. 5 (1912), 728; no. 12–13 (1914), 813.

46. These documents are available in the Cartas de Chamada section of the Museu da Imigração digital archive, http://www.inci.org.br/acervodigital/index.php. The Memória do Imigrante collection is maintained by APESP. Setting the parameters to the document origin from São Paulo and the dates from 1896 to 1927 yielded the chamadas sample. I accessed the archive on 15 May 2018.

47. Including 1914 in the count reflects a delayed response to World War I by immigrants living out of harm's way in São Paulo.

48. "Compadre" and "comadre" designate the relations between a child's biological parents and godparents, of particular importance in Spanish- and Portuguese-speaking America.

49. Baily, *Immigrants in the Lands of Promise*, 22–24, 58–60.

50. Trento, in Do *outro lado do Atlântico,* provides the most comprehensive study of Italians in Brazil.

51. The number of immigrants in the hospedaria divided by the total number of immigrants yields this share (*RSA*, various years). The *RSA* for 1923 contains a comprehensive table for 1899–1923 (p. 96). As for the share of unsubsidized immigrants during the war years and the latter half of the 1920s, the majority used the *hospedaria*, reaching a peak of 86 percent in 1917. In most years, 20–30 percent of unsubsidized immigrants used the hospedaria.

52. Holloway, *Immigrants on the Land,* 44.

53. Literacy rates will be underestimated due to this sample bias.

54. Immigrants were deemed to have settled in the city if "capital" was listed as the final destination.

55. The number of adult immigrants passing through the hospedaria between 1889 and 1902 was substantial, at 552,366, according to registros. From 1897 to 1899, a substantial number (14,755) and share (13.8%) were also contracted directly to the capital (Holloway, "Creating the Reserve Army?"); these immigrants are not captured in the analysis.

56. This timing varies slightly from the periods used to examine the chamadas. The difference is that chamadas originating in São Paulo lagged in response to World War I; by 1914 many immigrants arriving from Europe already had been directly affected by rising continental tensions like the Balkans Wars of 1912–1913. An increase in passport applications submitted in Porto from young men of conscription age also supports this interpretation (Processos de Passaporte, Arquivo Distrital do Porto, Portugal [hereafter PP, ADP]).

57. José Moya demonstrates how Brazil's subsidy program drew in Spanish emigrants (*Cousins and Strangers,* 83). Baily's *Immigrants in the Lands of Promise,* a study of Italians in Buenos Aires, largely ends with migrations to the city before World War I. Donna Gabaccia finds that Italians continued migrating to South America during the 1920s (*Italy's Many Diasporas,* 133–135). Blanca Sánchez-Alonso, in "The Other Europeans," considers national immigration trends to Brazil and Latin America within the great migration wave.

58. Jeffrey Lesser explains well the trends in Japanese migration starting in 1918 (*Negotiating National Identity,* 94–95). From 1925 onward, only Portuguese immigration outpaced Japanese immigration to Brazil (Lone, *Japanese Community in Brazil,* 54–56).

59. For Japanese immigrants, elementary enrollment was equated with literacy. In 1910 in Japan, 98 percent of elementary-age children were enrolled, but just 41 percent of males and 23 percent of females completed elementary school. Elementary enrollment is not a good measure of literacy because Japanese literacy entails learning two thousand characters and two fifty-character alphabets (Honda, "Differential Structure, Differential Health," 263).

60. For studies outside of Brazil, see Abramitzky, Boustan, and Eriksson, "A Nation of Immigrants," 467–506; Tortella, "Patterns of Economic Retardation and Recovery," 1–21. On Brazil, see Andrews, *Blacks and Whites in São Paulo*; Weinstein, *Color of Modernity.* Lesser focuses on Syrians and Lebanese for the period (*Negotiating National Identity*),

and Hildete Melo, João Araújo, and Teresa Marques analyze job opportunities and pay at Brahma Brewing Company in Rio de Janeiro ("Raça e nacionalidade").

61. Motoyama, *Tecnologia e industrialização no Brasil*, introduction.

62. Italian immigration to New York City and Buenos Aires between 1870 and 1914 illustrates the importance of the differences between the regional groups and their immigrant experiences. While more skilled northern Italians immigrated to Buenos Aires and found relative success there, unskilled southern Italians composed much of the immigrant flow to New York City and met with nativism and less opportunity (Baily, *Immigrants in the Lands of Promise*, 61–68, 218).

63. The textile sector, for the most part, did not make these improvements.

64. Passport applications from Porto for potential Portuguese emigrants increased substantially from 1911 to 1913 (PP, ADP). Considering the low Portuguese literacy rates (21.5%), São Paulo's early growth disproportionately demanded low-skilled workers. More than 63 percent of Portuguese immigrants staying in the capital in this period registered as "agriculturalists," a full 15 percentage points higher than the average for all immigrants during the 1903–1913 period, proportions that support this interpretation. On Portuguese impressment see Menezes, "A 'onda' emigratória de 1912," 237–247. Sr. Antônio states that his family did not return to Italy in 1910 for fear that his father and brother would be drafted (Bosi, *Memórias e sociedade,* 226).

65. Julio records are in registros book 88, p. 23, family 32490; Manuel, book 88, p. 69, family 37400.

66. Of the 2,705 Portuguese individuals coming to the city whose port of embarkation was recorded in registros, 45 percent came from Leixões and 35 percent from Lisbon. This order was switched for the state, where Lisbon embarkations outnumbered those from Leixões, 9,912 to 7,979.

67. Although their exact trajectory could not be confirmed, this is the most likely. A document dated 5 November 1912 identifies the Praça da Batalha as Porto's center for transportation agencies (box 320, processo 509, PP, ADP).

68. Portugal, *Censo da população do Reino de Portugal,* 1:6.

69. Registros, book 88, pp. 21–27; p. 23, family 32490, Julio Augusto and family; p. 22, family 32390, Joaquim Canelles and family.

70. Registros, book 88, pp. 63–76. Streets listed where immigrants moved include Rua Hipódromo, Rua Caetano Pinto, and Rua Santa Rosa, all in Brás.

71. Strauss's last name was transcribed as Stranco in the database, but the original document clearly reads "Strauss" (registros, book 96, p. 280).

72. The largest number of Germans in registros, 450, came to the capital in 1924. In other years there were 23 (1919), 52 (1920), 42 (1921), 90 (1922), 97 (1923), and 7 (1925). No Germans were contracted in 1926 and 1927.

73. For an overview of European emigration in the interwar years, see Kirk, *Europe's Population in the Interwar Years,* 83–89.

74. Origin data only exist for a little over half of the 761 Germans who signed contracts from 1919 to 1927. Of those, 278 claimed Prussian origin, which to Brazilian immigration officials likely referred to the Free State of Prussia, while only 30 were listed from Bavaria and 10 from the city of Berlin.

75. *RSA*, 1924, 72–73; "Classificação dos immigantes entrados pelo porto de Santos durante o anno de 1927," box C09835, SA-I, APESP.

76. While German emigration did not expand dramatically after World War I, by 1923 it had reached prewar levels (Bade, "From Emigration to Immigration," 514).

77. Age squared is also used as a proxy for experience because of diminishing returns over an individual's lifetime.

78. Appendix A shows full statistical regression results. A similar analysis using port of embarkation rather than nationality is included for robustness.

79. The *Estado de São Paulo* of 11 June 1892 ran a help-wanted ad (on page 4) for carpenters and stoneworkers. An immigrant carpenter's perspective on employment is documented in chamada A0000205, 14 September 1913.

80. This decision about categories was partially a reflection of the registros database. Semirestricted access to registros made queries related to these three professions feasible. See appendix A.

81. Among textile workers, 46.5 percent moved to the city; for mechanics and blacksmiths the share was 35.4 percent and for businessmen, 31.0 percent (registros).

82. Portuguese constituted 35 percent of all arrivals but just 7 percent of businessmen, 27 percent of textile workers, and 10 percent of metalworkers.

83. The statistical results of these robust logit regressions are reported in tables A.3–A.5 in appendix A.

84. The influential thesis of the sociologist Florestan Fernandes holds that immigrants were more skilled because slavery had left many Brazilians unprepared for capitalism (Bastide and Fernandes, *Brancos e negros em São Paulo*, 57–58). Direct contracts for skilled workers somewhat support this thesis. George Andrews gives an excellent review of Fernandes's thesis as it relates to Brazilians and immigrants (*Blacks and Whites in São Paulo*, 71–82). For refutations of the thesis, see Hall, "Origins of Mass Immigration to Brazil," 136–138, 179; Leff, *Underdevelopment and Development*, 1:61–65; Melo, Araújo, and Marques, "Raça e nacionalidade."

85. Raquel Rolnik details Afro-Brazilian residential structures in "City and the Law" (100–113). See also Lowrie, "Negro Element in the Population," 404.

86. Registros, book 2, p. 49. The entry reads Seará rather than Ceará.

87. Literacy rates for migrants from urban centers of Rio de Janeiro and São Paulo were also lower than those in Brazil's 1920 census. See appendix A. Nathaniel Leff empirically approaches regional inequalities and the question of northeastern "backwardness" (*Underdevelopment and Development*, 2:5–40). Barbara Weinstein extensively discusses how regional disparities featured into a Paulista and national identity, demonstrating the intersection of cultural and economic history (*Color of Modernity*, particularly chapter 6.)

88. In the 1903–1913 period, 44.3 percent of registered migrants were from the southeastern states of São Paulo, Espírito Santo, and Rio de Janeiro, and among them just 43 percent were literate. The literacy rate of migrants from the Paraíba Valley during the same period was only 18 percent. Migrants from the cities of São Paulo and Rio de Janeiro were considered separately.

89. On Argentine, see Faini and Venturini, "Italian Emigration in the Pre-War Period," 94. On general patterns of European migration to Latin America, see Sánchez-Alonso, "The Other Europeans."

90. Appendix A, table A.2 provides a list of literacy rates of heads of household, by state and region.

91. Lima, *Municípios do Rio Grande do Norte*.

92. Registros, book 90, pp. 219–220.

93. Most Brazilians contracted to work in the city had similar profiles to that of João André. They were males in their mid-twenties and likely to be literate, and while most were married, they often traveled alone.

94. Registros, book 90, pp. 219–220.

95. Registros, book 90, p. 220.

Chapter 2. The City of Opportunity?

1. Studies considering labor leadership for urban workers during this era include Fausto, *Trabalho urbano e conflito social*; Maram, *Anarquistas, imigrantes*; Pinheiro and Hall, *A classe operária no Brasil*. Eva Blay explores housing in *Eu não tenho onde morar*. Maria Alice Rosa Ribeiro examines the textile labor force structure in *Condições de trabalho na indústria têxtil paulista*. The source base in Andrews, *Blacks and Whites in São Paulo*, diversifies extensively for the post-1920 period. On the lower-class Brazilian and particularly Afro-Brazilian experience, see Santos, *Nem tudo era italiano*.

2. In *Cotidiano e sobrevivência*, Pinto draws extensively on Americano's *São Paulo nesse tempo*, Bosi's *Memória e sociedade*, and Penteado's *Belènzinho* to explore the marginal urban environment, including informal and uncertain employment.

3. There is evidence that the change that started in 1913 with the impact of the Balkan Wars and World War I marked a continuation of the business recession (Fritsch and Franco, "Aspects of the Brazilian Experience with the Gold Standard," 164; Stein, *Brazilian Cotton Manufacture*, 105).

4. For detailed description of price construction see Ball, "Prices, Wages, and the Cost of Living," 5–13.

5. On Latin American gendered educational differences, see Camou, Maubrigades, and Thorp's introduction to *Gender Inequality and Development in Latin America* and López-Uribe and Quintero Castellanos's "Women Rising" in the same edited volume.

6. Hanley, *Native Capital*, 75–83; Summerhill, *Inglorious Revolution*, 164–179.

7. Hanley, *Native Capital*, chapter 4; Musacchio, *Experiments in Financial Democracy*, 79–81. Companies could start operations with 10 percent of capital and could be traded with just 20 percent of capital (Tannuri, *O Encilhamento*).

8. Holloway, *Immigrants on the Land*, 179. The shares also reflect São Paulo's rising coffee production during this period and a decline in labor supply after world coffee prices dropped in 1891 (Luna and Klein, *Economic and Demographic History of São Paulo*, 91–94).

9. Rolnik, "City and the Law," 262–267. Also see Greenfield, "Challenge of Growth," chapter 2.

10. Hanley, *Native Capital*, 93–98, 105.

11. Torres, *O bairro do Brás*, 112.

12. *Estado de São Paulo*, 11 June 1892, 4.

13. The estimate is based on median 1892 nominal wage in the wage series described in Ball, "Prices, Wages, and the Cost of Living," multiplied by 9 hours. Prices are from *Estado de São Paulo*, 6 May 1892, 2.

14. *Estado de São Paulo*, 11 June 1892, 4.

15. Anne Hanley connects the valorization campaign to industrial investment ("Business Finance and the São Paulo Bolsa," 122). Bértola and Ocampo call the valorization the "most significant case of commodity price regulation in Latin America" (*Economic Development of Latin America*, 142).

16. Hanley, *Native Capital*, 97–100; Musacchio, *Experiments in Financial Democracy*, 59. Musacchio details access to credit through stocks and bonds in chapter 3.

17. I agree with Luis Bértola and José Ocampo's description of the 1870–1913 period as the first era of globalization in Latin America. The authors contend that commodity-export-led growth in Latin America continued through 1929 but that "the first wave [of globalization] began to wane . . . starting with the First World War" (*Economic Development of Latin America*, 8).

18. Haber, "Development Strategy or Endogenous Process?," 19–20; Hanley, *Native Capital*, 100–104; Stein, *Brazilian Cotton Manufacture*, 81–86.

19. A. Pinto, *A cidade de S. Paulo em 1900*, 208–222. A 1912 bulletin of the state Department of Labor reports at least 4,492 textile workers in the city and estimates 6,000 textile workers statewide (*BDET*, 1912, no. 1–2, 41–64). This figure is an underestimate, as it does not include many cottage industries, and not every factory is listed in the *BDET* workforce information.

20. M. Pinto, *Cotidiano e sobrevivência*, 74.

21. *A Tribuna*, 9 September 1909, cited in Maram, *Anarquistas, imigrantes*, 120.

22. Penteado, *Belènzinho*, 122, 100.

23. Pinheiro and Hall, *A classe operária no Brasil*, 1:41–59.

24. Hanley, "Business Finance and the São Paulo Bolsa," 120–131; *RSA* (1913), 183–185.

25. *Annual Report 1916*, 8, São Paulo Tramway, Light, and Power Company (hereafter cited as Light), Fundação de Energia e Saneamento do Estado de São Paulo (FESESP). Maria Pinto also speaks to this decline in construction jobs (*Cotidiano e sobrevivência*, 92–93).

26. Nakamura and Zarazaga, "Economic Growth in Argentina," 249.

27. Luna and Klein state that Brazil "did not suffer any serious decline of its exports during World War I" (*Economic and Demographic History of São Paulo*, 176). Yet they also demonstrate how coffee exports and prices declined considerably and "a period of instability occurred during World War I" (80–81). The authors discuss notable changes in coffee exports (180). On falling GDP per capita during the war, see Bértola and Ocampo, *Economic Development of Latin America*, 96.

28. Letter from Luiz Moreira Barbosa, 1912, box 136, processo 337, PP, ADP. Dates refer to dates letters were written and do not always coincide with date of the passport application. Passport applications for married women, minors, and individuals meeting up with family members in Brazil are more likely to contain letters. Applications are ordered chronologically and by process number within boxes. On a decrease in imports, see Dean, *Industrialization*, 90.

29. José describes the laundry shop in the Sé neighborhood at 5 Rua 11 de Agosto in a letter dated 23 September 1912 (box 325, processo 598, PP, ADP). The following passport applications refer to steady work: 7 February 1913, box 342, processo 413; 7 October 1912, box 326, processo 663.

30. Chamada A0000033, 14 September 1911.

31. A discussion of the labor market appears in Light's *Annual Report 1916*, 8, FESESP.

32. In nominal wages, a plasterer made 12$000 daily in 1912 and 8$000–10$000 in 1914. Similar declines occurred for painters and stoneworkers (Fausto, *Trabalho urbano e conflito social*, 157). Shares of real wages are calculated from Ball, "Prices, Wages, and the Cost of Living," 24.

33. Hanley, *Native Capital*, 112. The firms that did weather the downturn tended to be larger (*Almanach commercial brasileiro 1918*, 448–452).

34. Musacchio notes that after a fivefold increase in publicly traded textile firms, reaching 25 by 1913, the number of firms decreased to 21 in 1917 (*Experiments in Financial Democracy*, 80). Hanley finds a decline, from 185 in 1913 to 158 in 1917 (*Native Capital*, 111–113). Also, the *BDET* 1912 reports on 31 textile establishments in the city, while the *BDET* 1919 only compares 20.

35. In December 1913, Light employed 213 individuals, and by August 1914 the number had risen to 230 in the following areas: 4 in offices, 18 in the garage, 68 in car barns, and 140 in shops. By December 1914 the numbers had dwindled to 2, 5, 53, and 88, respectively (Light, *Annual Report 1916*, 118, FESESP).

36. *BDET*, 1915, first trimester.

37. Vangelista, *Os braços da lavoura*, table 2.7, 96.

38. Earlier, companies would sometimes just fail to pay employees, leading to a push for daily compensation. By 1917, workers demanded biweekly pay (Pinheiro and Hall, *A classe operária no Brasil*, 1:232–234). Wage evidence from companies shows that salaried employees received lower pay than wage employees for the same jobs.

39. Letter from Joaquim Teixeira de Souza, 3 May 1914, box 394, processo 713, PP, ADP.

40. Ball, "Prices, Wages, and the Cost of Living," 10.

41. "Typical" refers to a twenty-five-year-old, unskilled Brazilian male worker. Age and nationality are based on the descriptive statistics from the wage series analysis.

42. Annual inflation rates are calculated for each consumption basket index (Ball, "Prices, Wages, and the Cost of Living," 12–13).

43. Ball, "Prices, Wages, and the Cost of Living," 22–25.

44. Chamada A0000186, 14 September 1913. Other direct references to the availability of food are in chamadas A0000117, 15 May 1912; A0000033, 14 September 1911; A0000572, 29 July 1912; A0000293, 12 March 1914. Another such reference is dated 4 April 1915 (box 401, processo 182, PP, ADP). Building materials and tools were also readily accessible (chamada A0000205, 14 September 1913).

45. Quoted in Pereira, *Washington Luís*, 289.

46. Pereira, *Washington Luís*, 292–295.

47. Cardim reports the salary of a domestic as a household expense for the employer. Only the prices of potatoes and coffee increased at lower rates, 19.4 and 16.7 percent, than rents and wages. Lard prices also increased more rapidly than rents and wages (*Ensaio de analyse*, 22–23).

48. Cardim, *Ensaio de analyse*, 24–25.

49. My reading of clothes prices counters the argument that protecting industries benefited Brazil's population.

50. Haber, "Development Strategy or Endogenous Process?," 15; Stein, *Brazilian Cotton Manufacture*, 82–85.

51. Barbosa, 1912, box 0136, processo 337, PP, ADP.

52. Chamadas A0000223, 3 May 1911; A0000126, 22 July 1912; A0000205, 3 June 1913; A0000572, 29 July 1912; A0000612, 7 September 1912; A0000640, 5 May 1913; A0000803 15 October 1917.

53. Chamada A0000407, 8 November 1911. The original says, "Aqui tiene uste a su yja q^e es obligasion a manternerla a uste."

54. In Bosi, *Memória e sociedade*, 129–30.

55. Jacino, *Transição e exclusão*, 104–6.

56. Ribeiro, "Os cortiços no distrito de Santa Ifigênia," 44. Alternate spellings for the neighborhood include Ephigênia, Iphigênia, and Efigênia, but Ifigênia reflects the modern spelling.

57. Rolnik, "City and the Law," 59, 67–68, 98, 381. For a detailed breakdown of the 1893 *cortiço* census in São Paulo's Santa Ifigênia neighborhood, see Ribeiro, "Os cortiços no distrito de Santa Ifigênia," 60–78.

58. "Municipal Report," 1892, box 6, Polícia Administrativa e Higiene (PAH), Fundo de Intendência Municipal (FIM), Arquivo Histórico Municipal Washington Luís (AHMWL), São Paulo. Box 5, PAH, also for 1892, contains six documents related to the "Relação dos cortiços existentes nos distritos da Brás, Santa Efigênia, Consolação e Sé. Relatorios de engenheiros" (report on cortiços in the named districts).

59. Meade, *Civilizing Rio*, 90–96; Piccini, *Cortiços na cidade*, 28–36.

60. Kogan, "History of Floods," 78–79; Seabra, *Os meandros dos rios nos meandros do poder*.

61. Ball, "Wife, Mother, and Worker," 119. For a comprehensive look at the development of *vilas operárias*, see Blay's *Eu não tenho onde morar*.

62. "Contrato para casa vila operárias," 1908, box 5, "Obras," FIM, AMWL.

63. Rolnik, "City and the Law," 212.

64. *BDET*, 1919, no. 31–32, 202, table 2.

65. On a halt in construction, see Lemos, *Alvenaria burguesa*, 164–165; M. Pinto, *Cotidiano e sobrevivência*, 92; Rolnik, "City and the Law," 251.

66. Belenzinho was just one of three textile factories surveyed that reported having worker housing (*BDET*, 1919, no. 31–32, 202, table 2). A search for "vila operária" in Projeto SIRCA (Sistema de Registro, Controle e Acesso ao Acervo) of AHMWL shows more typical proposals (http://www.projetosirca.com.br/). Law 498 of 14 December 1900 permitted the construction of worker houses outside of the urban perimeter. One atypical construction contract from 1908 proposed a villa with a population of 10,000 (Contrato, 1908, box 5, "Obras," FIM, AHMWL.

67. Moura, *Trabalho feminino e condição social do menor*, 26, citing a report in the *Diario Oficial* from 1914.

68. Caldeira, *City of Walls*, 219; Holloway, *Immigrants on the Land*, 179.

69. Returning to Europe was no longer a viable option for many immigrants, but migrating to the interior was. Some families and individuals returned to the interior either through the *hospedaria* or independently to escape the burdens imposed by World War I ("Letter to Oscar," 6 November 1914, box C09858, Secretaria da Agricultura, Inspetoria de

Imigração de Santos (SA-I), APESP. The number of immigrants using the hospedaria annually attests to this dramatic shift: 5,802 during World War I, compared to 27,967 before the war and 13,462 from 1919 to 1927. The annual number of immigrants was 20 percent less during the war than in the previous decade. Numbers are derived from state Agriculture Department reports (*RSAs*).

70. Luna and Klein, *Economic and Demographic History of São Paulo*, 100.

71. Luna and Klein, *Economic and Demographic History of São Paulo*, 267, 272–276.

72. Bértola and Ocampo use Gini coefficients as a measure of income disparity in the region showing that Brazil has made little headway in terms of reducing their Gini (*Economic Development of Latin America*, 119–120). Historically high inequality in the region is supported in findings of studies such as Acemoglu, Johnson, and Robinson's "Colonial Origins of Comparative Development" and Engerman and Sokoloff's "Factor Endowments, Institutions, and Differential Paths."

73. On how diseases and epidemics shed light on mortality as a quality-of-life indicator see Read, "Do Diseases Talk?." For an example of this research in São Paulo state specifically, see Read, "Sickness, Recovery, and Death."

74. Bértola and Ocampo, *Economic Development of Latin America*, 119–120, 32–47; Franken, "Growing Taller, yet Falling Short," 160–172; Morrisson and Murtin, "Century of Education." Several contributions in Camou, Maubrigades, and Thorp's edited volume, *Gender Inequalities and Development in Latin America*, offer insights into this period, but most begin in the post-1930 era. Gaston Díaz's description of the emerging "Gender Inequality Historical Database for Latin America" has little evidence for the pre-1920 period.

75. Barbosa, 1912, box 136, processo 337, PP, ADP.

76. Letter, 1912, box 136, processo 331, PP, ADP.

77. Lilliecreutz et al., "Effect of Maternal Stress During Pregnancy"; Wisborg et al., "Psychological Stress during Pregnancy and Stillbirth."

78. São Paulo, Departamento de Estatística do Estado, "Movimento da população do município de São Paulo."

79. Blount, "A administração da saúde pública no estado," 45–46.

80. The study excludes 1918 in the calculation due to the flu pandemic that year (Blount, "A administração da saúde pública no estado").

81. Revised estimates also assume linear population growth; however, instead of using incrementation of 17,184 per annum between 1900 and 1920, a 19,200 annual increase is assumed between 1900 and 1914 and a 12,480 annual increase between 1914 and 1920.

82. São Paulo, *Annuario estatistico do estado*, 1905, 350–351; 1910, 210–211. Rates for the share of children under five years in 1901 were 78 percent for Brás and 66 percent for Belenzinho (1901, 426). For similar rates and analysis see Luna and Klein, *Economic and Demographic History of São Paulo*, 272–279.

83. Chamada A0000439, 7 March 1919.

84. Marcílio, *História da escola em São Paulo e no Brasil*, 100.

85. Buenos Aires, Ministerio de Desarrollo Económico, *La economía porteña en cifras*, 18. New York State Department of Health, *Annual Report* vol. 1; vol. 37, part 1, 284–285. The São Paulo rates are also lower than those for San Francisco in the *1900 US Census Reports*, vol. 3, lix–lx.

86. Tossounian, "Women's Associations and the Emergence of a Social State," 300n8.

87. New York City's 1916 rate is from New York State Department of Health, *Annual Report* vol. 1; vol. 37, part 1, 285. The 1900 rates are available in *Annual Report of the State Department of Health*, December 31, 1954, vol. 2, xlvii. On childbirth and stillbirths in Rio de Janeiro, see Roth, *Miscarriage of Justice*, chapter 3.

88. Sharon Sassler finds that second-generation immigrant women in the United States delayed marriage as a strategy for social mobility ("Women's Marital Timing at the Turn of the Century," 567–585). Claudia Goldin finds a revolutionary effect for the United States in the 1970s whereby women delaying marriage received more education ("Quiet Revolution," 18–19). Chiara Saraceno identifies this effect in Italy during the 1960s ("Constructing Families, Shaping Women's Lives," 266). For an overview of theoretical literature linking female education and higher marrying ages and decreased fertility, see Camou, Maubrigades, and Thorp, introduction, 9.

89. São Paulo, *Annuario estatistico do estado*, 1901, 403.

90. In 1910 and 1920, respectively, 29.8 and 31 percent of fifteen- to nineteen-year-old women were married, based on data analysis in IPUMS Abacus Beta (Ruggles et al.), using age, marriage status, and gender as variables.

91. Rates were the following in 1910 (including women twenty years old), 1915, 1919, and 1927 (all ages nineteen and younger): entire city, 51.7, 36.1, 33.3, 30.8; established downtown, 49.5, 34.3, 30.2, 24.7; outskirts/periphery, 58.0, 45.8, 43.5, 37.3 (São Paulo, *Annuario estatistico do estado*, 1910, 205; 1915, 84; 1919, 157; 1927, 136). The downtown area includes Consolação, Santa Ifigênia, Santa Cecília, and Sé. The neighborhoods of Bela Vista and Bom Retiro are excluded because of their large immigrant shares. Cambucí and Liberdade are excluded because of their large share of working-class individuals. The periphery neighborhoods include Jardim America, Sant'Anna, Lapa, Penha da França, São Miguel, Nossa Senhora do 'O, Butantan, Ipiranga, Osasco, Itaquera, Saúde, and Cantareira. Also see Luna and Klein, *Economic and Demographic History of São Paulo*, 289–290.

92. Colistete, "O atraso em meio à riqueza," 200.

93. Colistete estimates that if the same investment in education continued from Empire to Republic, all children would have effectively gained literacy ("O atraso em meio à riqueza," 208, 217).

94. Colistete, "O atraso em meio à riqueza," 201–205. Francisco Luna and Herbert Klein show budgetary increases through 1917 and an expenditures per capita peak in 1913 (*Economic and Demographic History of São Paulo*, 86–88).

95. Petitions came from rural and urban areas, demonstrating that requesting schools was an established practice and commitment to education in diverse communities (Colistete, "O atraso em meio à riqueza," 236–239).

96. Ball, "Inequality in São Paulo's Old Republic," 134–135. Rates are from Brazil, Directoria Geral de Estatística, *Recenseamento do Brasil, 1920* (hereafter cited as Brazil, *Recenseamento 1920*), vol. 4.4, 803–804. The long-term development benefits for girls' education would have been higher, but that was simply not the Paulistano reality.

97. Research demonstrates more positive externalities for female education and gendered education disparities as a marker of backwardness and a hindrance to growth. In the introduction to their edited volume, Camou, Maubrigrades, and Thorp observe, "If men and women have the same innate capacity, giving priority to the men would reduce the productivity of human capital as a whole" (3).

98. Marcílio, *História da escola em São Paulo e no Brasil*, 173, table 7. Maria Luiza Marcílio reports the following matriculation rates in 1908: entire city, 25%; Sé, 97%; Brás, 25%; Santa Ifigênia, 22%; Cambucí, 31%; Belenzinho, 24%. The Sé rates are elevated because children from other neighborhoods attended schools in the Sé district.

99. Marcílio, *História da escola em São Paulo e no Brasil*, 143, 203–204, 223–233; Penteado, *Belènzinho*, 15, 51–56.

100. São Paulo, Directoria Geral da Instrucção Publica, *Annuario do ensino do estado de São Paulo*, 1923, 573. The report calculates that 80 percent of private school students were enrolled in primary schools.

101. A. Costa, *A escola na República Velha*, 121; Marcílio, *História da escola em São Paulo e no Brasil*, 141–144. Law 1.750 of 8 December 1920 reduced compulsory schooling to two years.

102. Colistete, "O atraso em meio à riqueza," chapter 4.

103. Elizabeth Hutchison has found that in Chile at the turn of the twentieth century, census registrations often underestimated female participation in the labor force (*Labors Appropriate to Their Sex*, 38). A similar dynamic likely existed in São Paulo.

104. Decreto 1.313 of 17 January 1891; Ball, "Prices, Wages, and the Cost of Living," 111; Besse, *Restructuring Patriarchy*, 95–96; Pena, *Mulheres e trabalhadoras*, 151–154.

105. Workers clearly made time for leisure. Although they would have found it difficult to join middle- and upper-class soccer clubs, they invested in sport (Bocketti, *Beautiful Game*, 69, 73, 84), in theater (Levy, "Forging an Urban Public," 153–189, 202), and in circuses, church festivals, and parades (Penteado, *Belènzinho*, 165–170, 195–204).

106. Ball, "Wife, Mother, and Worker," 111–112.

107. Chamada A0000293, 12 March 1914.

108. The selection is based on available data and is not necessarily representative. Even so, the evidence is instructive. Regression analysis shows that median attendance records did not vary statistically by gender (female, 75%; male, 81%; coed, 78%) or neighborhood (Barra Funda, 63%; Belenzinho, 81%; Cambucí, 67%; Gazometro, 77%; Liberdade, 73%; Nossa Senhora da Penha, 77%; Sant'Anna, 87%; Visconde de Parnahyba, 76%). The dataset was created from the attendance record books Livros de Presência (LiP), E02182, E02202, E02215, E02227, E02243, E02332, E02447, E02812, E04465, Secretaria da Agricultura (SA), APESP.

109. LiP, E02447, SA, APESP.

110. An estimated attendance prediction based on the attendance observations points to increasing attendance over the period. Few inspectors commented on preparedness, but observations of illiteracy rates among the attending pupils indicate the failure to prepare students (LiP, E02812, E02182, SA, APESP).

111. *Guerra Sociale*, 24 March 1917, 10 April 1917, 24 April 1917. *Guerra Sociale* was an anarchist journal launched in São Paulo in 1912.

112. Stanley Stein details the growth of protections through duties levied on imported cloth and exemptions given to machinery imports (*Brazilian Cotton Manufacture*, 82–85). While Stein argues that World War I created a monopoly market, he fails to recognize how labor was manipulated in that market (106–107). Stephen Haber's evidence on machinery age demonstrates the challenges textile owners faced ("Development Strategy or Endogenous Process?," 11, 15.

113. *Guerra Sociale*, 10 April 1917.

114. *Guerra Sociale*, 24 April 1917.

115. Working children and women are described as "chupias" (*Guerra Sociale*, 24 March 1917).

116. "Passaporte pra Ignacia de Jesus Ribeiro," box 410, processo 182, PP, ADP. The full quote: "a nossa Eliza ganha para ella e para os irmãos porque ella o menos que pode ganar aqui como ajudanta de custureira são 60:000 a 70:000 por mês nem que ella saiba muito ouco." Although Alfredo goes on to state how the younger children can also earn some money, it is Eliza who will be the key contributor.

117. Emerson and Souza, "Is There a Child Labor Trap?," 376. Recent scholarship examining links between primary school and underdevelopment in Brazil demonstrates a historical underinvestment in education slowed down development (Colistete, "O atraso em meio à riqueza," chapter 4, n127).

118. Emerson and Souza, "Is There a Child Labor Trap?," figure 3, probit analysis.

119. Ball, "Wife, Mother, and Worker," 112; Veccia, "Family and Factory," 37–39.

120. Veccia, "Family and Factory," chapter 4; Wolfe, *Working Women, Working Men*, 11–12, 15.

121. "Para uma senhora ganhar dinheiro em casa," *Revista Feminina*, no. 31, December 1916; "As senhoras brasileiras," *Revista Feminina*, no. 34, March 1917.

122. Chamada A0000293, 12 March 1914.

123. Chamada A0000776, 3 July 1916. Low-skilled male wage in 1916 on a nine-hour workday was used to calculate difference between male and female wage (Ball, "Prices, Wages, and the Cost of Living," 24–25). Maria would have earned 70 percent of what an unskilled adult male could make in 1916.

124. On the prevalence and nature of the informal sector, see M. Pinto, *Cotidiano e sobrevivência*, chapters 3, 4.

125. In general, 1917 and 1918 were marked by more strikes and labor organization worldwide (Bollinger, on Peru, 609–610; Haas, on Argentina, 4; Loveman, 130–132, on Chile; Rial Roade, on Uruguay, 707).

126. *Estado de São Paulo*, 3 July 1916; Wolfe, "Anarchist Ideology, Worker Practice," 815–817.

127. For a description of the events, see Lopreato, *Espíritu da revolta*, 46–58. The book centers around the context and implications of the strike.

128. Wolfe, "Anarchist Ideology, Worker Practice," 821–827.

Chapter 3. Nonstriking Workers and São Paulo's *Sindicato Amarelo*

1. *Estado de São Paulo*, 24 December 1907, 4; *Lucta Proletária*, 17 January 1908.

2. *Lucta Proletária*, 8 February 1908.

3. *Lucta Proletária*, 14 March 1908. From this point on in text, I will avoid using the Italian "crumiro" and English "scab," terms with disparaging connotations, and opt for the terms "nonstriking worker," "replacement worker," and "strikebreaker." The creation and fate of the "yellow union" is unknown, demonstrating how difficult it is to explore labor organization beyond anarchist syndicalist organization.

4. Alexander, *History of Organized Labor in Uruguay and Paraguay*, 9–25, 93–106. In Greenfield and Maram's edited volume, *Latin American Labor Organizations,* see Haas,

"Argentina," 3, 20; Greenfield, "Brazil," 72–74; Loveman, "Chile," 130–132; and Rial Roade, 705–707. For Brazil, see Batalha, *O movimento operário na Primeira República*; Fausto, *Trabalho urbano e conflito social*; Maram, *Anarquistas, imigrantes*; Maram, "Labor and the Left in Brazil"; Pinheiro and Hall, *A classe operária no Brasil*; Weinstein, *For Social Peace in Brazil*, 38–50; Wolfe, *Working Women, Working Men*.

5. DeShazo, *Urban Workers and Labor Unions in Chile*, 253, 273–274.

6. Maria Valéria Pena highlights how strike leaders' patriarchal approach often alienated São Paulo's large female workforce (*Mulheres e trabalhadoras*, 182–204).

7. Alexander, *History of Organized Labor in Uruguay and Paraguay*, 15–17, 21; Haas, "Argentina," 3, 20; Greenfield, "Brazil," 72–128, and on São Paulo's weakened labor organization, 99, 118.

8. This demonstrates how an elastic labor supply to accommodate the export sector also weakened worker organization (Leff, *Underdevelopment and Development*, 1:63–70).

9. Maria Helena Machado considers Afro-Brazilian strikebreakers in "From Slave Rebels to Strikebreakers" (247–274). In Michigan, Mexicans and African Americans were used as strikebreakers in the 1919 Detroit steel strike (García, *Mexicans in the Midwest*, 79–80; Whatley, "African-American Strikebreaking," 526–527).

10. Batalha, *O movimento operário na Primeira República*, 50–51; Lopreato, *O espíritu da revolta;* Veccia, "Family and Factory," chapter 4; Wolfe "Anarchist Ideology, Worker Practice"; Wolfe, *Working Women, Working Men*, 11–15; Woodard, *Place in Politics*, 77–81.

11. Andrews, *Blacks and Whites in São Paulo*, 62; Gitahy, *Processo de trabalho e greves portuárias;* Honorato, *O polvo e o porto;* Machado, "From Slave Rebels to Strikebreakers," 270–274.

12. In economics, this would be considered an elastic labor supply. In the case of São Paulo, Leff argues that the immigration system provided elastic labor for the hinterlands (*Underdevelopment and Development*, 1:63–70). The role in the city's industrial labor market, however, has not been investigated.

13. There are fewer observations for port of embarkation before 1914. Shares are based on the following observations: Málaga, 17; Gibraltar, 37; Barcelona, 14; Genoa, 28; Naples, 27. These findings correlate with Baily's findings for variations between northern and southern Italian immigrant literacy (*Immigrants in the Lands of Promise*, 65). The Spanish migration to São Paulo was distinct from what Moya details for Argentina (*Cousins and Strangers*, 14–18). Most Spanish immigration during the era originated in the northern provinces (Nugent, *Crossings*, 101–110), but in Brazil as a whole, immigration from southern Spain dominated (Cánovas, "Imigrantes espanhóis na Paulicéia," 230; Klein, "Social and Economic Integration of Spanish Immigrants in Brazil," 507–508).

14. Taylor, "External Dependence, Demographic Burdens," 923–925.

15. Baily, *Immigrants in the Lands of Promise*, 150–153.

16. Among the 617 Portuguese individuals arriving, there were 155 heads of household, 117 of whom had accompanying wives, and 318 children, amounting to 2 children per head of household.

17. Percentages are derived from heads of household divided by number of wives by nationality in the hospedaria sample.

18. The share of children estimates resulted from dividing the number of children by

the number of heads of household in the sample: Portuguese, 2.046; Italian, 2.057; Spanish, 2.071.

19. Between 1903 and 1913, records show that 1,559 single and 4,033 married Portuguese immigrants moved to the city through the hospedaria. During the same period, 10,620 single and 10,388 married Portuguese moved elsewhere in the state.

20. Baily, *Immigrants in the Lands of Promise*, 149–150.

21. Spanish and Portuguese heads of household outnumbered Italian heads of household by a factor of 4.79.

22. Moya, *Cousins and Strangers*, 89–90.

23. The figure is based on the registros sample of head of household literacy, by nationality.

24. Tortella, "Patterns of Economic Retardation and Recovery," 11–12, 15.

25. Portuguese heads of household were also the most likely immigrant group to be agriculturalists, at 78 percent.

26. Portuguese represented 40 percent of the 17,789 individuals contracted from the hospedaria to work in the city from 1903 to 1913. During the same period, they were just 17.2 percent of immigrants contracted to the entire state. In that period, 31.6 percent of immigrants contracted to the city were Spanish and 15.1 percent were Italian (Ball, "Inequality in São Paulo's Old Republic," 56, table 2.3). This finding contradicts Cristina Peixoto-Mehrtens's characterization of São Paulo that Italians dominated the construction industry with 90 percent of construction jobs (*Urban Space and National Identity*, 94). Registros and employee data from São Paulo Tramway, Light, and Power Company and Paulista Railway demonstrate that this is an overestimate. Sheldon Maram notes a dominance of Italians in the stoneworkers labor union in the early twentieth century ("Labor and the Left in Brazil," 258–259), but that would create an ideal environment for Portuguese stoneworkers to be contracted to undermine organization. Jobs listed in *Boletins de Ocorrências* (medical incident reports) from the Old Republic also demonstrate a sizeable non-Italian presence in a variety of professions. The Italian presence was larger in the prewar period, but of the 179 incidents reported in November 1923 for which professions were recorded, Italians were far from 90 percent of workers. There were 35 Italians in nine professions; 19 Spaniards in five professions; 2 Germans in two professions; 25 Portuguese in seventeen professions; 71 white Brazilians in twenty-three professions; 13 black Brazilians in five professions; and 14 brown Brazilians in eight professions (E14100, *Boletins de Ocorrências* 56365–57136, APESP).

27. Calculations are based on the port of embarkation recorded in the hospedaria registros sample for families and single heads of household arriving before 1914. There were 283 Portuguese heads of household passing through the hospedaria between 1903 and 1913. Of these the average age was 33.5 years, 67 percent arrived with families, and 22 percent were literate. The 39 Leixões heads of household on average were 37 years old, 79.5 percent arrived with families, and 32.4 were literate. For the 38 Lisbon heads of household, the average age was 31 years, 65.8 percent arrived with families, and 29.0 percent were literate. For further rates, see appendix A.

28. Stepan, *Hour of Eugenics*, 85–100.

29. Stepan, *Hour of Eugenics*, 98–100.

30. Voyages: Trans-Atlantic Slave Trade Database (https://www.slavevoyages.org/) up-

dates numbers on the volume of the slave trade to Brazil. As of 28 July 2020, the database showed 4.86 million slave disembarkations in Brazil as compared to 5.63 million for the Americas between 1501 and 1875. The next-largest importer was Jamaica, at 1.02 million. On the importance of indigenous peoples in Brazil's early colonial period, Afonso Taunay's *Historia geral das bandeiras paulistas* typifies the lore surrounding the São Paulo region; chapters 2–5 of Metcalf's *Go-Betweens and the Colonization of Brazil* cover the early period in a less dramatic fashion.

31. Lesser, *Negotiating National Identity*, 81–89. Stewart Lone also observes a relatively welcoming reception for Japanese in the 1910s (*Japanese Community in Brazil*, 56).

32. Stepan, *Hour of Eugenics,* 42–47, 46 (quote).

33. *Almanach commercial brasileiro, 1918*, 75 ("hardworking"). Railroad engineer Gaspar Ricardo Junior speaks of Portuguese bravery in *Revista da Associação de Comércio de São Paulo* 2, no. 9 (September 1922): 487–489. On jobs, see Reis, *Almanach illustrado de São Paulo*, 93.

34. Martinho and Gorenstein, *Negociantes e caixeiros*. These shares also contrast findings that only 19 percent of Portuguese emigrants were female (Nugent, *Crossings*, 105). This dynamic is similar to what Moya describes for Spanish immigrants in Buenos Aires (*Cousins and Strangers*, 373–375).

35. Thomas Skidmore notes how Oliveira Vianna was a bridge between scientific racism and Freyre (*Black into White*, 200–203). Marshall Eakin, in *Becoming Brazilian*, considers Freyre's legacy in several realms of everyday Brazilian life.

36. Mariano was also the Brazilian ambassador to Portugal; he is quoted on São Paulo's 400th anniversary celebrations in Weinstein, *Color of Modernity* (273n22). In her chapter 7 Weinstein carefully analyzes intellectual approaches to the formation and complexities of a Paulista identity surrounding the city's quadricentennial.

37. Francisco Luna and Herbert Klein report 116,563 marriages in the city of São Paulo over the period, 27,717 in which one spouse was an immigrant and 41,287 in which immigrants married immigrants (*Economic and Demographic History of São Paulo*, 290–293).

38. Luna and Klein, *Economic and Demographic History of São Paulo*, 291–293.

39. Bosi's interviews with Amadeu and Ariosto show both men as Brazilians whose Italian parents met and married in Brazil (*Memoria e sociedade*, 124, 154).

40. São Paulo, *Annuario estatistico do estado*, 1901, 420–421; legitimacy rates of 93 percent for the city, 412–413.

41. Family dependence was enough to slow the Argentine economy in the early twentieth century (Taylor, "External Dependence, Demographic Burdens," 923–925). The impact of family decisions would have been even greater for Paulistas and Paulistanos.

42. Luna and Klein, *Economic and Demographic History of São Paulo*, 289–290.

43. São Paulo, *Annuario estatistico do estado*, 1901, 414–415. Shares are based on the mother's nationality and include legitimate and natural births. There were 8,001 registered legitimate births (Italian, 4,286; Portuguese, 1,085; Brazilian, 1,869) and 597 registered natural births (Italian, 110; Portuguese, 65; Brazilian, 365). Historians sometimes use last names as a marker of immigrant nationality, but again, Portuguese last names are indistinguishable from Brazilian last names (Ball, "Wife, Mother, and Worker," 115; Colistete, "O atraso em meio à riqueza," 239–244; Peixoto-Mehrtens, *Urban Space and National Identity*, 88–89).

44. São Paulo, *Annuario estatistico do estado*, 1901, 414–415. These were the neighborhoods registering the largest immigrant populations and births.

45. *RSA*, various years. For methodology, see Ball, "Inequality in São Paulo's Old Republic," 43.

46. Michael Hall and Marco Aurélio Garcia point to how the movement of immigrants to São Paulo weakened labor organization; they emphasize how controlling the labor supply was effective in "maintaining low wages and weakening the labor movement" ("Urban Labor," 163). The authors also address how factory owners exploited national and racial difference (163–164). Their scholarship has not detailed the direct link between the hospedaria and factory owners and fails to address the importance of the family unit.

47. *Lucta Proletária*, 22 February 1908.

48. *Lucta Proletária*, 29 February 1908.

49. Registros, book 1A, pp. 7–9, 1908, entries 341–344 and 347–350. The preceding and following days' entries show almost exclusively agricultural contracts.

50. *Estado de São Paulo*, 20 July 1905, 3; 23 July 1905, 2.

51. Registros, book 74, pp. 225–255; 244–255 for 27 and 28 July 1905.

52. *O Chapeleiro*, 29 July 1905, 2. Registros, book 74, pp. 259–266, on contracts signed on 2 August 1905.

53. State decree 1.460 of 10 April 1907 officially created the city's livestock research unit, but this contract attests to an earlier presence. The 1907 decree outlined personnel to include the following unskilled and semi-skilled positions: a guard, a gardener, five servants, and ten rural workers.

54. Registros, book 77, pp. 219–220.

55. *Lucta Proletária*, 1 September 1906. The Actas Oficiais, which reported active labor organizing, describe a workers meeting on 24 July at which it was mentioned that Paulista Railway was bringing in strikebreakers.

56. The cross-sector mobilization indicates that this was a general strike, but grievances were solved on a factory level, limiting the strength of the wider movement.

57. The 1,241 also included those who were not heads of households. Only 62 individuals were contracted to the city between May 5 and June 4, and 22 of these signed contracts in June (registros, book 78, pp. 218–246).

58. Pereira, *Washington Luís*, 146–150. Paulo Pinheiro and Michael Hall offer examples of police presence in labor strikes (*A classe operária no Brasil*, 1:250–253).

59. Articles in the *Estado de São Paulo* touch on questions of ensuring nonstriking workers' safety such as seventy workers in the Barão de Limeira Lavanderia (laundry), 9 May 1907, 3; Limpeza Pública (sanitation) workers, cart drivers, Vidraria Santa Maria (glass company) workers, 13 May 1907, 2; bakers and Anhaia textile factory workers, 15 May 1907, 2; bakers, 16 May 1907, 3; comb factory workers, 22 May 1907, 2; workers at the Mariangela and Penteado textile factories, 23 May 1907, 2.

60. *Estado de São Paulo*, 8 May 1907, 3 (quote); 13 May 1907, 2; 9 May 1907, 3.

61. *Estado de São Paulo*, 12 May 1907, 2.

62. *Estado de São Paulo*, 15 May 1907, 2; 16 May 1907, 2; 17 May 1907, 2.

63. *Estado de São Paulo*, 25 May 1907, 3.

64. *Estado de São Paulo*, 13 May 1907, 2. Striking workers protested official violence in the arrest of Brazilina Maria da Conceição (*Estado de São Paulo*, 17 May 1907, 3).

65. Police attacked and apprehended male strikers, but demonstrations by females were largely permitted to continue (Wolfe, "Anarchist Ideology, Worker Practice," 824–825).

66. *Estado de São Paulo*, 24 December 1907, 3–4. On the May 1907 strike, see Batalha, *O movimento operário na Primeira República*, 42–43.

67. *Estado de São Paulo*, 24 December 1907, 2. A later account reports that Domelio was Camillo's surname (*Estado de São Paulo*, 12 January 1908, 2). I have kept the names as they appear in the reports, without accents.

68. *Estado de São Paulo*, 10 January 1908, 3.

69. Their complaint was over unfairly distributed scheduling (*Estado de São Paulo*, 10 January 1908, 3; 11 January 1908, 2).

70. *Estado de São Paulo*, 15 January 1908. Six of the twenty-six ceramic factories in the city continued production with the labor of strikebreakers (*Lucta Proletária*, 29 February 1908).

71. Batalha, *O movimento operário na Primeira República*, 43.

72. *Estado de São Paulo*, 12 January 1908; 15 January 1908.

73. The two women remained in custody until someone posted their bail (*Estado de São Paulo*, 16 January 1908, 3).

74. *Estado de São Paulo*, 16 January 1908.

75. *Lucta Proletária*, 17 January 1908.

76. *Estado de São Paulo*, 17 January 1908, 4.

77. *Estado de São Paulo*, 12 February 1908, 2–3.

78. *Lucta Proletária* reported that 100 men, 21 women, and 8 children remained on strike (8 February 1908).

79. *Lucta Proletária*, 22 February 1908.

80. Rolnik, "City and the Law," 100–113; Veccia, "Family and Factory," 338.

81. *Lucta Proletária*, 29 February 1908, 14 March 1908.

82. On strikes' effectiveness, see Pinheiro and Hall, *A classe operária no Brasil*, 1:64–72.

83. *Estado de São Paulo* 13 May 1907, 2; 25 May 1907, 3. The middle of May also marked an increase in the number of violent conflicts registered in the *Estado de São Paulo*. While the incidents were not explicitly related to conflicts between striking and nonstriking workers, some articles mention individuals who were on strike, suggesting that labor conflicts featured into this increase.

84. *O Chapeleiro*, 29 July 1905, 2; 22 November 1906.

85. Threats of that nature came from Mundo Elegante workers (*Estado de São Paulo*, 25 May 1907, 3).

86. *Estado de São Paulo*, 14–17 October 1902.

87. *Estado de São Paulo*, 24 February 1901, 3; 26 February 1901, 4.

88. *Estado de São Paulo*, 17 February 1901, 1.

89. *Estado de São Paulo*, 23 February 1901, 3. The brother and sister were arrested on charges of aggravated assault.

90. *O Chapeleiro*, 29 July 1905, 2; Siqueira, "Entre sindicatos, clubes e botequins," 170–172.

91. *Lucta Proletária*, 21 March 1908.

92. An editorial equates those forced to be strikebreakers with being as poor as "Chi-

nese" and "Afro-Brazilians" (*O Chapeleiro*, 1 May 1904). Another in *O Chapeleiro* of 29 July 1905 says some strikebreakers should be shown compassion more than anything else.

93. On Pedrezzoli, see *O Chapeleiro* 29 July 1905. The "high treason" of Francisco Sarno is condemned in *O Chapeleiro*, 22 November 1906.

94. Veccia, "Family and Factory," 88.

95. *Estado de São Paulo*, 8 May 1907.

96. *Estado de São Paulo*, 8 May 1907, 3; 9 May 1908, 3.

97. *BDET*, 1912, 120–121.

98. The threat was open to official interpretation; in the case of Eduardo Rezski, soliciting neighbors to join the strike was enough to land him in jail (*Estado de São Paulo*, 17 January 1908, 4).

99. *Estado de São Paulo*, 14 May 1907, 2.

100. Jacino, *Transição e exclusão*, 182–184. Martins notes that Afro-Brazilians contested their exclusion from the Guarda Cívica in 1926; Lithuanians, Latvians, Polish, Austrians, and Germans, the new immigrant stream into the city, often constituted the rank and file of this new policing group (*A civilização do delegado*, 151–153).

101. Andrews, *Blacks and Whites in São Paulo*, 65. São Paulo Tramway, Light, and Power Company executives considered police protection critical to being able to get through the 1906 strike (29 May 1906, general letters box 13, FESESP). Penteado reports that Italians in Belenzinho called Portuguese "krumiros" (scabs) and "fura-greves" (strikebreakers) (*Belènzinho*, 127–131). A 1912 *BDET* report on the national composition of the state labor force indicates that only more skilled policemen for the city had submitted their reports, but in the lower-skilled workforce (inferred from the share of illiterate workers and relative reported salaries) of the water and sewer department and central zootechnic posts, Portuguese workers represented 204 of 837 (24%) and 15 of 54 (28%), respectively. Portuguese day laborers represented 22 of 24 forest service workers, although 20 were literate (109–121).

102. Quoted in Maram, "Labor and the Left in Brazil," 259. "Maneis" refers to the plural of Manoel.

Chapter 4. Discrimination in the Paulistano Labor Market

1. For a description of the São Paulo School of Sociology, see Andrews, *Blacks and Whites in São Paulo*, 7–10. Teresa Sales provides a clear discussion of historiographic nuances related to the bridge from the colonial to the modern era ("Raízes da desigualdade social," 26–37).

2. Bucciferro, "Racial Inequality in Brazil"; Jacino, *Transição e exclusão*.

3. On race in Rio de Janeiro, see Adamo, "Broken Promise"; Adamo, "Race and Povo;" Dávila, *Diploma of Whiteness*; Melo, Araújo, and Marques, "Raça e nacionalidade no mercado de trabalho carioca." Andrews, in *Blacks and Whites in São Paulo*, speaks to racial divides in São Paulo. Barbara Weinstein, in *Color of Modernity*, looks at the intersection of race and regional discrimination. See also Lovell and Wood, "Skin Color, Racial Identity, and Life Chances in Brazil."

4. On legal allowance for these women to work, see Ball, "Wife, Mother, and Worker," 112–113.

5. This is different from the long tenures recorded in the 1930s (Adamo, "Broken Prom-

ise," 59–63; Veccia, "Family and Factory," 327–333). Vargas's labor laws reserving positions for national workers are one possible explanation for this divergence.

6. Two studies based on US Census records are Boustan, *Competition in the Promised Land,* and Goldin, *The Gender Gap.*

7. This is similar to the approach in Margo and Villaflor, "Growth of Wages in Antebellum America" (873–895). Jacino, in *Transição e exclusão,* has used a new source, the *Boletins de Ocorrências,* to investigate racialized hiring practices. Justin Bucciferro draws on Jacino's research as well as that in Stein, *Vassouras,* and Ianni, *As metamorphoses do escravo* (Bucciferro, "Racial Inequality in Brazil," 179–183).

8. Simonsen's cost-of-living indicator begins during World War I (cited in Dean, *Industrialization of São Paulo,* 92). Lobo and colleagues' "Estudos das categorias socioprofissionais" and "Evolução dos preços e do padrão de vida" span the entire period for Rio de Janeiro. A detailed account of the construction of this new wage series, which spans the entirety of the Old Republic in São Paulo, can be found in Ball, "Prices, Wages, and the Cost of Living."

9. This contrasts the 12 to 16 percent city and state estimates in Samuel Lowrie's "Negro Element in the Population of São Paulo," 411–412, 416; it fits more closely with his demographic estimate (407). As Lowrie himself notes, race is in the eye of the beholder, and employers would be quicker to classify someone Afro-Brazilian than the individual himself or herself would. The larger estimation also fits more closely with the city's lower classes (416), who would have been vying for industrial positions.

10. Jacino also looks at help-wanted advertisements in his *Transição e exclusão.* I employ a more systematic approach that considers the entire period; my finding confirms Adamo's evidence for Rio de Janeiro ("Race and Povo," 192–206).

11. Andrews, *Blacks and Whites in São Paulo;* Jacino, *Transição e exclusão.* For Rio de Janeiro, see Adamo, "Broken Promise," chapter 2. Firm-level evidence for Andrews and Adamo are primarily from the 1930s and 1940s.

12. The series is based on 3,400 wage observations for 1,809 individuals employed at Paulista Railway; 1,893 entry-wage observations for individuals employed at Light; and employment information for 727 wage employees and 622 piece-rate employees at Jafet.

13. *Race* and *female* are dummy variables. Nationality signifies a series of dummy variables for different nationalities.

14. *Literacy* is not included in these analyses because of data restrictions, but tables B.4–B.8 in appendix B demonstrate that when a literacy dummy variable is included, the results show that mechanics were more likely to be literate and unskilled workers were less likely to be literate.

15. On differing national cultural norms in terms of female labor participation, see Ball, "Wife, Mother, and Worker," 122–125.

16. Percentage is based on table B.2 in appendix B. Estimate is based on female coefficients for models 3 and 2, respectively. These models were chosen based on the goodness of fit (R^2).

17. Goldin, *Gender Gap,* 59–65.

18. Age is included both as *age* and as *age*^{2} because although wages are expected to increase with age, they are not expected to increase in a linear fashion; at some point, a

decline in wages would be expected. Including *age*[2] allows both effects in the wage evidence to be seen.

19. The Portuguese estimates are based on models 3 and 2, respectively, in appendix B, table B.4. Model 3 includes literacy, and model 2 does not. The German estimate is based on model 2. Once literacy is included, the German dummy is no longer statistically significant.

20. This is consistent with findings for Rio in Adamo, "Race and Povo," 194, and in Melo, Araújo, and Marques, "Raça e nacionalidade no mercado de trabalho carioca." Studies on racial discrimination in Detroit also show discrimination at the hiring and promotion levels rather than wage discrimination (Maloney and Whatley, "Making the Effort," 486–488). Bértola and Ocampo allude to systemic inequality that must be understood as linked to systemic racial prejudice (*Economic Development of Latin America*, 117–120).

21. A dummy variable equals 1 if the answer is yes and 0 if the answer is no.

22. The laborer position corresponds to 99910 in the Historical International Standard Classification of Occupations (HISCO), the spinner to 75220. For the mechanic, the HISCO spans both 72000–72999 and 83000–87999. HISCO traditionally codes a spinner as a low-skilled worker, but unskilled is more appropriate for the Brazilian case.

23. Calculations are derived from odds ratios based on appendix B, table B.5, models 2 and 1 for mechanics and models 3 and 1 for unskilled workers.

24. See tables B.6 and B.7 in appendix B.

25. Estimates based on 1914–1930 models 2 and 4 in appendix B, table B.6.

26. The statistical results show white Brazilian males were just 5.5 percent less likely to be hired than black Brazilian males (model 3, table B.5), likely an underestimate.

27. Bucciferro, "Racial Inequality in Brazil," 181–183; Jacino, *Transição e exclusão,* chapter 3.

28. Maram, *Anarquistas, imigrantes;* Pinheiro and Hall, *A classe operária no Brasil;* Woodard, *Place in Politics.* Weinstein speaks for the need to highlight these understandings (*For Social Peace in Brazil,* 38–29). Andrews, in *Blacks and Whites in São Paulo,* and Adamo, in "Broken Promise," use the firm-level approach, but the focus is distinctly on racial discrimination.

29. A job in the formal labor market was important because it allowed workers access to company-level labor organization and some degree of job security.

30. Lamounier, *Ferrovias e mercado de trabalho;* Summerhill, *Order against Progress;* Saes, *As ferrovias de São Paulo.*

31. 1906 state law 1045-C and 1907 state decree 1.458. In 1910, state decree 1.921 reduced the rate of nonagriculturalists back to 5 percent.

32. "Chamada de imigrantes 'Artistas,'" 10 June 1912, C09855, SA-I, APESP. "Letter to Dr. Oscar Lögregues," 21 June 1910, in the same archive box makes a similar request from E. R. Noroeste, another railroad company. The need for subsidization is argued in "Letter to Oscar," 5 November 1909, box C09854, SA-I, APESP.

33. Batalha, *O movimento operário,* 42–43.

34. Lanna, *Ferrovia, cidade e trabalhadores,* n.p. Theodulo was hired in Jundiaí and eventually was transferred to Campinas to care for his sick mother. She cites box 75.4-41 of the lost Paulista Railway archive as the original source.

35. Lanna, "Trabalhadores das ferrovias."

36. Firm descriptive statistics are presented in appendix B, table B.1. For other racial job share estimates, see Adamo, "Race and Povo," 194; Jacino, *Transição e exclusão,* chapter 3.

37. The Jafet factory had Lebanese and Italian *pardo* workers.

38. Regression results are not statistically significant, but there was a negative correlation between being white and being hired as an unskilled worker at Paulista Railway (appendix B, table B.9, model 3).

39. Entering unskilled education levels for white workers were 38 percent illiterate or poor, 45 percent average, and 15 percent good. For nonwhite workers levels were 49 percent illiterate or poor, 39 percent average, and 11 percent good.

40. "Montagem de veículos importados dos Estados Unidos," photograph, 1925, original in Museu GM, São Paulo copy from General Motors Heritage Center, Detroit.

41. Andrews, *Blacks and Whites in São Paulo,* 65. In the accident reports, Portuguese do appear as soldiers; however, in general they are overrepresented in official jobs, either at the municipal or state level (E14100, E14042, E13968, *Boletins de Ocorrências,* APESP).

42. "Letter to Miss A. J. Hanley," 30 August 1905, General Letters, no. 13, Fundação de Energia e Saneamento do Estado de São Paulo (FESESP).

43. Of these 877 Light employees, 858 were hired between 1924 and 1929. Spanish workers represented 5 percent of hires, Germans and Austrians 6 percent, and other nationalities 14 percent (Ball, "Inequality in São Paulo's Old Republic," 96–98).

44. Andrews, *Blacks and Whites in São Paulo,* 259–262.

45. In the Light sample, 2.44 percent were fired. The share is 3.67 percent for Portuguese workers and 10.71 percent for Spanish workers.

46. Light *fichas,* São Paulo Tramway, Light and Power Company, FESESP. Maram, *Anarquistas, imigrantes,* 22 notes the importance of Spanish organizers.

47. Averaging the equations

$$(\Sigma w_f \Phi m - \overline{w_f})/(\overline{w_m} - \overline{w_f}) \text{ and } -(\Sigma w_m \Phi w - \overline{w_m})/(\overline{w_m} - \overline{w_f})$$

can indicate the importance of occupation distribution (in male (m) and female (f) wage (w) differentials. When testing the importance for boys and girls in the state of São Paulo using the 1920 Brazilian census, the results, -1.53 and 1.3, respectively, show girls highly concentrated in a few high-paying positions. This conclusion is based on the result that the quotient is both larger than 1 and negative for the first equation. For methodology, see Goldin, *Gender Gap,* 71–73.

48. Penteado, *Belènzinho,* 100–108; "Exploração de menores," *Guerra Sociale,* 10 April 1917; "Pela classe: Brandão d'um café, etc. etal," *O Internacional,* 15 June 1924; "Pela unificação dos empregados em cafés de São Paulo," *O Internacional,* 27 June 1925; "A situação dos jovens que trabalham em cafés," *O Internacional,* 1 May 1929.

49. Brazil, *Recenseamento 1920,* vol. 5.2, 386–417. The 1920 census only registered 9 jobs that were exclusively held by women and 142 by men.

50. "Pela unificação," *O Internacional,* 27 June 1925; "Pela classe," *O Internacional,* 15 June 1924.

51. In the Jafet textile factory, five fourteen-year-old boys were employed in bleaching positions. Two fifteen-year-olds were mechanics, one an assistant and one a full mechanic. The highest position given to girls was that of weaver, and women often tended fewer looms than men tended.

52. Antonio Stocco, 1980s interview, oficina 11, Memoria Fabril project, Museu da Cidade de São Paulo. Stocco reported making 660 réis per hour.

53. Brazil, *Recenseamento 1920*, vol. 5.2, 386–417.

54. Using the *Recenseamento 1920* to investigate gender pay differences of jobs that employed both men and women shows that in general, men could expect to earn 2$200 more per hour than women. This increases to 4$900 among the top-earning jobs (top quartile) and drops to 1$300 per hour in the lowest-earning jobs (bottom quartile). All these positions are registered in the lowest-earning jobs (bottom quartile).

55. In female wages over a male occupational distribution, the result reveals -.598. In male wages over a female distribution, the result is less extreme, at 0.051. For methodology, see Goldin, *Gender Gap*, 71–73.

56. Chamada A0000776, 3 July 1916.

57. Brazil, *Recenseamento 1920*, vol. 5.2, 386–417. Within the city, 6,072 women worked in textiles, 20,958 in beauty and clothing, and 12,729 in domestic work (vol. 4.5, 786–787).

58. The textile industrialist Jorge Street's approach represents an important exception to that of the typical textile industrialist because of his paternalistic attitude toward workers. In 1912, Jafet's capital value was 4,000 contos de réis, and the company employed 785 laborers. The average for São Paulo in 1912 was 1,989 contos de réis and 691 laborers (*Boletim da Directoria de Indústria e Commercio* [*BDIC*], 1912, 124–125). In 1917, Jafet's capital was 5,500 contos de réis, and the company employed 1,200 laborers. The average for São Paulo that year was 2,124 contos de réis and 486 laborers (*BDIC*, 1919, 120).

59. On Jafet's representativeness, see Ball, "Inequality in São Paulo's Old Republic," 67–69.

60. Based on the forty-two wage observations for boys and eighty-seven for girls under the age of fourteen in the Jafet 20 percent employee entry card sample. The gender pay difference increased slightly by including fourteen- and fifteen-year-olds.

61. Antononacci, "Atravesando o Altântico," 140; Ball, "Wife, Mother, and Worker," 122.

62. "Passaporte pra Ignacia de Jesus Ribeiro," box 410, processo 182, PP-ADP.

63. The jobs with the highest discrepancy in the male-to-female pay ratio were managerial positions (1.97), starchers (1.85), and threaders (1.75). The most similar pay appears to have been for weavers (1.125) (*BDET*, 1912, 76–77).

64. For a theoretical discussion of historical gender wage differentials, see Burnett, *Gender, Work, and Wages in Industrial Revolution Britain*, 80–84. Burnett argues that strength differences and less access to school for women led to lower female wages (104–123).

65. *Guerra Sociale*, 24 March 1917; *Revista de Comércio e Indústria* 5, no. 53 (May 1919), 143–144; Wolfe, *Working Women, Working Men*, 12–13.

66. Penteado implies relatively easy movement between different factories during the era (*Belènzinho*, 63–64), but his privilege allowed him a mobility unavailable to most women.

67. Pena, *Mulheres e trabalhadoras*, 35.

68. Besse, *Restructuring Patriarchy*, 121–122. Disputes over private matters were effectively decided by colonial laws and traditions. In 1858 Brazil's civil laws were compiled, but the Philippine Ordinances and institutionalized colonial practices still served as the basis for resolving legal disputes within the private sphere.

69. Tomasevicius Filho, "O legado do Código Civil de 1916," 87, 91 (quote). The 1916

Civil Code, also known as the Código Beviláqua, was in effect until 2003, when the updated 2002 code replaced it. The Instituto Histório Geográfico Brasileiro put out an edition dedicated to the code (*Revista IHGB* 178, no. 473 [January–March 2017]).

70. The original reads, "se o marido não ministrar os meios de subsistência à mulher e aos filhos." This caveat allows women to gain judicial authorization to work.

71. Ball, "Wife, Mother, and Worker," 112–113. For more descriptions of articles 242 and 245, see Pena, *Mulheres e trabalhadoras*, 147–149; Veccia, "Family and Factory," 37–39.

72. In the wage regression analysis, the *age* and *age*^{2} variables capture these two effects, respectively.

73. Veccia, "Family and Factory," 338. On earlier informality, see M. Pinto, *Cotidiano and sobrevivência*.

74. Mario Cardim reports the 1925 salary for a domestic as 120$000 (*Ensaio de analyse*, 24–25). The median hourly wage for an adult female nonapprentice worker at Jafet in 1925 was 0$500. Assuming nine-hour workdays, six days a week for four weeks a month yields a monthly income of 108$000.

75. Portuguese workers were also overrepresented, but the number of observations is too small to generalize, twelve adult male workers total, with two in medium-skilled positions. See appendix B, table B.10.

76. Ball, "Wife, Mother, and Worker" 116–119.

77. *BDET*, 1912, 74–75. On immigrant industrialists, see Dean, *Industrialization of São Paulo*, chapters 2, 4.

78. Penteado, *Belènzinho*, 111. The comparison of mechanic wages at Light, Paulista Railway, and Jafet is taken from the wage series (Ball, "Prices, Wages, and the Cost of Living").

79. Of the forty-three workers not considered white, three were not Brazilian; the Portuguese, Syrian, and Spanish workers were all considered *pardo*.

80. Suk, "Only the Fragile Sex Admitted," 601–606, 611.

81. Alvim and Peirão, *Mappin*, 21–22.

82. Alvim and Peirão, *Mappin*, 40–21.

83. Women who worked many years at Mappin include Maria Clayton, Leonor Perrone, Helene Rubenstein and Mme. Rosenthal (box 2, documents 42, 48, 52, Mappin Collection). Information is unavailable on the marital status of other high-ranking women at Mappin such as the clothing designer Dona Inês and the beauty assistant Lory Dawson, both of whom are mentioned in the interviews.

84. "Folha do pagamento," box 2, Mappin Collection.

85. These differences are consistent with those reported in Brazil, *Recenseamento 1920* (vol. 5.2, 386–417), in which male tailors (*cortadores de roupa*) made 1.87 times more than female tailors, and male seamsters made 1.24 times more than their female counterparts. Male tailors, thus, made 2.63 more than female seamsters. Male department heads and office personnel at Mappin made 2.2 more than their female counterparts.

86. Perrone comments on hiring practices (box 2, document 52, Mappin Collection).

87. Alvim and Peirão, *Mappin*, 53.

88. These nationalities might be overestimates because I accept the researcher's probable nationalities from the salary sheets. The evidence shows 35.46 percent Italians, 28.37

percent Portuguese, 8.51 percent British, and 3.55 percent Germans. Brazilians were just 23.4 percent of employees ("Folha de pagamento," Mappin Collection).

89. Andrews, *Blacks and Whites in São Paulo,* 67, 119–120, 126–127.

90. Suk, "Only the Fragile Sex Admitted," figures 1, 2.

91. Box 2, documents 42, 43, and 65, Mappin Collection.

92. Although there is no exact count of the time dos Santos stayed with the company, it was a significant portion of his working life (Alvim and Peirão, *Mappin,* 53).

93. Raquel Rolnik highlights Afro-Brazilian jobs from recorded municipal crimes in the capital, showing that Afro-Brazilians tended to be coachmen and cart drivers, day laborers, masons, cooks, construction workers, policemen, *catadores de lixo* (rag pickers), vendors, and loaders ("City and the Law," 63).

94. Brazil, *Recenseamento 1920,* vol. 4.5, 786–787; Veccia, "Family and Factory," 310–311. Less reputable professions were also viable options. "Prostitute," for example, appears as a profession in the 1923 *Boletins de Ocorrências* sample and Jacino's research, but likely due to circumstances, Afro-Paulistanas were overrepresented in this job (E14100, *Boletins de Ocorrências,* APESP; Jacino, *Transição e exclusão,* chapter 3).

95. Bosi, *Memória e sociedade,* 363–369.

96. "Revolting punishments" refers to a case reported in the newspaper in which Thereza da Conceição Ferreira was accused of abusing Anna Rosa, a minor, and then hiding her so the visual markings of the abuse would not be questioned (*Estado de São Paulo,* 16 May 1907, 2). Many patterns described by Sandra Graham would have persisted into the Old Republic (*House and Street,* 102–107).

97. Bosi, *Memória e sociedade,* 385, 389.

98. Interview transcripts from Veccia note that some women preferred textile factory jobs to domestic jobs, as the latter were associated with Afro-Brazilians ("Factory and Family," 310–311).

99. The stark absence of women from most of these incident reports in positions where the 1920 Brazilian census documents their employment, for example, as weavers, demonstrates that they do not fully and accurately represent the workforce.

100. Jacino, *Transição e exclusão,* 145–195.

101. Jacino, *Transição e exclusão,* 155–156.

102. The number of observations in figure 4.1 for each nationality and race in 1912, 1918, and 1923, respectively, is as follows: Italians (51, 32, 16); Portuguese (23, 21, 28); white Brazilians (35, 59, 52); Afro-Brazilians (25, 22, 21). They are drawn from E13968, entries 6299 to 6517; E14042, entries 56366 to 56650; E14100, entries 105287 to 105555, *Boletins de Ocorrências,* APESP.

103. This proportion does not include women who were termed "domestics," as there is ambiguity over whether the term referred to women who stayed home or were domestic service workers. The presence of "s.doméstica" in the records suggests the records made a distinction.

104. Decca, *A vida fora das fábricas,* 15–17, citing *BDET,* 1927.

105. Jacino, *Transição e exclusão,* 154–155.

106. Chamada A0000942, 15 July 1920.

107. *Estado de São Paulo,* 12 July 1891, 3.

108. *Estado de São Paulo,* 12 April 1891, 3; 11 January 1891.

109. Ads for white female cooks appear in *Estado de São Paulo*, 11 January 1891; 8 January 1893; 8 February 1891. While a help-wanted advertisement might be placed for more than one day, the month lag in the sampling minimizes double counting, an assumption confirmed in analyzing the sample.

110. Butler, *Freedoms Given, Freedoms Won*, 71–3.

111. Sources and count of advertisements are presented in appendix B, table B.11.

112. Alberto, *Terms of Inclusion*, 29–30. I diverge from Alberto in using the term "Afro-Brazilian" (22).

113. Butler, *Freedoms Given, Freedoms Won*, 71–75.

114. For discussion of "boa aparência," see Roth-Gordon, *Race and the Brazilian Body*, 42–48. The phrase *boa aparência* had been used in contexts prior to this period, but this era marked a transition toward implicit racial bias.

115. *Estado de São Paulo*, 1 January 1921; 10 January 1926; 13 July 1930.

116. Alberto, *Terms of Inclusion*, 99.

117. M. Martins, *A civilização do delegado*, 167–168.

118. This racial differentiation within the justice system supports Boris Fausto's evidence on types of crimes for which Afro-Brazilians were charged and arrested between 1880 and 1924. As a whole, Afro-Brazilians were proportionately incarcerated, but they were overrepresented in larceny cases and underrepresented in homicides (*Crime e cotidiano*, 63–71). Arrest rates by nationality are on 71–81.

119. The calculation is an underestimate based on five days per week, nine hours a day. The budget is based on Davis, "Padrão de vida dos operários," 163–165.

120. Most real estate listings did not include prices, but a *chácara* was listed for sale in the *Estado de São Paulo* of 13 January 1920 on page 10.

121. For a discussion of the models and channels by which education contributes to growth, see Barbosa Filho and Pessôa, "Educação e crescimento." David Lam and Suzanne Duryea link increased female education with fertility reduction and greater investment in children ("Effects of Schooling on Fertility, Labor Supply, and Investments in Children," 160–192). Sergio Ferreira and Fernando Veloso find lower intergenerational mobility in Brazil but demonstrate the relation between parent and child educational achievement ("Mobilidade intergeracional de educação no Brasil," 481–539).

122. A Barra Funda attendance book registers two girls leaving school to get jobs ("Livro de Presencia, Barra Funda," 1898, E02447, LiP, SA, APESP). On children in the workforce see Veccia, "Family and Factory," 300–317.

123. Ball, "Wife, Mother, and Worker," 120; Veccia, "My Duty as a Woman," 103–104.

124. Brazil, *Recenseamento 1920*, vol. 4.4, 803–804. The middle-class *centro* includes Sé, Consolação, Santa Cecília, and Santa Ifigênia. The working-class *centro* includes Bela Vista, Bom Retiro, Cambucí, Brás, Moóca, and Belenzinho. Latin American suburbs tend to be poorer and with less access to public goods and services and higher rates of informality, making them more akin to the English term outskirts. Working-class suburbs are Vila Marianna, Sant'Anna, Lapa, and Ipiranga. Small suburbs are defined as those non-*centro* neighborhoods with populations below 4,000; they include São Miguel, Osasco, Butantan, Perdizes, Penha da França, and Nossa Senhora do 'O. Liberdade is eliminated from the count because of its large Japanese population and greater literacy rates among Japanese immigrants (Honda, "Differential Structure, Differential Health," 263). It is worth noting

that by 1920 the literacy rate for girls was slightly higher in every neighborhood group but Brás, Moóca, and Belenzinho, further supporting evidence that working-class girls entered the labor force while boys went to school.

125. Calculations are from the real wage database and table 4.4. See also Ball, "Inequality in São Paulo's Old Republic," 150, table 5.4.

Chapter 5. The Textile Response: Labor Exploitation in the Postwar Era

1. Dean, *Industrialization of São Paulo*; J. Martins, *Empresário e empresa*; Teixeira, *A fábrica do sonho*.

2. On the 1882 law, see Summerhill, *Inglorious Revolution*, chapter 6; in chapter 2 Summerhill explores the connection between the Encilhamento and credit markets.

3. In 1906, the Brazilian government's decision to try to control world coffee supply and prices benefited the agricultural sector as a whole, leading to increased cotton plantings (Stein, *Brazilian Cotton Manufacture*, 99). The burgeoning crops provided cotton for textile production (Topik, *Political Economy of the Brazilian State*, 65).

4. Font, in *Coffee, Contention, and Change*, and Woodard, in *Place in Politics*, have demonstrated how growing tensions between coffee elites and urban interests contributed to the 1930 revolution. Luna and Klein also speak to this tension (*Economic and Demographic History of São Paulo*, 134–135). There were few rags-to-riches stories, as it was largely individuals from elite agricultural families or those involved in the export and import business who counted among the city's industrialists. On the industrial elite, see Dean, *Industrialization of São Paulo*, 49–60. Topik has observed debates surrounding exchange rate policies (*Political Economy of the Brazilian State*, 138–140), the industrial elite (153–155), and the connection between elites and the nonagricultural economy (143–146).

5. Topik, *Political Economy of the Brazilian State*, 146. Topik demonstrates the important fiscal and industrial changes and the gradual increase in industrial protection in the 1891–1915 period (144–146).

6. Luna and Klein, *Economic and Demographic History of São Paulo*, 80, 188–189; Topik, *Political Economy of the Brazilian State*, 143. On forward and backward linkages related to railroad construction and noncoffee agriculture, see Summerhill, *Order against Progress*, chapter 6.

7. Aldo Musacchio argues that postwar inflation in Brazil was high enough that investors were willing to give up investor protection "to protect labor against macroeconomic instability" (*Experiments in Financial Democracy*, 217).

8. Munck, with Falcon and Galitelli, *Argentina: From Anarchism to Peronism*, 76–89. Even in Montevideo, which had arguably the most developed labor organization in the region, labor unrest increased during the war, and 1917 saw a violent clash between the government and workers (Alexander, *History of Organized Labor in Uruguay and Paraguay*, 21–25). In Chile, 1917–1930 saw intensified labor organization; there, labor had better bargaining power than in Brazil, and negotiations proved more successful (DeShazo, *Urban Workers and Labor Unions in Chile*, chapter 6).

9. Weinstein, *For Social Peace in Brazil*, 13–50; Wolfe, *Working Women, Working Men*, 25–49; Ribeiro, *Condições de trabalho na indústria têxtil paulista*, chapter 4.

10. Bocketti, *Invention of the Beautiful Game*, 86–90; Decca, *A vida fora das fábricas*; Levy, "Forging an Urban Public."

11. Wolfe, *Working Women, Working Men*, 42–43.

12. Almost 35,000 of the city's 95,000 wage employees worked in the industrial sector (Luna and Klein, *Economic and Demographic History of São Paulo*, 198, 209).

13. This argument agrees with Weinstein in terms of variation within the working class (*For Social Peace in Brazil*, 38–42), and it challenges interpretations depicting a more unified laboring class during the Old Republic (Decca, *A vida fora das fábricas*, 129).

14. Luna and Klein, *Economic and Demographic History of São Paulo*, 284.

15. The estimate is based on *RSA* data from the following years and pages: 1920, 53; 1922, 85; 1923, 101–3; 1924, 76–82; 1925, 107; 1926, 130–131; 1927, 198–205; 1928, 366–375. This number is an underestimate, as there are no data for 1921. Using the ratio of capital to interior reentries from 1928, I estimate that 90 percent of the 66,311 reentries came from the capital.

16. In 1920, the hospedaria had 33,537 individuals registered, 8,957 of whom were reentries from the city. Only 1,685 of all registrations were contracted to work in the city (*RSA*, 1920, 53). The one-in-five ratio assumes that all city contracts were fulfilled by current city residents. This would not have been the case, meaning the odds were even smaller.

17. Luebke, *Germans in the New World*, chapter 8.

18. Dean, *Industrialization of São Paulo*, 51; Penteado, *Belènzinho*, 62, 109, 117, 120.

19. Light, *Annual Report*, 1925, 19; 1927, 109–110; 1928, 100, FESESP. Ficha evidence indicates that many workers left of their own volition, taking advantage of other job opportunities and higher pay.

20. Woodham, *Twentieth-Century Design*, 11–12. In 1887, just one year before Brazil abolished slavery on May 13, 1888, 15 percent of Brazil's enslaved population lived in the state (Stein, *Vassouras*; Vangelista, *Os braços da lavoura*, 38).

21. Ribeiro, *Condições de trabalho na indústria têxtil paulista*, 38–41.

22. Weinstein, *For Social Peace in Brazil*, 25–26.

23. Weinstein, *For Social Peace in Brazil*, 17.

24. Grandin, *Fordlândia*, 43–45.

25. Ribeiro, *Condições de trabalho na indústria têxtil paulista*, 42.

26. In Haber's "Efficiency Consequences of Institutional Change," he demonstrates the decline in spindles per worker. He notes that total factor productivity estimates cannot be compared across time due to unreliable price estimates (30, table 8). See also Haber, "Business Enterprise and the Great Depression in Brazil," 341–348; Topik, *Political Economy of the Brazilian State*, 154.

27. Gregory Clark espouses this correlation in "Why Isn't the Whole World Developed?" (149–152). In his calculations, Brazil's ratios place it most comparable to the following group of countries: France, Switzerland, Austro-Hungary, Spain, and Mexico.

28. Wolfe, *Working Women, Working Men*, 35.

29. Ribeiro, *Condições de trabalho na indústria têxtil paulista*, 70; Wolfe, *Working Women, Working Men*, 43. For Mexico, see Haber, *Industry and Underdevelopment*, 156–158, especially table 9.1. Spindles per worker can be considered a proxy for the capital-to-labor ratio (Razo and Haber, "Rate of Growth of Productivity in Mexico," 490).

30. Luna and Klein, *Economic and Demographic History of São Paulo*, 186–188. The efficiency decline in the sector suggests that the increase in machinery imports that Stanley Stein notes in the postwar years in *Brazilian Cotton Manufacture* were either not ad-

equately implemented or were not good matches for Brazilian conditions (Weinstein, *For Social Peace in Brazil*, 25n37).

31. Dean, *Industrialization of São Paulo*, chapter 6, contains a good discussion of competing views.

32. Weinstein emphasizes how older textile firm industrialists offered bonuses or benefits out of a paternalistic rather than rationalization approach (*For Social Peace in Brazil*, 25–26).

33. As early as 1920, a letter from Centro dos Industriaes de Fiação e Tecelagem de São Paulo (CIFTSP) industrialists complained that foreign imports threatened the Paulista textile sector ("Letter from CIFTSP to mayor of São Paulo," 30 October 1920). It is among Circulares Syndicato Patronal Industriais Têxteis de São Paulo, Associação Brasileira de Indústria Têxtil e de Confecção, São Paulo (hereafter cited as CIFTSP Circulares, ABIT). For discussion of stocks and the impact on the industry, see *RSA*, 1927, 16; 1928, 16–17.

34. Circular 63, 24 November 1921, 3, CIFTSP Circulares, ABIT. The original reads, "A guerra veio salvar as nossas industrias textis de ruína quasi certa: a importação desappareceu, os stocks europeus foram rapidamente exgottados e o nosso povo foi obrigado reconhecer que os tecidos nacionaes nada ficam a dever aos seus similares do extrangeiro."

35. Efforts to lobby for increasing taxes on imported cloth include "Letter to mayor," 30 October 1920, and Circulares 642, 644, 646, 724–726, 732 (CIFTSP Circulares, ABIT). Requests for lower import duties on inputs include "Copy of letter from 23 April 1924," 12 June 1924, and circular 229 (CIFTSP Circulares, ABIT).

36. "Letter from Sr. J. Lindolpho Camara to CIFTSP," 28 August 1924; response, 29 August 1924, Circular 351, CIFTSP Circulares, ABIT.

37. Topik, *Political Economy of the Brazilian State*, 151. Jennifer Eaglin discusses the tension between the sugar and coffee sectors of the economy and how valorizations in 1906, 1917, and the 1920s served as models for sugar during the Vargas era ("Sweet Fuel," 42–49).

38. Many CIFTSP circulars from 1922 address regulating cotton.

39. Discussion of the 1925 energy crisis dominated the circulars in February 1925 (Circular 413, 7 February 1925; Circular, 14 February 1925; Circular 427, 18 February 1925) and continued even through September (Circular 520, 22 September 1925). On reduced production hours, see Circulars 431, 19 February 1925; 452, 16 April 1925; 490, 3 July 1925, CIFTSP Circulares, ABIT.

40. Circular 612, 7 July 1926. Circulars discussing the 1926 crisis include 596, 31 May 1926; 603, 15 June 1926; 605, 19 June 1926; 606, 21 June 1926; 617, 16 July 1926; 631, 26 August 1926. Industrialist Francesco Matarazzo did not want to cut production, arguing that the Mariangela factory had many orders to fulfill ("Actas das assembleias geral extraordinarias," 11 June 1926; 6 July 1926, CIFTSP Circulares, ABIT).

41. Topik, *Political Economy of the Brazilian State*, 151–155. After the 1928 tariff was imposed, importation of textiles dropped considerably (Luna and Klein, *Economic and Demographic History of São Paulo*, 188, figure 7.3).

42. State law 2.028 of 1924 increased the annual tax burden for textiles to some of the highest among all industries, with the largest cotton and silk factories required to pay 5:000$000 and wool factories 10:000$000.

43. The scientific plantation is discussed in Dean, *Industrialization of São Paulo*, 131. Circular 74, 21 December 1921, mentions cotton residuals. The CIFTSP did begin publish-

ing a bulletin about worldwide cotton production, but its future was jeopardized in 1925 with the financial pressures from the energy crisis (Circular 233, 13 July 1923; "Letter from 13 January 1925"; "Relatorio e Balanço 1925–1926," CIFTSP Circulares, ABIT).

44. Wolfe, *Working Women, Working Men*, 34.

45. Dean, *Industrialization of São Paulo*, 114–117; Wolfe, *Autos and Progress*, 65.

46. Weinstein, *For Social Peace in Brazil*, 16–22.

47. Weinstein, *For Social Peace in Brazil*, 27–37.

48. Light, *Annual Report 1918*, 7–8, FESESP.

49. For a discussion of forward and backward linkages with Brazil's railroad industry, see Summerhill, *Order against Progress*, 25. In *Strategy of Economic Development*, Albert O. Hirschman introduces the concept that the production most linked with development was that which created both forward and backward linkages.

50. Light, *Annual Report 1918*, 7–8, FESESP.

51. Lecocq, "A fabricação de cimento no Brasil," *Revista de Comércio e Indústria* 7, no. 75 (March 1921): 77–79; *Revista da Associação Comercial de São Paulo* 2, no. 2:107.

52. On Cia. Brasileira de Cimento Portland, otherwise known as Perus, see Mascarenha, *A technologia e a retomado do desenvolvimento*, 17–19; Negri, "Concentração e desconcentração industrial em São Paulo," 38.

53. Peixoto-Mehrtens, *Urban Space and National Identity*, 26.

54. On the viability of ethanol development and the ethanol industry, see Eaglin, "Sweet Fuel," 50–52. Email correspondence between Jennifer Eaglin and the author, 29 March 2018. The state agriculture department reports on the ethanol initiative (*RSA*, 1922, 18). The state even tested a Ford car's ability to run 500 kilometers on the ethanol.

55. Weinstein, *For Social Peace in Brazil*, 31–36; Wolfe, *Autos and Progress*, 67. Peixoto-Mehrtens highlights construction workers' lack of technical knowledge (*Urban Space and National Identity*, 13–14).

56. Musacchio, *Experiments in Financial Democracy*, 218–220.

57. Dean, *Industrialization of São Paulo*, 144. The term "good and simple souls" is Simonsen's, but it is unclear whether the quote originates in "À margem da profissão" or "Rumo à verdade," an official speech delivered at the Escola Livre de Sociologia e Política de São Paulo, 27 May 1933.

58. Wolfe, *Working Women, Working Men*, 34; Weinstein, *For Social Peace in Brazil*, 38–50.

59. Weinstein, *For Social Peace in Brazil*, 17.

60. This subtle difference in underlying motivations had a large impact on the historiography of Brazil's economic history. Scholarship linking Brazil's past with slavery and the enslaved population's inability to transition to the industrial economy includes the São Paulo school of sociologists, notably Fernando Henrique Cardoso and Octavio Ianni Costa. Caio Prado Júnior, in *História econômica do Brasil*, argues that abolition and immigration played important roles.

61. Batalha, *O movimento operário na Primeira República*, 50–52; Lopreato, *O espíritu da revolta*.

62. Ribeiro, *Condições de trabalho na indústria têxtil paulista*, 78–79.

63. Circular 39, 25 July 1921, CIFTSP Circulares, ABIT. Ribeiro highlights many of the circulars (*Condições de trabalho na indústria têxtil paulista*, 84–100). However, this analy-

sis uses a broader lens to situate the CIFTSP response (Circular 39, 25 July 1921; Circular 217, 26 May 1923; Circulars 201, 302, 304, March 1924; Circular 316, April 1924, CIFTSP Circulares, ABIT).

64. "Letter from Cotonifício Rodolfo Crespi to CIFTSP," 25 March 1922, CIFTSP Circulares, ABIT.

65. Wolfe, "Anarchist Ideology, Worker Practice," 825–826; Wolfe, *Working Women, Working Men*, 38–54.

66. Circular 187, 3 March 1923, CIFTSP Circulares, ABIT, emphasis added. Ribeiro mentions the quote about making workers "disappear" but fails to discuss the significance of the wording (*Condições de trabalho na indústria têxtil paulista*, 86–95). The city of São Paulo reportedly had secret agents who specialized in repressing labor organization (Circular 366, 24 October 1924, CIFTSP Circulares, ABIT).

67. Some textile industrialists had been coffee plantation slave owners. A particularly damning report of Penteado's *bacalhau* tortures of his enslaved workforce confirms a long tradition of labor exploitation (Pinheiro and Hall, *A classe operária no Brasil*, 2:168–172). The report was originally published in the labor periodical *Terra Livre* as "Do escravocrata ao patrão," 1 June 1907, 2–3.

68. Circular 295, February 1924; Circular 302, 12 March 1924; Circular 304, 19 March 1924, CIFTSP Circulares, ABIT.

69. Circular 316, 23 April 1924, CIFTSP Circulares, ABIT.

70. Veccia, "Family and Factory," chapter 6, table 3.

71. "Letter to the state director of Department of Agriculture from the CIFTSP board," 18 June 1924, CIFTSP Circulares, ABIT. The original reads, "expurgar do seu seio os maus elementos que o infelicitam."

72. Circular 203, 12 April 1923, discussing rewarding workers who distinguished themselves at the International Centennial Exposition. "Letter to Sec da Ag from CIFTSP board," 17 June 1924, advocates for schools but says the state government should provide no social programs. Circular 872, 26 August 1929, reports on a symposium related to rationalization in industry.

73. Feeding a five-person family in 1925 cost between 1.4 and 1.6 times more than it had in 1920 (Ball, "Prices, Wages, and the Cost of Living," 12–15). Cardim shows that prices rose faster than wages between 1923 and 1928 ("Ensaio de analyse," 15).

74. Jorge Street's factory and Mappin department store did offer *férias* (holidays) to employees, but several interview transcripts suggest these were the only two large employers in the city offering that benefit (box 2, documents 52 and 65, Mappin Collection).

75. Circular 147, 6 November 1922; "Copy of letter to Exmo Sr. Deputado Arthur de Souza Lemos," 15 June 1929; Circular 853, 12 June 1929, CIFTSP Circulares, ABIT; Ribeiro, *Condições de trabalho na indústria têxtil paulista*, 157.

76. "Letter from CIFTSP," 29 July 1926, Circular 667, 31 December 1926, CIFTSP Circulares, ABIT. Circular 863, 22 July 1929, instructs members to finally enact the *lei de férias*, three years after the law was passed. One by-product of federal law 17.496 was that companies kept better employment records, which helps explain why scholarship on labor is more extensive since 1929.

77. The Rio proposal would have restricted this right to women with almost a year's service with the company (Circular 778, 7 May 1928, CIFTSP Circulares, ABIT).

78. Circular 778, 7 May 1928, CIFTSP Circulares, ABIT.

79. Ball, "Wife, Mother, and Worker," 118–119.

80. State decree 3.708 of April 1924 became state law 2.014 on 26 December 1924 (Circulars 323, 7 May 1924; 397, 31 December 1924; and 399, 6 January 1925; "Relatório e balanço 1925–6," CIFTSP Circulares, ABIT).

81. Bosi, *Memória e sociedade,* 326.

82. Weinstein, *For Social Peace in Brazil,* 33.

83. Ball, "Prices, Wages, and the Cost of Living," 12–15.

84. "Acta extraordinária," 31 October 1924; "Acta . . . extraordinária," 5 November 1924. A 10 percent concession had been planned and already granted earlier in the year (Circulars 282, 23 January 1924; 286, 31 January 1924; 294, 20 February 1924; 298, February 1924, CIFTSP Circulares, ABIT).

85. Circular 423, 14 February 1925. Reduced production set a precedent for future crises. Circulars 414, 423, and 426 discuss similar practices during the 1926–1927 crisis. "Acta da assembleia geral extraordinária," 6 July 1926, made clear that workers would not get paid normally as factories operated on reduced schedules.

86. Rolnik, "City and the Law," 194–202.

87. Pinheiro and Hall, *A classe operária no Brasil,* 1:251. Factory owners evicted all residents during a glassworkers strike in 1909.

88. On a preemptive 10 percent wage increase, see "Acta da assembleia geral extraordinária," 31 October 1924. On *operário* housing, see Circulars 573, 580, CIFTSP Circulares, ABIT.

89. The Polytechnic School held its first classes in 1894, and its first engineering class graduated in 1899. Roberto Simonsen graduated from the institution in 1909 (Weinstein, *For Social Peace in Brazil,* 17). Peixoto-Mehrtens, in *Urban Space and National Identity,* notes a need for these trained professionals.

90. Mascarenhas, *A technologia e a retomado do desenvolvimento,* 17–19.

91. In 1926, of 181 students who matriculated, 61 were in the one-year program, 43 in the two-year program (just 15 in the second year), and 45 in the civil engineering program (22 first year, 11 second year, 12 third year) (F. Azevedo, *Relatório do anno de 1926,* 4, 19).

92. *Escola Politécnica Relatórios,* 1920–1927.

93. *Escola Politécnica Relatório,* 1926, 2. On company contributions, see Mascarenhas, *A technologia e a retomado do desenvolvimento,* 21.

94. Mascarenhas, *A technologia e a retomado do desenvolvimento,* 20–23. The group of companies that invested in the expansion were Light (100:000$); Indústrias Reunidas F. Matarazzo (100:000$), various enterprises; Cia. Brasileira de Cimento Portland (50:000$), cement; Fábrica Votorantim (33:333$200), cement; Serva, Ribeiro & Cia. (15:000$), ironware and earthenware; Cia. Paulista de Louças Esmaltadas (10:000$), enamel tableware; Cotonifício Rodolfo Crespi (10:000$), textiles; Klabin & Irmãos (10:000$), paper.

95. Dean, *Industrialization of São Paulo,* 102–103.

96. "Pioneiros: Antonio Pereira Ignacio," Votorantim, 100 Anos, 2018, http://www.votorantim100.com/personagem/antonio-pereira-ignacio.

97. Votorantim was the second-largest textile factory in the state (Dean, *Industrialization of São Paulo,* 104).

98. Circulars 362, 20 October 1924; 368, 28 October 1924, CIFTSP Circulares, ABIT.

99. Circulars 667, 31 December 1926; 688, March 1927, CIFTSP Circulares, ABIT.

100. *Colorado School of Mines Magazine* 9, no. 1 (1918): 32. Moraes even wrote an article about Brazil for the school's magazine ("Occurrence of Nickel Ore").

101. "Pioneiros: Senador José Ermírio de Moraes," Votorantim 100 Anos, 2018, http://www.votorantim100.com/personagem/senador-jose-ermirio-de-moraes.

102. Monangueira, "Vila Maria Zélia"; Street and Moraes Filho, *Idéias sociais de Jorge Street*; Paula, "Os operários pedem passagem!"; Teixeira, *A fábrica do sonho*.

103. Teixeira, *A fábrico do sonho*; Weinstein, *For Social Peace in Brazil*, 23.

104. Barro and Bacelli, *História dos bairros de São Paulo: Ipiranga*, 107; Dean, *Industrialization of São Paulo*, 31.

105. By nationality, there were 220 Brazilians, 387 Italians, 150 Syrians, and 28 Spaniards (*BDET*, 1912, 74–75).

106. Dean, *Industrialization of São Paulo*, 30–31. State law 1.631 of 27 December 1918 officially made Ipiranga its own *distrito da paz* (judicial district) in the city, which would further facilitate providing goods and services.

107. São Paulo, Departamento Estadual de Estatística, *Catálogo das indústrias do município da capital*, 1943, entry 1032.

108. Dean, *Industrialization of São Paulo*, 170.

109. On the complexities of Lebanese nationalism, Greater Syria and Greater Lebanon independence movements, and the roles of emigrants in those movements, see Hakim, *Origins of the Lebanese National Idea*, chapter 8, particularly 224–225.

110. Jafet *fichas*. During her time at Jafet, Wadika experienced the death of her husband and the factory's adaptation of the *lei de férias* in the 1930s ("V & W," 1912–1930, Fiação, Tecelagem e Estamparia Ypiranga, Centro de Documentação de Informação Científic, Pontifícia Universidade Católica, São Paulo). For long-tenure anomaly, see Ball "Wife, Mother, and Worker," 118.

111. The Fiação e Malharia Ypiranga Assad textile company, which was founded in 1918 by the Assad brothers on Rua Sorocabanos, was just down the street from the Jafet factory. It also drew on the closeness of the Syrian community and the Jafet networks (São Paulo, Departamento Estadual de Estatística, *Catálogo das indústrias do município da capital*, 1943, entry 1004). Dean suggests that family ownership was a key component in Paulista industry and among successful firms (*Industrialization of São Paulo*, 113–121). The Assad and Jafet firms fit this model.

112. *BDIC*, 1912, 124–125; 1919, 120.

113. Wolfe, *Working Women, Working Men*, 23–24.

114. *Estado de São Paulo*, 11 August 1918, 11.

115. *Fichas* show that most workers attended two looms. Mariangela loom evidence is from Circular 758, 24 January 1928, CIFTSP Circulares, ABIT.

116. Wolfe, *Working Women, Working Men*, 36–39.

117. Wolfe, *Working Women, Working Men*, 35.

118. Circular 269, 14 December 1923, CIFTSP Circulares, ABIT; Jafet fichas.

119. Ball, "Prices, Wages, and the Cost of Living," 12–15.

120. Extraordinary General Assembly meetings reports, 31 October 1924, 5 November 1924, CIFTSP Circulares, ABIT. The wage increase is reflected in Jafet *ficha* evidence.

121. Here a tally from the Jafet *ficha* sample when workers revealed wage increases

shows 2 May 1923, 1 December 1923, and 1 January 1925 as the three points when Jafet granted factory-wide raises. Workers who got raises on 2 May 1923 include Justina Moneratti, João João de Moraes, Berenicia Bordini, Laurino Lopes, and Luiz Cansi.

122. Circulars 761, 10 February 1928; 764, 11 February 1928; 770, 17 March 1928, CIFTSP Circulares, ABIT.

123. Some firms even reduced their workforce. Jafet reduced work to three days per week and eight hours per day but made no apparent reduction in its workforce (Circular 637, 13 September 1926, CIFTSP Circulares, ABIT). Also see Street and Moraes Filho, *Idéias de Jorge Street*, 327–328.

124. The shares per year are as follows: 1923, 11.84 percent; 1924, 14.14 percent; 1925, 19.52 percent; 1926, 14.80 percent.

125. "Adult" here refers to workers over fifteen years of age. The most dramatic drop-off seems to have been from 1921 to 1922; however, there are few observations for those years.

126. These drops corresponded with the energy crises of the decade. Median tenures of adult workers at Jafet in the sample are reported by year and by gender.

127. Ball, "Wife, Mother, and Worker," 117–119.

128. For Jafet's support of reduced protection, see "Acta da assembleia geral extraordinária," 21 July 1926, CIFTSP Circulares, ABIT.

129. State decree 2.141 of 1911 prohibited child labor under age ten and night shifts for children under eighteen. It also required that children between ten and twelve only be assigned light tasks. The federal 1927 Código de Menores (Juvenile Code) prohibited all labor of children under age twelve.

130. Ball, "Inequality in São Paulo's Old Republic," 99. *BDET*, 1912, highlights that many children were employed and notes that the Jafets reported offering schooling subsidies (47). Perhaps subsidies were offered for Syrians' children (Bosi, *Memória e sociedade*, 324–326).

131. Rolnik, "City and the Law," 198. *BDET*, 1912, reports on Ipiranga under "N.5." (47). The numeration is 1 less than the tables on pages 70–77; however, the factory described clearly is the Jafet Ipiranga factory. On the Pombal, see Barro and Bacelli, *História dos bairros de São Paulo: Ipiranga*, 107–111. Jafet fichas name the Vila Jafet starting in the mid-1920s.

132. Bosi, *Memória e sociedade*, 326.

133. Musacchio finds greater capital concentration in firms occurring in the 1930s and through the end of the twentieth century (*Experiments in Financial Democracy*, chapter 10). He also notes the importance of family networks in successful firms during the Old Republic (123–124).

134. The CIFTSP instructed members to prepare for the *lei de férias* in July 1929. Fichas suggest an additional three-year lag for Jafet to implement the law.

135. Orberg, interview; Wolfe, *Autos and Progress*, 47, 51, 21.

136. Orberg recalls relative autonomy despite Ford's incorporation under US law (interview, 8–11); Wolfe, *Autos and Progress*, 49, 53.

137. Orberg, interview, 8–11, 26; Wolfe, *Autos and Progress*, 45–7.

138. Orberg, interview, 13.

139. Orberg, interview, 12. General Motors do Brasil was incorporated on 26 January 1925 with 2,000 common shares and 2 million cruzeiros ("Brasil," GM International

Relations: Argentina, Brazil, Uruguaya, Mexico binder, General Motors Heritage Center, Detroit).

140. *Panorama* 44, no. 1 (2005), historic eightieth-year edition.

141. Luna and Klein report more than 34,000 textile workers in the state and 53 percent of Brazilian textiles being produced in the city (*Economic and Demographic History of São Paulo*, 201–203). Thus, 15,000 is an underestimate of the city's textile labor force.

Chapter 6. The Middle-Class Glass Ceiling in the Postwar Era

1. Lesser, *Immigration, Ethnicity, and National Identity;* Lone, *Japanese Community in Brazil*, 48–56. The hospedaria registros sample reveals an increase in Russians, Hungarians, and Germans.

2. Here I am not speaking of employer goals but rather of workers' abilities to use mechanisms employers implemented to meet their own needs. The choice of "good" jobs and "bad" jobs recalls the language of dual labor market theories. While perhaps not a rigid dual labor market, the substantial pay differences, structures, and strategies in the textile sector compared to the transportation sector definitely made the former bad jobs and the latter good jobs. I diverge here from arguing that São Paulo had a pure dual labor market because workers with good jobs were clearly motivated by training, loyalty, and promotions. On dual labor market debate, see particularly Wachter's critique and Piore's rebuttal in Wachter et al., "Primary and Secondary Labor Markets."

3. Scholars have noted the presence of liberal professions in a growing middle class (Font, *Coffee, Contention, and Change,* 182; Woodard, *Place in Politics,* 179–183).

4. A working middle class emerged prior to the Vargas era, which challenges scholarship highlighting this group in the 1930s and throughout the Vargas era (Peixoto-Mehrtens, *Urban Space and National Identity,* 129–136; Weinstein, *Color of Modernity,* chapters 3, 6).

5. Bocketti, *Invention of the Beautiful Game;* Decca, *A vida fora das fábricas;* Levy, "Forging an Urban Public"; Ribeiro, *Condições de trabalho na indústria têxtil paulista;* Suk, "Becoming Modern at the Movies"; Wolfe, *Working Women, Working Men.*

6. Chamadas A0000436, 11 January 1919; A0000437, 15 February 1919.

7. Chamada A0000860, 21 November 1920; Holloway, *Immigrants on the Land,* 84–86.

8. Chamada A0000860, 21 November 1920. The original reads, "Desculpe em a carta hir em portugues, que a fez a delfina do Joaquim que estava na turma que tambem veio para aqui estamos vizinhos."

9. The translation diverges from the more common use of in the expression *dar um jeito,* which means "to make a way" or "to make it happen."

10. Chamada A0000860. Wages equivalent to nominal wages in Ball, "Prices, Wages, and the Cost of Living."

11. Roque Mestrieri, interview, ca. 1980, São Paulo, box 2, document 43, Mappin Collection. The collection includes interview transcripts that Alvim and Peirão conducted in São Paulo in the early 1980s to research and write *Mappin: Setenta Anos.*

12. The Jafet fichas show that employees from the interior were indistinguishable from other employees in age and literacy.

13. Jafet fichas list former employers and, so it is possible to distinguish those whose prior work was in interior textile factories from those coming from agricultural jobs in the

interior. Light fichas began systematically registering workers' previous employers in 1924, which included noting industrial employers in the interior.

14. Vangelista, *Os braços da lavoura*, 83.

15. *Colonos* did not necessarily anticipate that production would double in the 1927–1928 growing season (Luna and Klein, *Economic and Demographic History of São Paulo*, 109–111; *RSA*, 1928, 347).

16. Only 26 of the 1,123 employees registering prior employers in the Light sample came from the interior. Only 38 of 1,145 employees registered going to the interior as the reason they were leaving; this number is likely an underestimate because employees leaving due to low wages may also have returned or gone to the interior.

17. An article from 1921 explains that many *colonos* migrated to the city because they earned more there (*Revista Brasileira de Commercio*, no. 77 [May 1921]: 156–157).

18. For the forty-two Jafet employees who came from the interior, the median age was twenty and median tenure 282 days; their average age was twenty-five; 57 percent were female, 47 percent literate, 83 percent white, 57 percent Brazilian, and 31 percent piece-rate employees. For the 1,258 Jafet employees with prior employers in the sample, the median age was eighteen, median tenure 256.5 days, average age twenty-one; 65 percent were female, 52 percent literate, 93 percent white, 65 percent Brazilian, and 38 percent piece-rate employees. These percentages are based on fewer observations for tenure, race, and literacy. Adamo also notes that Afro-Brazilians were more likely than whites to migrate to cities ("Broken Promise," 22).

19. Weinstein, *Color of Modernity*, 225.

20. *RSA*, 1919, 28–31.

21. *RSA*, 1919, 29–31.

22. *RSA*, 1927, 339.

23. *RSA*, 1928, 338; *RSA*, 1926, 115.

24. *RSA*, 1919, 28.

25. *RSA*, 1920, 53; 1922, 85; 1923, 101–103; 1924, 76–82; 1925, 107; 1926, 130–131; 1927, 198–205; 1928, 366–375.

26. Chamada A0000439, 7 April 1919.

27. Jafet fichas sample; *RSA*, 1920, 53; 1922, 85; 1923, 101–103; 1924, 76–82; 1925, 107; 1926, 130–131; 1927, 198–205; 1928, 366–375.

28. Light ficha for Antonio Marcelino Pedro.

29. In the Light sample, thirty-five workers were contracted directly from Europe and twenty-six from the interior. Jafet did not hire many workers directly from Europe.

30. In the sample, seven of the twenty-three employees hired directly from Europe were "Syrian." The only other nation registering more than two direct contracts was Hungary.

31. Chamada A0000823, 21 April 1921.

32. Penteado describes moving from São Paulo to Buenos Aires and back to São Paulo (*Belènzinho*, 23–29).

33. *RSA*, 1908, 111; 1912–1913, 181–182.

34. *RSA*, 1916, 151.

35. *RSA*, 1916, 151.

36. *RSA*, 1920, 49; 1922, 83; 1923, 99, 100; 1926, 116, 125; 1927, 187, 192; 1928, 340.

37. Ester Namias Cansanção provides a similar story of migration from Argentina to Brazil (box 2, document 74, Mappin Collection).

38. Chamada A0000823, 21 April 1921.

39. Masterson, with Funada-Classen, *Japanese in Latin America*, 73–82.

40. Daniels, *Politics of Prejudice*, chapter 1; Lesser, *Immigration, Ethnicity, and National Identity*, 150–163.

41. Mae M. Ngai's essay "Architecture of Race in American Immigration Law" on the 1924 Immigration Act is interesting in her conceptualization of national origin.

42. Lesser, *Immigration, Ethnicity, and National Identity*, 129–130; *RSA*, 1920, 53; 1922, 85; 1924, 76–82.

43. In the Jafet 1920s sample, there were sixteen Hungarian employees and seven Russians. At Light, there were twenty-three Hungarians, five Romanians, and sixteen Russians.

44. *RSA*, 1922, 92. The *RSA* of 1920 addresses how Russians were granted subsidies in that year (41).

45. Chamada A0000992, 14 February 1922.

46. Gypsies were not allowed into Brazil. A petition speaks of gypsies coming from Uruguay who were refused entry (6 August 1913, C09857, SA-I, APESP).

47. It is not uncommon to find mislabeled destinations when the passport indicates arrival in one city and the accompanying documentation indicates another. Two examples are the passport for Maria de Jesus, (July 1914, box 99, processo 127, PP, ADP) and the passport for Ermelinda Martins dos Santos (1912, box 342, processo 782, PP, ADP).

48. On immigration restrictions see Skidmore, *Black into White*, 198–199. On quotas see Lesser, *Negotiating National Identity*, 120–121. Many first-generation Brazilians would benefit from the Nationalization of Labor Law enacted in 1931 (Andrews, *Blacks and Whites in São Paulo*, 97).

49. Ball, "Prices, Wages, and the Cost of Living," 24–25.

50. In the Mappin Collection, interview with Bartolomeu Perrota and Antonieta Dal Bello Perrota, box 2, document 53 has the number of female seamsters; interview with Angela Sgarro Specchio, document 66 has the number of female embroiderers.

51. Suk, "Only the Fragile Sex Admitted," 598–601.

52. Mappin Collection box 2, document 53 has information on piece-rate workers.

53. Suk, "Only the Fragile Sex Admitted," 598.

54. General Motors do Brasil offered 300$000 monthly for a mechanic position in 1925 (*Panorama*, May 1993, 11). The Light fichas sample shows median wage for nonapprentice mechanics at Light in the same year was 210$000.

55. Chamada A0000436. All the school-age children were enrolled.

56. Ball, "Wife, Mother, and Worker," 120.

57. Stocco, interview. On the popularity of soccer see Bocketti, *Invention of the Beautiful Game*.

58. Veccia, "My Duty as a Woman," 102–103; chamada A0001226, 10 December 1923.

59. Girls represented 8.55 percent of the Jafet workforce sample; boys represented 3.65 percent. Girls working outside of the home or not as domestics were employed in textile, food, and chemical factories or in the clothing and beauty sectors (Brazil, *Recenseamento* 1920, vol. 5.2, 386–417).

60. Dona Livinia, interview transcript, in Bosi, *Memória e sociedade*, 324.

61. Light fichas, Antonio Marcelino Pedro.

62. Almost 15 percent of Light employees left because of low wages and/or for other jobs. The share was almost 30 percent among German and Austrian workers.

63. In an interview with Vicente Sgarro's daughter, Angela Sgarro Specchio, she notes that she spoke with a Neopolitan accent (transcript, box 2, document 66, Mappin Collection).

64. Sgarro's daughter, Angela, recalled walking and grooming the horses (box 2, document 66, Mappin Collection).

65. Box 2, document 66, Mappin Collection.

66. The original reads, "Meu filho trabalhou no Mappin, no escritório. Depois saiu, porque foi mandado embora por ter outro emprego. Mas hoje é formado em economia e está muito bem" (box 2, document 66, Mappin Collection).

67. Leonor Perrone provides another example (box 2, document 52, Mappin Collection).

68. Box 2, document 62, Mappin Collection.

69. Employees received eight days of paid vacation; Mappin was the only place to offer paid vacation other than Jorge Street. Employees also only paid 10 percent over the wholesale price for products box 2, documents 65, 53, Mappin Collection).

70. Box 2, documents 43, 53, Mappin Collection.

71. Box 2, document 42, Mappin Collection.

72. Nelly Colson, interview, box 2, document 32, Mappin Collection.

73. *Panorama*, February 1966, 4. He became *superintendente da construcção de carroçarias, pintura e acabamento* (head of car construction, painting, and finishing).

74. *Panorama*, 1993, 11. Light fichas show that a mechanic at Light during that year could expect to earn 210$000 a month, and salaries ranged between 121$333 and 346$000. The median pay for nonapprentice mechanics in 1925 was 1$200 an hour (São Paulo Tramway, Light and Power Company, FESESP).

75. *Panorama*, May 1993, 11. Other family employment stories include those of the Minchini family (*Panorama*, February 1996) and Sergio Dal Pogetto and his father, Oriundo, and uncle Dante (*Panorama*, January 2005).

76. *Panorama*, May 1993, 11.

77. The weekly budget for food is estimated from Ball, "Prices, Wages, and the Cost of Living," 11–15. On Ford offering relatively high wages, see Orberg, interview, 13.

78. Laerte also left General Motors do Brasil for personal reasons in 1927, 1929–1934, and the end of the 1940s, but he was loyal to the company (*Panorama*, 1993, 11). São Paulo's 1932 revolution helped rescue General Motors do Brasil from the Depression as Paulistas demanded production for the revolution.

79. For the service school, see *GMWorld*, March 1950. On SESI and SENAI, see Weinstein, *For Social Peace in Brazil*, chapter 4.

80. Barro and Bacelli, *História dos bairros de São Paulo: Ipiranga*, 63.

81. "Report on GM do Brasil," 1952, GM International Relations: Argentina, Brazil, Uruguay, Mexico Binder; GM Heritage Center; *Panorama*, January 2006, 49.

82. The gold watch is a GM tradition, but the exact date of when the first gold watch was distributed in Brazil was in the early 1950s (*Panorama*, February 1996; *GMWorld* August–September 1953; *GMWorld*, March 1954.

83. *Panorama*, 1960s.

84. *Panorama*, 1994, special edition.

85. There is not a single Afro-Brazilian or female represented in the twenty-five *Panorama* photographs showing employees receiving the watches in the 1960s. By the 1980s, only 8 women (1.8%) and 14 Afro-Brazilians (3.2%) appeared among the 430 employees receiving watches. These may not include all recipients, as the pages were scanned by archivists at GM in Brazil, and some issues appeared to be missing.

86. Box 2, document 52, good appearance; document 48, standard for department heads, Mappin Collection.

87. Chamadas A0001136, A0001112, A0001226. It was only after five to eight years, on average, that immigrants asked aging family members to join them.

88. Chamada A0000878, 29 June 1920. In the chamadas database, his name appears as João Partaldi, but the document reads Partaloli.

89. Chamada A0000878, 29 June 1920. The job of banana vendors has been associated with Afro-Brazilians, so Partaloli's choice of a degraded profession seems particularly intriguing.

90. Chamada A0001089, 24 July 1922.

91. 25 June 1917, box 451, processo 991, PP, ADP.

92. 24 June 1917, box 452, processo 1113–1114, PP, ADP. The original reads, "Pois que aé dever ser mais baratas do que cá."

93. Chamada A0000803, 15 October 1917.

94. Chamada A0000823, 21 April 1921.

95. Ball, "Prices, Wages, and the Cost of Living"; Cardim, *Ensaio de analyse*.

96. Chamada A0000823, 21 April 1921.

97. Wolfe, *Working Women, Working Men*, 30–35.

98. Chamada A0000112, 24 March 1923.

99. Dona Risoleta interview, in Bosi, *Memória e sociedade*, 363–401, particularly p. 388.

100. Luna and Klein, *Economic and Demographic History of São Paulo*, 274–276.

101. Childhood mortality accounted for 52.8 percent of all deaths. Life expectancy for individuals born in 1920 was just 30.9 years for men and 36.6 years for women (Luna and Klein, *Economic and Demographic History of São Paulo*, 279–280).

102. Rolnik, "City and the Law," 275. In 1914 the population was 110 inhabitants per hectare; in 1930 the figure was just 47.

103. Rolnik, "City and the Law," 214–218.

104. Bosi, *Memória e sociedade*, 136; Rolnik, "City and the Law," 269–273.

105. Chamada A0001089, 24 July 1922.

106. Rolnik, "City and the Law," 95.

107. Rolnik, "City and the Law," 98, 129, 139–140; on the 1920s, 214–215.

108. Rolnik, "City and the Law," 264–266.

109. Woodard, *Place in Politics*, chapter 4.

110. Victor Nunes Leal's 1948 classic work *Coronelismo, enxada e voto* documents the phenomenon of the *café com leite* (coffee with milk) oligarchy characterized by political bosses and electoral fraud. Analyses of the period find considerable infighting within the ruling Partido Republicano Paulista (Font, *Coffee, Contention, and Change*; Woodard, *Place in Politics*).

111. Font, *Coffee, Contention, and Change,* 207–210; Rolnik, "City and the Law," 259–261; Woodard, *Place in Politics,* 140, 155, 166.

112. Rolnik, "City and the Law," 261–267. This was a part of the Prestes Maia Plano de Avenidas in 1924 that included the construction of Avenida 9 de Julho. On the implementation of the Plano de Avenidas in the 1930s and its complicated legacy in the city, see Peixoto-Mehrtens, *Urban Space and National Identity,* 103–107.

113. Odette Seabra's *Os meandros dos rios nos meandros do poder,* the 2019 publication of her much-cited 1987 dissertation, extensively covers the flooding of those rivers.

114. Rolnik, "City and the Law," 269–270, italics in the original.

115. Kogan, "Socio-Environmental History of the Floods in São Paulo," 51, 78–79.

116. Kogan, "Socio-Environmental History of the Floods in São Paulo," 93.

117. Seabra, *Os meandros dos rios nos meandros do poder.* On the influence of urban developer Companhia City and the development of the Jardins, see Peixoto-Mehrtens, *Urban Space and National Identity,* 33–39.

118. *Estado de São Paulo,* 19 February 1929, 7.

119. The government offered free barge service for residents from points in the following neighborhoods: Vila Elza, Vila Maria, Vila Guilherme, Casa Verde, Bairro da Corôa, Bairro da Limão, Freguesia do Ó, Piquery, Lapa, Vila Anastácio, Cidade Jardim, Canindé, Bom Retiro, and Ipiranga (*Estado de São Paulo,* 19 February 1929, 7).

120. On recent research of the 1929 flood, see the Universidade Federal de São Paulo's Hímaco research project database, Base de Dados da Enchente de 1929, http://www2.unifesp.br/himaco/enchente_1929.php#.

121. *Estado de São Paulo,* 19 February 1929, 7.

122. *Estado de São Paulo,* 19 February 1929, 7.

Appendix A. Livros de registros de matrícula de entrada de imigrantes na Hospedaria de Imigrantes

1. Informally, the database is also known as the Banco de Dados Maria José, named after a researcher who helped developed it.

2. I added a filter to isolate heads of households and then an additional filter to distinguish individuals coming with families (*chefe*) versus those coming alone (*só*).

3. The total number of adults arriving between 1903 and 1927 to the city was 17,796. The total number in our head-of-household and individual sample is 850.

4. Literacy rates are from Brazil, *Recenseamento 1920,* vol. 4.4, x–xi, 803–804.

Appendix B. Chapter 4 Data

1. For details of the construction of the database, see Ball, "Prices, Wages, and Cost of Living." Andrews describes the records for Jafet and Light (*Blacks and Whites,* appendix C). Lanna, in *Ferrovia, cidade e trabalhadores,* provides a description of the Paulista evidence.

Bibliography

Archives

Annaes da Sessão Extraordinária e Ordinária. Associação Legislativo do Estado de São Paulo. São Paulo.

Boletins de Ocorrências. Secretaria da Segurança Pública do Estado de São Paulo. Arquivo Público do Estado de São Paulo (APESP). São Paulo.

Cartas de chamada. Memória do Imigrante. http://www.inci.org.br/acervodigital/. Arquivo Público do Estado de São Paulo (APESP). São Paulo.

Circulares. Sindicato Patronal Industriais Têxteis de São Paulo. Library, Associação Brasileira de Indústria Têxtil e de Confecção. São Paulo.

Division newsletter. General Motors Operations. General Motors Heritage Center (GMHC). Sterling Heights, MI.

Fiação, Tecelagem e Estamparia Ypiranga. Centro de Documentação de Informação Cientific. Pontifícia Universidade Católica, São Paulo.

Fundo de Intendência Municipal (FIM). Arquivo Histórico Municipal Washington Luís (AHMWL). São Paulo.

General Motors International Relations. Brazil. General Motors Heritage Center (GMHC). Sterling Heights, MI.

General Motors Overseas Operations History. General Motors Heritage Center (GMHC). Sterling Heights, MI.

Inspetoria de Imigração de Santos. Secretaria da Agricultura. Arquivo Público do Estado de São Paulo (APESP). São Paulo.

Leuenroth, Edgard. Edgard Leuenroth Archive. Instituto de Filosofia e Ciências Humanas. Universidade Estadual de Campinas, Brazil.

Livros de Presência. Secretaria da Agricultura. Arquivo Público do Estado de São Paulo (APESP). São Paulo.

Livros de registros de matrícula de entrada de imigrantes na hospedaria (registros). Memória do Imigrante. Arquivo Público do Estado de São Paulo (APESP). São Paulo. http://inci.org.br/acervodigital/livros.php.

Mappin Collection. Ca. 1980. Documentação Histórica e Iconografia do Museu do Ipiranga. Museu Paulista. São Paulo.

Memoria Fabril. Museu da Cidade de São Paulo. São Paulo.

Orberg, Kristian. Interview by Owen Bombard. 25 May 1953, São Paulo. Acc. 65, box 51, transcript. Oral Histories. Benson Ford Research Center. Detroit, MI.

Polícia Administrativa e Higiene (PAH). Arquivo Histórico Municipal Washington Luís (AHMWL). São Paulo.

Processos de Passaporte. Arquivo Distrital do Porto, Portugal.

São Paulo Tramway, Light, and Power Company. Fundação Energia e Saneamento. São Paulo.

Turmas de Visita. Secretaria da Agricultura. Arquivo Público do Estado de São Paulo (APESP). São Paulo.

Secondary Sources

Abramitzky, Ran, Leah Platt Boustan, and Katherine Eriksson. "A Nation of Immigrants: Assimilation and Economic Outcomes in the Age of Mass Migration." *Journal of Political Economy* 122, no. 3 (2014): 467–506. https://doi.org/10.1086/675805.

Acemoglu, Daron, Simon Johnson, and James A. Robinson. "The Colonial Origins of Comparative Development: An Empirical Investigation," *American Economic Review* 91, no. 5 (2001): 1369–1401.

Adamo, Samuel. "The Broken Promise: Race, Health, and Justice in Rio de Janeiro, 1890–1940." PhD diss., University of New Mexico, 1983.

———. "Race and Povo." In *Modern Brazil*, edited by Conniff and McCann, 192–208.

Alberto, Paulina. *Terms of Inclusion: Black Intellectuals in Twentieth-Century Brazil*. Chapel Hill: University of North Carolina Press, 2011.

Alexander, Robert. *History of Organized Labor in Uruguay and Paraguay*. Westport, CT: Praeger, 2005.

Almanach commercial brasileiro, 1918. São Paulo, Brazil: O Ribeiro, 1918.

Alvim, Zuleika M. F., and Solange Peirão. *Mappin: Setenta anos*. São Paulo: Ex Libris, 1985.

Americano, Jorge. *São Paulo nesse tempo: 1915–1935*. São Paulo: Melhoramentos, 1962.

Andrews, George Reid. *Blacks and Whites in São Paulo, Brazil, 1888–1988*. Madison: University of Wisconsin Press, 1991.

Antononacci, Maria Antonietta. "Atravessando o Altântico: Memórias de imigrantes espanholas no fazer-se de São Paulo." *Revista de História UFC* 1, no. 2 (2002): 131–164. http://www.repositorio.ufc.br/handle/riufc/17195.

Autor, David H., and Susan N. Houseman. "Do Temporary-Help Jobs Improve Labor Market Outcome for Low-Skilled Workers? Evidence from "Work First." *American Economic Journal: Applied Economics* 2, no. 3 (July 2010): 96–128. aeaweb.org/articles?id=10.1257/app.2.3.96.

Azevedo, Aluísio de. *O cortiço*. São Paulo: Círculo do Livro, 1991 [1890].

Azevedo, Francisco P. Ramos. *Relatório do anno de 1926 apresentado ao Exmo. Sr. Dr. José Manuel Lobo, D.D., Secretário d'Estado dos Negócios do Interior*. São Paulo, 1926.

Bade, Klaus J. "From Emigration to Immigration: The German Experience in the Nineteenth and Twentieth Centuries." *Central European History* 28, no. 4 (1995): 507–535.

Baer, Werner. *The Brazilian Economy: Growth and Development*, 4th ed. Westport, CT: Praeger, 1995.

Baily, Samuel L. *Immigrants in the Lands of Promise: Italians in Buenos Aires and New York City, 1870–1914*. Ithaca, NY: Cornell University Press, 2004.

Bales, Kevin. "The Dual Labor Market of the Criminal Economy." *Sociology Theory* 2 (1984): 140–164.

Ball, Molly Catherine. "Inequality in São Paulo's Old Republic: A Wage Perspective, 1891–1930." PhD diss., University of California, Los Angeles, 2013.

———. "Prices, Wages, and the Cost of Living in Old Republic São Paulo: 1891–1930." *Research in Economic History* 34 (2018): 1–34. doi.org/10.1108/S0363-326820180000034001.

———. "Wife, Mother, and Worker: The Decision to Work in Early Twentieth-Century São Paulo." *Journal of Women's History* 29, no. 4 (2017): 109–132. doi:10.1353/jwh.2017.0053.

Barbosa Filho, Fernando de Holanda, and Samuel de Abreu Pessôa. "Educação e crescimento: O que a evidência empírica e teórica mostra?" *Economia* 11, no. 2 (2010): 265–303.

Barro, Máximo, and Roney Bacelli. *História dos bairros de São Paulo: Ipiranga*. São Paulo: Prefeitura Municipal de São Paulo, 1981.

Bastide, Roger, and Florestan Fernandes, eds. *Brancos e negros em São Paulo*. 2nd ed. São Paulo: Nacional, 1959.

Batalha, Claudio H. M. *O movimento operário na Primeira República*. Rio de Janeiro: Jorge Zahar, 2000.

Becker, Gary. *The Economics of Discrimination*. Chicago: University of Chicago Press, 1957.

Bértola, Luis, and José Antonio Ocampo. *Economic Development of Latin America since Independence*. Oxford, England: Oxford University Press, 2012.

Bértola, Luís, Melissa Hernández, and Sabrina Siniscalchi. "Un índice histórico e desarrollo humano de América Latina y algunos países de otras regions: Metodología, fuentes y bases de datos." Serie Documento de Trabajo no. 28, Facultad de Ciencias Sociales, Programa de História Económica y Social, Universidad de la República, Montevideo, Uruguay, 2011. https://EconPapers.repec.org/RePEc:ude:doctra:28.

Besse, Susan. *Restructuring Patriarchy: The Modernization of Gender Inequality in Brazil, 1914–1940*. Chapel Hill: University of North Carolina Press, 1996.

Bethell, Leslie, and José Murilo de Carvalho. "1822–1850." In *Brazil: Empire and Republic 1822–1930*, edited by Leslie Bethell, 45–112. New York: Cambridge University Press, 1989.

Blay, Eva Alterman. *Eu não tenho onde morar: Vilas operárias na cidade de São Paulo*. São Paulo: Studio Nobel, 1985.

Blount, John Allen III. "A administração da saúde pública no estado de São Paulo: O serviço sanitário, 1892–1918." *Revista de Administração de Empresas* 12, no. 4 (October–December 1972): 40–48. http://dx.doi.org/10.1590/S0034-75901972000400003.

Bocketti, Gregg. *The Invention of the Beautiful Game: Football and the Making of Modern Brazil*. Gainesville: University Press of Florida, 2016.

Bollinger, William. "Peru." In *Latin American Labor Organizations*, edited by Greenfield and Maram, 307–388.

Bosi, Ecléa. *Memória e sociedade: Lembranças de velhos*. 3rd ed. São Paulo: Companhia das Letras, 1994.

Boustan, Leah Platt. *Competition in the Promised Land: Black Migrants In Northern Cities and Labor Markets*. Princeton, NJ: Princeton University Press, 2016.

Brazil, Directoria Geral de Estatística. *Recenseamento do Brasil em 1872*. 12 vols. Rio de

Janeiro: Typ. G. Leuzinger, 1874. https://biblioteca.ibge.gov.br/biblioteca-catalogo. html?id=225477&view=detalhes.

———. *Recenseamento do Brasil, realizado em 1 de setembro de 1920*. 40 vols. Rio de Janeiro, 1922–1930.

Bucciferro, Justin R. "Racial Inequality in Brazil from Independence to the Present." In *Has Latin American Inequality Changed Direction? Looking over the Long Run*, edited by Luis Bértola and Jeffrey Williamson, 171–194. Cham, Switzerland: Springer Open Access, 2017. https://doi.org/10.1007/978-3-319-44621-9.

Buenos Aires, Ministerio de Desarrollo Económico. *La economía porteña en cifras*. Buenos Aires: Gobierno de la Ciudad de Buenos Aires, 2010.

Burnett, Joyce. *Gender, Work, and Wages in Industrial Revolution Britain*. New York: Cambridge University Press, 2008.

Butler, Kim D. *Freedoms Given, Freedoms Won: Afro-Brazilians in Post-Abolition São Paulo and Salvador*. New Brunswick, NJ: Rutgers University Press, 1998.

Caldeira, Teresa P. R. *City of Walls: Crime, Segregation, and Citizenship in São Paulo*. Berkeley: University of California Press, 2000.

Camou, María Magdalena, Silvana Maubrigades, and Rosemary Thorp. *Gender Inequalities and Development in Latin America during the Twentieth Century*. New York: Routledge, 2016.

———. Introduction to *Gender Inequalities and Development in Latin America*, edited by Camou, Maubrigades, and Thorp, 2–23.

Cano, Wilson. *Raízes da concentração industrial em São Paulo*. São Paulo: DIFEL, 1977.

Cánovas, Marília Dalva Klaumann. "Imigrantes espanhóis na Paulicéia: Trabalho e sociabilidade urbana, 1890–1922." PhD diss., Universidade de São Paulo, 2007.

Cardim, Mario. *Ensaio de analyse de factores economicos e financeiros do estado de São Paulo e do Brasil no periodo de 1913–1934 pelo methodo de numeros indices*. São Paulo: Secretaria da Agricultura, Indústria e Commércio, Estado de São Paulo, Directoria de Publicidade Agrícola, 1936.

Chazkel, Amy. *Laws of Chance: Clandestine Lottery and the Making of Urban Public Life*. Durham, NC: Duke University Press, 2011.

Clark, Gregory. "Why Isn't the Whole World Developed? Lessons from the Cotton Mills." *Journal of Economic History* 47, no. 1 (1987): 141–73. doi:10.1017/S0022050700047458.

Coatsworth, John H. "Indispensable Railroads in a Backward Economy: The Case of Mexico." *Journal of Economic History* 39, no. 4 (1979): 939–960.

Coatsworth, John H., and Alan M. Taylor, eds. *Latin America and the World Economy since 1800*. Cambridge, MA: Harvard University Press, 1998.

Colistete, Renato Perim. "O atraso em meio à riqueza: Uma história econômica da educação primária em São Paulo, 1835 a 1920." Faculdade de Economia, Administração, Contabilidade e Atuária, Universidade de São Paulo, 2016.

Cometti, Elizabeth. "Trends in Italian Emigration." *Western Political Quarterly* 11, no. 4 (1958): 820–834.

Conniff, Michael L., and Frank D. McCann, eds. *Modern Brazil: Elites and Masses in Historical Perspective*. Lincoln: University of Nebraska Press, 1989.

Costa, Ana Maria C. Infantosi. *A escola na República Velha: Expansão do ensino primário em São Paulo*. São Paulo: Edec, 1983.

Costa, Emilia Viotti da. *The Brazilian Empire: Myths and Histories.* Chicago: University of Chicago Press, 1985.

——. *Da senzala à colônia.* 3rd ed. São Paulo: Editora UNESP, 1997.

Daniels, Roger. *The Politics of Prejudice: The Anti-Japanese Movement in California and the Struggle for Japanese Exclusion.* Berkeley: University of California Press, 1962.

Dantas, Mariana L. R. "Picturing Families between Black and White: Mixed Descent and Social Mobility in Colonial Minas Gerais, Brazil." *The Americas* 73, no. 4 (2016): 405–426.

Dávila, Jerry. *Diploma of Whiteness: Race and Social Policy in Brazil, 1917–1945.* Durham, NC: Duke University Press, 2003.

Davis, Horace B. "Padrão de vida dos operários da cidade de São Paulo." *Revista do Arquivo Municipal* 13 (1935): 113–166.

Dean, Warren. *Industrialization of São Paulo, 1880–1945.* Austin: University of Texas Press, 1970.

Decca, Maria Auxiliadora Guzzo. *A vida fora das fábricas: Cotidiano operário em São Paulo (1920/1934).* Rio de Janeiro: Paz e Terra, 1987.

DeShazo, Peter. *Urban Workers and Labor Unions in Chile, 1902–1927.* Madison: University of Wisconsin Press, 1983.

Díaz, Gaston. "A Gender Inequality Historical Database for Latin America." In *Gender Inequalities and Developments in Latin America during the Twentieth Century,* edited by Camou, Maubrigades, and Thorp, 249–259.

Eaglin, Jennifer. "Sweet Fuel: Ethanol's Socio-Political Origins in Ribeirão Preto, São Paulo, 1933–1985." PhD diss., Michigan State University, 2015.

Eakin, Marshall C. *Becoming Brazilian: Race and National Identity in Twentieth-Century Brazil.* New York: Cambridge University Press, 2017.

Eltis, David, and David Richardson, eds. *Extending the Frontiers: Essays on the New Transatlantic Slave Trade Database.* New Haven, CT: Yale University Press, 2008.

Emerson, Patrick M., and André Portela Souza. "Is There a Child Labor Trap? Intergenerational Persistence of Child Labor in Brazil." *Economic Development and Cultural Change* 51, no. 2 (January 2003): 375–398. doi.org/10.1086/346003.

Engerman, Stanley L., and Kenneth L. Sokoloff. "Factor Endowments, Institutions, and Differential Paths of Growth among New World Economics." In *How Latin America Fell Behind,* edited by Haber, 260–304.

Faini, Ricardo, and Allesandra Venturini. "Italian Immigration in the Pre-War Period." In *Migration and the International Labor Market,* edited by Hatton and Williamson, 72–90.

Fausto, Boris. *Crime e cotidiano: A criminalidade em São Paulo (1880–1924).* São Paulo: Brasiliense, 1984.

——. *Trabalho urbano e conflito social, 1890–1920.* São Paulo: Companhia das Letras, 1976.

Fay, Marianne, and Charlotte Opal. *Urbanization without Growth: A Not-So-Uncommon Phenomenon.* Washington, DC: World Bank, 1999.

Ferreira, Roquinaldo. "The Suppression of the Slave Trade and Slave Departures from Angola, 1830's–1860's." In *Extending the Frontiers,* edited by Eltis and Richardson, 331–334.

Ferreira, Sergio Guimarães, and Fernando A. Veloso. "Mobilidade intergeracional de educação no Brasil." *Pesquisa e Planejamento Econômico* 33, no. 3 (2003): 481–539.

Figart, Deborah M. "Discrimination." In *Handbook of Economics and Ethics*, edited by Jan Peil and Irene van Staveren, 91–98. Northampton, MA: Edward Elgar, 2009.

Fink, Leon, ed. *Workers across the Americas: The Transnational Turn in Labor History.* New York: Oxford University Press, 2011.

Fogel, Robert W. *Railroads and American Economic Growth: Essays in Econometric History.* Baltimore, MD: Johns Hopkins Press, 1964.

Fogel, Robert W., and Stanley L. Engerman. *Time on the Cross: The Economics of American Negro Slavery.* Boston: Little, Brown, 1974.

Font, Mauricio A. *Coffee, Contention, and Change in the Making of Modern Brazil.* Cambridge, England: Basil Blackwell, 1990.

Franken, Daniel William. "Growing Taller, yet Falling Short: Policy, Health, and Living Standards in Brazil, 1850–1950." PhD diss., University of California, Los Angeles, 2016.

Freitas, Sônia Maria de. *Presença portuguesa em São Paulo.* São Paulo: Memorial do Imigrantes, 2006.

Freyre, Gilberto. *Casa grande e senzala.* 12th ed. Brasília: Editora Universidade de Brasília, 1963.

Fritsch, Winston, and Gustavo H. B. Franco. "Aspects of the Brazilian Experience with the Gold Standard." In *Monetary Standards in the Periphery: Paper, Silver, and Gold, 1854–1933*, edited by Pablo Martin Acena and Jaime Reis, 152–171. London: Macmillan, 2000.

Fuentes, Marisa J. *Dispossessed Lives: Enslaved Women, Violence, and the Archive.* Philadelphia: University of Pennsylvania Press, 2016.

Furtado, Celso. *Formação econômica do Brasil.* 40th ed. São Paulo: Brasiliense, 1993.

Gabaccia, Donna R. *Italy's Many Diasporas.* London: University College London Press, 2000.

Gamio, Manuel. *Forjando patria: Pro-nacionalismo/Forging a Nation.* Bilingual ed. Translated and edited by Fernando Armstrong-Fumero. Boulder: University Press of Colorado, 2010.

García, Juan R. *Mexicans in the Midwest, 1900–1932.* Tucson: University of Arizona Press. 1996.

Gitahy, Maria Lucia C. *Processo de trabalho e greves portuárias—1889–1910: Estudo sobre a formação da classe operária no porto de Santos.* São Paulo: Ciências Sociais Hoje, Vértice, 1987.

Goldin, Claudia. *Understanding the Gender Gap: An Economic History of American Women.* New York: Cambridge University Press, 1990.

———. "The Quiet Revolution That Transformed Women's Employment, Education, and Family." *American Economic Review* 96, no. 2 (2006): 1–21.

González, Ondina, and Bianca Premo, eds. *Raising an Empire: Children in Early Modern Iberia and Colonial Latin America.* Albuquerque: University of New Mexico Press, 2007.

Graham, Sandra Lauderdale. *House and Street: The Domestic World of Servants and Masters in Nineteenth-Century Rio de Janeiro.* Austin: University of Texas Press, 1992.

Grandin, Greg. *Fordlândia: The Rise and Fall of Henry Ford's Forgotten Jungle City.* New York: Macmillan, 2009.

Grandío Moraguez, Oscar. "The African Origins of Slaves Arriving in Cuba." In *Extending the Frontiers*, edited by Eltis and Richardson, 176–204.

Greenfield, Gerald Michael. "Brazil." In *Latin American Labor Organizations*, edited by Greenfield and Maram, 63–128.

———. "The Challenge of Growth: The Growth of Urban Public Services in São Paulo, 1885–1913." PhD diss., Indiana University, 1975.

Greenfield, Gerald Michael, and Sheldon L. Maram, eds. *Latin American Labor Organizations*. New York: Greenwood, 1987.

Guy, Donna. *Sex and Danger in Buenos Aires: Prostitution, Family, and Nation in Argentina*. Lincoln: University of Nebraska Press, 1991.

Guzmán, Tracy Devine. *Native and National in Brazil: Indigeneity after Independence*. Chapel Hill: University of North Carolina Press, 2013.

Haas, Lisbeth. "Argentina." In *Latin American Labor Organizations*, edited by Greenfield and Maram, 1–25.

Haber, Stephen H. "Business Enterprise and the Great Depression in Brazil: A Study of Profits and Losses in Textile Manufacturing." *Business History Review* 66, no. 2 (1992): 335–363.

———. "Development Strategy or Endogenous Process? The Industrialization of Latin America." Stanford Center for International Development Working Paper No. 269, November 2005, 1–86.

———. "The Efficiency Consequences of Institutional Change: Financial Market Regulation and Industrial Productivity Growth in Brazil, 1866–1934." National Bureau of Economic Research Working Paper No. 94, November 1996.

———, ed. *How Latin America Fell Behind*. Stanford, CA: Stanford University Press, 1997.

———. Introduction to *How Latin America Fell Behind*, edited by Haber, 1–33.

———. *Industry and Underdevelopment: The Industrialization of Mexico, 1890–1940*. Stanford, CA: Stanford University Press, 1995.

Hall, Michael. "The Origins of Mass Immigration to Brazil." PhD diss., Columbia University, 1969.

Hall, Michael, and Marco Aurélio Garcia. "Urban Labor." In *Modern Brazil*, edited by Conniff and McCann, 161–191.

Hakim, Carol. *The Origins of the Lebanese National Idea, 1840-1920*. Berkeley, CA: University of California Press, 2013.

Hanley, Anne G. "Business Finance and the São Paulo Bolsa, 1886–1917." In *Latin America and the World Economy since 1800*, edited by Coatsworth and Taylor, 115–138.

———. *Native Capital: Financial Institutions and Economic Development in São Paulo, Brazil, 1850–1920*. Stanford, CA: Stanford University Press, 2005.

———. *The Public Good and the Brazilian State: Municipal Finance and Public Services in São Paulo, 1822–1930*. Chicago: University of Chicago Press, 2018.

Hatton, Timothy J., and Jeffrey G. Williamson, eds. *Migration and the International Labor Market, 1850–1939*. New York: Routledge, 1994.

Herranz-Locán, Alfonso. "The Role of Railways in Export-Led Growth: The Case of Uruguay, 1870–1913." *Economic History of Developing Regions* 26, no. 2 (2011): 1–32.

Hirschman, Albert O. *The Strategy of Economic Development*. New Haven, CT: Yale University Press, 1958.

Holloway, Thomas. "Creating the Reserve Army? The Immigration Program of São Paulo, 1886–1930." *International Migration Review* 12, no. 2 (1978): 187–209.

———. *Immigrants on the Land: Coffee and Society in São Paulo, 1886–1930.* Chapel Hill: University of North Carolina Press, 1980.

Honda, Gail. "Differential Structure, Differential Health: Industrialization in Japan, 1868–1940." In *Health and Welfare during Industrialization: A National Bureau of Economic Research Project Report,* edited by Richard H. Steckel and Roderick Floud, 251–284. Chicago: University of Chicago Press, 1997.

Honorato, Cezar Teixeira. *O polvo e o porto: A Cia. Docas de Santos, 1888–1914.* São Paulo: Hucitec, 1996.

Huberman, Michael. "Working Hours of the World Unite? New International Evidence of Worktime, 1870–1913." *Journal of Economic History* 64, no. 4 (2004): 964–1001.

Hutchison, Elizabeth Quay. *Labors Appropriate to Their Sex: Gender, Labor, and Politics in Urban Chile, 1900–1930.* Durham, NC: Duke University Press, 2001.

Ianni, Octavio. *As metamorphoses do escravo: Apogeu e crise da escravatura no Brasil meridional.* São Paulo: Difusão Européia do Livro, 1962.

Jacino, Ramatis. *Transição e exclusão: O negro no mercado de trabalho em São Paulo pós abolição, 1912/1930.* São Paulo: Nefertiti, 2014.

James, Daniel. *Resistance and Integration: Peronism and the Argentine Working Class, 1946–1976.* New York: Cambridge University Press, 1988.

Jedwab, Remi, and Dietrich Vollrath. "Urbanization without Growth in Historical Perspective." *Explorations in Economic History* 58 (2015): 1–21.

Kirk, Dudley. *Europe's Population in the Interwar Years.* New York: Gordon and Breach, Science, 1946.

Klein, Herbert S. *La inmigración española en Brasil: Siglos XIX y XX.* Vol. 16. Columbres, Spain: Archivo de Indianos, 1996.

———. "The Social and Economic Integration of Spanish Immigrants in Brazil." *Journal of Social History* 25, no. 3 (Spring 1992): 505–529.

Kogan, Gabriel. "The Socio-Environmental History of the Floods in São Paulo 1887–1930." Master's thesis, UNESCO-IHE, 2013.

Kuznesof, Elizabeth A. *Household Economic and Urban Development: São Paulo 1765 to 1836.* Boulder, CO: Westview, 1986.

———. "The Role of the Merchants in the Economic Development of São Paulo, 1765–1850." *Hispanic American Historical Review* 60, no. 4 (1980): 571–592.

Lam, David, and Suzanne Duryea. "Effects of Schooling on Fertility, Labor Supply, and Investments in Children, with Evidence from Brazil." *Journal of Human Resources* 34, no. 1 (1999): 160–192.

Lamounier, Maria Lucia de. *Ferrovias e mercado de trabalho no Brasil do século XIX.* São Paulo: Edusp, 2012.

Lanna, Ana Lucia Duarte. *Ferrovia, cidade e trabalhadores: A conquista do oeste (1850–1920).* CD-ROM. São Paulo: Universidade de São Paulo Faculdade de Arquitetura e Urbanismo, 2000.

———. "Trabalhadores das ferrovias: A Companhia Paulista de Estrada de Ferro, São Paulo, 1870–1920." *Varia Historia* 32, no. 59 (2016): 505–545.

Leal, Victor Nunes. *Coronelismo, enxada e voto: O município e o regime representativo no Brasil*. São Paulo: Companhia das Letras, 2012.

Leff, Nathaniel. *Underdevelopment and Development in Brazil*. 2 vols. Boston: George Allen and Unwin, 1982.

Lemos, Carlos Alberto. *Alvenaria burguesa: Breve história da arquitectura residencial de tijolos em São Paulo a partir do ciclo econômico liderado pelo café*, 2nd ed. São Paulo: Nobel, 1989.

Lesser, Jeffrey. *Immigration, Ethnicity, and National Identity in Brazil*. New York: Cambridge University Press, 2013.

———. *Negotiating National Identity: Immigrants, Minorities, and the Struggle for Ethnicity in Brazil*. Durham, NC: Duke University Press, 2001.

Levy, Aiala Teresa. "Forging an Urban Public: Theaters, Audiences, and the City in São Paulo, Brazil, 1854–1924." PhD diss., University of Chicago, 2016.

Lilliecreutz, Caroline, Johanna Larén, Gunilla Sydsjö, and Ann Josefsson. "Effect of Maternal Stress during Pregnancy on the Risk for Preterm Birth." *BMC Pregnancy Childbirth* 15, no. 5 (2016): 1–8. https://doi.org/10.1186/s12884-015-0775-x.

Lima, Nestor. *Municípios do Rio Grande do Norte: Baixa Verde, Caicó, Canguaretama e Caraúbas*. Mossoró, Brazil: Fundação Guimarães Duque, 1990.

Lindert, Peter H., and Jeffrey G. Williamson. *Globalization and Inequality: A Long History*. Washington, DC: World Bank, 2001.

Lobo, Eulalia Maria Lahmeyer, Lucena Barbosa Madureira, Octavio Canavarros, Zakia Feres, and Sonia Gonçalves. "Evolução dos preços e do padrão de vida no Rio de Janeiro, 1820–1930: Resultados preliminares." *Revista Brasileira de Economia* 25, no. 4 (1971): 235–265.

Lobo, Eulalia Maria Lahmeyer, Otavio Canavarros, Zakia Feres Elias, Simone Novais, and Lucena Barbosa Madureira. "Estudo das categorias socioprofissionais, dos salários e do custo da alimentação no Rio de Janeiro de 1820 a 1930." What *Revista Brasileira de Economia* 27, no. 4 (1973): 129–176.

Lone, Stewart. *The Japanese Community in Brazil, 1908–1940: Between Samurai and Carnival*. New York: Palgrave, 2001.

López-Uribe, María del Pilar, and Diana Quintero Castellanos. "Women Rising: Dynamics of the Education System and the Labour Market in Colombia, 1900–2000." In *Gender Inequalities and Developments in Latin America during the Twentieth Century*, edited by Camou, Maubrigades, and Thorp, 162–191.

Lopreato, Christina da Silva Roquette. *O espíritu da revolta: A greve geral anarquista de 1917*. São Paulo: Annablume, 2000.

Lovell, Peggy A., and Charles H. Wood. "Skin Color, Racial Identity, and Life Chances in Brazil." *Latin American Perspectives* 25, no. 3 (1998): 90–109.

Loveman, Brian. "Chile." In *Latin American Labor Organizations*, edited by Greenfield and Maram, 129–178.

Lowrie, Samuel. "The Negro Element in the Population of São Paulo, a Southernly State of Brazil," *Phylon* 3, no. 4 (4th quarter, 1942): 398–416.

Luebke, Frederick C. *Germans in the New World: Essays in the History of Immigration*. Urbana: University of Illinois Press, 1999.

Luna, Francisco Vidal, and Herbert S. Klein. *An Economic and Demographic History of São Paulo 1850–1950*. Stanford, CA: Stanford University Press, 2018.

———. *Slavery and the Economy of São Paulo 1750–1850*. Stanford, CA: Stanford University Press, 2003.

Lurtz, Casey. "Insecure Labor, Insecure Debt: The Struggle over Debt Peonage in the Soconusco, Chiapas." *Hispanic American Historical Review* 96, no. 2 (Spring 2016): 291–318.

Machado, Maria Helena Pereira Toledo. "From Slave Rebels to Strikebreakers: The Quilombo of Jabaquara and the Problem of Citizenship in Late Nineteenth-Century Brazil." *Hispanic American Historical Review* 86, no. 2 (2006): 247–274.

Mallon, Florencia E. *The Defense of Community in Peru's Central Highlands: Peasant Struggle and Capitalist Transition, 1860-1940*. Princeton, NJ: Princeton University Press, 1983.

Maloney, Thomas N., and Warren C. Whatley. "Making the Effort: The Contours of Racial Discrimination in Detroit's Labor Markets, 1920–1940." *Journal of Economic History* 55, no. 3 (1995): 465–493.

Maram, Sheldon Leslie. *Anarquistas, imigrantes e o movimento operário brasileiro, 1890–1920*. Translated by José Eduardo Ribeiro Moretzsohn. Rio de Janeiro: Paz e Terra, 1979.

———. "Labor and the Left in Brazil, 1890-1921: A Movement Aborted." *Hispanic American Historical Review* 57, no. 2 (1977): 254–272.

Marcílio, Maria Luiza. *História da escola em São Paulo e no Brasil*. São Paulo: Instituto Braudel, 2005.

Margo, Robert A., and Georgia C. Villaflor. "The Growth of Wages in Antebellum America: New Evidence." *Journal of Economic History*, 47, no. 4 (1987): 873–895.

Martinho, Lenira Menezes, and Riva Gorenstein. *Negociantes e caixeiros na sociedade da independência*. Rio de Janeiro: Prefeitura da Cidade do Rio de Janeiro, 1992.

Martins, José de Souza. *Empresário e empresa na biografia do Conde Matarazzo*. Vol. 2. São Paulo: Instituto de Ciências Sociais, 1967.

Martins, Marcelo Thadeu Quintanilha. *A civilização do delegado: Modernidade, polícia e sociedade em São Paulo nas primeiras décadas da República, 1889–1930*. São Paulo: Alameda Cada, 2014.

Mascarenhas, Maria de Graça. *A technologia e a retomado do desenvolvimento: 100 anos do IPT*. São Paulo: Instituto de Pesquisas Tecnológicas do Estado de São Paulo, 1999.

Masterson, Daniel M., with Sayaka Funada-Classen. *The Japanese in Latin America*. Urbana: University of Illinois Press, 2004.

Meade, Teresa A. *Civilizing Rio: Reform and Resistance in a Brazilian City, 1889–1930*. University Park: Pennsylvania State University Press, 2010.

Melo, Hildete P. de, João L. de Araújo, and Teresa Cristina de N. Marques. "Raça e nacionalidade no mercado de trabalho carioca na Primeira República: O caso da cervejaria Brahma." *Revista Brasileira de Economia* 57, no. 3 (2003): 535–568. http://dx.doi.org/10.1590/S0034-71402003000300003.

Menezes, Lená Medeiros de. "A 'onda' emigratória de 1912: Dos números às trajetorias." In *Nas duas margens: Os portugueses no Brasil*, edited by Fernando de Sousa, Isménia Martins, and Izilda Matos, 237–247. Porto, Portugal: CEPESE/Edições Afrontamento, 2009. https://www.cepese.pt/portal/pt/publicacoes/obras/nas-duas-margens.-os-portugueses-no-brasil.

Metcalf, Alida C. *Go-Betweens and the Colonization of Brazil: 1500–1600*. Austin: University of Texas Press, 2005.

Miki, Yoku. *Frontiers of Citizenship: A Black and Indigenous History of Postcolonial Brazil*. New York: Cambridge University Press, 2018.

Miller, Shawn William. *The Street Is Ours: Community, the Car, and the Nature of Public Space in Rio de Janeiro*. New York: Cambridge University Press, 2018.

Monangueira, V. S. "Vila Maria Zélia: Visões de uma vila operária em São Paulo (1917–1940)." Master's thesis, Universidade de São Paulo, 2006.

Moraes, José Ermírio Albuquerque de. "The Occurrence of Nickel Ore near the Village of Livramento, Minas Geraes, Brazil, South America." *Colorado School of Mines Magazine* 10, no. 12 (1919): 32–33.

Morrisson, Christian, and Fabrice Murtin. "The Century of Education." *Journal of Human Capital* 3, no. 1 (2009): 1–42.

Morse, Richard McGee. *From Community to Metropolis: A Biography of São Paulo, Brazil*. New York: Octagon, 1974.

———. "Latin American Cities: Aspects of Function and Structure." *Comparative Studies in Society and History* 4, no. 4 (1962): 473–493.

Motoyama, Shozo. *Tecnologia e industrialização no Brasil: Uma perspectiva histórica*. São Paulo: Editora UNESP, 1994.

Moura, Esmeralda Blanco Bolsonaro de. *Trabalho feminino e condição social do menor em São Paulo (1890–1920)*. São Paulo: Centro de Demografia Histórica da América Latina, 1988

Moya, José C. *Cousins and Strangers: Spanish Immigrants in Buenos Aires, 1850–1930*. Berkeley: University of California Press, 1998.

Munck, Ronaldo, with Ricardo Falcon and Bernardo Galitelli. *Argentina: From Anarchism to Peronism: Workers, Unions, and Politics, 1855–1985*. New Jersey: Zed, 1987.

Musacchio, Aldo. *Experiments in Financial Democracy: Corporate Governance and Financial Development in Brazil, 1882–1950*. New York: Cambridge University Press, 2009.

Nakamura, Leonard I., and Carlos E. J. M. Zarazaga. "Economic Growth in Argentina in the Period 1900–1930: Some Evidence from Stock Returns." In *Latin America and the World Economy since 1800*, edited by Coatsworth and Taylor, 247–270.

Negri, Barjas. "Concentração e desconcentração industrial em São Paulo (1880–1990)." PhD diss., Universidade Estadual de Campinas, 1994.

Ngai, Mae M. "The Architecture of Race in American Immigration Law: A Reexamination of the Immigration Act of 1924." *Journal of American History* 86, no. 1 (1999): 67–92.

North, Douglass C. "Institutions." *Journal of Economic Perspectives* 5, no. 1 (1991): 97–112.

North, Douglass C., and Barry R. Weingast. "Constitutions and Commitment: The Evolution of Institutions Governing Public Choice in Seventeenth-Century England." *Journal of Economic History* 49, no. 4 (1989): 803–832.

Nugent, Walter T. K. *Crossings: The Great Transatlantic Migrations, 1870–1914*. Bloomington: Indiana University Press, 1992.

Nussbaum, Martha, and Amartya Sen. *The Quality of Life*. New York: Cambridge University Press, 1993.

Paiva, Odair da Cruz, and Soraya Moura. *Hospedaria de Imigrantes de São Paulo*. São Paulo: Paz e Terra, 2008.

Paula, Amir El Hakim de. "Os operários pedem passagem! Geografia do operário na cidade de São Paulo (1900–1917)." Master's thesis, Universidade de São Paulo, 2005.

Peixoto-Mehrtens, Cristina. *Urban Space and National Identity in Early Twentieth-Century São Paulo, Brazil: Crafting Modernity*. New York: Palgrave Macmillan, 2010.

Pena, Maria Valéria Junho. *Mulheres e trabalhadoras: Presença feminina na constituição do sistema fabril*. São Paulo: Paz e Terra, 1981.

Penteado, Jacob. *Belènzinho, 1910: Retrato de uma* época. 2nd ed. São Paulo: Carrenho, 2003.

Pereira, Robson Mendoça. *Washington Luís na administração de São Paulo (1914–1919)*. São Paulo: Editora UNESP, 2010.

Pérez Meléndez, José Juan. "The Business of Peopling: Colonization and Politics in Imperial Brazil, 1822–1860." PhD diss., University of Chicago, 2016.

Piccini, Andrea. *Cortiços na cidade: Conceito e preconceito na reestruturação do centro urbano de São Paulo*. São Paulo: Annablume, 1999.

Pinheiro, Paulo Sérgio de Moraes Sarmento, and Michael M. Hall. *A classe operária no Brasil: Documentos (1889 a 1930)*. 2 vols. São Paulo: Alfa Omega, 1979–1981.

Pinto, Alfredo Moreira. *A cidade de S. Paulo em 1900: Impressões de viagem*. São Paulo: Governo do Estado de São Paulo, 1979.

Pinto, Maria Inez Machado Borges. *Cotidiano e sobrevivência: A vida do trabalhador pobre na cidade de São Paulo, 1890–1914*. São Paulo: Edusp, 1994.

Piore, Michael. "Jobs and Training." In *The State and the Poor*, edited by Samuel H. Beer and Richard E. Barringer, 53–83. Cambridge, MA: Winthrop, 1970.

Portugal, Direcção Geral da Estatística e dos Proprios Nacionaes. *Censo da população do Reino de Portugal no 1° de dezembro de 1900: Quarto recenseamento geral da população*. 3 vols. Lisbon: Imprensa Nacional, 1905–1906.

Prado Júnior, Caio. *História econômica do Brasil*. 16th ed. São Paulo: Brasiliense, 1973.

Premo, Bianca. "Familiar: Thinking beyond Lineage and across Race in Spanish Atlantic Family History." *William and Mary Quarterly* 70, no. 2 (2013): 295–316.

Razo, Armando, and Stephen Haber. "The Rate of Growth of Productivity in Mexico, 1850–1933: Evidence from the Cotton Textile Industry." *Journal of Latin American Studies* 30, no. 3 (1998): 481–517.

Read, Ian. "Do Diseases Talk? Writing the Cultural and Epidemiological History of Disease in Latin America." *Latin America Perspectives* 44, no. 4 (2016): 192–200.

———. "Sickness, Recovery, and Death among the Enslaved and Free People of Santos, Brazil, 1860–1888." *The Americas* 66, no. 1 (2009): 57–80.

Reis, Carlos A., ed. *Almanach illustrado de São Paulo*. São Paulo: Typ. Andrade e Mello, 1904.

Rial Roade, Juan. "Uruguay." Translated by Lisa Ebener and Gerald Michael Greenfield. In *Latin American Labor Organizations*, edited by Greenfield and Maram, 701–726.

Ribeiro, Maria Alice Rosa. *Condições de trabalho na indústria têxtil paulista (1870–1930)*. São Paulo: Hucitec, 1988.

———. "Os cortiços no distrito de Santa Ifigênia (1893)." In *Os cortiços de Santa Ifigênia: Sanitarismo e urbanização (1893)*, edited by Simone Lucena Cordeiro, 39–78. São Paulo: Imprensa Oficial, 2010.

Rolnik, Raquel. "The City and the Law: Legislation, Urban Policy, and Territories in the City of São Paulo (1886–1936)." PhD diss., New York University, 1995.

Roth, Cassia. *A Miscarriage of Justice: Women's Reproductive Lives and the Law in Early Twentieth-Century Brazil.* Stanford, CA: Stanford University Press, 2020.

Roth-Gordon, Jennifer. *Race and the Brazilian Body: Blackness, Whiteness, and Everyday Language in Rio de Janeiro.* Berkeley: University of California Press, 2017.

Ruggles, Steven, Sarah Flood, Ronald Goeken, Josiah Grover, Erin Meyer, Jose Pacas, and Matthew Sobek. *Integrated Public Use Microdata Series: Version 9.0.* Dataset. Minneapolis: University of Minnesota, 2019. http://doi.org/10.18128/D010.V9.0.

Saes, Flavio Azevedo Marques de. *As ferrovias de São Paulo, 1870–1940.* São Paulo: Hucitec, 1981.

Sales, Teresa. "Raízes da desigualdade social na cultura política brasileira." *Revista Brasileira de Ciências Sociais* 9, no. 25 (1994): 26–37. http://www.anpocs.com/images/stories/RBCS/25/rbcs25_02.pdf.

Sánchez-Alonso, Blanca. "The Other Europeans: Immigration into Latin America (1870–1930)." Universidad Carlos III de Madrid Working Papers in Economic History. Madrid, November 2007.

———. "Those Who Left and Those Who Stayed Behind." *Journal of Economic History* 60, no. 3 (September 2000): 730–755.

Santos, Jose Carlos Ferreira dos. *Nem tudo era italiano: São Paulo e pobreza, 1890–1915.* São Paulo: Annablume, 1998.

São Paulo, Departamento de Estatística do Estado. *Movimento da população do município de São Paulo: Resumo do movimento do Registro Civil 1894/1957.* São Paulo: Typografia do Diario Official, 1960.

São Paulo, Departamento Estadual de Estatística. *Catálogo das indústrias do município da capital.* São Paulo, 1943.

São Paulo, Directoria Geral da Instrucção Pública. *Annuario do ensino do estado de São Paulo 1923.* São Paulo: Typografia do Diario Official, 1924.

São Paulo, Secretaria da Agricultura. *Boletim do Departamento Estadual do Trabalho.* São Paulo, 1911–1919.

———. *Boletim da Directoria de Indústria e Commércio.* São Paulo, 1907–1929.

São Paulo, Secretaria de Estado dos Negocios da Agricultura, Commercio e Obras Publicas. *Relatorio do Secretario da Agricultura, Commercio e Obras Publicas.* São Paulo, 1903–1928.

São Paulo, Repartição de Estatística e Archivo do Estado. *Annuario estatístico do estado de São Paulo.* São Paulo, 1901–1927.

Saraceno, Chiara. "Constructing Families, Shaping Women's Lives: The Making of Italian Families between Market Economy and State Interventions." In *The European Experience of Declining Fertility, 1850–1970: The Quiet Revolution,* edited by John R. Gillis, Louise A. Tilly, and David Levine, 251–269. Cambridge: Blackwell, 1992.

Sassler, Sharon. "Women's Marital Timing at the Turn of the Century: Generational and Ethnic Differences." *Sociological Quarterly* 38, no. 4 (Fall 1997): 567–585.

Seabra, Odette Carvalho de Lima. *Os meandros dos rios nos meandros do poder: Tietê e Pinheiros; valorização dos rios e das várzeas na cidade de São Paulo.* São Paulo: Alameda, 2019.

Simonsen, Roberto Cochrane. *Brazil's Industrial Evolution*. São Paulo: Escola Livre de Sociologia e Política, 1939.

———. *À margem da profissão*. São Paulo: São Paulo Limitada, 1932.

Siqueira, Uassyr de. "Entre sindicatos, clubes e botequins: Identidades, associações e lazer dos trabalhadores paulistanos (1890–1920)." PhD diss., Universidade Estadual de Campinas, 2008.

Siriani, Silvia Cristina Lambert. *Uma São Paulo alemã: Vida quotidiana dos imigrantes germânicos*. São Paulo: Imprensa Oficial, 2003.

Skidmore, Thomas E. *Black into White: Race and Nationality in Brazilian Thought*. Durham, NC: Duke University Press, 1993.

Slenes, Robert W. *Na senzala, uma flor: Esperanças e recordações na formação da família escrava; Brasil sudeste, século XIX*. São Paulo: Nova Fronteira, 1999.

Stein, Stanley J. *The Brazilian Cotton Manufacture*. New York: Cambridge University Press, 1957.

———. *Vassouras, a Brazilian Coffee County, 1850–1900: The Roles of Planter and Slave in a Plantation Society*. Princeton, NJ: Princeton University Press, 1957.

Stepan, Nancy. *"The Hour of Eugenics": Race, Gender, and Nation in Latin America*. Ithaca, NY: Cornell University Press, 1991.

Stolcke, Verena. "The Exploitation of Family Morality: Labor Systems and Family Structure on São Paulo Coffee Plantations, 1850–1979." In *Kinship Ideology and Practice in Latin America*, edited by Raymond Thomas Smith, 264–296. Chapel Hill: University of North Carolina Press, 1984.

Street, Jorge, and Evaristo de Moraes Filho. *Idéias sociais de Jorge Street*. Rio de Janeiro: Fundação Casa de Rui Barbosa, 1980.

Suk, Lena Oak. "Becoming Modern at the Movies: Gender, Class and Urban Space in Twentieth Century Brazil," PhD diss., Emory University, 2014.

———. "'Only the Fragile Sex Admitted': The Women's Restaurant in 1920s São Paulo, Brazil." *Journal of Social History* 51, no. 3 (2018): 592–620.

Summerhill, William R. *Inglorious Revolution: Political Institutions, Sovereign Debt, and Financial Underdevelopment in Imperial Brazil*. New Haven, CT: Yale University Press, 2015.

———. *Order against Progress: Government, Foreign Investment, and Railroads in Brazil, 1854–1913*. Stanford, CA: Stanford University Press, 2003.

Suzigan, Wilson. *Indústria brasileira: Origem e desenvolvimento*. São Paulo: Brasiliense, 1986.

Tannuri, Luiz Antonio. *O Encilhamento*. São Paulo: Hucitec-Funcamp, 1981.

Taunay, Afonso de Escragnolle. *Historia geral das bandeiras paulistas*. 3 volumes. São Paulo: Typ. Ideal, H. L. Canton, 1927.

Taylor, Alan M. "External Dependence, Demographic Burdens, and Argentine Economic Decline after the Belle Epoque." *Journal of Economic History* 52, no. 4 (1992): 907–936.

Teixeira, Palmira Petratti. *A fábrica do sonho: Trajetória do industrial Jorge Street*. São Paulo: Paz e Terra, 1990.

Tomasevicius Filho, Eduardo. "O legado do Código Civil de 1916." *Revista da Faculdade de Direito da Universidade de São Paulo* 111 (2016): 85–100.

Topik, Steven. *The Political Economy of the Brazilian State, 1889–1930*. Austin: University of Texas Press, 1987.

Torres, Maria Celestina Teixeira Mendes. *O bairro do Brás*. São Paulo: Prefeitura do Município de São Paulo, Secretaria Municipal de Cultura, Departamento do Patrimônio Histórico, Divisão do Arquivo Histórico, 1985.

Tortella, Gabriel. "Patterns of Economic Retardation and Recovery in South-Western Europe in the Nineteenth and Twentieth Centuries." *The Economic History Review* 47, no. 1 (1994): 1–21.

Tossounian, Cecilia. "Women's Associations and the Emergence of a Social State: Protection for Mothers and Children in Buenos Aires, 1920–1940." *Journal of Latin American Studies* 45, no. 2 (2013): 297–324.

Trento, Angelo. *Do outro lado do Atlântico: Um século de imigração italiana no Brasil*. Translated by Mariarosaria Fabris and Luiz Eduardo de Lima Brandão. São Paulo: Studio Nobel, 1989.

Triner, Gail. *Banking and Economic Development: Brazil, 1889–1930*. New York: Palgrave, 2000.

———. *Mining and the State in Brazilian Development*. London: Pickering and Chatto, 2011.

United States Department of Commerce, Bureau of Foreign and Domestic Commerce. *Trade Directory of South America: For the Promotion of American Export Trade*. Miscellaneous Series nǫ. 13. Washington, DC: Government Printing Office, 1914.

United States, Department of the Interior. *Twelfth Census of the United States Taken in the Year 1900*. Washington, DC: US Census Office, 1901.

Vampré, Danton. *São Paulo Futuro*. Play. São Paulo: Revista de Costumes Paulistas, 1914.

Van Leeuwen, Marco H. D., and Ineke Maas. *HISCLASS: A Historical International Social Class Scheme*. Leuven, Belgium: Leuven University Press, 2011.

Van Leeuwen, Marco H. D, Ineke Maas, and Andrew Miles. *HISCO: Historical International Standard Classification Of Occupations*. Leuven, Belgium: Leuven University Press, 2002.

Vangelista, Chiara. *Os braços da lavoura: Imigrantes e "caipiras" na formação do Mercado de trabalho paulista (1850–1930)*. São Paulo: Hucitec, 1991.

Vasconcelos, José. *The Cosmic Race/La raza cósmica*. Bilingual ed. Translated by Didier T. Jaén. Baltimore, MD: Johns Hopkins University Press, 1997.

Veccia, Theresa. "Family and Factory: Textile Work and Women's Lives in São Paulo, Brazil, 1880–1940." PhD diss., University of Wisconsin at Madison, 1995.

———. "'My Duty as a Woman': Gender Ideology, Work, and Working-Class Women's Lives in São Paulo, Brazil, 1900–1950." In *The Gendered Worlds of Latin American Women Workers*, edited by John D. French and Daniel James, 100–146. Durham, NC: Duke University Press, 1997.

Versiani, Flávio Rabelo. "Imigrantes, trabalho qualificado e industrialização: Rio e São Paulo no início do século." *Revista de Economia Política* 13, no. 4 (1993): 77–96.

Villaça, Flávio. "A estrutura territorial da metropole sul-brasileira." PhD diss., Universidade de São Paulo, 1978.

Villela, Annibal V., and Wilson Suzigan. *Política do governo e crescimento da economia brasileira, 1889–1945*. Rio de Janeiro: Institution de Pesquisa Económica Aplicada and Instituto de Planejamento Económico e Social, 1973.

Wachter, Michael L., R. A. Gordon, Michael J. Piore, and Robert Hall. "Primary and Secondary Labor Markets: A Critique of the Dual Approach." *Brookings Papers on Economic Activity*, 1974, no. 3, 637–693.

Weinstein, Barbara. *The Color of Modernity: São Paulo and the Making of Race and Nation in Brazil*. Durham, NC: Duke University Press, 2015.

———. *For Social Peace in Brazil: Industrialists and the Remaking of the Working Class in São Paulo, 1920–1964*. Chapel Hill: University of North Carolina Press, 1996.

Whatley, Warren C. "African-American Strikebreaking from the Civil War to the New Deal." *Social Science History* 17, no. 4 (1993): 525–558.

Winn, Peter. *Weavers of Revolution: the Yarur Workers and Chile's Road to Socialism*. New York: Oxford University Press, 1986.

Wisborg, Kirsten, Anne Barklin, Morten Hedegaard, and Tine Brink Henriksen. "Psychological Stress during Pregnancy and Stillbirth: Prospective Study." *BJOG: An International Journal of Obstetrics and Gynaecology* 115, no. 7 (2008): 882–885.

Wolfe, Joel. "Anarchist Ideology, Worker Practice: The 1917 General Strike and the Formation of São Paulo's Working Class." *Hispanic America Historical Review* 71, no. 4 (November 1991): 809–846.

———. *Autos and Progress: The Brazilian Search for Modernity*. New York: Oxford University Press, 2010.

———. *Working Women, Working Men: São Paulo and the Rise of Brazil's Industrial Working Class, 1900–1955*. Durham, NC: Duke University Press, 1993.

Woodard, James. *A Place in Politics: São Paulo, Brazil, from Seigneurial Republicanism to Regionalist Revolt*. Durham, NC: Duke University Press, 2009.

Woodham, Jonathan M. *Twentieth-Century Design*. New York: Oxford University Press, 1997.

Zimmerman, Kari. "'As Pertaining to the Female Sex': The Legal and Social Norms of Female Entrepreneurship in Nineteenth-Century Rio de Janeiro, Brazil." *Hispanic American Historical Review* 96, no. 1 (2016): 39–72.

Index

MOLLY C. BALL teaches Latin American, comparative, economic, and public history courses at the University of Rochester. Her research focuses on the history of nineteenth- and twentieth-century Brazil. She holds a PhD in history from the University of California, Los Angeles. She is also the mother of three wonderful children.